FEB 25 '98

MORAL
DEVELOPMENT

A Compendium

Series Editor

BILL PUKA
Rensselaer Institute

A GARLAND SERIES

SERIES CONTENTS

VOLUME

4

THE GREAT JUSTICE DEBATE

KOHLBERG CRITICISM

Edited with introductions by
BILL PUKA

GARLAND PUBLISHING, INC.
New York & London
1994

Library of Congress Cataloging-in-Publication Data

Moral development : a compendium / edited with introductions by Bill
Puka.
    p.   cm.
    Includes bibliographical references.
    Contents: v. 1. Defining perspectives in moral development — v.
2. Fundamental research in moral development — v. 3. Kohlberg's
original study of moral development — v. 4. The great justice
debate — v. 5. New research in moral development — v. 6. Caring
voices and women's moral frames — v. 7. Reaching out.
    ISBN 0–8153–1551–1 (v. 4 : alk. paper).
    1. Moral development.   I. Puka, Bill.
BF723.M54M66   1994
155.2'5—dc20   94–462
                                          CIP

Printed on acid-free, 250-year-life paper
Manufactured in the United States of America

CONTENTS

SERIES INTRODUCTION

Moral development is an interdisciplinary field that researches moral common sense and interpersonal know-how. It investigates how children evolve a sense of right and wrong, good and bad, and how adults hone their abilities to handle ethical issues in daily life. This includes resolving value conflicts, fermenting trusting, cooperative, and tolerant relationships, and setting ethical goals. It focuses most on how we think about these ethical issues (using our cognitive competences) and how we act as a result.

These seven volumes are designed to function as a standard, comprehensive sourcebook. They focus on central concerns and controversies in moral development, such as the relation between moral socialization and development, moral judgment and action, and the effects of culture, class, or gender on moral orientation. They also focus on central research programs in the field, such as the enduring Kohlberg research on moral stages, Gilligan research on ethical caring and women's development, and related prosocial research on altruism.

The studies contained here were compiled from the "wish lists" of researchers and educators in the field. These are the publications cited as most important (and, often, least available) for effective teaching and research training and for conveying the field to others. Unfortunately, the most crucial studies and essays in moral development are widely scattered across hard-to-find (sometimes out-of-print) volumes. Compiling them for a course is difficult and costly. This compendium eases these problems by gathering needed sources in one place, for a single charge. Regrettably, rising reprint fees frustrated plans to include *all* needed resources here, halving the original contents of these volumes and requiring torturous excising decisions. Even so, compared to other collections, this series approaches a true "handbook" of moral development, providing key sources on central issues rather than "further essays" on specialized topics.

A major aim of this series is to represent moral development accurately to related fields. Controversies in moral development have sparked lively interest in the disciplines of philosophy, education, sociology and anthropology, literary criticism, political science, gender and cultural studies, critical legal studies, criminology and corrections, and peace studies. Unfortunately, members of these fields were often introduced to moral development through the highly theoretical musings of Lawrence Kohlberg, Carol Gilligan, or Jean Piaget—or by highly theoretical commentaries on them. Jumping into the fray over gender or culture bias in stage theory, theorists in the humanities show virtually no familiarity with the empirical research that gave rise to it. Indeed, many commentators seem unaware that these controversies arise in a distinct research field and are context-dependent.

This compendium displays moral development as a social science, generating research findings in cognitive developmental, and social psychology. (Students are invited to recognize and approach the field as such.) Theory is heavily involved in this research—helping define the fundamental notions of "moral" and "development," for example. But even when philosophically or ethically cast, it remains psychological or social scientific theory. It utilizes but does not engage in moral philosophy per se. Otherwise, it is not moral development theory, but meta-theory. (Several extensively criticized Kohlberg articles on justice are meta-theory.) The confusion of these types and levels of theory has been a source of pervasive confusion in the field. The mistaken assessment of psychological theory by moral-philosophical standards has generated extremely damaging and misguided controversy in moral development. Other types of theory (moral, social, interpretive, anthropological) should be directed at moral development science, focusing on empirical research methods and their empirical interpretation. It should be theory of data, that is, not meta-theoretical reflection on the "amateur" philosophizing and hermeneutics interpolations of psychological researchers. (Likewise, social scientific research should not focus on the empirical generalizations of philosophers when trying to probe social reality or seek guidance in doing so from this theoretical discipline.) The bulk of entries in this compendium present the proper, empirically raw material for such "outside" theoretical enterprise.

To researchers, theorists, and students in related fields, this series extends an invitation to share our interest in the fascinating phenomena of moral development, and to share our findings thus far. Your help is welcomed also in refining our treacherously qualitative research methods and theories. In my dual disciplines of psychology and philosophy, I have found no more inspiring area of study. Alongside its somewhat dispassionate research orientation, this field carries on the ancient "cause" of its pre-scientific past. This is to show that human nature is naturally good—that the human psyche spontaneously unfolds in good will, cleaving toward fair-mindedness, compassion, and cooperative concern.

The first volume, *Defining Perspectives*, presents the major approaches to moral development and socialization in the words of chief proponents: Kohlberg, Bandura, Aronfreed, Mischel, Eysenck, and Perry. (Piaget is discussed in detail.) This first volume is required reading for those needing to orient to this field or regain orientation. It is crucial for clarifying the relations and differences between moral development and socialization that define research.

The second volume, *Fundamental Research*, compiles the classic research studies on moral levels and stages of development. These studies expose the crucial relation of role-taking and social perspective to moral judgment and of moral judgment to action. They also divine the important role of moral self-identity (viewing oneself as morally interested) in moral motivation.

The third volume contains *Kohlberg's Original Study*, his massive doctoral research project. The study, which has never before been published, sets the parameters for moral development research, theory, and controversy. (Major critical alternatives to Kohlberg's approach share far more in common with it than they diverge.) Here the reader sees "how it all started," glimpsing the sweep of Kohlberg's aspiration: to uncover the chief adaptation of humankind, the evolving systems of reasoning and meaning-making that, even in children, guide effective choice and action. Most major Kohlberg critiques fault features of this original study, especially in the all-male, all-white, all-American cast of his research sample. (Why look here for traits that characterize all humans in all cultures through all time?) It is worth checking these criticisms against the text, in context, as depictions of unpublished work often blur into hearsay. It is also worth viewing this study through the massive reanalysis of its data (Colby, Kohlberg, et al.) and the full mass of Kohlberg research that shaped stage theory. Both are liberally sampled in Volume Five.

The Great Justice Debate, the fourth volume, gathers the broad range of criticisms leveled at moral stage theory. It takes up the range of "bias charges" in developmental research—bias by gender, social class, culture, political ideology, and partisan intellectual persuasion. Chief among these reputed biases is the equation of moral competence and development with justice and rights. Here key features of compassion and benevolence seem overlooked or underrated. Here a seemingly male standard of ethical preference downplays women's sensibilities and skills. Responses to these charges appear here as well.

Volume Five, *New Research*, focuses on cross-cultural research in moral development. Studies in India, Turkey, Israel, Korea, Poland, and China are included. While interesting in itself, such research also supports the generalizability of moral stages, challenged above. Indeed, Volume Five attempts to reconceive or re-start the central research program of moral development from the inception of its matured research methods and statistically well-validated findings. From this point research is more data-based than theory-driven. It can address criticism with hard evidence. Regarding controversy in moral development, Volumes Four and Five go together as challenge and retort.

Volume Six, *Caring Voices*, is devoted to the popular "different voice" hypothesis. This hypothesis posits a distinct ethical orientation of caring relationship, naturally preferred by women, that complements justice. Compiled here is the main record of Gilligan's (and colleagues') research, including recent experiments with "narrative" research method. The significant critical literature on care is well-represented as well, with responses. While Gilligan's empirical research program is more formative than Kohlberg's, her interpretive observations have influenced several fields, especially in feminist studies. Few research sources have more common-sense significance and "consciousness-raising" potential. The student reader may find Gilligan's approach the most personally relevant and useful in moral development.

Reaching Out, the final volume, extends moral development concerns to "prosocial" research on altruism. Altruistic helping behavior bears close relation to caring and to certain ideals of liberal justice. This volume emphasizes the role of emotions in helping (and not helping), focusing on empathic distress, forgiveness, and guilt. It also looks at early friendship and family influences. Moral emotions are related to ethical virtues here, which are considered alongside the "vices" of apathy and learned helplessness. Leading researchers are included such as Hoffman, Eisenberg, Batson, and Staub.

INTRODUCTION

This volume details the voluminous criticism of moral development research and its defense, focusing on charges of ideological
bias in moral stage theory. "Controversial" is perhaps the most
common qualifier accompanying "Kohlberg's theory" or "moral development," the field it dominates. The chief, substantive controversy here is whether justice or rights are preeminent over other
ethics like group welfare or benevolent virtue. Is the most developed
moral judgment a matter of merely giving people their due, or going
"beyond the call" in a spirit of generosity? Kohlberg's most polemi-
cal "philosophical" writings reduce morality to justice, identifying
competent and mature moral reasoning with justice reasoning.
Benevolent ethical strains are closed off in a derided "bag of virtues"
and then laid aside as ethically discretionary, idiosyncratic, or
irrelevant.

From the 1960s forward, the most common critical reaction to
Kohlberg's stages was that they fell short on kindness and love.
This seemed especially true of Kohlberg's highest stage of justice, a
poor rival to benevolent ideals. (My own first publications in moral
development, "Moral Education and Its Cure" and "Altruism and
Moral Development," took up this refrain.)

The 1970s saw a flowering of criticisms focused on additional
"Kohlberg biases." These targeted ideological biases (by culture,
political partisanship, socioeconomic class and system, and gender)
and philosophical biases (showing partisanship to certain epistemological, social, normative-ethical, and meta-ethical schools of thought).
Kohlbergian researchers and theorists were accused of undue political liberalism, western-style/competitive-market individualism,
classism, and patriarchal attitudes. These biases purportedly slanted
the way they originally chose or sampled research subjects (white
males), posed moral issues for subjects to discuss (conflicts of individual interest), and constructed moral interviews that contained
these conflicts (with forced-choice, right-wrong formats). These biases also slanted the way researchers categorized or coded the
resulting responses (by moral relevance) and interpreted them (by
moral validity and cognitive competence). The ideological critiques
of Simpson and Sullivan, included here, are perhaps best known.

Kohlberg was singled out for showing further "philosophical" partisanship that tainted research method and theory. The moral depictions in his stages reputedly leaned toward ethical rationalism, Kantianism, social contractarianism, meta-ethical objectivism, and formalism. As critics saw it, this tendency was progressively "read in" to the data.

Such criticisms were especially easy to formulate since Kohlberg explicitly avowed allegiance to these particular tenets and schools of thought. In addition, he glibly derided notable alternatives like ethical intuitionism, utilitarianism, and relativism. Over time, he also pledged allegiance to various ideological "biases" as well, such as "Western-style liberalism."

Allegiance to Piagetian structuralism also branded Kohlberg researchers "rigid formalists" on the psychological front. (Why else would they squeeze the myriad subtleties and varieties of moral thought and feeling into a single, invariant, logically hierarchical sequence of universal stages?) Kohlberg's "Stage 6" was singled out for abuse as the embodiment of all Kohlberg bias. Locke's, Staughan's, and my criticisms focus on Stage 6, covering the gamut of bias charges.

These theoretical challenges dovetailed neatly with criticisms of Kohlberg's research methodology—his highly qualitative interpretation of research data and its inhospitableness to statistical analysis. "Kurtines and Grief" (included here) became the best-known methodological critique of Kohlberg methods. Born of similar methodological doubts, Murphy's and Gilligan's criticism of moral "theme bias" became the most widely known theoretical critique, suggesting patriarchal bias as well. Holstein's data on male-favoring sex differences in Kohlberg studies buttressed the latter suggestion, which became more vocal and gained more attention over time.

Unfortunately, replies to these criticisms are far less well known, as are Kohlberg's accommodations to critics, and his self-instigated revisions of methods and theory. Broughton's important reply to Kurtines and Grief is included here. My essay "Toward the Redevelopment of Kohlberg's Theory" notes the virtual irrelevance of most theoretical criticism—ideological and philosophical criticism—to Kohlberg's data-based stage theory. Such controversies rage at a meta-theoretical level, leaving newly reformulated stage depictions unscathed. These new, data-based depictions and the research revisions they reflect are included in Volume Five with Kohlberg's reply to critics.

Some notable criticisms of the Piaget-Kohlberg framework are a bit less radical, seeking only piecemeal clarifications and revisions.

I include here the contributions of Gibbs, on the unrecognized Piagetian reflectivity of higher moral stages, and of Peters, who argues for the compatibility of stage and virtue theory. (Indeed, Peters argues that Kohlberg's stages *are* complex virtues.) Van Haaften attempts to further elaborate the much-neglected logic of developmental transformation.

The Great
Justice
Debate

THE CLAIM TO MORAL ADEQUACY OF A HIGHEST STAGE
OF MORAL JUDGMENT *

IN previous publications I have outlined: (a) the extensive research facts concerning culturally universal stages of moral
judgment,[1] (b) the psychological theory of development which
best fits those facts,[2] and (c) a metaethical view which attempts to
bridge the gap between naturalistic and nonnaturalistic theories of
moral judgment and their grounds of adequacy.[3] The present paper
elaborates a claim made in the previous paper [3]: the claim that a
higher or later stage of moral judgment is "objectively" preferable
to or more adequate than an earlier stage of judgment according to
certain *moral* criteria. Since these criteria of adequacy are those central to judgment at our most advanced stage, "stage 6," the problem
becomes one of justifying the structure of moral judgment at stage
6. First, however, we shall briefly review the position taken in our
earlier paper, and introduce the claims of the present one.

I. REVIEW OF PSYCHOLOGICAL THEORY

Over a period of almost twenty years of empirical research, my colleagues and I have rather firmly established a culturally universal
invariant sequence of stages of moral judgment; these stages are

[2] I treat these matters in greatest detail in my papers "Propositional Verbs and
Knowledge," this JOURNAL, LXIX, 11 (June 1, 1972): 301–312, and "The Wages of
Scepticism," *American Philosophical Quarterly*, x, 3 (July 1973): 177–187.

* To be presented in an APA symposium on Moral Development and Moral
Philosophy, December 28, 1973; commentators will be Kurt Baier and Richard G.
Henson; see this JOURNAL, this issue, 646–648 and 648–649, respectively.

[1] *Moralization: The Cognitive-Developmental Approach* (New York: Holt,
Rinehart & Winston, 1974).

[2] "Stage and Sequence: The Cognitive-Developmental Approach to Socialization," in D. Goslin, ed., *Handbook of Socialization Theory and Research* (New
York: Rand McNally, 1969).

[3] "From Is to Ought: How to Commit the Naturalistic Fallacy and Get Away
with It in the Study of Moral Development," in T. Mischel, ed., *Cognitive Development and Epistemology* (New York: Academic Press, 1971).

grossly summarized in Table 1:

Table 1. Definition of Moral Stages

I. Preconventional level

At this level the child is responsive to cultural rules and labels of good and bad, right or wrong, but interprets these labels either in terms of the physical or the hedonistic consequences of action (punishment, reward, exchange of favors) or in terms of the physical power of those who enunciate the rules and labels. The level is divided into the following two stages:

Stage 1: *The punishment-and-obedience orientation.* The physical consequences of action determine its goodness or badness regardless of the human meaning or value of these consequences. Avoidance of punishment and unquestioning deference to power are valued in their own right, not in terms of respect for an underlying moral order supported by punishment and authority (the latter being stage 4).

Stage 2: *The instrumental-relativist orientation.* Right action consists of that which instrumentally satisfies one's own needs and occasionally the needs of others. Human relations are viewed in terms like those of the market place. Elements of fairness, of reciprocity, and of equal sharing are present, but they are always interpreted in a physical pragmatic way. Reciprocity is a matter of "you scratch my back and I'll scratch yours," not of loyalty, gratitude, or justice.

II. Conventional level

At this level, maintaining the expectations of the individual's family, group, or nation is perceived as valuable in its own right, regardless of immediate and obvious consequences. The attitude is not only one of *conformity* to personal expectations and social order, but of loyalty to it, of actively *maintaining*, supporting, and justifying the order, and of identifying with the persons or group involved in it. At this level, there are the following two stages:

Stage 3: *The interpersonal concordance or "good boy---nice girl" orientation.* Good behavior is that which pleases or helps others and is approved by them. There is much conformity to stereotypical images of what is majority or "natural" behavior. Behavior is frequently judged by intention—"he means well" becomes important for the first time. One earns approval by being "nice."

Stage 4: *The "law and order" orientation.* There is orientation toward authority, fixed rules, and the maintenance of the social order. Right behavior consists of doing one's duty, showing respect for authority, and maintaining the given social order for its own sake.

III. Postconventional, autonomous, or principled level

At this level, there is a clear effort to define moral values and principles that have validity and application apart from the authority of the groups or persons holding these principles and apart from the individual's own identification with these groups. This level again has two stages:

Stage 5: *The social-contract legalistic orientation,* generally with utilitarian overtones. Right action tends to be defined in terms of general individual rights, and standards which have been critically examined and agreed upon by the whole society. There is a clear awareness of the relativism of personal values and opinions and a corresponding emphasis upon procedural rules for reaching consensus. Aside from what is constitutionally and democratically agreed upon, the right is a matter of personal "values" and "opinion." The result is an emphasis upon the "legal point of view," but with an emphasis upon the possibility of changing law in terms of rational considerations of social utility (rather than freezing it in terms of stage 4 "law and order"). Outside the legal realm, free agreement and contract is the binding element of obligation. This is the "official" morality of the American government and constitution.

Stage 6: *The universal-ethical-principle orientation.* Right is defined by the decision of conscience in accord with self-chosen *ethical principles* appealing to logical comprehensiveness, universality, and consistency. These principles are abstract and ethical (the Golden Rule, the categorical imperative); they are not concrete moral rules like the Ten Commandments. At heart, these are universal principles of *justice*, of the *recriprocity* and *equality* of human *rights*, and of respect for the dignity of human beings as *individual persons* ("From Is to Ought," pp. 164/5).

As Table 1 indicates, the last stage, stage 6, has a distinctively Kantian ring, centering moral judgment on concepts of obligation as these are defined by principles of respect for persons and of justice. In part, this corresponds to an initial "formalist" or "structuralist" bias of both our moral and our psychological theory. Our psychological theory of morality derives largely from Piaget,[4] who claims that both logic and morality develop through stages and that each stage is a structure which, formally considered, is in better equilibrium than its predecessor. It assumes, that is, that each new (logical or moral) stage is a new structure which includes elements of earlier structures but transforms them in such a way as to represent a more stable and extensive equilibrium. Our theory assumes that new moral structures presuppose new logical structures, i.e., that a new logical stage (or substage) is a necessary but not sufficient condition for a new moral stage. It assumes, however, that moral judgments (or moral equilibrium) involves two related processes or conditions absent in the logical domain. First, moral judgments in-

[4] Jean Piaget, *The Moral Judgment of the Child* (Glencoe, Ill.: Free Press, 1948; first edition, 1932).

volve role-taking, taking the point of view of others conceived as *subjects* and coordinating those points of view, whereas logic involves only coordinating points of view upon objects. Second, equilibrated moral judgments involve principles of justice or fairness. A moral situation in disequilibrium is one in which there are unresolved conflicting claims. A resolution of the situation is one in which each is "given his due" according to some principle of justice that can be recognized as fair by all the conflicting parties involved. These "equilibration" assumptions of our psychological theory are naturally allied to the formalistic tradition in philosophic ethics from Kant to Rawls. This isomorphism of psychological and normative theory generates the claim that a psychologically more advanced stage of moral judgment is more morally adequate, by moral-philosophic criteria. The isomorphism assumption is a two-way street. While moral philosophical criteria of adequacy of moral judgment help define a standard of psychological adequacy or advance, the study of psychological advance feeds back and clarifies these criteria. Our psychological theory as to why individuals move from one stage to the next is grounded on a moral-philosophical theory which specifies that the later stage is morally better or more adequate than the earlier stage. Our psychological theory claims that individuals prefer the highest stage of reasoning they comprehend, a claim supported by research.[5] This claim of our psychological theory derives from a philosophical claim that a later stage is "objectively" preferable or more adequate by certain *moral* criteria. This philosophic claim, however, would for us be thrown into question if the facts of moral advance were inconsistent with its psychological implications.

Our assumption of isomorphism implies first the assumption of continuity between the context of discovery of moral viewpoints (studied by the psychology of moral development) and the context of justification of moral viewpoints (studied by formal moral philosophy). This implies that the philosopher's *justification* of a higher stage of moral reasoning maps into the psychologist's *explanation* of movement to that stage, and vice versa. The isomorphism assumption is plausible if one believes that the developing human being and the moral philosopher are engaged in fundamentally the same moral task.

II. MORAL THEORIES AND NATURAL STRUCTURES

Our notions of moral philosophic adequacy derive, then, from the notion that moral theories are derivative from the natural struc-

[5] See my *Moralization, op. cit.*

tures we term "stages." The structures are "natural," not in the sense of being innate, but in the sense of being the sequential results of processing moral experience, not derivative from particular teachings or particular moral ideologies or theories. In this sense notions of natural rights, social contract, and utility are "natural structures" emerging in nonphilosophers from reflection upon the limits of customary morality in very varied cultural and educational circumstances. To clarify the relation of philosophic moral theories to this, we have interviewed moral philosophers concerning our moral dilemmas and tried to relate their published theory to their reasoning on the dilemmas. We feel that our results justify the notion that a philosopher's formal moral theory is an elaboration of certain portions of his "natural" moral-stage structure. Not only do philosophers use their published moral theories to reason about interview dilemmas, but we see that their theories interlock with "natural" or unformalized elements of their moral reasoning unstated in their published theories but required for actually making moral decisions. Further, hardly to our surprise, all philosophers interviewed reason at the two highest stages, being stage 5, stage 6, or some mixture of the two. We believe our data on philosophers are consistent with our assumptions, that: (1) stages are natural structures generating families of moral theories, and (2) the two major families of formal normative moral theory tend to be generated by two natural structures which we term "stage 5" and "stage 6."

Our own approach to moral theory is to view it as a constructive systematization of these natural structures. Without formal moral theory men naturally attain to a "stage 5" in which they judge laws by the light of a social contract, by rule-utilitarianism, and by some notion of universal or natural rights. Much moral philosophy may be understood as a systematization of this mode of thought, and most moral philosophers have, in some sense, assumed this to be their task. Other philosophers, however, have attempted to generalize, or raise to a higher level, these "stage 5" postulates, to define a basis for individually principled moral decision. As George Herbert Mead [6] put it:

> Kant generalized the position involved in the theory of natural rights and social contract, which was that one could claim for himself only that which he recognized equally for others. He made a generalization of this the basis for his moral doctrine, the categorical imperative that

[6] *Movements of Thought in the Nineteenth Century* (Chicago: University Press, 1936).

every act should be of such a character that it could be made universal for everyone under the same conditions.

As John Rawls [7] states it:

My aim is to present a conception of justice which generalizes and carries to a higher level of abstraction the familiar theory of the social contract as found, say, in Locke, Rousseau and Kant.

In our view, there is a family of theories that have the purpose just stated of Kant and Rawls. This family of theories may be looked at as derivatives of a natural structure I term "stage 6." Rawls's theory, when traced back to its natural structural roots, is not merely a "generalization" and "abstraction" of the theory of social contract, but derives from a new way of thought, a new system of assumptions, a new decision-making process. This is true in the same sense that "the familiar theory of social contract" is not merely a "generalization" and "abstraction" of the stage 4 conception of an overriding need for social order, but is an expression of a natural structure we term "stage 5."

The purpose of this paper, then, is to describe the stage 6 natural structure underlying various theories like Rawls's and to justify the sense in which it is better than structures of reasoning based on the "more familiar" conception of the social contract and of utilitarianism.

In terms of description, this means that we view Rawls's theory as further elaborating a natural decision-making structure only partly specified by Kant and that Rawls's theory can be further elaborated and specified as a decision-structure applicable to resolving individual moral dilemmas, as we attempt to do in this paper.

A second claim of this paper is that the adequacy of a moral structure is to be judged primarily in terms of the adequacy of an interlocked series of assumptions for making moral choice. The criteria of adequacy used by stage 6 are implicit in "stage 5" structures, since these are trying to do the same job as stage 6. Both aim at determining moral decisions and judgments on which all rational men involved in sociomoral action could ideally agree. Stage 6 can do this better than stage 5.

III. DIFFERENTIATION AND INTEGRATION AT STAGE 6

Assuming for the moment the existence of a natural structure called "stage 6," how can developmental analysis aid in justifying its claim

[7] A Theory of Justice (Cambridge, Mass.: Harvard, 1971).

to adequacy? By claiming that stage 6 is more adequate than stage 5 by certain formal criteria which also make stage 5 more adequate than stage 4. Two such criteria are differentiation and integration. In our earlier paper ("From Is to Ought") we elaborated the formal concepts of differentiation and integration that apply to both the psychological and the normative analysis of moral deliberation, and linked the concepts to formalistic concepts of moral judgments as prescriptive and universal. Increased differentiation and integration are anchored in the "is" side by their explanatory power in the study of the development of directed thinking, and on the "ought" side by their necessary inclusion in rational justification and choice. To illustrate how and why this might be the case, we shall consider some usages of the categories of "rights" and "duties" at stages 5 and 6, and the sense in which this suggests that moral theories derived from stage 6 structures are more advanced than moral theories derived from stage 5 structures. Table 2 shows usage of "rights" and "duties" at each stage:

Table 2. Six Stages in the Usage of Categories of Rights and Obligations

Stage 1. *Having a Right:* Means having the power or authority to control something or someone, or it is confused with being right (in accordance with authority).

Obligation: Or "should" is what one "has to do" because of the demands of external authorities, rules, or the external situation.

Stage 2. *Having a Right:* Implies freedom of the self to choose and to control the self and its possessions. One has a right to ignore the positive claims or welfare of another as long as one does not directly violate his freedom, or injure him. (Having a right differentiated from being right, and from being given the power to, by a status one holds.)

Obligation: Obligation or "should" is a hypothetical imperative contingent on choice in terms of an end. In this sense, obligations are limited to oneself and one's ends. ("Should" or obligation differentiated from "has to" from external or authoritative compulsion.)

Stage 3. *Having a Right:* Implies an expectation of control and freedom which a "good" or natural person would claim. A right is based either on a rule or on a legitimate expectation toward others, e.g., you have a right to have your property respected since you worked hard to acquire the property. Rights are earned. (Having a right differentiated from the freedom to control and choose.)

Obligation: "Should" or "duty" equals a role-obligation, what it is incumbent on a member of a social position to do for his role-partners as defined by rules, by the expectation of the role-partner, or by what a good role-occupant (a good husband, a good doctor) would do. (Obligation differentiated from being a means to a desired end.)

8

Stage 4. *Having a Right:* Rights are: (a) categorical general freedoms and expectations which all members of society have, and (b) rights awarded to particular roles by society. General rights usually take primacy over role-rights. (Having a right differentiated from a particular legitimate expectation.)

Obligation: Obligations are responsibilities, i.e., welfare states of others or of society for which one is accountable. These responsibilities arise through: (a) being a member of society, and (b) voluntarily entering into roles which entail these responsibilities. (Obligation or duty as commitment and responsibility differentiated from what is typically expected of a role-occupant.)

Stage 5. *Having a Right:* Has an awareness of human or natural rights or liberties which are prior to society and which society is to protect. It is usually thought by stage 5 that freedoms should be limited by society and law only when they are incompatible with the like freedoms of others. (Natural rights differentiated from societally awarded rights.)

Obligation: Obligations are what one has contracted to fulfill in order to have one's own rights respected and protected. These obligations are defined in terms of a rational concern for the welfare of others. (Obligations as required rational concern for welfare differentiated from fixed responsibilities.)

Stage 6. *Having a Right:* There are universal rights of just treatment which go beyond liberties and which represent universalizable claims of one individual upon another.

Obligation: Any right or just claim by an individual gives use to a corresponding duty to another individual.

Table 2 suggests that each higher stage's usage of the categories of rights and duties is *more differentiated and integrated* than the prior stage. We list, in the parentheses, the differentiation of the concept of "right" and "obligation" made by each stage not made at the prior stages. At stage 2, a right as a freedom is differentiated from a physical or social power; at stage 3 it is differentiated as an expectation to be supported by others from an actual physical or psychological freedom, etc. The sense in which each stage is *better integrated* is seen in the fact that only at stage 6 are rights and duties completely correlative. The meaning of correlativity of rights and duties is suggested in the following passage by Raphael.[8]

We have accepted the deontological view that the moral use of "ought" is a basic concept that cannot be derived from the idea of goodness.— We turn next to the notion of "rights." There are two senses of the word, the first meaning, "I have no duty to refrain from so acting,"

[8] D. Daiches Raphael, *Moral Judgement* (London: Allen & Unwin, 1955).

the second in which I describe the same fact as I describe by saying, "Someone else has a duty to me." The second kind of a right might be called "a right of recipience." Whenever I have a right of action, I also have a right of recipience. In virtue of the second definition of rights, the two forms of expression: "A has a duty to B" and "B has a right (of recipience) against A" are correlative in the sense of analytically implying each other. They may not be connotatively tautologous in ordinary speech, though they are in the more precise language we are recommending (pp. 47–49).

Let us accept, for the moment, Raphael's view that using rights and duties on correlative terms is either more "precise" or more "integrated." We have found that such usage, consistently maintained, is found only at stage 6. At stage 5, "rights" categories are completely reciprocal; i.e., the concept and limits of rights are completely reciprocal with the rights of others, but individual rights and individual duties are not completely correlative.

An example is case 2, age twenty-four, who said:

Morality to me means recognizing the rights of others first to life and then to do as they please as long as it doesn't interfere with somebody else's rights.

Although case 2 is able to define rights clearly, he is unable to specify clearly the conditions under which awareness of rights generates correlative duties. At stage 5, for every right, society has some duty to protect that right. Duties to other individuals, however, are not clearly specified in the absence of either individual contract or social contract. At stage 5 there are obligations to the law and there are obligations to the welfare of others, of a rule- or act-utilitarian sort. But recognition of individual rights does not directly generate individual duties; i.e., rights and duties are not directly correlative. Even moral philosophers, like our "natural" stage 5 subjects, need not accept that rights directly imply duties. This is indicated in philosophers' responses to the following dilemma:

In Europe, a woman was near death from a very bad disease, a special kind of cancer. There was one drug that the doctors thought might save her. It was a form of radium for which a druggist was charging ten times what the drug cost him to make. The sick woman's husband, Heinz, went to everyone he knew to borrow the money, but he could only get together about half of what it cost. He told the druggist that his wife was dying, and asked him to sell it cheaper or let him pay later. But the druggist said, "No, I discovered the drug and I'm going to make money from it." So Heinz got desperate and broke into the man's store to steal the drug for his wife.

In general, subjects whom we classify on other grounds as stage 5 recognize the woman's right to live, but do not believe that it directly generates an obligation to steal to save her. Or they may recognize a duty to steal for the wife, based on contract, but recognize no duty to steal for the friend or stranger who equally has a right to life. This, too, is the position taken by a number of moral philosophers, two of whom are quoted elsewhere ("From Is to Ought," 206–207).

Examples are as follows:

Philosopher 1:

> What Heinz did was not wrong. The distribution of scarce drugs should be regulated by principles of fairness. In the absence of such regulations, the druggist was within his legal rights, but in the circumstances he has no moral complaint. He still was within his moral rights, however, unless it was within his society a strongly disapproved thing to do. While what Heinz did was not wrong, it was not his duty to do it. In this case it is not wrong for Heinz to steal the drug, but it goes beyond the call of duty; it is a deed of supererogation.

Philosopher 2:

> It is a husband's duty to steal the drug. The principle that husbands should look after their wives to the best of their ability is one whose general observance does more good than harm. He should also steal it for a friend, if he were a very close friend (close enough for it to be understood that they would do this sort of thing for each other). The reasons are similar to those in the case of wives. If the person with cancer were a less close friend, or even a stranger, Heinz would be doing a good act if he stole the drug, but he has no duty to.

These philosophers agree that stealing to save a life in the situation is right, but disagree on when it is a duty. Using rule-utilitarian criteria of duty, it is difficult to make duties and rights correlative. In contrast, here is the response of philosopher 3, who responds quite differently to duty questions about this dilemma:

IF THE HUSBAND DOES NOT FEEL VERY CLOSE OR AFFECTIONATE TO HIS WIFE, SHOULD HE STEAL THE DRUG?
Yes. The value of her life is independent of any personal ties. The value of human life is based on the fact that it offers the only possible source of a categorical moral "ought" to a rational being acting in the role of a moral agent. _
SUPPOSE IT WERE A FRIEND OR AN ACQUAINTANCE?
Yes, the value of a human life remains the same.

In general, philosopher 3's conceptions of rights and duties were correlative. In this sense his thinking appears more differentiated and integrated than that of the other two philosophers. We must note, however, that the greater integration of a structure making rights and duties correlative is not a mere matter of increased logical or analytical tidiness, as Raphael suggests, but that it imposes a severe price. The price in question is, baldly, that philosopher 3 has to be prepared to go to jail to steal for a friend or acquaintance, and philosophers 1 and 2 do not. According to Raphael (*op. cit.*):

> From an objective point of view, the so-called duties of supererogation are not duties. For the agent, they are duties but from the objective standpoint, i.e., from the standpoint of what we take to be the average moral agent, they are thought to go beyond duty. Correspondingly, in the eyes of the agent, the beneficiary has a right while from the objective standpoint (of the average impartial spectator) the person benefited does not have a right (51).

We would question whether duties and rights could be made correlative, as Raphael wishes, if the moral point of view adopted is that recommended by Raphael, i.e., "the average moral agent" or "the average impartial spectator." To make duties and rights correlative, we must take not the standpoint of the "average moral agent," but philosopher 3's standpoint of the "rational moral agent." The rational moral agent is not a self-sacrificial saint, since the saint's duties do not imply that he has corresponding rights. The rational moral agent is fair, not saintly, he does as a duty only what his is rationally prepared to demand that others do as a duty, or that to which he has a right. The fact that a dying acquaintance in need of the medicine has the right to life does not define a duty for the average moral agent, but it may for the rational or just moral agent.

In summary, there are certain basic categories used by every moral stage-structure or every moral theory, such as the categories of rights and duties. Development through the stages indicates a progressive differentiation of categories from one another, e.g., of rights from duties, and a progressive integration of them, expressed in the correlativity of rights and duties. This correlativity is not merely a matter of the analytic tidiness of an abstract normative or metaethical theory, but leads to very different judgmetns of obligation, judgments that are in better equilibrium with judgments of rights.

As a result, stage 6 moral judgments are- able to differentiate, among the amorphous wastebasket of "actions of supererogation," those actions which are duties prescribed by the rights of others from those which are not.

As stated, a problem remains for stage 6 moral judgment. If the rights of every human define duties for an individual moral agent, this seems to open up the abyss of the existence of infinite and simultaneous duties to support the rights of every human being wherever he is. The problem here entailed is partially solvable, though complex. The individual moral agent has rights, and these rights are incompatible with having duties to every right of every other. Because a human being has a right to life, other humans have a duty to save that life. The conditions under which one human being has a duty to save the life of another human being require clarification of what it means for a "rational moral agent" to choose between conflicting duties since he cannot be an omnipotent saint.

IV. UNIVERSALIZABILITY AND REVERSIBILITY AT STAGE 6

Since Kant, formalists have argued that rational moral judgments must be reversible, consistent, and universalizable, and that this implies the prescriptivity of such judgments. We claim that only the substantive moral judgments made at stage 6 fully meet these conditions, and that each higher stage meets these conditions better than each lower stage. In fully meeting these conditions, stage 6 moral structures are ultimately equilibrated.

For developmental theory, meeting these conditions of moral judgment is parallel with the equilibration of fully logical thought in the realm of physical or logical facts. According to Piaget and others, the keystone of logic is reversibility. A logical train of thought is one in which one can move back and forth between premises and conclusions without distortion. Mathematical thinking is an example; $A + B$ is the same as $B + A$. Or again, the operation $A + B = C$ is reversible by the operation $C - B = A$. In one sense, the elements of reversible moral thought are the moral categories as these apply to the universe of moral actors. To say that rights and duties are correlative is to say that one can move from rights to duties and back without change or distortion. Universalizability and consistency are fully attained by the reversibility of prescriptions of actions. Reversibility of moral judgment is what is ultimately meant by the criterion of the fairness of a moral decision. Procedurally, fairness as impartiality means reversibility in the sense of a decision on which all interested parties could agree insofar as they can consider their own claims impartially, as the just decider would. If we have a reversible solution, we have one that could be reached as right starting from anyone's perspective in the situation, given each person's intent to put himself in the shoes of the other.

13

Reversibility meets a second criterion of formalism: universalizability. As reversibility starts with the slogan, "Put yourself in the other guy's shoes when you decide," universalizability starts with the slogan, "What if everyone did it; what if everyone used this principle of choice?" It is clear that universalizability is implied by reversibility. If something is fair or right to do from the conflicting points of view of all those involved in the situation, it is something we can wish all men to do in all similar situations. Reversibility tells us more than universalizability, then, in resolving dilemmas, but it implies universalizability.

The concept of reversibility explains the intuitive plausibility of Rawls's conception of justice (op. cit.) as a rational choice in an original position in which one is under a veil of ignorance as to one's role or identity. Rawls argues that this conception leads to the choice of a justice principle of equality, with inequalities accepted only when it is to the benefit of the least advantaged. This conception of choice in the veil of ignorance is a formalization of the conception of fairness involved in having one person cut the cake and a second person distribute it. This conception leads to a mini-maximization solution in the sense that the division must be such that the least advantaged person is better off, i.e., that the cake is so cut that the person cutting the cake is willing to live with getting the smallest piece.

Our conception of stage 6 helps to clarify the intuitive plausibility of Rawls's notion of the original position. This is because the concept of fairness as reversibility is the ultimate elaboration of the concept that fairness is reciprocity, a conception held at every stage. At stage 1, the conception of reciprocity is mechanical equivalence, an eye for an eye and a tooth for a tooth. At stage 2, reciprocity is mediated by awareness that self and others are subjectively evaluating actors with different interests and aware of one another's interests. The result is a notion of fairness as positive (or negative) exchange of gratifications: if you contribute to my needs and interests, it's fair for me to contribute to yours. At stage 3, reversibility becomes the Golden Rule, i.e., putting yourself in the other guy's shoes regardless of exchange of interests or values. The difficult attainment of this Golden Rule conception is illustrated by the following interpretation of the Golden Rule by a ten-year-old:

> Well, it's like your brain has to leave your head and go into the other guy's head and then come back into your head but you still see it like it was in the other guy's head and then you decide that way.

14

Stage 3 interpretations of Golden Rule reversibility, however, do not yield fair decisions nor are they completely reversible. As a result, they lead to no determinate moral resolution of a situation. In the "Heinz steals the drug" dilemma, the husband reaches one solution if he puts himself in his wife's shoes, another in the druggist's. Or again, in the Talmudic dilemma of a man with a water bottle encountering another man equally in danger of dying of thirst, a stage 3 interpretation of the Golden Rule logically leads to their passing the water bottle back and forth like Alphonse and Gaston.

At higher stages, e.g., stage 5, these problems are handled by the conceptions of prior rights and contractual agreements. Reversibility at stage 5 means reciprocity of rights. In the stage 5 subject's words:

> Morality means recognizing the rights of other individuals to do as they please as long as it doesn't interfere with somebody else's rights.

At stage 6, reversibility is attained by a second-order conception of Golden Rule role-taking. In the Heinz dilemma, Heinz must imagine whether the druggist could put himself in the wife's position and still maintain his claim and whether the wife could put herself in the druggist's position and still maintain her claim. Intuitively we feel the wife could, the druggist could not. As a result, it is fair for the husband to act on the basis of the wife's claim. We call the process by which a reversible moral decision is reached, "ideal role-taking." Stage 6 moral judgment is based on role-taking the claim of each actor under the assumption that all other actors' claims are also governed by the Golden Rule and accommodated accordingly. This is what is meant by calling stage 6 reversibility the second-order application of the Golden Rule. The steps for an actor involved in making such a decision based on ideal role-taking are:

1. To imagine onself in each person's position in that situation (including the self) and to consider all the claims he could make (or which the self could make in his position).
2. Then to imagine that the individual does not know which person he is in the situation and to ask whether he would still uphold that claim.
3. Then to act in accordance with these reversible claims in the situation.

This is clearly similar to Rawls's notion of choice under a veil of ignorance as to who in a moral situation one is to be. Differences involved spring from the facts that: (1) we are trying to arrive at concrete decisions in addition to a choice of principles governing a society, and (2) An ideal moral agent decides with knowledge of all the facts of interest and claims, and is under the veil of ignorance only as to who he is in the situation. Also eliminated is the opposition between a mini-maximization and a maximization basis of making a decision.

For the purpose of solving individual moral dilemmas, we do not want to assume that the individual is ignorant of the probabilities of outcome of a given decision to each person involved, only that he is ignorant of the probability of being any particular person in the situation, i.e., that he is likely to be any particular person in that situation.

Returning to the stealing-the-drug situation, let us imagine someone making the decision under the veil of ignorance, i.e., not knowing whether he is to be assigned the role of husband, wife, or druggist. Clearly, the rational solution is to steal the drug; i.e., this leads to the least loss (or the most gain) to an individual who could be in any role. This corresponds to our intuition of the primacy of the woman's right to life over the druggist's right to property and makes it a duty to act in terms of those rights. If the situation is that the dying person is a friend or acquaintaince, the same holds true. Here a solution achieved under the veil of ignorance is equivalent to one obtained by ideal role-taking, or "moral musical chairs" as described earlier.

The notion of stage 6 as a natural structure implies the following:

1. A decision reached by playing moral musical chairs corresponds to a decision as to what is ultimately "just" or "fair." Ideal role-taking is the decision procedure ultimately required by the attitudes of respect for persons and of justice as equity recognized at higher stages. This is suggested by Rawls's derivation of principles of justice as equity from the original position.

2. Accordingly, the decision reached by ideal role-taking defines duties correlative to rights rather than acts of supererogation.

3. If we engage in ideal role-taking in most situations, we reach a determinate decision. Our stage 6 moral judges do agree on a choice alternative in our dilemmas where facts and probabilities are specified.

4. A decision reached in that way is in "equilibrium" in the sense that it is "right" from the point of view of all involved insofar as they are concerned to be governed by a moral attitude or a concep-

tion of justice, i.e., insofar as they are willing to take the roles of others.

5. The procedure integrates "absolute rights" or equality notions and utilitarian conceptions in conflict at stage 5.

To support these claims convincingly involves elaborating a "stage 6" analysis and choice in various moral dilemmas, a procedure not possible in a limited space. An example of the integration of utility and deontological justice more difficult than that of stealing the drug is that of an individual drowning in the river. A passerby can save him, but at a 25% risk of death (and a 75% chance that both will be saved). Stated in terms of ideal role-taking, from the point of view of the drowning person, he should. If the drowning person put himself in the bystander's shoes and returned to his own position, he still could make the claim. If the passerby took the drowning person's position, he could not maintain his claim to inaction. Stated in terms of the "veil of ignorance," if an individual did not know whether he was the bystander or the drowning person, he would judge the right decision that of jumping in as long as the risk of death for jumping was definitely less than 50%. Utility maximization (or minimaximization) leads to the choice of jumping in if the actor does not know the probabilities of which party he will end up being, but does know the probabilities of the outcome of each alternative (jumping/not-jumping) for both parties. In other words, in these situations "stage 5" utilitarian considerations are perceived from the point of view of stage 6 notions of correlative rights and duties based upon the fundamental equality of persons.

The notion that these claims correspond to a greater psychological equilibration of moral judgment becomes truly plausible in empirical study. A. Erdynast [9] gave subjects instructions to assume the original position. This could not be done or was meaningless to highly intelligent subjects below stage 5. Stage 5 subjects, however, would often change their choices after assuming the original position and would feel that the new solution was more adequate. A number of Harvard undergraduates engaged in small-group discussions in which original-position solutions were elaborated by the group leader and were discussed in relation to alternative ultimates of decision. A number of those who were initially stage 5 retained and elaborated this mode of moral thought, a change we called a

[9] "Relationships between Moral Stage and Reversibility of Moral Judgment in an Original Position." Unpublished Ph.D. thesis, Harvard University, 1973.

movement from stage 5 to stage 6. The fact that only students pre-viously at stage 5 adopted this mode of thinking suggests that it is a stepwise progression of an intuitive natural structure rather than one more moral theory.

LAWRENCE KOHLBERG
Laboratory of Human Development, Harvard University

Human Develop. *17:* 81–106 (1974)

Moral Development Research

A Case Study of Scientific Cultural Bias

ELIZABETH LÉONIE SIMPSON

University of Southern California, Los Angeles, Calif.

Abstract. From the moral development scale scoring manual, Kohlberg's published works, and the research of his collaborators and others, an analysis was made of the evidence supporting the hierarchy of moral reasoning (from the lowest stage of blind acceptance of powerful authority to the application of abstract principles of justice and equality) and the claims put forth for the cross-cultural universality of the cognitive-developmental theory. Findings suggest that the definitions of stages and the assumptions underlying them, including the view that the scheme is universally applicable, are ethnocentric and culturally-biased. Conceptual and methodological problems of cross-disciplinary and cross-cultural research are discussed.

Key Words

Moral development
Cultural bias
Cross-cultural universality
Developmental theory
Developmental stages
Ethnocentrism
Cross-cultural
Cross-disciplinary

Two thousand years ago *human brotherhood* as a concept broke out of faith as the first swell of a wave which is still ascending. Ideological in origin, the term then as today was intended to represent those commonalities which hold species-wide – to declare unimportant the manifest differences which divide individuals and groups. A statement of belief and hope, the concept included only scattered reports of personal testimony that *human brother-hood* actually existed, had been observed and experienced as alive and, if not as well as might be desired, at least describable. Universality suffered a major setback when, as their developing science unfolded, in a more structured way anthropologists inferred from their widening field experience that no *empirical* base supported broad generalizations about human behavior, that groups shaped their own patterns of thought and actions and that these varied for historical, genetic, and environmental reasons. Generalization grounded on too little evidence had turned out to be normative statements of what Western social scientists believed to be the way that members of specific cultures *ought* to behave if they were 'primitive', 'folk', or 'civilized' societies. A neat hierarchy placed the scientists' own cultures at the top of the list with others trailing at various levels of inferiority. The concept of *human brotherhood* or *universality* was driven to the slaughter-house to be eaten as *cultural relativism,* and the American Anthropological Association issued a statement that cultural superiority was intellectually blind and socially destructive since which time, among anthropologists at least, the attempt to generalize culturally-specific structures or processes into species-wide ones has proceeded with considerable caution.

Care is warranted. It is hard not to believe that, beneath the humanist's intuitive acceptance of his fellow man, there lies a solid empirically-derived plinth of commonality. Different can mean equal, but it is rarely seen that way and we are easier with each other when we find our similarities. During the past 15 years some of these have been described by KOHLBERG and his associates who have been studying the developmental sequence and stages of moral reasoning in children and young adults. Their work, and that of an increasing number of others in cross-cultural research, insistently press some unanswered questions upon us: how are claims to universality to be established? Just how are group differences to be accounted for? As a case in point, I would like to consider the methodology and interpretation of findings which are specific to KOHLBERG's cognitive-developmental research. These, I believe, serve as a focus for examining more broadly some of the problems of cross-cultural studies in any field, not just the emotion-laden one of morality.

Philosophical and Psychological Bases of Morality

Morality may be examined from a number of perspectives, some more suited to the philosopher than to the scientist and some the contrary. All the phenomena of morality – the patterns of behavior, principles, concepts, rules employed by individuals and groups in dealing with moral issues and decision-making – may be studied through descriptive empirical inquiry into *what is*. Normative investigation into what *should* represent moral obligation, right, and good in human relationships and the analytic answering of logical, epistemological, and semantic questions about ethics – these two are philosophical attempts to understand the process. The three are all legitimate but differing modes of thinking. The demands of accurate communication include making clear which mode is being utilized so that the claims to authority of science are not confused with those of theology and philosophy. One of the difficulties with KOHLBERG's work (as I will elaborate later) is that, although developing parallel and, in some senses, isomorphic philosophical and psychological statements of cognition and morality, in his prolific writing he does not make clear the empirical sources of his claims to universality in the empirical realm. The distinction between normative philosophy and empirical psychology remains blurred, and normative thinking especially governs the description of what he calls empirically derived categories of 'post-conventional' or principled reasoning.

In brief, KOHLBERG believes that, building on PIAGET's [1955] work on the developmental acquisition of morality, he has isolated the *structure* of morality from its *content*. He has described a typology of stages through which all maturing individuals pass in invariant sequence, although at differential rates which are affected by interaction with the social environment. KOHLBERG's cognitive scheme describes a structure of morality in which the acquisition of new modes of thought is dependent upon the reorganization and displacement of preceding modes through a self-constructive process. Three levels succeed one another: the *pre-conventional,* the *conventional,* and the *post-conventional.* Each has two stages. For the pre-conventional, the first is one in which goodness is defined in terms of the physical consequences which actions provoke and the second one in which instrumental actions are good because, through reciprocity, they supply what is wanted from others. At the conventional level, goodness is defined as conformity to the expectations of others. At stage 3, good behavior is that which is pleasing to others and approved by them; at stage 4, respect for authority and the belief that the social order should be maintained – a law-and-order orientation – govern moral reasoning. Stages 5 and 6 occur at the post-conventional level where morality is seen as apart from the authority invested in persons or groups at any one time. What is 'right', at stage 5, is a matter of social contract or agreement among men and may be changed by them for rational considerations of social utility. At stage 6 morality is based in the autonomous functioning of conscience in accordance with abstract principles of justice, equality, and reciprocity which is dependent not merely upon the exchange of advantages but also upon respect for the dignity of human beings as individual persons. KOHLBERG refers to the stage types he has delineated as an invariant developmental sequence, although related research has only tentatively supported that claim.[1]

KOHLBERG suggests that those who are learning to score protocols based on the moral dilemma stories which make up the moral development interviews read FRANKENA's [1963] little book, 'Ethics', to gain some understanding of the philosophical underpinnings

[1] To show sequentiality based on empirical evidence, stage-6 individuals, for example, would have to pass through 4 and 5, stage-5 individuals through 4, and stage-4 individuals through neither of the others. Recent writing by KOHLBERG and his colleagues takes it for granted that this has been established, although the data most often quoted [TURIEL, 1966] reports only stages 2, 3, and 4 and the hypothesis of irreversible forward movement through the stages was supported *only* by reporting the *net* shift (experimental results minus control) which approached statistical significance and was in the right direction. REST *et al.* [1969] also report that children presented with statements at different moral levels tend to prefer those above, rather than their own, but alternative explanations besides the attractiveness of higher level concepts are also plausible [HOFFMAN, 1970, pp. 279–280].

of the theory. Near the beginning of this work, FRANKENA writes that 'morality is a social enterprise ...social in its origins, sanction, and functions'. It is a social institution which also promotes the rational self-guidance or self-determination of its members, an individualistic or protestant aspect of its nature which the philosopher sees clearly may be confined to the Western world. 'In MATHEW ARNOLD's words, it asks us to be... "self-govern'd, at the feet of Law"' [FRANKENA, 1963, p. 5].

According to both moral philosophy and recent social psychology, morality begins for each individual as a set of culturally defined goals and of rules governing achievement of the goals, which are more or less external to the individual and imposed on him or inculcated as habits. This internalization process may be an entirely irrational one on the learner's part, but it is usually accompanied by culturally-held beliefs which are given as reasons. Later, there is movement toward rationality, the examined life, and autonomy, with the individual becoming a moral agent of his own.

FRANKENA does not carry his awareness of cultural difference far enough to see that learning to examine one's own life analytically and to function as an autonomous moral agent may also be the result of group values and training. As a philosopher, he leans briefly into the world of sensory observation and meets KOHLBERG bending energetically his way. 'I was aware', KOHLBERG [1971, p. 152] writes, of orienting to philosophical concepts of morality'. Like his predecessor, PIAGET, he takes his theory of cognitive stages to be a theory of genetic epistemology, rather than a purely psychological one. As the empirical psychologist is a contributor to the solution of epistemological problems, so the philosopher provides the ethical implications of psychological theory: '...an adequate psychological explanation of cognition or of morality must include an explanation of these concepts throughout humanity, an explanation that cannot be purely psychological in the usual sense.' The 'epistemological blinders psychologists have worn have hidden from them the fact that the concept of morality is itself a philosophical (ethical) rather than a behavioral concept'.

So far so good. The marriage between the two disciplines has been completed and its consumation is underway. But one of the partners turns out to be somewhat less than up to the expectations aroused by KOHLBERG's statement that 'One can be pluralistic as to philosophic concepts and arrive at the same research conclusions...'. His cosmopolitanism is hemispheric, for KOHLBERG's 'pluralism' is strictly confined to *Western* philosophy: '...whether one starts from Kant, Mill, Hare, Ross or Rawls in defining morality, one gets similar research results.' (Elsewhere DEWEY is added to the list). Surely an adequate explanation of the concept of morality 'throughout humanity' implies the examination of its meaning in the *non*-Western world as well – a very large portion of humanity. Any philosophical system which supports a *universal* theory of development must account for conceptual differences which arise in the varying perceptions and explanations of reality adhering to the customs and broad social environments of diverse groups. Western and Eastern philosophies differ far more *between* themselves than *within,* both in substance and methodology. The reconciliation of this variance in order to build a unified, synthetic theory of human moral development would be a difficult task – perhaps even an impossible one – without major assimilation of one general system by another and the destruction of its integrity. The *tertium quid* resulting might then become the philosophical foundation for claims of universality. This situation does not exist today, however, even if indeed it may in the future, and in the meantime Western philosophy does not represent systems of thought common to the entire world.

Moral Development as Socialization

BRANDT [1959, p. 87], seeking to describe what it is that disparate groups of men have in common in regard to ethical theory, concludes that there are culturally universal meanings to moral *terms* – that is, that all cultures have *legal* or *formal* rules and *moral* or *informal* rules or both. All have also certain modes of making moral judgments and concepts which express these modes (such as obligation, moral evaluation, punishment and reward, etc.), although the content to which these modes apply and which is judged moral varies from culture to culture. To KOHLBERG, this argument is only a justification for the 'fact' that morality is a socio-cultural product derived from the mores of a particular society and originating at the social-system level, not at the individual level. It is difficult to see how morality could be other than the product of interaction with the social environment and, in that sense, a socio-cultural product. KOHLBERG as much as says so himself in attributing development to a self-constructive process of organism-environment interaction. But this is not to say that a specific culture's moral system is unicellular, for any society may have more than one set of overlapping mores. The moral content of a particular subgroup may not even be consistent with that of others; in a pluralistic society his reference groups may be more important for the moral development of any one individual or group than the generalized system attributed to the majority of the larger culture. Conforming thinking or behavior may be referenced to small groups within a complex culture and still be conventional thought or action.

In his argument against the conceptualization of moral development as socialization into the behavior patterns of a particular group, KOHLBERG remarks that studies of learned conformity to standards generally ignore the relationship of conformity to age-development. Citing studies which fail to show an increase in experimental honesty ('resistance to temptation'), he suggests that conformity to moral standards does not in fact define trends of age-development. The problem here, of course, as I have suggested above, may be in the definition of cultural conformity. It is possible that the failure of honesty to increase developmentally was indeed an indication of increased socialization into the norms of a particular group, e.g., that the *enacted* (and therefore *observed*) values of the group were *not* those of resistance to temptation and honesty and that, during the developmental process the children were truly learning actual, although not verbally expressed, values. Any attempt to account for the direction and type of development and the learning effects of group membership must take into consideration how a specific trait is regarded – that is, rewarded or punished – in its behavioral manifestations and not what the expressed cultural ideal is. Children get the message of the former as thoroughly or more so than the latter; in a corrupt society with a well-developed ideology both action and words may be learned.

Cultural Universality

Like each of us, KOHLBERG himself, his interest in cognitive development and moral reasoning, his choice of a Kantian or Deweyian infrastructure for this theory and his predilection for abstractions of such principles as

23

justice, equality, and reciprocity are all, in a sense, accidents of time and place and the interaction of his personality with a specifiable social environment and the norms of the subgroups within that environment. His rebuttal to BRANDT and others who emphasize cultural differences along with their superordinate more abstract commonalities is more a statement of faith than an evidence-based conclusion. Not only are there universal moral concepts, values, or principles, he writes, there is less variation between individuals and cultures than has usually been maintained in the sense that (1) 'almost all individuals in all cultures use the same thirty basic moral categories, concepts, or principles and (2) all individuals in all cultures go through the same order or sequences of gross stages of development, though varying in rate and terminal point of development' [KOHLBERG, 1971, p. 175]. (Earlier – p. 166 – we find the former statement expressed unqualifiedly: 'In all cultures we find the same aspects or categories of moral judgment and valuing...'.)

Whether or not (1) is an accurate statement, it is so broad as to be of extremely limited utility. What matters is not that there are thirty basic categories, concepts, or principles which are widely shared. (Perhaps there are more? Fewer?) If we wish to understand the actual process of morality what concerns us is *how* these are used, by *whom* (the old? the male? the sick? the married?) and *when*. As for (2), the evidence is suggestive, but hardly conclusive enough for the use of those firm, dogmatic 'all's'. Not that much work has been done. In one article [KOHLBERG, 1967], work in five cultures is referred to; in later work, still only twelve cultures are given as the basis for generalizing to mankind as a whole. (The latter is in reference to age trends toward *intentionality* – considering what the intentions of the moral actor were – which have been found in research by either PIAGET or KOHLBERG and their collaborators in the literate cultures of Switzerland, Belgium, Britain, Israel, United States, and Taiwan, as well as in all but one of the pre- or semi-literate cultures of the Atayal, Hopi, Zuni, Pagago, Mayan, and Sioux [KOHLBERG, 1969, p. 408].) Undifferentiated statements such as the following: 'Development of Negro slum groups is more like that found in Mexico than that found in the stable upper lower-class American group' [KOHLBERG, 1969, p. 401] do not add to our sense that the investigators are sensitively attuned to cultural variables. Is development is Mexico's highly sophisticated capital, on haciendas, in Indian villages, the jungles, and the tourist towns all equivalent to the same degree to development in American Negro slums? (Rural or urban? Northern or southern?)

Additionally, to render claims for universality valid, two aspects of the studies remain to be accounted for: (1) regression to previously held stages which deviates from the universal pattern of development and (2) the fact that post-conventional or principled reasoning is not found in some groups.[2] One cannot reasonably extrapolate from evidence of invariant sequentiality at the lower levels of moral reasoning to fill out the hierarchy at the higher levels. If principled reasoning as defined by KOHLBERG does not occur in some cultures, for whatever reason, then one third of the paradigm is missing and the assumption that, under different conditions, these stages *would* appear in these groups is not necessarily warranted. This is a researchable question, but one which has not been settled to date.

The ascendancy of the normative philosopher over the empirical scientist becomes very clear in KOHLBERG'S acknowledgment that his stage 6 describes a utopian ideal, rather than a reality: 'There is a universal set of moral principles held by men in various cultures, our stage 6. (These principles, we shall agree, *could* logically and consistently be held by all men in all societies; they would in fact be universal to all mankind if the conditions for socio-moral development were optimal for all individuals in all cultures.)

In responding to written and oral interviews based on situations and issues, a very small percentage of the subjects studied in a number of cultures utilize the reasoning processes and the principled content which *I prefer* to think is the highest developmental stage of which human beings are capable, and which *I believe* all *should* utilize and would under specifiable conditions.' (Italics added.)

The preacher has succeeded the philosopher.

Clearly, cultures and individuals may be systematically described as to their stage or developmental status. At this point, however, as we have seen,

---

[2] Post-conventional reasoning, the highest level of KOHLBERG's hierarchy, presupposes the capacity to perform the formal operations of abstract thought. But the empirical parameters of formal thinking are defined by cultural manifestations of combinatorial and propositional logic [PELUFFO, 1967; GOODNOW and BETHON, 1966; KIMBALL, 1968], functional mental capacity [JACKSON, 1963; STEPHENS et al., 1971] and what PIAGET [1972] has termed 'extremely disadvantageous conditions' which may delay its appearance to twenty years of age, and, indeed, even prevent its appearance. Problems involving high ego-involvement [HIGGINS-TRENK and GAITE, 1971], ethical decision-making [PERRY, 1968], and certain types of culture-specific subject matter [ELKIND, 1962] also affect capacity to operate on the formal level. If formal operational thinking – a precondition for principled reasoning – does not occur in every culture, it seems illogical to expect principled reasoning to appear universally. But even where these conditions are generally met, ROSS [1972] points out that fewer than 50% in adolescent samples are able to achieve this level of reasoning.

Kohlberg leans a little farther into philosophy and assumes a judgmental, normative stance which is in danger of toppling him out of scientific psychology entirely. We can, he writes, 'characterize moral differences between groups and individuals as being more or less adequate morally' [Kohlberg, 1969, pp. 176–177]. In other words, not only is morality culturally universal in its form or structure; its basic content principles are also universal – or rather, *should* be. Here he disagrees with Alston [1971, p. 275] who sees that position on the reasoning hierarchy does not necessarily ascribe more virtue to one stage than to others. '...the necessary logical order thesis in itself... has absolutely no bearing on the question with which we are presently concerned. The mere fact that one concept logically depends on another has no tendency to show that moral thinking involving the former is superior to moral thinking involving the latter.'

It remains to be seen whether or not, once the empirical sequences have been established, it is possible to establish these evaluative distinctions of higher or lower levels.

Cultural or Developmental Differences?

For Kohlberg, cultural differences are actually fundamental differences in principles or modes of moral evaluation. The moral stages he has delimited, however, constitute 'principles' which represent 'major consistencies within the individual not directly due to factual belief' [Kohlberg, 1971, p. 177]. His biological development is more important than what the individual has learned culturally about the nature of the world. Unfortunately, Kohlberg's stand suggests that, while trivial factual beliefs learned culturally do not seem to affect major consistencies in stage development directly, that the existential superordinate beliefs learned in a social environment do not, either. It is very hard to imagine, however, that the unpleasant members of pre-conventional cultures such as the Mundugumor described by Mead [1935], or Turnbull's [1972] mountain people have any possibility at all of attaining the farther reaches of morality any more than the stage 2 ghetto child whose existential beliefs are grounded in a reality of instrumental relativism. The need to survive in those particular environments has taught members of these cultures beliefs and values which are not at all likely to be counteracted by the developmental process.

The moral development of women is also clearly related to cultural influences. 'Most' adults of stage 3 are women with a 'good-girl' orientation and an emphasis on love and romantic relationships involving idealization of the other, identification or sharing between selves and unselfish or sacrificial concern for the love object. Women get to stage 3 faster and stay there longer; in defining their roles, they learn to find their prestige in goodness ('niceness'), as opposed to the prestige of power [KOHLBERG, 1969, p. 423]. To paraphrase an old line, a good woman is hard to find – at least one at the principled level of reasoning – because she has been taught that she is expected not to think or act that way.

Similarly, when KOHLBERG describes the 4- and 5-year-olds as failing to say that copying someone else's work is 'bad', while the majority of a group of 6-year-olds (n = 24) thought it was ('copying someone else's work isn't good', 'you should do your own work', etc.), it is difficult to attribute the change to 'a growing orientation to stable normative patterns of an "ideal self"' – that is, to natural, developmental progression within the individual – in a society in which 6-year-olds entering school are getting their first massive and integrated indoctrination of the competitive, rather than the cooperative, ideal. Direct imitation is discouraged as cheating and the child conforms to the expectation of his microsociety. Whether this represents, as KOHLBERG suggests, developmental transformation into more structured identification with normative models (as reflected in the 'good boy' reasoning of the stage-3 child who wishes to please persons important to him) or whether it merely indicates the impact of a very clear, directly taught, and continuously rewarded cultural message is not so easily decided.

Here again, claims for the universality of the cognitive shift need to be substantiated by evidence, in this case, that it takes place even in groups where the ideal taught is one of cooperation and mutual assistance. Even if sharing one's work is conceived as culturally desirable, if the cognitive transformation is a 'normal' progression, the 6-year-olds should continue to make it and think that imitation is bad. By the same token, we would want to know whether the *low* degree of imitation in school children which AUSUBEL *et al.* [1954] found correlated with *high* parental identification (high 'satellizing' attitudes) still appears consistently when the type of imitation occurring and parental child-rearing practices vary from culture to culture and group to group. Overall, it seems plausible to agree with KOHLBERG that the general development of concepts of roles and rules through modeling and identification in individual family experiences occurs during the years 3–8 much as BALDWIN [1906] and AUSUBEL *et al.* [1954] describe, while remaining skeptical that 'much is also universally derived from the common basic meanings of age and sex-roles at a given cognitive stage' [KOHL-

BERG, 1969, p. 433]. The universality of these 'common basic meanings' has yet to be shown.

Moral Inferiority

As we have seen, insistence on minimizing differential cultural effects places a heavy normative burden on the simple, observable fact of perceptual and interpretive group differences. Differences in values are frequently not the consequence of diversity in ethical principles, but of differences in the comprehension and definition of a situation according to the meaning which it has for specific groups [ASCH, 1952]. This is an explanation which is quite compatible with the views of ethnographic psychologists. Others have emerged in the writing of BRONFENBRENNER [1962] (to whom KOHLBERG refers as an 'extreme proponent of cultural relativism of values'). On the basis of his careful review of the literature, BRONFENBRENNER argues that class, sex, and culture are all more important determinants of moral development than advancing age or experience. LERNER [1937] and HARROWER [1934], for example, found that upper-class children in America and England, respectively, advanced through the developmental stages more rapidly than did lower-class ones. LICKONA [1969] suggests that class differences are best dealt with in terms of variation in general intellectual development which has been found to be closely related to moral judgment, but in any case, explanations of group differences involving intelligence or the attributed inferiority associated with socio-economic status must be thoughtfully reviewed for, as COLE et al. [1971, pp. XII–XIII] have written, '...one cannot assume that psychological tasks, be they derived from theories of cognitive development or the structures of intelligence, evoke the same kinds of behaviors in subjects from different cultures. When we present a task to a subject and he appears to respond randomly or stupidly, the first question we must ask is "what is the subject doing?" Behavior is never random, although it may seem random to an observer with a particular orientation. Only after it is determined that subjects from two groups are engaged in the same activity (applying the same processes), can one ask questions about their relative abilities.'

LÉVI-STRAUSS [1966] has described the thinking of pre-industrial peoples in quite different terms. He sees difference in cognitive processes as variation in the kinds of categories which disparate groups produce. The principal thought processes which groups generate are neither lower nor higher than those of one another. Instead, they represent widely varying strategies used to explore and explain the world rationally. These coherent systems may differ widely, but all involve the gathering of information, its ordering or systematizing, and classification. While the same sort of mental observations take place, among preliterate groups the attributes which are used for forming categories are primarily based on what may be seen and experienced, rather than on abstractions. Both, classification – which depends on inferences drawn about the relationship of properties in the structure of the object categorized – and problem-solving are limited by the concrete experience of the group.

Some investigators suggest that certain cultures promote problem-solving abilities by emphasizing cognitive training both earlier and over a long period of time. Where children attend Western-style schools (where problem-solving is highly valued), the growth of these skills is accelerated. These schoolchildren learn to read and write and also to deal with abstractions – events and objects which are not present – in solving school problems [BRUNER et al., 1966]. Lack of opportunity may delay or preclude development of certain skills. Problems which depend upon familiarity with their own environment also accelerate the acquisition of cognitive skills [PRICE-WILLIAMS, 1969].

The COLE et al. [1971, pp. 193–195] research in Liberia supports both of these previous studies since the ability of the Kpelle people to make verbal logical judgments depends upon the level of education of the subject and the way in which the problem is posed. Nonliterate Kpelle depend on the particular content of the problem when the premises are given by others and they must come to a conclusion for themselves. With education, there is a tendency for respondents to act on the basis of logical relations contained in the problems themselves. Further inquiry showed that problems can be posed in such a way as to lead nonliterates to respond to the logical relations within the problems rather than to their content – a finding which suggests that alternative forms of problem-presentation might be tried before conclusions as to problem-solving capacities, including those in the moral domain, are reached.

COLE et al. [1971] replicated the KENDLER and KENDLER [1967] experiments on inferential behavior (the spontaneous integration of two separately learned behavior segments to obtain a goal) among the Kpelle. Their first experiment showed Kpelle children falling far behind Americans in this capacity. In a second, 'ethnic', replication, they used materials which were all familiar to the children. The results showed that virtually all the Kpelle subjects (including nonliterate adults and school children from 7- to 14-years-old) demonstrated integrated inferential behavior.

In many ways, KOHLBERG's views may be compared to those of WERNER [1948] to whom cognitive development in general implied qualitative changes in both structure and the dynamic properties of behavior. Like KOHLBERG, he described the developing organism as showing increasing differentiation as he passed through a series of stages on a hierarchy. As in KOHLBERG's more sophisticated and elaborate version of cognitive development, WERNER found good reason for equating the abilities of Western children and the members of tribal cultures (whom he also compared to the mentally ill). The primitive thinking manifest in civilized children and preliterate adults was considered to be low on the developmental continuum.

KOHLBERG makes much the same statement in a more complex way when he writes that preliterates go through the lower stages of hierarchical development more slowly than Western, urban children and then do not reach the highest level of morality – that of principled, post-conventional moral judgment. Moral maturity, as defined by both WERNER and KOHLBERG, is not accessible to the 'savage' mind. As KOHLBERG [1971, p. 178] himself writes, the absence of the post-conventional, two highest stages in preliterate or semiliterate village culture, suggests 'a mild [!] doctrine of social evolutionism'. He cites the philosopher HOBHOUSE's [1906] work on moral evolution in his support. He might also have referenced an anthropologist, LEVY-BRUHL [1910]. As KOHLBERG believes that a simple, noncomplex, nondifferentiated society implies an inability of its members to reach the highest stages of ethical reasoning and moral maturity, so LEVY-BRUHL believed that primitive culture implies primitive thought. The primitive person has a prelogical mind in which beliefs about the world are infused with, and governed by emotion. His mental processes follow naturally from a highly simplified and religious culture.

The Appropriate Framework

Is this the case? At this point, the evidence is far from all in. Rather than accept large numbers of human groups (for the rural and the 'socially disadvantaged' Western blacks and ethnics are included here, too) as somehow deficient morally, it seems more appropriate to ask whether the same paradigm is suitable for use as a moral index with members of widely differing cultures if the methods involved (e.g., formal operational thinking) require modes of classification and problem-solving not utilized within each specific group. Ethnoscientists would undoubtedly respond with some passion to this question since the anthropological method clearly excludes the establishment of a structural parallel between cognitive processes of varying groups by using the category system of one of them to describe another. The desire to be able to compare and coordinate the knowledge and development of one people with that of others does not legitimize the practice.

The work of one of KOHLBERG's collaborators serves as another example of the way in which ethnocentric distortion has confused this body of research. REST [unpublished] describes his definition of the stages of moral development as sociological, rather than philosophical like KOHLBERG's. Each stage is seen as a new conception of the social system which is based on a new logical achievement – a conception which leads a stage to stress particular issues or values and to interpret them in particular ways. Stage 4 supports the known and established social arrangements of one's own society by default because 'it' has no criteria for weighing competing social orders or rule-systems. By definition, stage 5 occurs only in a democracy and a constitutional democracy at that: (1) the individual *agrees* to be bound by the laws of the society he lives in. (The implication, of course, is that as a citizen and not a subject such agreement is a matter for his continuing decision.) (2) He recognizes the functional need for agreed-upon law as distinct from the need for repression of evil and violence. (The purposes of law and government are the protection of peaceful interaction and the general welfare, rather than the exercise of power and privilege.) (3) The stage-5 individual has attained the notion that in a democracy all are lawmakers and hence contractually bound to follow laws democratically or constitutionally made. (Since this notion is both alien and irrelevant to the masses of human beings who are not members of a constitutional democracy, its use as a criterion for the attainment of stage 5 is somewhat suspect.)

According to KOHLBERG, the stages are defined *structurally*. REST's definition of the principled stages is clearly based on content which is taught culturally as facts, beliefs, and values. Stage 6 is equally culture-bound, but more directly correspondent with KOHLBERG's definition: law and social authority are seen as limited by prior natural human rights. There is an inner natural law containing a set of precepts such as the value of human life which are valid for all humanity and whose source is God or the nature of the universe. But many social scientists and philosophers believe that natural law and human rights originate with man. For one example, see the excellent discussion of the intimate connection between the possession of 'natural' human rights and membership in groups in ARENDT [1958].

Both men suppose those at stages 5 and 6 to be transcending their socialization, that is, cultural indoctrination, and to have abandoned behavioral, affective, or cognitive conformity. 'The claim of principled morality is that it defines the right for anyone in any situation' [KOHLBERG, 1971, p. 185]. This is opposed to pre- and conventional morality

30

which define situational behavior. But the more universalized rules, derived from Judaeo-Christian tradition, are 'moral'! Guides to all relevant moral situations in all cultures, these are principles of justice and respect for personality and human dignity. 'Guidance by principle must generate decisions which anyone could adopt as moral ... no exceptions to principles.'[3]

The Cultural Definition of Principles

Moral principles, as principles of choice for resolving conflicts of obligation, are 'active reconstructions of experience' [KOHLBERG, 1971, p. 225]. They imply a 'sensitivity' to justice, a concept (and in many places a principle) which is 'content-free' and merely implies that principles should be impartially applied to all [KOHLBERG, 1971, p. 230]. But justice as a distributive mechanism – to see that each person gets exactly what another in his place would get – is still content and, as a process, is the varying product of each creative group whose invention it is. In the behavioral, as well as the cognitive, world it has both a process and a content meaning: that each should get what he deserves in his particular roles and situation, and that he should get what he should have according to the values of the group, either to punish him, to protect the group, and/or to facilitate his changed behavior. Whether KOHLBERG is talking about principles of justice as defined by elements of liberty, equality, and reciprocity [Scoring Manual, p. 187] or describing justice as process, he is still referring to cultural content since neither concepts nor processes can operate without it. There is no such thing as process alone, or a concept emptied of the specific items which generalize to its whole, and a morality which 'defines the right' in all situations defines the right in none.

Principled reasoners are seen as autonomous, internally-oriented actors and thinkers. In his discussion of internality and social learning studies, KOHLBERG [1969, pp. 411–412] compares his use of internality to that of

---

[3] In his earlier work KOHLBERG pointed out the failure of previous researchers to find significant associations between moral attitudes and values and behavioral decisions and limited his research to the process of moral reasoning, with the assumption that the individual who understands the nature of justice will behave more justly than one who does not. Recently he has become more concerned with the value-behavior relationship and, although the data have not yet been published, has written '...principled moral reasoning has been found to be a precondition for principled moral action' [KOHLBERG, 1972, p. 491].

31

McDougall [1908], who describes an internal component of moral maturity as the highest of three stages where 'conduct is regulated by an ideal that enables a man to act in the way that seems right to him regardless of the praise or blame of his immediate social environment'. As a description of a structural element of the principled actor's conduct, this is an eloquent statement, but we are no closer to knowing how he would actually behave, what decisions he would make, and how he learned that such choices were available to him.

How may it be determined that the behavior or thinking displayed is the product of an individual, rather than deriving from his past experiences as a member of various social groups? At the conventional level, the standards being adhered to and advocated by moral reasoners represent those of the majority – by definition; reasoning adheres to the customary patterned responses (norms) of each discrete culture. At the post-conventional level the principles displayed may simply be the learned values of a *different* and *smaller* reference group so well internalized that its members believe themselves to be functioning autonomously. They may still be, as Aronfreed [1961] puts it, 'relatively stable end-results of different patterns of social reinforcement'. What are the sources for the definition of the 'social good or utility' for which contracts or laws may be broken by stage 5 reasoners? For definitions of which principles should be applied universally? Members can probably even identify the groups (from dyads to the subcultures of intellectual elites) in which they learned to reason abstractly about morality and to employ the kind of terminology which admits them to elevated ethical status. In some groups, internality – in the sense of autonomy in respect to the dominant culture – is learned as a norm, and admission and continued membership are contingent upon that knowledge.

Language as Criterion

The language used in the protocols of stage-5 and stage-6 subjects raises other questions about the structural aspects of the moral development interviews. The ability to make a principled 'hit', as Rest calls a clear score, seems to depend upon the capacity to refer to hierarchies and principles, to universal ideas, and especially to concepts such as justice, equality, and reciprocity at a high level of abstraction. Requirements for the highly trained use of analytic and theoretical modes of thought and language would automatically disqualify most of the world population (including

Americans) at any age. Consider, for example, one subject's (Jim's) response to the questions 'Should the husband steal the drug to save his wife's life? Should he do it for someone he just knows?'

'Yes. A human life takes precedence over any other moral or legal value, whoever it is. A human life has inherent value whether or not it is valued by a particular individual.'

He adds: 'The inherent worth of the individual human being is the central value in a set of values where the principles of justice and love are normative for all human relationships.'

Is this a measure of success at Philosophy 800, given formally or informally, or is it a measure of the development of moral reasoning? Oh pity the poor savages in our state colleges, our ghettos, in villages and tribes abroad who cannot express themselves so neatly, so profoundly, and so elegantly! By KOHLBERG definition, they may never know principled reasoning. The sentence last quoted is such a pure work of art as to call forth the suspicion that it was memorized or edited. It is incredibly round, full, and firmly packed for natural, responsive, human speech. Is this sophisticated verbalism? Perhaps, too, the extent to which principled reasoning has been truly learned, rather than merely articulated, cannot be known without behavioral indices.

This example may serve also to demonstrate why there is a strong, consistent correlation between moral development stage and IQ since IQ is essentially a measure of the ability to succeed in school doing those things which require, among other capabilities, considerable verbal facility. KOHLBERG'S stage 6s are not functioning independently of their socialization; they have been very thoroughly socialized into the company of intellectual elites who value and practice analytic, abstract, and logical reasoning.

Conceptual Differences

As we have said, cultural differences are seen by KOHLBERG as relatively unimportant in the moral development of the individual. However, just as there are times when a presumably principled reasoner may choose not to reason that way, he concedes that so there are occasions when social expectations may override the judgment of the individual. Where unwanted and rejected cultural differences appear anyway in moral principles, they are written off as an 'accommodation to cultural givens', to what most people do. Above all, they do not mean that 'core moral concepts of conventional morality are merely culturally variable internalizations' [KOHLBERG, 1971, p. 178].

But the content which generalizes to build concepts *is* culturally-derived – unless one can imagine that learning is free from the restrictions and qualifications imposed upon it by membership in specific groups at a specific time and place. Highly abstract concepts such as justice have so little commonality in meaning from one group to another as to be practically useless as cross-cultural generalizations. Concept development simply does not mean the same thing from one class or one culture to another. In large part, it does not entail learning the same body of particular knowledge, so that the relational bases for the generalizing which builds the broad abstractions are fragile.

In the United States, for example, the concept of *equality* has a wide range of specific meanings which is affected by class membership. Working-class Americans define equality as economic but not social; upper middle-class Americans tend to conceptualize it as social, not economic [LIPSET, 1959]. In another context, BOHANNAN [1965] gives an example of the concept *responsibility* – a word which consistently appears in some form in all European languages derived from Latin. Also translated into languages with predominantly Germanic vocabularies, it is a concept which is, nevertheless, very difficult to express in most African tongues. While African cultures recognize obligations toward kinsmen and officials that Europeans would call 'responsibilities', these for Africans are directed towards people, not towards principles, ideas, or a 'system'. Most of all, the African idea does not extend to meaning that the one who has responsibilities is the one who is to be blamed.

Two illustrations from the 'Scoring Manual' will bring us closer to the problem at hand. Although the moral dilemma interview stories were modified for the cross-cultural studies, the manual for scoring *responses* was not [JENNINGS, personal commun., 1972]. Interview protocols are scored according to a series of issues which have been selected because they are deemed to have universal applicability; it is that universality which is in question. First, the issue of *property rights*. The general or conceptual meaning of this issue is not difficult to infer. But men do not deal with generalities in their interactions and the Americans who believe that one has a right to anything one can pay for and that taxes on income and private property and restrictive use laws are wrong or bad have very little content in common with members of a culture where little or no property is seen as private and rights over it are group rights and held in common.

34

Value of Life as an issue suffers from the same ambiguities. To Americans, its *expressed* meaning is that *human* (not all) life is sacred. Its *enacted* meaning is so full of exceptions as to render the principle meaningless: men, women, and children may be killed to protect them from others; those who kill or rape others (depending upon the identities of victim and killer) or steal secrets from the government to give to other governments and those who cannot pay for emergency medical care may be killed, as may the hopelessly damaged. Many groups, including the Eskimo, kill the aged and the newly born who might consume needed resources. These are only a few of the categories of those who may be killed. In other cultures and sub-cultures those categories might take quite another shape – among the Hindu and the Quakers, for instance. In every group it is not that life is valued overall or not valued, but *that it is valued situationally in highly culturally-specific ways.*

KOHLBERG'S [1971, p. 174] strong statement, 'anyone who understands the values of life and property will recognize that life is morally more valuable than property', comes as a shock and also as a contradiction, since elsewhere he had depicted the American's view of life as strictly stage 2 – instrumental to the needs of its possessors or other persons. Other than its expression of belief, does this statement have grounding in a researchable reality? Is there anyone who believes that under all conditions life is more valuable than property? Those describable conditions must include explanations as to whose life and whose property are involved, as well as to what class (role) of persons is doing the destruction. Over the course of social history in the United States alone many who believed they knew the value of life and property have died, sent others off to kill, or killed themselves for property. Men committed suicide when they lost their property during the Great Depression; on the terrible *Noche Triste* Cortez's soldiers drowned trying to flee from the Aztecs because they would not abandon the gold they were stealing.

The situation in one interview involves a druggist who wants an exorbitant amount for a drug he has invented and which he refuses to sell more cheaply to the poor husband of a woman who will die without it. 'Even at stage 2 (instrumental relativism), boys know that the druggist in the story would rather save his own life than his property, so that the druggist's property is less valuable than the woman's life' [KOHLBERG, 1971, p. 174]. The statement quoted does not follow logically, but the point remains: not to the druggist it isn't, since he is willing to have her die rather than give up his property. History is also full of examples of men and women who have freely given of their lives for the preservation of their own property or the property of others. The point is that the relative value of property and life is decided situationally and culturally and is not a matter of natural and universal knowledge.

One could go further. The concepts of *civil rights and liberties* and *rules and laws* may be extremely trivial issues in a traditional society where the type and degree to which these exist as functional content are so taken for granted that self-conscious analysis about them does not occur. Can a moral issue (in KOHLBERG's principled sense) exist without a high degree of consciousness about cultural interactional patterns? For that matter, can it exist where the practice of analysis itself is not encouraged and valued?[4] The way in which a problem such as a moral dilemma is reconstructed by the individual and the ranking of the importance of the issues contained in it are culturally determined.

ALSTON [1971, p. 272], following his analysis that KOHLBERG's stages of moral reasoning are also stages of conceptual development since that process utilizes the concepts, suggests that a test of concept acquisition is needed. Such a measure would solve the problem which ALSTON sees – that some persons may understand the concepts but not utilize them in the context of the particular situational reasoning required by the moral development interviews. It would also make clear the highly differential cultural content which underlies the 'universality' of higher-order concepts – in other words, what people actually mean when they *do* utilize certain concepts.

KOHLBERG [1969, p. 385] himself has suggested that stages 4, 5, and 6 may be viewed as alternative types of mature moral response, rather than as a sequence. Such a conception would relieve some of the tension caused by the attempt to define the higher three stages as culture-free and universally attained through normal development. It would also render the

---

[4] That such analysis has been increasingly valued within the United States is manifest in new precollegiate curricula which are intended to foster the development of critical, reflective, and rational modes of thought and decision-making. Programs have been developed in political education, for example, to teach thinking skills through discussion of controversial cases or public issues [FENTON, 1967; HUNT and METCALF, 1968; OLIVER and SHAVER, 1966]. OLIVER, who may express the educational avant-garde, has since repudiated this approach on the grounds of its inappropriateness for most students, especially those who are members of groups where analysis is not valued, and its irrelevance to central educational problems: the development of social responsibility, respect for diversity, and community.

hierarchy a typology and represent the stages (at least above the first three) as lateral, rather than vertical growth so that the present pious loading would be shoveled off principled reasoning.

Irreversibility

Besides cultural universality, another claim made for KOHLBERG'S hierarchy of moral stages is its *irreversibility*. As we have said, situational and cultural factors may delay or abort progress toward moral maturity, but the order of progression is invariant. In general, it does appear that, as KOHLBERG reports, the 'normal' course of social experience leads to progress through the sequence as delineated. The meaning of 'normal' needs to be carefully explored, however, since regression – that is, a break in the usual developmental pattern – occurs among adolescents under a variety of conditions. KRAMER [1968] reports return to lower-level moral functioning among groups of both middle-class and delinquent American boys. Similarly, adolescents among the Atayal, a Malaysian aboriginal group on Taiwan, regress cognitively to hold concepts about the nature of dreams which they had held at an earlier age. In their studies of children from six different Indian tribes, HAVIGHURST and NEUGARTEN [1955] found a clear departure from the 'invariant sequence' in which PIAGET [1963], like KOHLBERG'S orderly age-progression toward reciprocity, found faith in 'immanent justice' – automatic punishment for wrong-doing – left behind. According to these investigators, faith in immanent justice among Indian children tended to increase, rather than to decrease, with age and, in doing so, to reflect the prevailing belief system of the adult culture.

To explain these disorderly phenomena, KOHLBERG [1971, p. 360] says that some behavioral changes are structural and directed – that is, universal, progressive through sequential stages, and irreversible – and some are 'reversible situation-specific learnings'. The former require a form of analysis different from the latter. Just as cultural differences in morality are seen as an accommodation to 'cultural givens', so social training may be 'superimposed' upon structural development [TURIEL, 1969]. LANGER [1967] concluded from his research that discrepancies in experience resulting from cognitive conflict may lead to *either* progressive or regressive change or fixation – that is, to forward, backward, or lack of movement and TURIEL'S [1969] explanation seems hardly adequate to account for discontinuities and reversals in an 'invariant sequence' which is theoretically culture-independent. If the posited movement does not occur, then the burden is on the theoretician to account for the failure evidentially, while remaining within the framework of the theory.

Reporting Data

One of the problems in examining this body of empirically-derived evidence on moral development and assessing comparative findings is that the conventional procedures of reporting, in as spare and elegant a fashion as possible, descriptions of the samples, methodology (including modifications of the interview stories from culture to culture and of the elaborate and detailed scoring manual), and results have not been systematically followed. Interested investigators have available only rather free-wheeling discussions of the data from other societies and the inferences and generalization which have been drawn from the broad range of often only partially referenced sources. Percentages are given without demarcation of group size or its demographic characteristics; definitions of social class are uniformly lacking. Most vital perhaps is failure to describe the testing and scoring methodology utilized cross-culturally.

Acceptance of scientific theory should rest upon sources of authority which are traditional to science, e.g., the systematic, controlled, replicable, and consistent accumulation of data among well-defined groups. Where are the tentativeness, the waiting on solid replication, the care about generalizing beyond the data, and, above all, the accuracy in reporting fully the data upon which the massive mountain of inference, philosophical speculation, normative statement, and extrapolation has been built? The paragraphs cited at the middle of page 7 serves as an unfortunately typical example of this kind of reporting even in more detailed discussions of results of investigations. We are never told what modifications in the story situations and scoring procedures of the interviews have been made to account for cultural differences, how many subjects have been studied, or what their individual and group characteristics are. KOHLBERG is much more complete in describing the studies which a few of his colleagues have made than he is in his own work, especially its cross-cultural aspects. Without changing the labels, the discursive writing and wide-ranging, if extremely interesting and provocative, discussions slide freely from unsubstantiated references to results to theorizing and prescription whose relatedness to the actual data base involves several levels of discourse. This is a disservice to KOHL-BERG's conceptual and theoretical contributions and his claims to authority, and it is a disservice to social science seeking to build a body of theory and law solidly upon data.

I do not wish to be misunderstood. Clearly, there are other sources of authority than those used by science – among them faith and the belief that wells from personal, intuitive, and inner knowledge. As powerful heuristic tools, the cognitive-developmental theory and the elaborations, controversies, applications, and analyses which have been engendered since its inception have inherent value. The typology of moral development and the body of thought behind it would have been useful if they had been received through revelation, although, of course, they would not have been accepted and utilized by the large body of workers who consider themselves scientists and who depend upon sources other than 'swift, inward inspiration' and spiritual enlightenment to substantiate their claims to knowledge. If the assertion of universality is based on scientific evidence, we are entitled to know in detail the extent and shape of those data. It is time for the cross-cultural data to be fully published so that the comparability of methodology and results may be carefully examined. As it is, access to existing data poses a serious impediment to evaluating the work done in this field. The two major publications cited by KOHLBERG (Stages in the Development of Moral Thought and Action, 1969 and, with TURIEL, Recent Research in Moral Development, 1971, both Holt, New York) are not listed in *Books in Print*. KOHLBERG is hardly responsible for publisher's delays, but in the meantime questions remain which it is presumed these books will answer since the numerous articles and chapters have not.

Cross-Cultural Research

What are the requirements of valid cross-cultural research? First of all, a balanced cognizance of the potency of group variation and the capacity to look through cultural meanings, and not directly at the behavior of actors. BOHANNAN [1965, p. 27] again provides an African example: the British colonists, not understanding that the indigenous procedures they observed were the functional patterns of a legal system, felt compelled to write down for African use – and hence to codify into rigidity – the supple and responsive unwritten system of their own nation. Almost endless instances of transcultural miscommunication could be added. Cultural difference and cross-cultural misunderstandings are so pervasive that, to be convincing, claims for universality in any area of human behavior must be supported by studies which show – at the very least – a deep awareness and appreciation of variation both in perception and in the systematic patterns and processes which groups develop for the handling of their differential values and needs. The interviews, stories, or whatever means of testing used must be sensible, relevant, and realistic in the eyes of the members of each society; the scoring manuals or procedures must be shaped to the expectations of each group of human beings toward each other (and the investigators) in the roles defined by those groups.

Perhaps the only proper measures for use in cross-cultural research are those of ethnographic analysis available to the field anthropologist who may then determine whether or not a particular type of behavior and/or reasoning occurs consistently in the patterned interactions among members of a particular culture (or among them and others). Frequency of occurrence would suggest that this behavior and/or type of reasoning should be well-developed. If such skills are perceived by investigators as comparable to those of other groups, but the tests which commonly measure their appearance in those groups do not demonstrate their presence in the group being studied, then the burden of explanation is on the investigator. As COLE et al. [1971, p. 216] have written, tests and experiments are 'specially contrived occasions for the manifestation of cognitive skills'. Whether the skill appears may be highly dependent upon the context in which it is elicited. They give an example from the Kpelle of Liberia who are skillful at measuring rice, which is frequently required in their social environment, but not at measuring distance, which is not. Another example [GLADWIN, 1970] is of navigators who use a complex natural compass but nevertheless do not perform the way that high-school students in the United States do on a standard psychological test.

If a skill which appears in one group does not appear in members of another cultural group, two explanations, then, are possible: one, that it is indeed absent and the two groups, for whatever reasons, have essential differences (which, in a judgmental world, will probably be immediately ranked in value) or two, that the investigators have failed to observe situations in which this skill appears naturally or to experimentally provide those opportunities which will provoke it. Different groups may use the same skills in highly differential patterns. Conceptual thinking, for example, and its applications as a problem-solving mode do occur among nonliterate groups such as the Kpelle, but the situations in which they apply it are different even from those of their *educated* age-mates [COLE *et al.,* 1971, p. 225].

This point of view is opposed to those which state that westernization and accultura-tion bring with them general cultural advancement including new abilities and cognitive skills [DOOB, 1960]. Literacy and the activities encountered in western-style schools are seen as providing analytic and conceptual tools which do not exist in non-western cultures [GREENFIELD and BRUNER, 1966; GOODY and WATT, 1962]. In effect, these changes in the outer environment create a transformation in cognitive processes. Much of KOHLBERG's work is consistent with the latter interpretation of group differences, except that the deprived groups he describes as lacking in differentiated, logical, and principled moral reasoning include subgroups of rural, as well as urban ghetto, types. Unlike COLE *et al.* [1971], he does find age differences in the cognitive performance of preliterates and other 'deprived' subgroups, although the progression shown is comparatively slow and the stage of post-conventional reasoning is not reached. Whether principled reasoning and behavior would show up using a combination of ethnographic and experimental techni-ques is a very interesting question. How would one go about such research? First, the use of these procedures in mundane activities would have to be observed, their presence established, and the occasions on which they were utilized carefully delineated. Then, the attempt would have to be made to develop controllable situations in which such thinking and behavior were elicited in response to specific stimuli. Results from such a study would make it possible to contrast the use of these reasoning processes in a number of groups and to compare with some accuracy the differential distribution in frequency and situation of their occurrence.

At best, cross-cultural experimentation and description have built-in problems of meaning communication – problems which plague and harry at each step of the research process. Even in complex, industrial societies, the mere presence of investigators alters the patterns and processes of what is being explored. In preliterate or non analytic groups, even when the task at hand is clearly understood, the presence of the experimenter seeking answers to questions or solutions to problems disrupts the established culture through the violation of traditional norms. Can a measure of 'normal' cognitive functioning, in the moral domain or elsewhere, be obtained under those circumstances any more than accurate data about animal behavior may be obtained in the laboratory? Ethologists, understanding the close functional relationship between behavior and the physical and social environment, would agree that it would be difficult indeed. If not eliminating the distortion which alteration in the natural environment produces, the task of the scientist is first to seek to minimize it and, secondly, to carefully evaluate its extent.

When findings are in, difficulties involving inference remain. Subtleties of meaning and the ability to rank cultural values accurately may loom large in the elimination of alternative explanations. COLE *et al.* [1971, p. 22] suggest the need to use multiple indicators to reduce the number of tenable rival explanations since accurate inferences depend upon data from all patterns of performance to reduce irrelevant explanations. And, above all, behavior or reasoning which appears inappropriate or meaningless should encourage further inquiry, rather than the labeling of inferiority.

Afterword

Perhaps rather than seeking to compare all men when such comparisons are inappropriate or to synthesize diversity on a Procrustean bed into compact uniformity, we should examine more carefully the distinctions which various groups maintain between methods of solving moral dilemmas. Perhaps our scientific search should be less for eternal verities and universal invariance than for alternate and creative modes of coping with the truly universal and eternal problems of justice and liberty. Whether there is any inevitable human sequence beyond conventional moral thought remains an open question. Whether it is desirable to assist the growth of children in widely varying social and physical environments toward the internalization of the specifically Western principles and the cultural content now associated with the highest level of the moral hierarchy remains another.

Because the saber-toothed tiger survived for forty million years, the teeth which finally grew inward and destroyed him could hardly be called maladaptive. But the moral reasoning which we see actively applied today by the Western world, quite apart from high-minded professional philosophy, bids fair to destroy man far short of a life span of forty million years. Is there a society with as many concepts for *the good* as the Eskimos have for *snow* or the Arabs for *horse*? Are there functional methods of conflict resolution and resource allocation in use which would serve people whose present methods are failing? We would do better to explore and analyze differences wherever found, to borrow and adapt, and to nurture invention and cultural mutation as it occurs than to perpetuate the ideology of a suicidal world trying to reconcile its differences through the use of a theoretical framework ill-suited for containing and ordering real human diversity.

Acknowledgement

I am grateful to Joseph Adelson (clinical psychologist), Langdon Longstreth (developmental psychologist), M. Brewster Smith (social psychologist), and William Winslade (philosopher) for encouraging and critical readings of an earlier version of this paper.

References

Alston, W.P.: Comments on Kohlberg's 'From is to ought'; in Mischel, Cognitive development and epistemology (Academic Press, New York 1971).

Arendt, H.: The origins of totalitarianism; 2nd ed. (World, Cleveland 1958).

41

Aronfreed, J.: The nature, variety, and social patterning of moral responses to transgression. J. abnorm. soc. Psychol. *63:* 223–240 (1961).

Asch, S.E.: Social psychology (Prentice-Hall, Englewood Cliffs 1952).

Ausubel, D.P., *et al.:* Perceived parent attitudes as determinants of children's ego structure. Child Develop. *25:* 173–183 (1954).

Baldwin, J.M.: Social and ethical interpretations in mental development (Macmillan, New York 1906).

Bohannan, P.: Lessons from cross-cultural communication. Co-Existence *3:* 24–32 (1965).

Brandt, R.B.: Ethical theory: the problems of normative and critical ethics (Prentice-Hall, Englewood Cliffs 1959).

Bronfenbrenner, U.: The role of age, sex, class, and culture in studies of moral development. Rel. Educ. *57:* suppl. (1962).

Bruner, J.S.; Olver, R., and Greenfield, P.: Studies in cognitive growth (Wiley, New York 1966).

Cole, M.; Gay, J.; Glick, J., and Sharp, D.: The cultural context of learning and thinking (Basic Books, New York 1971).

Doob, L.: Becoming more civilized (Yale Univ. Press, New Haven 1960).

Elkind, D.: Quantity conceptions in college students. J. soc. Psychol. *57:* 459–465 (1962).

Fenton, E.: Teaching the new social studies in secondary schools (Holt, Rinehart & Winston, New York 1966).

Frankena, W.K.: Ethics (Prentice-Hall, Englewood Cliffs 1963).

Gladwin, T.: East is a big bird (Belknap Press, Cambridge 1970).

Goodnow, J.J. and Bethon, G.: Piaget's tasks: the effects of schooling and intelligence. Child Develop. *37:* 573–582 (1966).

Goody, J. and Watt, I.: The consequences of literacy. Comp. Stud. Soc. Hist. *5:* 304–345 (1962).

Greenfield, P.M. and Bruner, J.S.: Culture and cognitive growth. Int. J. Psychol. *1:* 89–107 (1966).

Harrower, M.R.: Social status and moral development. Brit. J. educ. Psychol. *4:* 75–95 (1934).

Havighurst, R. and Neugarten, B.: American Indian and white children (Univ. Chicago Press, Chicago 1955).

Higgins-Trenk, A. and Gaite, A.J.: Elusiveness of formal operational thought in adolescents. Proc. Meet. Amer. Psychol. Ass., Washington 1971.

Hobhouse, L.T.: Morals in evolution (Chapman & Hall, London 1906).

Hoffman, M.: Moral development; in Mussen Carmichael's manual of child psychology; 3rd ed., pp. 261–359 (Wiley, New York 1970).

Hunt, M.P. and Metcalf, L.E.: Teaching high school social studies; 2nd ed. (Harper & Row, New York 1968).

Jackson, S.: The growth of logical thinking in normal and subnormal children; master's thesis Manchester (unpublished, 1963).

Kendler, T.S. and Kendler, H.H.: Experimental analysis of inferential behavior in children; in Lipsitt and Spiker Advances in child development and behavior, vol. 3 (Academic Press, New York 1967).

Kimball, R.L.: A background concept study in Malawi. Domasi: Science Centre, 1968; cited by Ross (1972).

KOHLBERG, L.: Moral and religious education and the public schools. A developmental view; in SIZER Religion and public education (Houghton-Mifflin, Boston 1967).

KOHLBERG, L.: Stage and sequence. The cognitive-developmental approach to socialization; in GOSLIN Handbook of socialization theory and research (Rand McNally, New York 1969).

KOHLBERG, L.: From is to ought. How to commit the naturalistic fallacy and get away with it in the study of moral development; in MISCHEL Cognitive development and epistomology (Academic Press, New York 1971).

KOHLBERG, L. and MAYER, R.: Development as the aim of education. Harvard educ. Rev. 42: 449–496 (1972).

KRAMER, R.: Moral development in young adulthood; doctoral dissertation Chicago (unpublished, 1968).

LANGER, J.: Disequilibrium as a source of cognitive development. Proc. meet. Soc. Res. Child Develop., 1967.

LERNER, E.: Constraint areas and moral judgment of children (Banta, Menasha 1937).

LÉVI-STRAUSS, C.: The savage mind (Univ. of Chicago Press, Chicago 1966).

LEVY-BRUHL, C.: How natives think (Washington Square Press, New York 1966; first publ. 1910).

LIPSET, S.M.: Political man (Doubleday, Garden City 1959).

MEAD, M.: Sex and temperament in three primitive societies (Morrow, New York 1935; Laurel Edition, Dell Publishing, New York 1968).

McDOUGALL, W.: An introduction to social psychology (Methuen, London 1908).

OLIVER, D.W. and SHAVER, J.P.: Teaching public issues in the high school (Houghton-Mifflin, New York 1966).

PELUFFO, N.: Culture and cognitive problems. Int. J. Psychol. 2: 187–198 (1967).

PERRY, W.G., jr.: Forms of intellectual and ethical development in the college years. A scheme (Holt, Rinehart & Winston, New York 1968).

PIAGET, J.: The moral judgment of the child (Macmillan, New York 1955).

PIAGET, J.: The origins of intelligence in children (Norton, New York 1963).

PIAGET, J.: Intellectual evolution from adolescence to adulthood. Human Develop. 15: 1–12 (1972).

PRICE-WILLIAMS, D.; GORDON, W., and RAMIREZ, M.: Skill and conservations. A study of pottery-making children. Develop. Psychol. 1: 769 (1969).

REST, J.: The hierarchical nature of moral judgment. A study of patterns of comprehension and preference of moral stages. Harvard Lab. Human Develop., Moral Develop. Study (unpublished).

REST, J.; TURIEL, E., and KOHLBERG, L.: Relations between level of moral judgment and preference and comprehension of the moral judgment of others. J. Personality (1969).

ROSS, R.J.: The empirical status of the formal operation. Proc. Ann. Conf. Piagetian Thought, Univ. Southern Calif., Los Angeles 1972.

STEPHENS, B.; McLAUGHLIN, J.A., and MAHANEY, E.J.: Ages at which Piagetian concepts are achieved. Proc. Meet. Amer. Psychol. Ass., Washington 1971.

TURIEL, E.: An experimental text of the sequentiality of developmental stages in the child's moral judgments. J. Pers. soc. Psychol. 3: 611–618 (1966).

Turiel, E.: Developmental processes in the child's moral thinking; in Mussen, Langer and Covington Trends and issues in developmental psychology (Holt, Rinehart & Winston, New York 1969).

Turnbull, C.: Mountain people (Simon & Schuster, New York 1972).

Werner, H.: Comparative psychology of mental development (Int. Univ. Press, New York 1948).

Request reprints from: Elizabeth Léonie Simpson, 850 Second Street, *Santa Monica, CA 90403* (USA)

Hum. Dev. *20:* 352–376 (1977)

A Study of Kohlberg's Structural Theory of Moral Development: a Critique of Liberal Social Science Ideology[1]

Edmund V. Sullivan[2]

Applied Psychology and History and Philosophy, Ontario Institute for Studies in Education, Toronto, Ont.

Key Words. False consciousness · Figurative knowledge · Ideology · Liberal ideology · Moral development · Scotosis · Structuralism

Abstract. This article attempts a critical analysis of *Kohlberg*'s stage theory of moral development in the context of an ideology critique. From this point of view, *Kohlberg*'s stage theory is characterized as a species of 'liberal ideology'. The analysis of his postconventional stages relies on *Rawls'* criticism of the conception of a 'just community'. The critique of *Rawls'* is reflecting upon *Kohlberg*'s theory since it draws heavily from this 'liberal' conception of justice. A critical analysis of *Piaget*'s structuralism is briefly noted relating it to *Kohlberg*'s developmental structuralism. The separations of *thought* from *action, is* from *ought,* are analyzed as weaknesses stemming from this structural point of view.

This article will critically examine the growth metaphor advanced by *Kohlberg* relating specifically to the topic of the development of moral ideology. A critical analysis is appropriate at this time since this theoretical perspective has

[1] Adapted from a longer monograph of the same title from the Ontario Institute for Studies in Education Monograph Series, 1976.

[2] I would like to thank several of my colleagues for their written comments on a pre-publication draft of this article: *John Broughton, Cliff Christensen, Richard Hersh, Robert Hogan, Roger Hutchinsen, Patrick Lee, Rowland Lorimer, David Olson,* and *Jack Quarter.* To *Larry Kohlberg:*

'Well, we've been lucky devils both,
and there's no need of pledge or oath.

To bind our lovely friendship fast,
By firmer stuff
Close bound enough.'

Robert Graves

had uncritical acclaim for at least a decade. It is done with the belief that the academy does itself justice when it carefully evaluates its own creations however appealing and attractive they may be; and *Kohlberg*'s cognitive-developmental stage theory of moral development has certainly had its appeal and attraction up to this point in time.

Without detracting from the seminal contribution of *Kohlberg*'s work in psychology and education, it is important to note that this theory has existed in an era (or at least a recent past era) which made any developmental theory a very attractive option in North America (*Ausubel and Sullivan,* 1970). Since the concept of development implies progress, one can understand why a culture that demands progress should draw from theoretical perspectives which build this notion into their very ontology; and the decade of the sixties demanded theories that dealt with both intellectual and moral progress. Notwithstanding their own internal brilliance, it is safe to say, at least, that some of the appeal of the work of *Kohlberg, Erikson,* and *Piaget* has been that their perspectives have resonated to the demands of contemporary culture. Specifically in *Kohlberg*'s case, his theory filled a vacuum prevalent in the social sciences dealing with the whole topic area of values. As the sixties decried the 'value-free' emptiness of the social sciences, *Kohlberg*'s theory entered the scene as knight in shining armor. In a culture deeply involved in moral problems related to race, poverty, and war, this theory offered a concept of justice which promised to deal with the quagmire of value relativity. In the social sciences it was welcomed with open arms. In education, where *Kohlberg*'s work has flourished, his conception of development has been linked to the pioneering work of *Dewey* (*Kohlberg and Mayer,* 1972). The point of this brief introduction is to attest to the compelling quality of 'developmental metaphors' and specifically to indicate some specific reasons for *Kohlberg*'s popularity aside from the competence of the theory itself (*Hunt and Sullivan,* 1974).

A Critique of Liberal Social Science Ideology

This study will look at *Kohlberg*'s stage theory as an ideology; that is, as a 'style of thinking' (*Mannheim,* 1936). There 'ideology' is a study of a 'style of thinking' in an attempt to show how the context of a style of thought is rooted in certain types of societal interests (*Habermas,* 1971). This article should therefore be partly considered as a 'sociology of psychological knowledge' (*Buss,* 1975). The main thrust of a sociology of psychological knowledge is an attempt to reveal that within a social context psychological theories are tied to the infrastructure of a society or socially defined groups (*Buck-Morss,* 1975; *Buss,* 1975). Hopefully, by attempting to come to terms with the social basis of psychology's theories and activities, a sociology of psychological knowledge may lead to greater self-understandings (*Buss,* 1975).

'Ideology critique' can be considered as an 'emancipatory interest'; that is an attempt to analyze science and technology from a critical perspective (*Habermas,* 1970). One of the assumptions of a 'critical theoretical' perspective is that the development of 'science and technology' in the 20th century, in advanced capitalist societies, is for the legitimizing and stabilizing of certain political 'powers and interests' (*Habermas,* 1970). Critique is therefore an attempt to expose the interest base of research and theories and their legitimizing functions for societal institutions and specifically their legitimizing of certain dominant groups. The notion of 'critique' advanced is therefore an attempt to expose a dominant ideology; in this instance a 'liberal ideology'. Critique of a tradition must be based within a tradition. Much of the critique in this paper is informed by a perspective called 'critical social theory'. The critique, however, is not Marxian in the orthodox sense of this term. Nevertheless, it draws from a treatment of the development of ideology (*Marx and Engels,* 1970) which dramatizes differences in modes of thought, not only in different historical periods but also in different cultures. From a radical analysis, one can at least entertain the present popularity of both *Kohlberg* and *Piagetian* structuralism as a result of present historical-cultural demands. This perspective entertains the possibility that not only does the content of thought change but also its categorical structure. As *Marx and Engels* (1970) were at pains to point out in *The German Ideology,* in the past as well as the present, the dominant modes of thought are supplanted by new categories when the social basis of the group of which these thought forms are characteristic, disintegrates or is transformed under the impact of social change. Liberal ideology refers to a 'style of thought' developed at the time of the French Revolution (*Mannheim,* 1953). It is a form of 'natural-law' thought associated with revolutionary theorizing which had ascendency at the time of the French Revolution. *Mannheim* (1953, p. 117) has this summary characterization:

'A. The contents of natural-law thought
    i.   The doctrine of the "stage of nature."
    ii.   The doctrine of the social contract.
    iii. The doctrine of popular sovereignty.
    iv. The doctrine of the inalienable Rights of Man (life, liberty, property, the right to resist tyranny, etc.).
B. The methodological characteristics of natural-law thought
    i.   Rationalism as a method of solving problems.
    ii.   Deductive procedure from one general principle to the particular cases.
    iii. A claim of universal validity for every individual.
    iv. A claim to universal applicability of all laws to all historical and social units.
    v.   Atomism and mechanism: collective units (the state, the law, etc.), are constructed out of isolated individuals of factors.
    vi. Static thinking (right reason conceived as a self-sufficient, autonomous sphere unaffected by history).'

Kohlberg's stage theory of moral ideology draws its impetus from this tradition. Before turning to the specifics it is necessary at this point to indicate for purposes of analysis the broad outlines of this theory.

Kohlberg's *Cognitive-Developmental Structuralism*

Kohlberg (1969, 1971a, b) has developed his stage theory of moral development with a considerable amount of philosophical sophistication and with a broad understanding of the place of his work in modern psychology. The power of his analysis stems from his ability to combine philosophy, psychology, education, political science, etc. within the purview of his extensive empirical work. The details of this theoretical perspective can only be touched upon in this paper and the untutored reader would do well to read original sources. *Kohlberg* (1971b) postulates a series of six stages and three levels in the development and articulation of moral judgment from childhood into adulthood. The definition of these stages and levels is as follows:

Preconventional Level

At this level, the child is responsive to cultural rules and labels of good and bad, right or wrong, but interprets these labels in terms of either the physical or the hedonistic consequences of action (punishment, reward, exchange of favors) or in terms of the physical power of those who enunciate the rules and labels. The level comprises the following two stages:

Stage 1, punishment and obedience orientation. The physical consequences of action determine its goodness or badness regardless of the human meaning or value of these consequences. Avoidance of punishment and unquestioning deference to power are valued in their own right, not in terms of respect for an underlying moral order supported by punishment and authority (the latter being stage 4).

Stage 2, instrumental relativist orientation. Right action consists of that which instrumentally satisfies one's own needs and occasionally the needs of others. Human relations are viewed in terms similar to those of the market place. Elements of fairness, of reciprocity, and equal sharing are present, but they are always interpreted in a physical pragmatic way. Reciprocity is a matter of 'you scratch my back and I'll scratch yours', not of loyalty, gratitude, or justice.

Conventional Level

At this level, maintaining the expectations of the individual's family, group, or nation is perceived as valuable in its own right, regardless of immediate and obvious consequences. The attitude is one not only of conformity to personal expectations and social order, but of loyalty to it, of actively maintaining, supporting, and justifying the order and of identifying with the persons or group involving in it. This level comprises the following two stages:

49

Stage 3, interpersonal concordance or 'good-boy, nice-girl' orientation. Good behavior is that which pleases or helps others and is approved by them. There is much conformity to stereotypical images of what is majority or 'natural' behavior. Behavior is frequently judged by intention: 'he means well' becomes important for the first time. One earns approval by being 'nice'.

Stage 4, 'law and order' orientation. There is orientation toward authority, fixed rules, and the maintenance of the social order. Right behavior consists of doing one's duty, showing respect for authority, and maintaining the given social order for its own sake.

Postconventional, Autonomous, or Principled Level

At this level there is a clear effort to define moral values and principles that have validity and application apart from the authority of the groups or persons holding these principles and apart from the individual's own identification with these groups. This level again has two stages:

Stage 5, social-contract legalistic orientation. Generally, this stage has utilitarian overtones. Right action tends to be defined in terms of general individual rights and in terms of standards that have been critically examined and agreed upon by the whole society. There is clear awareness of the relativism of personal values and opinions and a corresponding emphasis on procedural rules for reaching consensus. Aside from what is constitutionally and democratically agreed upon, the right is a matter of personal 'values' and 'opinion'. The result is an emphasis upon the 'legal point of view', but with an emphasis upon the possibility of changing law in terms of rational considerations of social utility (rather than freezing in terms of stage 4 'law and order'). Outside the legal realm, free agreement and contract is the binding element of obligation. This is the 'official' morality of the United States government and constitution.

Stage 6, universal ethical-principle orientation. Right is defined by the decision of conscience in accord with self-chosen ethical principles appealing to logical comprehensiveness, universality, and consistency. These principles are abstract and ethical (the Golden Rule, the categorical imperative); they are not concrete moral rules like the Ten Commandments. At heart, these are universal principles of justice, of the reciprocity and equality of human rights and of respect for the dignity of human beings as individual persons (*Kohlberg*, 1971b, pp. 86–88).

Kohlberg (1971a) notes that the progression, or set of stages, just described, implies something more than age trends. First, it implies an invariant sequence. Each individual child must go step by step through each of the kinds of moral judgment outlined. The child can move at varying speeds and stop (i.e. fixate) at any level of development, but if he continues to move upward, he must move in accord with these steps. The longitudinal study of American boys and also cross-cultural data suggest that this is the case (*Kohlberg*, 1971a). Second, stages define 'structured wholes', that is, total ways of thinking which are identified as structures. Hence his theory is very much in line with the structuralism of *Piaget* to which he acknowledges a considerable debt. Third, a stage concept implies universality of sequence under varying cultural conditions. It implies that moral development is not merely a matter of learning the verbal values or rules of the child's culture but reflects something more universal in development, something that would occur in any culture. In short, his stages in moral judgment imply a cultural universal.

With this brief introduction to the broad outline of his stages completed, I would now like to turn to two specific aspects of this perspective which will provide the scope of the present critique. The two aspects are defined as follows: (1) The 'model of man'[3] in a stage-6 orientation and (2) a critical analysis of 'structuralism' *per se* when applied to moral ideology.

'Model of Man' in a Stage-6 Orientation

For *Kohlberg,* stage 6 is the end point of morality and therefore the ideal to which morality strives. Because of the universal significance that he attributes to the stages of morality, his stage 6 becomes 'the model of moral man' rather than 'a model of moral man'. 'An adequate psychological explanation of cognition or of morality must include an explanation of the universality of these concepts throughout humanity, an explanation which cannot be purely psychological in the usual sense' (*Kohlberg,* 1971a, p. 154). 'It has already been noted that we started our studies of moral development fifteen years ago with the notion (a) that there were unusual ontogenic trends toward the development of morality as it has been conceived by Western moral philosophers, and (b) that the development of such "rational" or "mature morality" is a process different from the learning of various "irrational" or "arbitrary" cultural rules and values' (*Kohlberg,* 1971a, p. 155).

At this point I would simply want it to be noted that *Kohlberg* sees the end point of moral development in a particular type of moral judgment that has universal significance for the species as a key definer of the 'rational' and the 'morally mature'.

Stage-6 Universal Ethical-Principle Orientation

In defining morality as a 'formal principle' *Kohlberg* (1973) puts himself in line with formalist philosophers from *Kant* through *Hare, Raphael* and more specifically *Rawls.* Referring back to the description of stage 6, the last stage has a distinctly Kantian ring. Stage 6 centers moral judgment 'on concepts of obligation as these are defined by principles of respect for persons and of justice. In part, this corresponds to an initial "formalist" or "structuralist" bias of both our moral and our psychological theory' (*Kohlberg,* 1973, p. 632).

---

[3] I don't use 'model of person' or 'model of human' because 'model of man' is the directional bias of most psychological theories.

Kohlberg's concept of stages is derived largely from *Piaget* where it is claimed that logic and morality develop through stages and that each stage is a structure which formally considered, is in better equilibrium than the preceding stage. It is also assumed that each new stage is a new structure which includes elements of earlier structures (i.e. stages) but transforms them in such a way to represent an equilibrium at a higher level. In contrast to *Piaget*'s cognitive stage theory, *Kohlberg*'s moral judgment stages entail (a) a process of role-taking, that is, taking the point of view of others conceived as subjects and coordinating those points of view and (b) a distinctive principle of justice as fairness. This principle operates in moral situations in which disequilibrium brings about a condition of unresolved conflicting claims. A resolution of the situation is one in which each is 'given his due' according to some principle of justice that can be recognized as fair by all the conflicting parties involved. *Kohlberg*'s (1973, p. 635) 'equilibrium' assumptions are allied to the philosophic tradition from *Kant* to *Rawls*. 'In our view, there is a family of theories that have the purpose just stated of Kant and Rawls. This family of theories may be looked at as derivatives of a natural structure I term "stage 6". Rawls's theory, when traced back to its natural structural roots, is not merely a "generalization" and "abstraction" of the theory of social contract, but derives from a new way of thought, a new system of assumptions, a new decision-making process. This is true in the same sense that "the familiar theory of social contract" is not merely a "generalization" and "abstraction" of the stage 4 conception of an overriding need for social order, but is an expression of a natural structure we term "stage 5" ' (*Kohlberg,* 1973, p. 635).

Kohlberg sees the stage-6 structure as synonymous with the Rawlsian conception of justice and in this sense he agrees with *Rawls* that this structure (stage 6) is better than structures of reasoning based on the 'more familiar' conception of the social contract and of utilitarianism (i.e. stage 5).

The original position. *Rawls'* (1971) concept of justice as fairness is derived from an ideal (not real) philosophical state called the 'original position'. The original position is a hypothetical way of defining the 'state of nature' which assumes that there are individuals before societies (i.e. the social contract). In the 'original position', persons of equal status, knowing nothing about their own actual positions in society, form a compact about the principles governing possible social arrangements. In *Rawls'* view, the virtue of a principle of 'justice as fairness' seems most logical and rational in this hypothetical position. It involves two principles. The first principle assumes that each person has a right to the most extensive basic liberty compatible with a like liberty for others. The principle relates to the distribution of wealth and to arrangements of power and authority. *Rawls* argues that inequalities can reasonably be expected to work out to the advantage of those who are worst off. *Rawls* neither sees it just or unjust that men are born with differing natural abilities into different social positions, they are simply natural facts. He never questions that these differences may not be as a result of natural abilities in the vein of acquired or inherited wealth. He, as well as *Kohlberg,* assumes that this is the best of all possible worlds up to now and will get better with the application of the principle of justice as fairness (i.e. stage 6 à la *Kohlberg*). The second principle also stresses the 'liberal' freedom of conscience, since it argues for diversity of conscience, in view of a lexico-graphical ordering in which basic freedoms are to take priority over welfare (*Rawls,* 1971).

Universalizability and reversibility at stage 6. In the context of *Kohlberg*'s stage 6, he argues that his position is a 'formalist' one, in line with *Kant* and *Rawls,* which considers moral judgments as reversible, consistent, and univer-salizable, and entailing prescriptivity for such judgments. A stage-6 structure is said to meet these criteria. Concretely, *Kohlberg* (1973, pp. 641–642) states:

'For developmental theory, meeting these conditions of moral judgment is parallel with the equilibration of fully logical thought in the realm of physical or logical facts. According to Piaget and others, the keystone of logic is reversibility. A logical train of thought is one in which one can move back and forth between premises and conclusions without distortion. Mathematical thinking is an example; A + B is the same as B + A. Or again, the operation A + B = C is reversible by the operation C – B = A. In one sense, the elements of reversible moral thought are the moral categories as these apply to the universe of moral actors. To say that rights and duties are correlative is to say that one can move from rights to duties and back without change or distortion. Universalizability and consistency are fully attained by the reversibility of prescriptions of actions. Reversibility of moral judgment is what is ultimately meant by the criterion of the fairness of a moral decision. Procedurally, fairness as impartiality means reversibility in the sense of a decision on which all interested parties could agree insofar as they can consider their own claims impartially, as the just decider would. If we have a reversible solution, we have one that could be reached as right starting from anyone's perspective in the situation, given each person's intent to put himself in the shoes of the other. Reversibility meets a second criterion of formalism: universalizability. As reversibility starts with the slogan, "Put yourself in the other guy's shoes when you decide," universalizability starts with the slogan, "What if everyone did it; what if everyone used this principle of choice?" It is clear that universalizability is implied by reversibility. If something is fair or right to do from the conflicting points of view of all those involved in the situation, it is something we can wish all men to do in all similar situations. Reversibility tells us more than universalizability, then, in resolving dilemmas, but it implies universalizability.

The concept of reversibility explains the intuitive plausibility of Rawls's conception of justice *(op.cit.)* as a rational choice in an original position in which one is under a veil of ignorance as to one's role or identity. Rawls argues that this conception leads to the choice of a justice principle of equality, with inequalities accepted only when it is to the benefit of the least advantaged. This conception of choice in the veil of ignorance is a formalization of the conception of fairness involved in having one person cut the cake and a second person distribute it. This conception leads to a mini-maximization solution in the sense that the division must be such that the least advantaged person is better off, i.e. that the cake is so cut that the person cutting the cake is willing to live with getting the smallest piece.'

53

As the extensive quote above indicates, *Kohlberg*'s end point of moral maturity is completely aligned to the Rawlsian concept of justice.

Critique of the Stage-6 'Model of Man'

If you look back to the *Mannheim* (1953) quote you will see that both *Rawls* and *Kohlberg* adopt a modified 'natural law' theory. I would like to make the case here that the 'model of man' adopted is to some extent parochial rather than universal in character and wedded historically to the liberal conceptions of natural law at the time of the French Revolution and developed to maturity in the writings of *Kant*. The Rawlsian conception of justice rests on a model of justice which assumes a principle which is said to be disinterested, abstract, formal, ideal, and universal. The essense of rationality is a disinterested abstract principle. In this, he, as well as *Kohlberg* in his argument for stage 6, is right in line with Kantian formalism. Instead of seeing the Kantian categories as disinterested rationality, *Marx and Engels* (1970) and subsequently *Lukacs* (1971) argued that abstract formalism was the organizing principle structuring social relations of production within Western capitalism. *Marx and Engels* (1970) lay at *Kant*'s door an abstract formalism implying a universality that masked a middle-class ideology which was present in Western capitalism. Where *Kant* claimed disinterest *Marx* saw class interests. *Lukacs* (1971) attempted to further argue and document this Marxian contention. It is not essential that the reader share a Marxian critique of Kantian formalism, but only to know that it has been made and by a theory of society which challenges the universal character and pretentions of liberal abstract formalism.

The original position revisited. First of all, is the original position as rational and in line with human nature as *Rawls* and *Kohlberg* imply? A radical perspective would reject the position of liberal theory because it treats the person as an isolated, independent entity in the datum of social analysis and social policy (*Duncan,* 1973).

In this context, is the 'original position' in any way in line with the interests of the 'least advantaged' as is proposed by *Rawls*? *Fisk* (1975) contends that a social contract contrived in the original position is hardly feasible. He attempts to demonstrate that on any other than the atomic conception of humans that is involved in the idea of natural freedom, contract theory must fail. Consider *Fisk*'s (1975, p. 63) hypothetical example. 'Assume that I know I am a member of a major group in a society, though I do not know which, and that these groups are locked in a struggle over factors controlling inequality. Why should I agree to a coercive mechanism to keep this struggle within limits of social stability? I might turn out to be a member of a group that can protect its members' interests only by fundamentally altering the social structure. If so, a state would simply prevent my group from effectively engaging its natural enemies. Since more likely than not I will enter history as a member of a disadvantaged group, I would not willingly risk giving up the benefits of solidarity with that group by agreeing to social harmony.'

Rawls' formalism, as *Kant*'s, his distinguished predecessor, simply immunizes him from sociological modes of understanding (*Barber,* 1975; *Daniels,* 1975). The limits on *Rawls* are the limits of *Kohlberg*'s stage-6 ideal. *Kohlberg* and *Rawls'* formalism bind the criterion of generality of norms to the further criterion of autonomy, that is, independence from contingent motives. 'The limits of formalistic ethics can be seen in the fact that inclinations incompatible with duties must be excluded from the domain of the morally relevant, and they must be suppressed. The interpretation of needs that are current at any given contingent stage of socialization must thereby be accepted as given' (*Habermas,* 1973, p. 89).

From a radical historical rather than abstract hypothetical position, there is every reason to reject the claim that the realization of *Rawls'* standard of social justice would be tolerable to a typical member of every income group in every society in the circumstances of justice (*Miller,* 1975). This applies clearly to groups that are oppressed and disenfranchised (e.g. Black America). *Rawls'* disinterested theory is not in their interest. Now insofar as *Kohlberg* argues that his theory is based on an abstract universal principle synonymous with *Rawls',* his theory of stages of justice faces similar criticism. In short, a case can be made that *Kohlberg*'s stage theory of moral development is essentially conservative in nature and masks an unreflective liberal ideology. Like most developmental theories in contemporary psychology, it also suffers from ahistoricism (*Kenniston,* 1974; *Riegel,* 1972). I would now like to dwell on this in more detail.

The 'impersonal' person and the 'a-historical' community. In a critical assessment such as the present study, it is essential to examine the 'model of man' that seems to be implicit in liberal social theory. One of the characteristics of this model is a conception of society based on the development of social contractual arrangements. The 'original position' of *Rawls* constitutes the ideal situation in which people negotiate social contracts. As is indicated, there is no historical basis for an 'original position' and it purposely attempts to be a-historical to eliminate the problems of man in his natural social settings. But what happens when one develops a theory of man-in-society which tries to negate his concrete historical circumstances? Is this an improvement or aberration in man's thinking about himself in society; or is it possibly both? I would contend that the liberal position represents a blatantly distorted conception of man when considered as a totality. The distortion of 'a-historical', 'ideality' (i.e. the liberal mentality) subsequently leads to an aberrant conception of the personal and interpersonal. In stark contrast to an ideal conception of man as seen in the liberal tradition and exemplified in *Rawls'* 'original position', a radical conception assumes that a conception of society stems from historical conditions (*Marx and Engels,* 1970). Man comes into the world which is already in momentum and where there is a solid, weighty, and dense social structure operating on the individual well before the time they act consciously in it or against it (*Duncan, 1973*). The liberal conception of man as a 'universalizing' creature who makes contractual arrangements from a-historical positions is probably more ambiguous than universal (*Macpherson, 1973*). One criticism of this conception (i.e. *Rawls*) is that there are remnants of 'bourgeois' man who both puts a high value on individual liberty and therefore tends to accept as inevitable a class-divided society in which class determines life prospects (*Macpherson, 1973*). If *Rawls* and *Kohlberg*'s universality is disinterested and ideal, it is nevertheless peculiar that this 'universalization' leaves unchallenged some of the deleterious effects of corporate capitalism. Moreover, a 'bourgeois' conception of man assumes a creature that is simply involved in social conflicts of interest. Although there is some validity to this position, it is nevertheless important to question the extensiveness of 'conflict of interests' in the development of a just social order. Is morality simply the development of a system of social arrangements which can deal with conflicts of interest in an ideal and disinterested way? If this is so, can a society or community be said to be based on a moral system which simply assumes that man at his deepest level enters into social arrangements out of conflicts of interests? This conception of man in society has been criticized by both radical and conservative theorists alike. *Rawls* criticizes the 'intuitionists' because they confuse prosocial tendencies in man (e.g. altruism) with part of the moral realm. *Kohlberg*'s argument for a prior claim for 'just ideality' agrees with *Rawls* on this account (*Beck et al., 1971*). The essence of liberalism is a vision of society made up of independent autonomous units who cooperate only when the terms of cooperation are such as to make it further the ends of each of the parties (*Barry, 1973*). Needless to say, this conception of man and society is being heavily criticized today. The critique challenges the very heart of a liberal concept of man and challenges a concept of man that is patently egocentric (*Macmurray, 1957*). The 'impersonality' of liberal theory represents a crisis of the personal. 'At this level, the crisis of the personal is the crisis of liberalism, which was an effort, however ambiguous, to subordinate the functional organization of society to the personal life of its members. Yet nothing could be more revealing of the depth of the crisis we are facing than one fact. Communism rests upon a criticism of liberal democracy. Liberalism, it maintains contradicts itself. While it stands in theory, for human freedom, in practice, it is a defense of exploitation' (*Macmurray, 1957, p. 30*).

Today there is a growing resentment of the 'instrumental rationalism' exemplified in liberal social thought (*Weisskopf, 1973*). The key features of a liberal concept of justice place a high value on the mastery of a restrictive intellectuality of a cognitive, analytical, measuring, and technical nature. This rationality can be seen as destructive of a deeper kind of philosophical reason which could deal with ends, goals, purposes, and ultimate meanings (*Weisskopf,*

(1973). *Kohlberg* (personal commun., 1972) acknowledges the latter type of reasoning as a religious perspective which he separates from morality and therefore justice. It therefore does not enter systematically in his thinking about a just social order.

A Critical Analysis of 'Structuralism' per se when Applied to Moral Ideology

Structuralism as a 'Universal Model' in Psychology

Our analysis to this point has concentrated on the philosophical underpinnings of a stage-6 'structure'. We have assumed in this section the notion of 'structure' without focusing on the concept of 'structure'. It is now important to discuss the notion of 'structure', particularly as a movement of thought in the social sciences called 'structuralism'. This is necessary if one is to appreciate and assess *Kohlberg*'s contribution as a psychologist, since he is a cognitive-developmental 'structuralist' par excellence. Structuralism is a method of analysis – the analysis of structures (*Dagenais,* 1972). Fundamentally, a 'structure' is an autonomous entity characterized by internal dependencies. As such, a structure is a system of transformations which, as a system, implies lawfulness of organization independent of the elements which compose it. A system is characterized, first of all, by its being a totality, that is, whatever the 'composing elements' in the system, they are subordinated to the laws which define the system as system. Second, a system is characterized by multiple transformations (e.g. stages), interdependent with each other and with the totality, that is, they are dependent upon the structure itself. Finally, a third characteristic of structure, that it is self-regulating, tends toward the conservation and enhancement of the system itself, on the one hand, and closedness toward all other systems on the other (*Dagenais,* 1972). In the context of the above definition, *Kohlberg*'s stage theory of morality is clearly a structural theory.

For a student growing up in this era, structuralism had many attractive features when compared with the more defunct adversary behaviorism. It became part of the 'Zeitgeist' in the social sciences and in education (*Sullivan,* 1967, 1969). For some, it obviously became 'the model of man' rather than 'a model of man'. Specifically, the critique under this heading will deal with some problem areas that 'structuralism' seems to create as a methodology. This section will touch on some of these issues insofar as they relate to *Kohlberg*'s conception of moral development. I will attempt to develop the idea that *Kohlberg*'s structural conception of morality tends to create dichotomies when treating the relationships between thought and action, form and content, and the abstract and the concrete. I shall then attempt to show how these bifurcations affect the area of moral commitment. Furthermore, the critique will attempt to demonstrate the tendency in *Kohlberg*'s 'structuralism' to separate the 'emotional life' from the 'intellectual' life where morality is concerned. In creating this type of dichotomy, the emotions are relegated to an epiphenomenal status in the under-standing of morality. This bias then creates its own caricatures, making the treatment of virtues ludicrous. The critique will attempt to develop a place for what *Kohlberg* calls 'the bag of virtues psychology' by looking at some of the implications for moral commitment when the issue of moral imagination and blindness are considered. All in all, the critique in this section is a counter-position to certain aspects of *Kohlberg*'s structuralism.

In order to analyze critically *Kohlberg*'s stage theory, it is necessary to understand a few things about *Piaget*. In his writings, *Piaget* (1948) seems to see the development of ethical judgments as following from the study of logical structures. *Kohlberg* (1969) follows *Piaget* in attempting to show that the devel-opment of 'moral judgments' can be studied to a considerable extent by a 'genetic epistemological' model. In a sense, *Piaget* (1948) and *Kohlberg*'s work are extensions of *Piaget*'s earlier work in the Kantian area of 'the practical reason'. *Kohlberg*'s stages of moral judgment are simply a more sophisticated and articulate extension of *Piaget*'s earlier inquiry into the understanding of moral judgment or practical reasoning. In *Kohlberg*'s and *Piaget*'s work in the area of moral judgment, there is a preoccupation with epistemological categories. There appears to be some question about this type of preoccupation since it may lock one into a specific direction which may have unintended consequences. From my own perspective, it appears that *Kohlberg*'s moral stages are simply an offshoot of the development of scientific understanding. In that sense, moral logic becomes simply an extension of scientific logic and this conclusion can easily be drawn from *Kohlberg*'s (1969) writings when he discusses the rela-tionship of moral stages to Piagetian stages of intellectual development. From this, I would be inclined to say that *Kohlberg*'s psychologism is a particular type of scientific outlook identified with the development of Kantian philosophy. Specifically, in his stage items, *Kohlberg* seems to indicate that stage-6 is *a priori* and all lower stages are forms of empiricisms leading to the stage-6 *a priori* (*Kohlberg,* 1971b). In one sense morality really begins at stage 6 when a prac-tical reflective process has reached full maturity. This strikes me as one of the reasons why there is a preoccupation of reflection over action within *Kohlberg*'s perspective. Reflection and action never seem to be in dynamic tension.

Moral Commitment

One of the first questions raised in relation to *Kohlberg*'s stage theory of moral judgment is what is the relationship between a person's moral judgment and his actions. The very nature of the formulation of this theory invites a question of this nature because most people identify morality with moral com-mitment or action. In *Kohlberg*'s formulation, the moral aspect is defined by the nature of the moral judgment. I will try to develop, in this section, several shortcomings in the way *Kohlberg* treats the relationship between moral judgment and moral action. The very nature of the theory creates a false dichotomy between thought (judgment) and action. Let us first turn to *Kohlberg* (1971b) to understand his treatment of the relationship of moral thought to moral action.

Kohlberg (1971b) identifies two main sources of consistency between moral judgment and action. The first source of consistency is the level of the structure or stage itself. He quotes several studies which apparently show the relationship of consistency between judgment and action, by showing that people at higher stages are more morally consistent. One study by *Krebs* on cheating in sixth graders indicated that the majority of children were below the principled level in moral judgment. 75% of these children cheated. In contrast, only 20% of the principled subjects (i.e. stages 5 and 6) cheated (*Kohlberg*, 1971b). Similar findings in the same direction are quoted on a college population. He also indicates that principled-level students were able to resist shocking people in the now famous Milgram experiment and also involve themselves in types of campus action where 'civil disobedience' ensued (*Kohlberg*, 1971b). In short, the higher the stage the greater the consistency between thought and action.

The second source of consistency between judgment and action are non-moral factors identified as attention, will, and ego-strength (*Kohlberg*, 1971b). This factor somewhat transcends the consistency produced simply by the structure. *Kohlberg* (1971b) cites a study which indicates that if children have an amoral philosophy (stage 2) they are much more likely to cheat if they are high on ego strength. If children have a conventional morality (stage 4) they are much less likely to cheat if they are high on a measure of ego strength. If children have reached the postconventional level (i.e. 5 or 6), high ego strength is less necessary, for even these principled children who are low in 'ego strength' do not seem to cheat. *Kohlberg* (1971b) concludes that in this sense, the basic virtue may be called 'autonomy' as well as 'justice'.

My first impression is that all of his contentions are simple, straightforward and logical. It may be too simple in dealing with the issue of moral consistency. *Kohlberg*'s conclusion about autonomy is certainly open to serious question as it is a troublesome concept taken all by itself (*Hogan*, 1973). *Hogan* develops this question in much greater detail. What is more important for our purposes at this point, is the whole question of whether *Kohlberg*'s 'structuralism' creates its own peculiar problems which are idiosyncratic to the theoretical position itself. My position is, in spite of their statements to the contrary, that *Kohlberg* and his predecessor Piaget produce a thought-action dichotomy which indicates the collapse of an inherently dialectical process.

Thought-action dichotomy. Kohlberg and *Piaget* follow in the tradition of Kant when dealing with the relationships between thought and action. I would like here to quote *Lukacs* (1971, p. 38) in a reflection he makes on *Kant* because it directly applies to *Kohlberg* and specifically to the issue at hand.

59

'Within such a world only two possible modes of action commend themselves and they are both apparent rather than real ways of actively changing the world. Firstly, there is the exploitation for particular human ends (as in technology, for example) of the fatalistically accepted and *immutable laws* (my italics) which are seen in the manner we have already described. Secondly, there is action directed wholly inwards. This is the attempt to change the world at its only remaining free point, namely man himself (ethics). But as the world becomes mechanized its subject, man, necessarily becomes mechanized too and so this ethics likewise remains *abstract* (my italics). Confronted by the totality of man in isolation from the world it remains merely normative and fails to be truly *active* (my italics) in the creation of objects. It is only prescriptive and imperative in character.'

Like *Kant, Kohlberg* and other cognitive-developmentalists are primarily interested in the development of abstract and universal laws (i.e. structures). The theory really does not focus on action or commitment and what ultimately follows is a thought-action dichotomy which is prevalent in the historical development of modern thought (*Habermas,* 1971). Now I am aware that both *Kohlberg* and *Piaget* would deny what I am saying here since the process of assimilation and accommodation which they subscribe to is supposedly dynamic and action-oriented. After all are not thought structures actions which are internalized? I would contend, as *Lukacs* does of *Kant,* that in *Kohlberg* the moral thought structures (i.e. stages) become reified; that is, take on a life of their own. Also in *Kohlberg*'s case it would appear that for him a thought structure always logically precedes action. In my opinion, we are always trying to get from thought (judgment) to action in *Kohlberg*'s stage theory and I consider this only a half-truth and a collapse of an inherently dialectical process. To me, thought directs action and action directs thought and so on and so on. I am really talking about the dialectics of a process called praxis. In *Friere*'s (1970) terms praxis is the fusion of action-reflection. Reflection then is one pole of a continuing process. If that pole is emphasized to the detriment of the other (i.e. action) then the dialectic collapses and thought and action separate. *Friere* indicates that reflection separated from action is simply pure verbalism. I would be inclined to see *Kohlberg*'s stages of thought structures in this light. One falls in love with morally pure and abstract thought categories. After all it is not important morally what particular choice you make (i.e. content) but rather the moral is determined by the form (i.e. maturity of the stage). It strikes me that *Kohlberg*'s theory deals with moral ambiguity in one way and one way only. The moral man thinks through clearly (thought) and then acts. I do not disagree with this but I question the completeness of the direction. It strikes me that all of us mere humans must act in ambiguity in many situations and that in the process of acting we really begin to clarify how we think. Furthermore, most people are more like St. Paul than *Kant,* 'We work out our salvation in fear and trembling'. In many instances we act with unclear guide posts and in the process of this activity the very nature of our thought processes changes. *Kohlberg*'s research never looks at the process in this direction because the theory is contemplative (*Mannheim,* 1953). Are only universal, abstract, thought structures (i.e. stages) the forms of activity? Is there a form to concrete, unique actions sensitive to the individual human story (i.e. the personal) and the specific cultural history (i.e. community)? Whatever the advantages there are in finding abstract, thought structures, I wonder if this should be to the detriment of the concrete, idiosyncratic, and contextual. Phenomenology has adamantly defended the latter (e.g. *Merleau-Ponty,* 1962). It is explicitly clear from *Piaget*'s (1971) own writing that he has an aversion to the concrete and contextual when he theorizes (*Sullivan,* 1975). I think the same thing can be said for *Kohlberg* with his passion for abstract, formal structures. Let it be clear that I am not arguing that there is no merit in their approach, rather, I am trying to point to its one-sidedness, its one-dimensionality. Is abstract formalism, then, an unmixed contribution to the development of Western thought or does it bring its own inherent problems? I will attempt to deal with this question by looking at the form-content distinction.

Form-content distinction. I would like to entertain the possibility that the question of form-content, abstract-concrete, and thought-action are all related issues. Although *Kohlberg* appears contradictory and equivocal on this matter (*Crittenden,* 1972), it nevertheless is apparent from the corpus of his writings that he has a penchant for form over content, as if it were possible to separate the two poles of this distinction. The higher stages are more abstract, and in approaching the ultimate ideal (i.e. stage 6), each stage is the achievement of a purer form of the moral. So it would follow that the lower stages are more content-oriented and more concrete. In the light of his theoretical thrust, abstract and formal are more valued as moral structures. *Kohlberg* follows *Piaget* here and therefore shares some of *Piaget*'s inherent Kantian formalism. And it should be noted here that movement of thought associated with 'abstract formalism' is not unequivocal in its virtues. *Scheler* (1973a), who was attracted to Kantian formalism, devoted a whole volume to some of the problems it presents for the development of ethical inquiry. He was struck by the fact that there is a tendency in the process of 'abstraction' to make light of the concrete context from which 'abstraction' receives its very life blood. *Piaget* (1971) systematically set out to do this methodologically and *Kohlberg* seems to fully accept *Piaget*'s methodological attack. This is a systematic weakness in cognitive-development 'structuralism' as is pointed out by *Turner* (1973) in noting *Piaget*'s weakness concerning 'figurative' knowledge. He indicates that *Piaget* downgrades the use of concrete imagery as it is always associated with less mature stages of thought. Mature development is always associated with more abstraction and less concretion. *Kohlberg*'s stage theory of moral development takes exactly the same tack as *Piaget*'s stage formulation of intellectual development. It therefore suffers some of the same shortcomings that are becoming apparent in the Piagetian formulation. Since this section is about moral commitment, I would like to point out here how 'structuralism' has generally dealt shabbily with human affect or the emotional life. In the case of *Piaget,* it comes to a criticism of the very process of 'decentering' which is always associated with the development of abstraction. A quote from *Turner* (1973, p. 354) sums it up beautifully:

'The identity (in the full sense of the personality of "self") of the subject, on the other hand, exists at a relatively concrete and particular level: its essential functional property is the integration of cognitive world-picture and logical operations with affect and value in the forms of purposive action. Affect is inherently concrete, particular, and associated with the unique relationship of the self to its objective environment. For this reason the integration and shaping of the personality or subjective self, on both conscious and unconsciousness levels, cannot be achieved by a decentered, abstract, and generalized mode of thought alone. A more concrete symbolic medium, centered upon the particular position of the subject and capable of condensing affective with cognitive associations, is required. It is this need that is filled by figurative imagery and symbolic forms. Figurative symbolism and "decentered" logical thought thus fulfill complementary functions and ideally reinforce one another. "Recentered" forms such as ritual or myth, for example, afford mechanisms by which structural principles of "decentered" cognitive systems (e.g., social or moral norms) can be invested with affective and motivational power. Alternatively, "recentered" forms can compensate for the depersonalization of "decentered" structures of social or cosmic reality at either the collective or the individual level by creating concrete, affectively charged worlds of meaning of a subjectively "centered" character.'

As I pointed out earlier, *Kohlberg*'s stage-6 ideal-principled person is a moral entity without 'flesh or bones'. In this ideal 'decentered' state, the stage-6 person is the Beatles' 'nowhere' man. *Kohlberg* and *Rawls* only identify the process of 'universalization' with that of an 'impartial judge' in a jurisprudential procedure. This is possibly one of the reasons why stage 6 seems only present in Western cultural samples since his stage 6 reflects a bias toward a jurisprudential process more prevalent in Western cultures. But can it be said that where that jurisprudential process is absent, that there is no attempt at universality. My own position is that *Kohlberg*'s and *Rawls'* process of universalization is sensitized to a jurisprudential model which is concretely developed in Western democracies and when this sensitivity is combined with scoring other cultures lower on moral development, it is a culturally biased model (*Simpson,* 1974). I think it should be noted that even within our own culture, this particular type of 'universalization' has limited value. The judge in our culture represents the 'generalized other' and his impartiality may be important for certain types of moral and legal claims. But does the possibility of a more universal ethics depend only on the possibility of all people developing the mentality of an impersonal judicial procedure? In other words should all moral claims be adjudicated by this ideal? It seems to me that most of us mere humans have to develop more inclusive ethics (i.e. universal) from our own personal rather than impersonal point in time and space (i.e. history). In this sense it is important not to become detached or decentered but to see the full force of my attachments and centerings and then to acknowledge their limited nature. By entering more deeply into my own personal and historical viewpoint it is hoped that I will realize that other viewpoints are limited, yet possibly looking at segments of reality that I have not considered. If this process were reciprocal then no party would lay claim to a more universal viewpoint (e.g. like the judge) but the very process itself would be a 'universalization' which would deepen in different ways the personal lives of all involved. This movement of 'universalization' is different from the impersonal process of *Rawls* or *Kohlberg*. In a contemporary context, this process of justice may issue from the call or a cry rather than an impersonal defused voice. Particular examples of what I am alluding to can be called out of *Friere*'s (1970) *Pedagogy of the Oppressed* or *Fanon*'s *Wretched of the Earth*. Here the call for justice comes from an 'opposed group' whose cry of anguish beckons a deeper sense of community and therefore a deeper universality. The call is itself part of a judgmental process but not by a judge who makes no personal claims. It is not synonymous with a jurisprudential process but rather a call to the community which appears close to what the Prophets did in the Old Testament. It calls for a deeper interest on the part of an oppressor group which extends the scope of the human community. Since it involves a radical personal and social change, it can hardly be identified with the impersonality of a judge in a judicial hearing. So for all its sophistication, *Kohlberg*'s stage 6 is a 'limited perspective' with a limited type of universalization despite his claims to the contrary. Moreover, the decentered autonomy subscribed to by *Piaget* and *Kohlberg* has the potential for creating as many problems as it appears to solve (*Hogan,* 1973). It is possible that 'autonomy' as a singular ideal can contribute to the development of a moral agent who lacks sociability and who disregards the pragmatic value of rules as well, might well be autocratic and anti-conforming, 'a great scoundrel and a rogue' (*Hogan,* 1973). So autonomy separated from other dimensions of the moral is conceivably an aberrant process. Insofar as autonomy and abstraction are considered as ideal states, there is a possibility that the moral agent may 'decenter' him/herself from any concrete moral commitments. It is at this point that a fusion of the figurative (concrete) and the abstract becomes essential for moral commitment. I would identify the figurative here with a faculty of imagination. Looking at *Kohlberg*'s (1973) stage-6 autonomous protocols one can see a person completely lacking in 'imagination'; a process that I would deem essential to effective moral commitment. Because of its importance, let me conclude with a short treatment on moral commitment and its relation to the 'imagination' and 'blindness'. The treatment will hopefully indicate a vacuum area in *Kohlberg*'s conception of the moral that cannot be passed over lightly.

Morality and the Imagination

There is something lacking in all of the conceptual elegance of both *Piaget* and *Kohlberg*'s structuralism. One significant area is their lack of treatment of the 'esthetic imagination' and the potential role it may play in the development of intellectual and moral understanding (*Simpson,* 1976). It can be said of *Kohlberg,* as it is said of *Piaget,* that his theory is confined to an analysis of 'decentering' in logical, and moral structures (*Turner,* 1973). In this light, *Turner* suggests that a theory of this kind must be supplemented by a theory of 'recentered' figurative symbolic structures before it can provide a comprehensive account of cultural and psychological structures (i.e. a theory of moral perception as well as action). *Kohlberg*'s theory in its present states collapses the dialectical tension here at the 'decentered' pole. This is probably why his formulation so easily lends itself to a thought-action dichotomy. To balance *Kohlberg*'s formulation, we need a fusion of thought-action, form-content, and the abstract and concrete. Both *Kohlberg*'s and *Piaget*'s 'structuralism' lack this fusion. What is needed is a complementary process which fuses the process of 'decentering' and 'recentering'.

The imagination is the thorn in the development of most theoretical rationalists. We noted earlier that *Piaget* seems to pass off figurative knowledge as simply a lower form of intellectual development. *Kohlberg*'s theory has no systematic place for it. In our everyday life, value synthesis is not a science but probably encompasses, when done well, the virtuosity of an artist. *Hampden-Turner* (1976, p. 291) probably speaks for most people when he concludes that 'no science can tell you, or ever will tell you, what you should do in a human encounter a few moments from now. You can be given the axioms and the principles involved, but the exact proportions of their combination is your existential decision. If a potential suicide arrives on your doorstep, the degree that you permit him to depend on you, and that you urge him to the independence he needs to survive, are two elements in the art of judgment.'

This art of judgment is not of necessity a blind art as naive romanticism would claim (*Macmurray,* 1957). A one-sided approach to intelligence which lacks the dimension of imagination or gives it a poor showing will be subject to the following judgment made by *Novak* (1971, pp. 57–58) in a discussion of the role of the imagination.

'What is it that intelligence aims to understand if not human experience? In whose service is it if not in the service of human action? The imagination organizes the matrix of patterns and structures and relationships in which insight occurs. Many people of good intelligence lack imagination, and hence insight ... there are a great many things, in any case, which simply cannot occur until the underlying experiential and imaginative base has been prepared. Reading Shakespeare at forty is not like reading him at twenty (It is surprising how much Shakespeare has learned in the intervening years). As Aristotle pointed out, young people find ethics (by which he meant discernment in singular concrete situations) very difficult to understand. They are too idealistic, see things too abstractly, lack the precise experience that is required. Wisdom, the ability to go to the heart of the matter in concrete situations, is acquired slowly; it is a discipline of experience, imagination and story, not of naked intelligence. Often in America, unfortunately, one's intelligence develops more swiftly than one's experience, imagination, and story.'

Let me briefly illustrate from a speech of *Martin Luther King* how this 'imagery' is employed to foster commitment to action.

'I say to you today, my friends, Let Freedom ring! From the hilltops of New Hampshire, from mighty mountains of New York ... from every hill and molehill in Mississippi ... Let Freedom ring from every house and hamlet, from every street in every city ... When Freedom rings we shall be able to speed that day, when all God's children, black men and white men, Jews and Gentiles, Protestants and Catholics, will be able to join hands and sing in the words of the old Negro Spiritual. Free at last! Free at last! Great God Almighty, we are free at last! We got some difficult days ahead. Some people are concerned as to what would happen to me from some of our sick white brothers. Well I don't know what will happen to me now ... But it really doesn't matter to me now ... because I've been to the Mountain Top ... Like everybody I would like to live a long life ... Longevity has its place ... But I'm not concerned with that now ... He's allowed me to go to the Mountain Top — and I've looked over and I've seen the Promised Land. I may not get there with you ... but I want you to know, tonight, that we, as a people, will get to the Promised Land. So I'm happy now, I'm not worried about anything. Mine eyes have seen the Glory of the coming of the Lord!'

King's universalization is imaginatively tied to the concrete figurative. In contrast to principles stated in an abstract manner, *King* illustrates the dynamic force of imaginative symbolism which has a compelling intensional quality. They tend to evoke action and commitment in a way abstract principles could never do, except in exceptional cases. His possession of principles is tied to a moral imagination which clearly fuses the concrete with the abstract.

Moral Blindness: the Possibilities for Self-Deception

I would like to conclude this article with a brief treatment of the role of self-deception since it is the point wherein moral reasons become rationalizations. This raises some fundamental questions about moral reasoning and its possible ambiguity.

What do we do about the inherent ambiguity of human commitment? How do we deal with a condition that is familiar to all of us and discussed by *James* (1958) under the title of 'a certain blindness in human beings'. *Kohlberg*'s structuralism, in line with 20th-century rationalism, suggests we eliminate ambiguity by advancing to higher stages of development. He is thoroughly Cartesian in his rationality since he sees moral maturity as a deeper integration of 'clear and distinct ideas'. Most of us have at least a vague suspicion that this type of rationality is lacking in certain respects. St. Paul hits the issue head on in speaking of his own problems of moral commitment. 'In fact, this seems to be the rule, that every single time I want to do good it is something evil that comes to hand. In my inmost self, I dearly love God's law, but I can see that my body follows a different law that battles against the law which reason dictates' (Romans 7: 21–23).

Now the problem that Paul alludes to did not stop with Paul; it is a problem he attributed to his sinful condition. For this form of psychological blindness, a more updated term would be 'alienation'. This term and its corresponding process are never alluded to in *Kohlberg*'s theory. What I would like to indicate in this section is that, in lacking a substantial treatment of alienation (i.e. moral blindness), *Kohlberg*'s theory suffers from some grave difficulties. Moral blindness is a form of what the Marxists would call 'false consciousness'.

In many of *Kohlberg*'s writings, there is a section devoted to a topic that he calls the 'bag of virtues'. *Kohlberg* identifies the 'bag of virtues' as a particular type of moral psychology and he advances his own structural theory at its expense. He presents this conception of moral psychology in such a pejorative light that it seems ludicrous that any one in his right mind would identify with such an approach. (See *Peters* 1971, for a more balanced treatment of the virtues.) Let me quote *Kohlberg* (1971b, pp. 74–75) to demonstrate my point.

'According to Aristotle, "virtue is of two kinds, intellectual and moral. While intellectual virtue owes its birth and growth to teaching, moral virtue comes about as a result of habit. The moral virtues we get by first exercising them; we become just by doing just acts, temperate by doing temperate acts, brave by doing brave acts." Aristotle, then, is claiming that there are two spheres, the moral and the intellectual, and that learning by doing is the only real method in the moral sphere.[4]

American educational psychology also divides the personality into cognitive abilities, passions or motives, and traits of character. Moral character consists of a bag of virtues and vices. For example, one of the earliest major American studies of moral character, conducted in the late twenties (Hartshorne and May, 1928–30), included honesty, sincerity, and self-control in the bag of virtues.

If we accept such a bag of virtues, it is evident how we should build character. Children should be exhorted to practice these virtues and should be told that happiness, fortune, and good repute will follow in their wake; adults around them should be living examples of these virtues, and children should be given daily opportunities to practice them. Daily chores should be used to build responsibility, the opportunity to give to the Red Cross should serve to build responsibility, service, altruism, and so on.

The psychologist's objection to the bag of virtues is that there is no such a thing. Virtues and vices are labels by which people award praise or blame to others, but the ways people use praise and blame towards others are not the ways in which people think when making moral decisions themselves.'

[4] Incidently, it can be seen by my treatment of the notion of 'praxis' that I am in complete agreement with *Aristotle*. I am sure he would be most happy to know that, so if you see him tell him.

If one concentrates on the last section of this quote, it is clear to me that *Kohlberg* oversimplifies the issue to make a point. He treats the virtue and vice issue in such a manner that it makes one feel that the use of these terms in one's vocabulary makes one primitive or at best naive. *Kohlberg* demonstrates here the unreflective secularism of the enlightment (*Sullivan,* 1975). He shares with *Piaget* an unreflective myth of 'liberal progress' (*Rieff,* 1961). Historically, the 'bag of virtues', as *Kohlberg* calls them, are more than labels by which people award praise or blame. After all, is that all *Dante* was doing in his *Divine Comedy?* It is obviously to me that *Dante,* in a masterful treatment of human emotions, sustained a dialectical conception of moral emotions with virtues and vices being the two poles of this complex dialectic. In the context of the present discussion, vices are aspects of human emotions which lead to moral blindness and virtues are emotions which help to achieve moral vision (i.e. imagination). In contrast to *Dante,* who achieves a dialectic between Apollo and Dionysis, *Kohlberg's* structuralism is one-sided in its Apollonian vigor. Any psychological theory which pretends to capture a substantial understanding of human intellectual and moral development must contend with those dynamic factors which lead to intellectual and moral blindness. Structuralism à la *Kohlberg* has no systematic place for this process in its explanatory scheme. Lacking an adequate treatment, he ends up by treating the area as epiphenomenal. Dionysis, however, will have his day when left unattended, when rational deliberation turns into rationalization, a term for what the Marxists called 'false consciousness'. *Scheler* (1972) does a masterful treatment of this process of rationalization in his phenomenological analysis of the emotion 'ressentiment'. His analysis of 'ressentiment' as well as sympathy (*Scheler,* 1973b) bears scrutiny since it shows the latent possibilities of the tradition of 'virtue and vices'. *Scheler* attempts to elaborate a phenomenology of feeling states, of sympathy and love, of shame and repentence, of pain and joy which can be summed up as a 'logic of the heart' (*Coser,* 1972). The richness of this treatment makes 'structuralism' look pale in its wake.

As I already pointed out, the issues of moral blindness and vision have important theoretical as well as practical implications. *Lonergan* (1957) outlines this in the development of a cognitional theory as a process called scotosis or 'flight from understanding'. *Becker* (1968) describes a similar process in his discussion of ethical theory. Both of the above theorists draw substantially from the tradition of Freudian psychology without in any way being Freudians. In the work of *Peters* (1971), *Freud* gets a fairer treatment as to his possible role in the development of moral psychology.[5] The whole area of moral failure looks peculiar when you are simply advancing in cognitive moral stages. *Peters* (1971,

---

[5] See *Kohlberg* (1964, 1969) for a much less sympathetic treatment of *Freud*. He sees his theory as transcending the contribution of Freudian psychology on moral matters.

pp. 265–266) ventures that, at least on the side of the vices, Freudian psychology has something substantial to say about moral failures:

'The same sort of point can be made about Freud's theory of character traits. This does not begin to look like a theory of how traits such as honesty, which were studied in the Hartshorne-May enquiry, are developed. Nor is it a theory about the development of higher-order traits such as consistency, determination, and courage, to which we are usually alluding when we speak of people having character. ...

Freud thought that he spotted a similarity between types of character and various forms of neuroses, and assigned a common cause to both in his theory of infantile sexuality. Here again we do not have a competing explanation of the sort of phenomena in which Kohlberg is interested, namely, the determinants of a rational, principled form of morality. Rather we have an attempt to explain types of character that fall a long way short of this in some systematic way.'

If *Kohlberg* has a 'blindness' for the contribution of *Freud* at the level of individual moral psychology, he also shares with his predecessors in the liberal tradition a blindness to the role of class consciousness. There is nothing in his structural conception of morality which indicates an appreciation of the blindness produced by one's place in the social structure (i.e. class consciousness and blindness). Without elaborating in detail, his conception therefore comes under the same criticisms leveled at *Kant* on the class blindness of his world view (see *Lukacs*, 1971; *Marx and Engels*, 1970).

References

Ausubel, D. and Sullivan, E.V.: Theory and problems of child development; 2nd ed. (Grune & Stratton, New York 1970).

Barber, B.: Justifying justice: problems of psychology, politics and measurement in Rawls; in *Daniels* Reading Rawls (Blackwell, Oxford 1975).

Barry, B.: The liberal theory of justice: a critical examination of the principled doctrines; in A theory of justice by John Rawls (Clarendon Press, Oxford 1973).

Beck, C.; Crittenden, B., and Sullivan, E.V. (eds.): Moral education: interdisciplinary approaches (University of Toronto Press, Toronto 1971).

Becker, E.: The structure of evil (Braziller, New York 1968).

Buck-Morss, S.: Socio-economic bias in Piaget's theory and its implications for cross-cultural studies. Hum. Dev. *18:* 35–49 (1975).

Buss, A.R.: The emerging field of the sociology of psychological knowledge. Am. Psychol. *30:* 988–1002 (1975).

Coser, L.A.: Introduction; in *Scheler* Ressentiment; translated by *W.W. Holdheim* (Schocken, New York 1972).

Crittenden, B.: Form and content in moral education (Ontario Institute for Studies in Education, Toronto 1972).

Dagenais, J.J.: Models of man (Martinus Nijhaff, The Hague 1972).

Daniels, N.: Equal liberty and unequal worth of liberty; in *Daniels* Reading Rawls (Blackwell, Oxford 1975).

Duncan, G.: Marx and Mill: two views of social conflict and social harmony (Cambridge University Press, Cambridge 1973).

Fanon, F.: The wretched of the earth (Grove Press, New York 1968).

Fisk, M.: History and reason in Rawls' moral theory; in *Daniels* Reading Rawls (Blackwell, Oxford 1975).

Friere, P.: Pedagogy of the oppressed; translated by *M.B. Ramos* (Herder & Herder, New York 1970).

Habermas, J.: Toward a rational society; translated by *J.J. Shapiro* (Beacon Press, Boston 1970).

Habermas, J.: Knowledge and human interests; translated by *J.J. Shapiro* (Beacon Press, Boston 1971).

Habermas, J.: Legitimation crisis; translated by *T. McCarty* (Beacon Press, Boston 1973).

Hampden-Turner, C.: The sane asylum (San Francisco Book Co., San Francisco 1976).

Hogan, R.: Moral conduct and moral character: a psychological perspective. Psychol. Bull. *79:* 217–232 (1973).

Hunt, D.E. and Sullivan, E.V.: Between psychology and education (Dryden, Hillsdale 1974).

James, W.: Talks to teachers on psychology and to students on some of life's ideals (1899; Norton, New York 1958).

Keniston, K.: Psychological development and historical change; in *Lifton and Olson* Explorations in psychohistory (Simon & Schuster, New York 1974).

Kohlberg, L.: Development of moral character and moral ideology; in *Hoffman and Hoffman* Review of child development research, vol. 1 (Russell Sage, New York 1964).

Kohlberg, L.: Stage and sequence: the cognitive-developmental approach to socialization; in *Goslin* Handbook of socialization theory and research (Rand McNally, Chicago 1969).

Kohlberg, L.: From is to ought: how to commit the naturalistic fallacy and get away with it in the study of moral development; in *Mischel* Cognitive development and epistemology (Academic Press, New York 1971a).

Kohlberg, L.: Stages of moral development as a basis for moral education; in *Beck Crittenden and Sullivan* Moral education: interdisciplinary approaches (University of Toronto Press, Toronto 1971b).

Kohlberg, L.: The claim to moral adequacy of a highest stage of moral judgment. J. Phil. *70:* 630–646 (1973).

Kohlberg, L. and Mayer, R.: Development as the aim of education. Harv. educat. Rev. *42:* 449–496 (1972).

Lonergan, B.: Insight: a study of human understanding (Longmans, London 1957).

Lukacs, G.: History and class consciousness: studies in Marxist dialectics; translated by *R. Livingstone* (MIT Press, Cambridge 1971).

Macmurray, J.: The self as agent (Faber & Faber, London 1957).

Macpherson, C.G.: Rawls's models of man and society. Phil. soc. Sci. *3:* 341–347 (1973).

Mannheim, K.: Ideology and utopia; translated by *L. Wirth and E. Shils* (Harcourt, Brace & World, New York 1936).

Mannheim, K.: Conservative thought; in *Kecskemeti* Essays on sociology and social psychology (Routledge & Kegan Paul, London 1953).

Marx, K. and Engels, F.: The German ideology (International Publishers, New York 1970).

Merleau-Ponty, M.: Phenomenology of perception (Routledge & Kegan Paul, London 1962).

Miller, R.: Rawls and Marxism; in *Daniels* Reading Rawls (Blackwell, Oxford 1975).

Novak, M.: Ascent of the mountain, flight of the dove (Harper & Row, New York 1971).

Peters, R.S.: Moral development: a plea for pluralism; in *Mischel* Cognitive development and epistemology (Academic Press, New York 1971).

Piaget, J.: The moral judgment of the child; translated by *M. Gabain* (1932; Free Press, Glencoe 1948).

Piaget, J.: Insights and illusions of philosophy; translated by *W. Mays* (World, New York 1971).

Rawls, J.: A theory of justice (Harvard University Press, Cambridge, 1971).

Rieff, P.: Freud: the mind of a moralist (Anchor, New York 1961).

Riegel, K.F.: Influence of economic and political ideologies on the development of development psychology. Psychol. Bull. *78:* 129–141 (1972).

Scheler, M.: in *Coser* Ressentiment; translated by *W.W. Holdheim* (1912; Schocken, New York 1972).

Scheler, M.: Formalism in ethics and non-formal ethics of values; 5th ed.; translated by *M.S. Frings and R.L. Funk* (1921; Northwestern University Press, Evanston 1973a).

Scheler, M.: The nature of sympathy; translated by *P. Heath* (1923; Archon Books, Hamden 1973b).

Simpson, E.L.: Moral development research: a case study of scientific cultural bias. Hum. Dev. *17:* 81–106 (1974).

Simpson, E.L.: A holistic approach to moral development and behavior; in *Lickona* Moral development and behavior; theory, research, and social issues (Holt, Rinehart & Winston, New York 1976).

Sullivan, E.V.: Piaget and the school curriculum: a critical appraisal (Ontario Institute for Studies in Education, Toronto 1967).

Sullivan, E.V.: Piagetian theory in the educational milieu: a critical appraisal. Can. J. behav. Sci. *1:* 129–155 (1969).

Sullivan, E.V.: Comment: phenomenology and structuralism: a war of the worlds. Interchange *6/4:* 52–54 (1975).

Sullivan, E.V.; Beck, C.; Joy, M., and Pagliuso, S.: Moral learning (Paulist, Press, Paramus 1975).

Turner, T.: Piaget's structuralism. Am. Anthrop. *75:* 351–373 (1973).

Weisskopf, W.A.: The dialectics of equality. Ann. Am. Acad. polit. soc. Sci. *409:* 163–173 (1973).

E.V. Sullivan, PhD, Ontario Institute for Studies in Education, 252 Bloor Street West, *Toronto, Ont.* (Canada)

Liberalism as Destiny

Lawrence Kohlberg
The Philosophy of Moral
Development: Moral Stages and the
Idea of Justice, Vol. 1. Essays on
Moral Development
San Francisco: Harper & Row, 1981.
476 pp. $21.95

Review by
Richard A. Shweder

Lawrence Kohlberg is professor of education and social psychology at Harvard University. The recipient of the National Institute of Mental Health's 1969 Research Scientist Award, he is also author of Meaning and Measurement of Moral Development. ■ *Richard A. Shweder is associate professor of human development at the University of Chicago. He is coauthor of the chapter* "The Moral Intuitions of the Child" *(with E. Turiel and N. Much) in* J. H. Flavell and L. Ross's Social Cognitive Development *and the chapter* "Does the Concept of the Person Vary Cross-Culturally?" *(with E. Bourne) in* A. J. Marsella and G. White's Cultural Conceptions of Mental Health and Therapy.

K ohlberg believes that reason is on the side of those who oppose capital punishment, hierarchy, tribalism, and divine authority (pp. 21, 30, 176, 289). Moved by the spirit of developmentalism (pp. 87, 134, 136, 137), he holds out secular humanism, egalitarianism, and the Bill of Rights as rational ideals or objective end points for the evolution of moral ideas (pp. 164, 165, 215). For Kohlberg, the history of the world (p. 227) and the history of childhood (in all societies) (p. 25) is the story of the progressive discovery of the principles of the American Revolution (pp. 8, 38, 154, 237). Hegel's Prussian state has been replaced by Western liberal democracy. Liberalism has become destiny (pp. 227, 253).

Three great works of moral philosophy have been written in the past 10 years: John Rawls's A Theory of Justice, Alan Gewirth's Reason and Morality, and Alasdair MacIntyre's After Virtue. Rawls and Gewirth seek to establish the rational foundations for an objective morality. Their basic idea is that what *deserves* to be considered moral is the same across cultures and history, and that knowledge of that external, objective morality is possible by means available to all people, namely, the canons of deductive and/or inductive logic.

Kohlberg's essays in The Philosophy of Moral Development are reflections on the developmental implications of that idea. Of the 10 essays published in the volume, some are already classics, for example, "Development as the Aim of Education" and "From Is to Ought."

Other essays are perhaps less well known but are equally substantial, for example, "Justice as Reversibility" and "Capital Punishment, Moral Development, and the Constitution."

The defense of objective morality

Kohlberg advances many provocative claims in these essays. The three most important claims are (a) that "even if there are observed cultural divergences of moral standards, there are rational principles and methods that can reconcile these divergences or lead to agreement" (p. 98), (b) that moral thinking is in fact historically and ontogenetically ordered in a sequence of general stages (pp. 227, 243), and (c) that later stages can be shown to be " 'objectively' preferable" to earlier stages (p. 190)—which explains why they tend to be chosen. Kohlberg believes that with the development of processes of rational reasoning (e.g., operational thinking) and with the right kind of education (Socratic dialogue to promote stage growth), there ought to be, and has been, a historical, cross-cultural, and ontogenetic convergence of beliefs about what is moral.

The dominant theme in Kohlberg's essays is that what is moral is not a matter of taste or opinion. Kohlberg abhors relativism. He shudders at the idea that the moral codes of man might be like the languages and foods of man—different but equal. Kohlberg's project in these essays is to establish that there is an objective morality that reason can reveal, to define that objective morality in terms

71

of justice, equity, equal respect for all persons, and the "natural" rights of man, and to defend that formulation against relativists, behaviorists, romantics, emotivists, psychoanalysts, and advocates of capital punishment and character education. What Kohlberg seeks is a conceptualization of what is moral derived from premises that no rational person could possibly deny by means that no rational person could possibly avoid—preferably deductive logic (pp. 226, 293). Rawls provides the philosophical inspiration (p. 192). Dewey provides the educational inspiration (p. 94). Piaget provides the psychological inspiration (p. 136). Martin Luther King provides the spiritual inspiration—Kohlberg believes that King was put to death because he was a stage 6 thinker (p. 85).

The failure of objective morality: MacIntyre's views

In my view, Kohlberg's project is a provocative and stimulating failure. The best statement of why it had to fail can be found in Alasdair MacIntyre's *After Virtue*, and thus, to evaluate Kohlberg's project, I must discuss MacIntyre's work at some length. MacIntyre never mentions Kohlberg. Instead he sets out to show that no rational justification for moral allegiances is possible within the framework of Western culture established at the time of the Enlightenment. As MacIntyre puts it, "moral debate [e.g., over such matters as abortion] is rationally interminable" (pp. 11, 70), and 200 years of brilliant reflection has yet to produce any consensus about the nature of that purported "objective" morality.

MacIntyre reveals the incommensurability of divergent contemporary moral positions. Claims about individual rights compete with claims about social utility, which compete with claims about virtue or just desert, and no scale exists for weighing these claims. He writes that the only *telos* left to the modern secular person is to maximize happiness, yet "the notion of happiness is *not* a unitary, simple notion and cannot provide us with a criterion for making our key choices" (p. 61); there is no non-arbitrary way to decide which "happiness" (the "insight" or the "orgasm") ought to guide us. Having disposed of the idea of "utility" (stage 5 thinking), MacIntyre turns to the concept of "human rights" (stage 6 thinking). It is shown to be a fiction: "Every attempt to give good reasons for believing there *are* such rights has failed" (p.

67). Kant's "categorical imperative" (act as you would will that everyone else act in the same situation) suffers an inglorious fate. It is shown to be useless for discriminating moral from nonmoral judgments, whereas Kant's principle of "universalizability" (treat all of humanity as an end, not as a means) is shown to be an assumption that rational persons can deny without inconsistency.

MacIntyre persuasively argues that every notable attempt since the Enlightenment (including Rawls and Gewirth) to construct a rational foundation for an objective morality has been built out of nonrational premises, premises that any rational person might reasonably deny. Consider, for example, the work of John Rawls, Kohlberg's inspirer. Rawls argues that under a "veil of ignorance" any rational person would agree to a social contract committing everyone to grant to everyone else liberty and equality. Under this prior-to-society "veil of ignorance," each of us is imagined to negotiate a social contract ignorant of all the ways we are different from others, ignorant of our place in society, our power, intelligence, and so forth.

Immediately, forceful objections arise in the philosophical literature. Gewirth (*Reason and Morality*, p. 108) argues that the assumption of a "veil of ignorance" is "factually false" and hence provides no rational justification for rational persons living in the real world where moral decisions must be made. Ronald Dworkins (*Taking Rights Seriously*) notes that Rawls does not explain why, given that one would have agreed to such a contract under a "veil of ignorance," that one should now consent knowing fully that one is talented, intelligent, handsome, rich, and powerful. MacIntyre himself criticizes Rawls for ignoring the "past" (p. 231) and overlooking the possibility that received inequalities are one's just desert. No rational consensus emerges, even among sophisticated thinkers.

If MacIntyre is right about the "recent" history of Western moral philosophy, alternative philosophies coexist for hundreds of years cycling in and out of philosophical prominence. Pace Kohlberg, Kant's defense of stage 6 reasoning is *followed* by Bentham's utilitarianism (stage 5), then by Moore's emotivism (stage 2, or is it stage 4½?), and now by MacIntyre's defense of pre-Kantian concepts of virtue (stage 4?). None of these philosophies goes away, nor does any ra-

tional criterion emerge for securing moral agreement. Quite the contrary. As MacIntyre argues, the modern secular individualist, having lost his concept of the ends (the *telos*) of life and having conceived of the "self" as either "prior to" or "outside" society and community, is left with no fixed reference point for constructing a rational moral code. Existentialism and relativism become the most genuine expressions of secular consciousness.

The paradoxes of moral discourse

If MacIntyre is right, diverse moral philosophies (e.g., Kohlberg's "stages") do not line up along some Jacob's ladder ascending to the rational recognition of the inalienable rights of man. Instead, diverse moral philosophies are coexisting and incommensurate points, and to adopt any one philosophy (e.g., stage 6 individual rights over stage 5 social utility over stage 4 virtue) is merely to assert one's personal or collective preference. Indeed, if MacIntyre is right, moral discourse is rife with paradox.

There is the paradox of "subjectivity versus objectivity." Whereas moral discourse is ultimately a disguise for personal or collective preferences, it is carried on in impersonal terms. When we say it is "right" (or "wrong") to abort a fetus or have more than one wife, we don't simply *mean* "I approve (or disapprove): do so as well." We seem to imply that there are objective standards that justify our conclusion. Kohlberg quite properly criticizes "emotivist" theories about the *meaning* of moral terms, and instead defines moral concepts by their impersonality and their implication that as a person with reason you are obligated to behave in such-and-such a way. That is what we mean when we say "that's good" (or "bad"), but if MacIntyre is right, we have no rational warrant for meaning it. We speak to each other (or at least to those with whom we are still on speaking terms) as though our moral choices had a rational foundation. Upon examination, that rational foundation turns out to be the soft sand of preferred (and often shared) assumptions. At its limit, moral discourse becomes ideology, a deceptive form of "mock rationality."

There is also the paradox of "form versus content." Simply put, there is a trade-off between rationality and relevance. On the one hand, if moral concepts are to be made fully rational, they must be emptied of content. They must be made devoid of relevance to everyday decisions. On the other hand, if moral concepts are to be made relevant to concrete moral decisions (abort or don't abort?), they must be enriched with nonrational assumptions. For example, the *formal* concept of justice is a rational concept. As Kohlberg notes (p. 176), "It merely prescribes that principles should be impartially applied to all." MacIntyre puts it this way: "If I claim a right in virtue of my possession of certain characteristics, then I am logically committed to holding that anyone else with the same characteristics also possesses this right" (p. 65). In other words, the formal principle of justice merely states "treat like cases alike and different cases differently." Note, it does *not* state which likenesses and differences count; the formal principle of justice says nothing about how particular people are to be treated. As a rational principle the *formal* principle of justice does not dictate that all sentient beings are to be treated in identical fashion; children, for example, may be different from adults in ways that call for special treatment such as denial of voting rights. To decide how particular people are to be treated as alike or different is to introduce nonrational assumptions; for example, that to be just is to treat everyone as though they had the same natural and inalienable rights. That quite substantive idea of justice is faithfully endorsed by secular humanists but is not required by fact or reason.

Conceptual inconsistencies

How does Kohlberg fare on the impossible quest for a rationally dictated objective morality? I am tempted to say "as expected." As expected, he has conceptual and empirical difficulties.

On crucial conceptual issues Kohlberg wavers. For example, he seeks a universal morality on which all rational people can agree (p. 161). Question: Does that universal morality prescribe a way of thinking about moral decisions or does it prescribe particular moral choices? Answer: First Kohlberg tells us he is studying the structure of thought, not the content (pp. 16, 170, 172, 184). Whether or not you pay your taxes is not the relevant issue, he says. It is what you think about what you are doing that matters; for example, did you withhold taxes as a matter of "conscience" or "expedience" (p. 184)? We are told that stage 6 ethics cannot tell us what is virtuous or worthy of praise

or blame (p. 172). Then Kohlberg states the opposite (pp. 192, 272). We are told that stage 6 reasoning leads to " 'morally right' conclusions about specific dilemmas" (p. 193), for example, opposition to capital punishment and opposition to the anti–Vietnam War sit-in at Harvard to prevent Dow Chemical Corporation, the manufacturer of napalm, from recruiting employees (p. 45).

Kohlberg argues that the higher stages of his scheme are more advanced. Question: What makes them more adequate? Answer: First we are told that later stages are more adequate because they are more differentiated and complex (pp. 84, 134, 135) (MacIntyre, by the way, sees this as their shortcoming). Second we are told they are more adequate because they are useful for solving social problems (e.g., how to behave to an outsider) (pp. 85, 152), although this is later denied (p. 170). Third we are told that later stages are better because they require formal operational thinking (p. 76) (as if "stage" 4 philosophers and "stage" 6 philosophers differ in their operational capabilities). Fourth we are told they are better because they promote agreement about concrete moral decisions (pp. 161, 272) (agreement becomes a criterion of adequacy!). At one point we are told that the criteria of adequacy are "the *formal* criteria that developmental theory holds as defining all mature structures" (p. 135). Later we are told the criterion of adequacy "is that of morality itself, not a conception of rationality or sophistication imported from other domains" (p. 169). So forget about differentiation, complexity, social problem solving, formal operational thinking, and so forth.

And what is that purely moral criterion? The test seems to be that you believe in "equal and universal rights" (p. 39) and view them as "natural" rights (pp. 154, 191, 237), that your allegiance be to "humanity" in general rather than to your tribe, community, or nation (pp. 135, 165), that you totally renounce the exercise of power, influence, and force in getting others to do what you want and never treat others as the instrument of your will (p. 165), that you think all differences between people (sex, age, intelligence, lineage, ethnicity) should be overlooked when deciding how they should be treated (pp. 135, 144, 176), and that you hold a secular (not religious) belief that life is sacred (pp. 19, 20). Somehow, in some way that eludes me, those rather substantive ideas are sup-

posed to qualify as abstract or formal modes of reasoning. To me, they look like the ideas of an articulate liberal secular humanist, and as far as I can tell, not one of those substantive ideas is required by logic or experience.

Some of the inconsistencies in Kohlberg's essays are jarring. One feels the need for a running commentary on the evolution of his thinking about morality. In one essay, B. F. Skinner is criticized for not answering the question, "What is the good?" (p. 67), yet in a later essay Kohlberg explicitly states that his own theory does not address and cannot answer such a question (pp. 169, 172). In one essay we are told that "a culture cannot be located at a single stage" (p. 129). In a later essay we are told that cultures are "highly stage consistent across legal, religious and ethical systems" (p. 237). In one essay we are told that moral principles "are not scales for evaluating collective entities" (p. 111). In a later essay we are told that "societies undergo moral stage evolution" (p. 234, also p. 227). In one essay we are told that "if the facts of development do not indicate that individuals move towards philosophically desired principles of justice, then the initial philosophic definition of the direction of development is in error and must be revised" (p. 86, also p. 178). In a later essay we are told that Rawls's theory successfully describes "the substantive principles used in the considered moral judgments of all human beings in any culture, with one major qualification. The qualification is that it successfully generates the judgments of only the human beings who have completed the sequence of moral development and are at the highest stage of moral judgment (stage 6, attained by less than 5 percent of American adults)" (p. 192). In one essay we are told that "moral concepts are essentially concepts of social relationships as manifested in social institutions" (p. 141). In the very same essay we are told that the term *moral* refers to a type of "decision-making process" not a "social institution" (p. 169). In one essay we are told that "if all people were stage 6, they would unanimously agree that the death penalty is morally wrong" (p. 289). In the very same essay, a quotation from Rawls provides a compelling stage 6 argument that could be used to defend capital punishment (p. 284). Reading these essays side by side, one gets the impression that Kohlberg is deeply uncertain about how to seek that purported objective morality.

Reason may be less cunning than Hegel or Kohlberg supposes.

Finally, there is the question of how Kohlberg's evidence is to be interpreted. Kohlberg's essays are not data-oriented essays, although summary data are presented from cross-cultural and longitudinal studies, and many published and unpublished research findings are cited. I have the following observations on the data that are presented.

The nature of the evidential support

First, Kohlberg's own evidence (pp. 24, 25, 255, 256) suggests that very few people in the world conceive of society as a social contract or conceive of individuals as possessing natural and inalienable rights prior to or outside society. Those stage 5 and stage 6 ideas seem to be culture specific; if they are advocated at all, and they rarely are, it is among Western educated middle-class adults. From a cross-cultural and developmental perspective, moral exegesis seems to *stabilize* around the not unreasonable ideas that social roles carry with them an obligation to behave in a certain way, that society is not of our own making, and that self and society are somehow intimately linked (stages 3 and 4).

Second, the way children or adults talk about a concept is probably a poor measure of the availability of that concept to the mind of the child or the adult. For example, we know that young children know a lot more about (e.g.) causation, number, grammar, and so forth, than they can articulate. Children who differ dramatically in their ability to articulate a concept (e.g., that a cause *precedes* its consequences) often do not differ in their ability to use that concept to draw inferences about the world. Kohlberg's emphasis on moral articulation and argumentation tends to obscure the moral competency of his informants. Young children know a lot more about the categorical imperative and the impersonality of rules than Kohlberg's methods have revealed.

Third, I wish Kohlberg had been more Socratic in his interviews. Language should not always be taken at its face value. For example, Kohlberg (p. 223) asks a 10-year-old child, "Why shouldn't someone steal from a store, anyhow? When the child replies, "It's not good because there might be someone who could see you and call the police," it is classified as a stage 1 response. I'd make the following wager with Kohlberg. I will bet that 7- to 10-year-old children do not *define* rightness and wrongness by punishment. I will bet that Kohlberg's 10-year-old does not mean that because you might get punished it is wrong to steal, but instead means to state that someone will call the police because it is wrong to steal. In other words, the call to the police and the resulting punishment is seen as a demonstration of the wrongness of theft. In my experience when the issue is pressed further and children are asked questions like, "What if there were no punishment?" or "What if no one could call the police?" they maintain the act would still be wrong. In the mind of the child transgressions are punished because they are wrong, not vice versa. That's my wager.

Finally, the world of cognitive developmental psychology has changed over the past 10 years. It is now widely acknowledged that Piaget underestimated the operational capacity of 2- through 7-year-old children. The idea of general stages has taken a beating. There have been numerous demonstrations that task content is decisive for how you think and that by manipulating the cognitive task it is possible to elicit either preoperational thinking, concrete operational thinking, or formal operational thinking from a subject. Thinking is task-specific, and most operational structures seem to be *available* to the mind of a 5-year-old. Kohlberg adopts an orthodox view of the operational incapacities of young children and the reality of abstract general stages (pp. 57, 58, 120, 137). It is no longer 1970. In 1982 the waning of the orthodox Piagetian paradigm cannot be ignored. At least one expects an argument. Kohlberg's silence on the issue is deafening.

The Philosophy of Moral Development is the first of three prospective volumes of Kohlberg's collected essays. Volume 2 will be entitled *The Psychology of Moral Development*. Volume 3 will be entitled *Education and Moral Development*. Kohlberg and I disagree about many things. Nevertheless, his work is provocative and stimulating; and as one sociologist of knowledge has commented, it may be just as important to be interesting as to be right. ∎

Hum. Dev. *23:* 77–104 (1980)

Moral Development in Late Adolescence and Adulthood: a Critique and Reconstruction of Kohlberg's Theory

John Michael Murphy and Carol Gilligan

Harvard University, Cambridge, Mass.

Key Words. Adolescent development · Adult development · Cognitive development · Epistemological development · Formal operations · Moral development

Abstract. This article provides an alternative conception of postconventional moral development which fits existing data on late adolescent and adult moral judgment better than *Kohlberg*'s higher stage descriptions. Moral judgment data from a longitudinal study of 26 undergraduates are scored by *Kohlberg*'s newly revised manual and replicate his original finding that a significant percentage of subjects appear to regress from adolescence to adulthood. The persistence of relativistic regression in these data suggests the need to revise the theory. The same hypothetical moral dilemmas are also scored according to an alternative coding scheme based on the hypothesis of an adult form of cognitive development. Results indicate that the *Kohlberg* regressors are progressors when evaluated against a standard of commitment in relativism instead of absolute principles of justice. Real-life data on the same subjects suggest that this progression is related to actual experiences of moral conflict and choice which lead to the restructuring of moral judgment to a more dialectical mode. It is suggested that this alternative notion of postconventional development is necessary for understanding (and scoring) adult moral judgment.

Moral development, in structural theory, is divided into three parts: pre-conventional, conventional, and postconventional. While the first two are the subject of considerable agreement among developmental psychologists, the third remains a territory of both empirical and theoretical dispute. It is to this latter region, then, that we bring new evidence and a new interpretation. On this basis we offer an integration of existing theory and data that extends the sequence of moral development beyond adolescence into adulthood.

While this essay is written within the framework of *Kohlberg*'s stage theory of moral development, it is critical of that framework in an attempt to make it more broadly applicable to judgments about real-life as well as hypothetical moral dilemmas and to the changes that occur in late adolescent and adult moral thought. This attempt is grounded empirically in the difficulty encountered in trying to fit the moral judgments of late adolescents and adults about both real and hypothetical dilemmas into the stage descriptions of *Kohlberg*'s sequence.

Although some psychologists (*Kurtines and Grief*, 1974) have recommended the wholesale abandonment of *Kohlberg*'s theory, claiming that more than a decade of empirical research has failed to provide the data necessary to confirm it, other critics have been less harsh, focusing instead on the upper half or third of the stages as problematic (*Brown and Hernstein*, 1975; *Gilligan*, 1977; *Puka*, 1976; *Reid and Yanarella*, 1977; *Sullivan*, 1977). This line of criticism has been supported both longitudinally (*Holstein*, 1976) and cross-culturally (*Edwards*, 1975; *Simpson*, 1974) by empirical work which has confirmed the sequentiality of the first three of *Kohlberg*'s six stages, while at the same time presenting evidence against invariant sequence for stages 4, 5, and 6. Based on these and other studies, one of *Kohlberg*'s closest associates (*Gibbs*, 1977, 1979) claims that stages 5 and 6 are best considered not as naturally occurring stages in the strict Piagetian sense, but rather as metaethical or philosophical reflections upon the normative judgments of earlier stages. While *Gibbs*'s position may solve the problem of discrepant data, it fails to deal with one very important implication. Without the postconventional level, moral stage development ends in adolescence, at least for bright subjects. This position seems so contrary to fact that it warrants another hypothesis, the possibility of cognitive transformation in late adolescence or early adulthood that would provide the new structures of thought necessary to the development of a different form of moral judgment. *Kohlberg* once proposed this idea himself and explored it at some length before rejecting it (*Kohlberg and Kramer*, 1969). Work not available at the time of that paper makes the hypothesis of an adult cognitive stage more plausible now and thus provides the basis for a reexamination of *Kohlberg and Kramer*'s argument and for the alternative conception of adult moral development proposed here.

In examining the implications for moral development of an adult stage of cognitive development, there are a number of different conceptions of such a stage to consider. All, however, concur in describing that stage as more dialectical and contextually relative than exclusively formal. Most recently, *Arlin* (1975) proposed a fifth cognitive stage which she called 'problem finding' to distinguish it from the 'problem solving' orientation of formal operations. Two other approaches have begun to generate bodies of research in an attempt to elucidate the structurally new form of mature thought.

In 1973, *Riegel* (1973, 1975) launched what has become a continuing argument for a dialectical psychology that would encompass the characteristics of adult thought more accurately than *Piaget*'s formal operations. Other researchers have followed the leads set out by *Perry* (1968, p. 205), who suggested 'adding an advanced period to *Piaget*'s outline'. In addition to seeing more in adult thought than formal operations, both groups have explored the implications of such thought for moral development. *Perry* (1968, p. 205) described the transition to maturity as a shift from 'the moral environment to the ethical, from the formal to the existential'. While *Arlin* (1975) hypothesized that the adult stage of cognitive development was one of problem finding, *Perry* is quite specific in naming the problem found as the recognition of the contextual relativism of all knowledge which leads to a revolutionary transformation in intellectual and ethical thought. There are striking similarities between *Perry*'s description of the post-relativistic quality of adult ethical thought and *Meacham*'s (1975, p. 162) discussion of a dialectical approach to moral judgment which 'considers the multiple aspects of behaviors and recognizes that they can be both good and bad, moral and immoral, depending upon the framework within which they are evaluated'. Another aspect of mature thought recognized by both *Perry* and the dialectical theoreticians is the 'epistemological loneliness' that can accompany the emergence of formal operations. This 'often involves a kind of conceptual overkill which achieves objectivity at the expense of conviction, commitment, mutuality, and the comfort of participating in a consensus of shared beliefs' (*Chandler,* 1975, p. 172). *Perry* seems to be talking about the same phenomenon when he notes that, 'If one comes to look on all knowing and all valuing as contingent on context, and if one is then confronted with an infinite universe of potential contexts for truth and care, one is threatened with a loss of identity. From one context to another, what one will see as true and what one will care about will be discontinuous' (*Perry,* 1968, p. 134).

In the remainder of this paper we will entertain the contrary-to-accepted-fact hypothesis of an adult cognitive transformation along the general lines suggested by *Perry* and *Riegel.* This cognitive shift would then provide the basis for a new form of moral judgment in adulthood, structurally different from that of adolescent thought. The experiential base for such a stage change would lie in the different experiences of moral choice and moral responsibility typically encountered only after adolescence. While there may be little difference between *Inhelder and Piaget's* (1958) discussion of adult equilibrated formal operations and the post-formal cognition envisioned here or between our view and many more traditional accounts of mature reasoning (*Guindon,* 1978; *Schwab,* 1978), there is a very real difference between *Piaget's* claim that formal operational thought is characterized by a lattice structure and the hypothesis considered here that mature cognition is characterized by a structure open to context, albeit one that may employ formal operations in solving problems. It is interesting to note that this is precisely the point that *Vygotsky* (1962) raised in his early critique of *Piaget.*

Thus, although there may be little difference between what *Piaget* (1972) means when he writes about mature cognition and what is meant here, the failure to describe adequately the structural properties of mature thought and to differentiate it from adolescent thought has led to considerable confusion in the literature on one of the major applications of Piagetian theory – *Kohlberg's* theory of moral development. While *Piaget* (1965, p. 317) noted in his early work on moral judgment that the emergence of 'the feeling of equity' is 'a development of equalitarianism in the direction of relativity' that renders moral judgment more contextual and results in a more generous and refined form of justice, these relativistic and contextual properties of mature thought have never been incorporated into *Kohlberg's* higher stage definitions (or into *Piaget's* for that matter). There are, among older adolescents and adults, people who are fully formal in their logical thinking and fully principled in their moral judgments (stage 5 and 6); and yet, as this paper attempts to demonstrate, they are not fully mature in their moral understanding. Conversely, those people whose thinking becomes more relativistic in the sense of being more open to the contextual properties of moral judgments and moral dilemmas frequently fail to be scored at the highest stages of *Kohlberg's* sequence. Instead, the relativising of their thinking over time is construed as regression or moral equivocation, rather than as a developmental advance. The present paper is an attempt to deal with both of these problems.

Background

The problem we address was first introduced into the cognitive developmental literature on moral judgment as an anomalous regression at the higher levels of moral development reported by *Kohlberg and Kramer* (1969). This regression among some of *Kohlberg's* subjects who had previously been scored as stages 4 and 5 took the form of a reassertion of moral hedonism that resembled judgments characteristic of stage 2. This was interpreted by *Kohlberg and Kramer* as a functional regression resulting from the adolescent identity crisis rather than a structural regression in moral thought. This interpretation was supported by their finding that such moral subjectivism had disappeared by age 25, having been replaced by the discovery that moral principles of equality and reciprocity provided an objective basis for resolving moral problems. However, the persistence of relativistic moral thought in other samples following the attainment of principled moral judgment (*Fishkin*, 1975; *Gilligan and Kohlberg,* 1977; *Gilligan*, 1978) led *Kohlberg* in 1973 to reconsider his earlier argument. Retracting his earlier conclusion that moral development ends in adolescence, he posited instead a kind of structural stage change in adulthood. While he had in 1969 rejected this notion, claiming that the attainment of formal operational logic in adolescence provided no basis for further structural changes in moral judgment, he argued, in 1973, that the attainment of principled moral judgment is a phenomenon of adult development and results from 'the experience of sustained responsibility for the welfare of others and the experiences of irreversible moral choice' (*Kohlberg*, 1973, p. 196).

While this major interpretive revision eliminated the problem of adolescent relativistic regression in his data by considering all relativistic judgments as preceding the attainment of principled thought, it left unchanged the definition of the higher stages. Thus, in his revised argument, *Kohlberg* never explained how the adult experiences of commitment and responsibility that followed the discovery of the moral consequences of choice could be made to fit structures of moral judgment that he had initially derived from adolescents' responses to hypothetical dilemmas. It is difficult to believe that the adult experiences could lead to exactly the same form of moral reasoning that was originally found in some of *Kohlberg*'s bright high-school students. These students had articulated formal moral justifications on the basis of the logical reversibility and universalizability of such hypothetico-deductive concepts as social contract and natural rights. While the logical concepts of equality and reciprocity can support a principled morality of universal rights and respect, experiences of moral conflict and choice seem to point rather to special obligations and responsibility for consequences that can be anticipated and understood only within a more contextual frame of reference. The balancing of these two points of view appeared to us to be the key to understanding adult moral development. In our view, this would require a restructuring of moral thought which would include but supercede the principled understanding of *Kohlberg*'s highest stages.

The radical revisions of his scoring manual which followed *Kohlberg*'s (1973) paper have eliminated virtually all stage 5 and 6 reasoning from the empirical moral judgment data. For instance, only 1 of *Kohlberg*'s 58 reported longitudinal subjects has reached an unmixed score of stage 5 by the age of 30, while 7 are consigned to the transitional stage 4/5 range (*Kohlberg, 1979*). We argue that the problems with sequence that led to the revision of the scoring manual stem from the failure to distinguish between two essentially different kinds of moral relativism which stand in different relation to postconventional or principled moral judgment. In making this distinction, we rely on the contrast described by *Perry* (1968)[1] between relativistic *multiplicity* (position 4 in *Perry*'s scheme), the position that there are many right answers to moral

---

[1] The complete description of these positions can be found in *Perry* (1968, pp. 57– 200). The following highly abbreviated outline of the positions is taken from pp. 9–10 of that volume:

Position 1: The student sees the world in polar terms of we-right-good vs. other-wrong-bad. Right Answers for everything exist in the Absolute, known to Authority whose role is to mediate (teach) them. Knowledge and goodness are perceived as quantitative accretions of discrete rightnesses to be collected by hard work and obedience (paradigm: a spelling test).

Position 2: The student perceives diversity of opinion, and uncertainty, and accounts for them as unwarranted confusion in poorly qualified Authorities or as mere exercises set by Authority 'so we can learn to find The Answer for ourselves'.

Position 3: The student accepts diversity and uncertainty as legitimate but still *temporary* in areas where Authority 'hasn't found The Answer yet'. He supposes Authority grades him in these areas on 'good expression' but remains puzzled as to standards.

Position 4: (a) The student perceives legitimate uncertainty (and therefore diversity of opinion) to be extensive and raises it to the status of an unstructured epistemological realm of its own in which 'anyone has a right to his own opinion', a realm which he sets over against Authority's realm where right-wrong still prevails, or (b) the student discovers qualitative contextual relativistic reasoning as a special case of 'what They want' within Authority's realm.

Position 5: The student perceives all knowledge and values (including authority's) as contextual and relativistic and subordinates dualistic right-wrong functions to the status of a special case, in context.

Position 6: The student apprehends the necessity of orienting himself in a relativistic world through some form of personal Commitment (as distinct from unquestioned or unconsidered commitment to simple belief in certainty).

Position 7: The student makes an initial Commitment in some area.

Position 8: The student experiences the implications of Commitment and explores the subjective and stylistic issues of responsibility.

Position 9: The student experiences the affirmation of identity among multiple responsibilities and realizes Commitment as an ongoing, unfolding activity through which he express his life style.

problems and no way of choosing among them, and *contextual relativism* (position 5), the position that while no answer may be objectively right in the sense of being context-free, some answers and some ways of thinking are better than others. *Perry*'s highest four positions of mature reasoning (6–9) add forms of commitment to this basic contextual relativism.

While *Perry*'s position 4 corresponds in many ways to *Kohlberg*'s description of stage $4\frac{1}{2}$ relativism as a form of moral equivocation that is incompatible with principled moral judgment, *Perry*'s positions of contextual relativism are quite different. For *Perry,* the realization of contextual relativism superceded conventional moral understanding and ushered in a period of ethical responsibility, compatible with principled moral judgments but also indicative of a new understanding of the contexts in which principles could operate and thus of a new responsibility for moral choice.

While *Kohlberg* attempted to solve the problem of relativistic regression in moral judgment data by radically altering his criteria for principled moral judgment in order to retain his conception that principles of justice were context-free and could generate an objectively right solution to moral problems, our data show that this solution still results in the problem of stage regression. In this paper, we show how our different analysis of the phenomenon of relativism in moral development leads to a further distinction between two types of postconventional moral judgment. Although it will not be discussed until much later in this paper, a brief outline of a two-category typology we have used may be helpful here. The first, which we call PCF (postconventional formal), solves the problem of relativism by constructing a formal logical system that derives solutions to all moral problems from concepts like the social contract or natural rights. The second, which we call PCC (postconventional contextual), finds the problem in that solution which now appears as only one of several potential contexts in which moral judgments can be framed. PCC reasoning derives from an understanding of the contextual relativism of moral judgment and the ineluctable uncertainty of moral choice. On that basis, it articulates an ethic of responsibility that focuses on the actual consequences of choice. In the shift from PCF to PCC, the criterion for the adequacy of moral principles changes from objective truth to 'best fit', and can only be established within the context of the dilemma itself. According to PCC reasoning, the choice of principles for solving moral problems is an example of commitment in relativism, a commitment for which one bears personal responsibility and which allows the possibility of alternate formulations that could be equally or more adequate in a given case.

81

Method

Although there have been numerous critiques of his theory, *Kohlberg* (1976) claims that the only valid argument against it is evidence in longitudinal data of regressions or stage skipping. Since the critiques have centered on the higher adult stages and since adult data of any kind are so rare, the longitudinal data from ages 19 to 26 which we report here for a higher-stage sample will allow us to address empirically many of the critical questions which have been raised about *Kohlberg*'s theory. Since our cases have also been scored by both the original and the revised manuals, we will be able to see whether the recent scoring revisions have solved the alleged problems with the stage sequence.

Sample

Subjects in this sample were 56 Harvard-Radcliffe undergraduates, primarily soph-omores, who enrolled in a course on moral and political choice given by *Kohlberg* and *Gilligan* in the fall of 1970 (*Gilligan and Kohlberg,* 1977). Both before (T1) and after (T2) the course, these students were given the standard *Kohlberg* hypothetical moral judgment interview in written form. Two years later, in the spring of 1973 (T3), 29 of the 44 students who had completed both pre- and posttests were asked to participate in a reinterview. No systematic selection criteria were employed, since the researchers' intentions were simply to interview as many of the original subjects as time and money would permit. One student refused to participate, one was never interviewed, and one interview was unusable due to poor technical quality. Thus, the total sample at T3 consisted of 26 undergraduates, 21 male and 5 female, which reflects the predominantly male enrollment in the course (42 males and 14 females), and in the university at that time.

At T3 a structured open-ended interview was used which, in addition to the standard hypothetical moral dilemmas, included questions about personal experiences of moral conflict and choice. Questions about ego identity and basic life history were also asked. The interviews were conducted by graduate students, tape recorded and transcribed, and averaged 2.5 h with most of the interview devoted to the real life rather than hypothetical reasoning. This material allows us to place our subjects' hypothetical moral reasoning within the broader context of their lives and other kinds of reasoning; we will return to it somewhat later in the argument. In the spring of 1978 (T4), the subjects were contacted and all 26 agreed to participate in a reinterview. Since an interview could not be arranged with one subject, only 25 cases are reported in the T4 analyses.

The sample is small and nonrepresentative. Obviously, a Harvard sample cannot be equated with the general population, and this particular group was unique even to Harvard. First of all, they were students who were concerned enough about morality and ethics to take an elective in that area. Secondly, the fact that they had studied *Kohlberg*'s theory biases all but their T1 responses — even though the theory holds that this should not be significant in an analysis of the structure of their reasoning. Finally, by the time of the 1978 interview, 25 out of 26 subjects already had degrees beyond the baccalaureate. Two-thirds of the sample were already employed, and all but one of the rest were enrolled in graduate school. There were 11 lawyers, 5 physicians, 4 psychologists, 2 architects, 1 state govern-ment employee, 1 marketing executive, 1 film maker, and 1 union organizer. This is an exceptionally motivated and successful group, even by Harvard standards. Roughly half of the men and women were married (9 and 3, respectively), one of each had a child, and most of the rest anticipated marriage and children. 3 of the men had been conscientious objectors to the war in Vietnam and 2 others had participated in the Peace Corps or Vista. In 1978, 6 said they were actively religious (2 Catholics, 2 Jews, and 2 Protestants). All of the subjects were from lower-middle to upper-middle class backgrounds. Only 1 subject was nonwhite (a somewhat lower minority ratio than at the university in 1973).

While the results of this study are thus not generalizable, even to an Ivy League population, the sample is well suited to the questions of this study – higher-stage development from adolescence to adulthood. If cognitive development turns out to be the key variable in these questions, it would be difficult to find a more intelligent sample. If, on the other hand, it is the experiences of choice and commitment that lead to development, this sample is also well above average. As for their exposure to the theory after the pretest (T1), an argument could be made that the course artifactually inflated the students' T3 scores and thus led to higher rates of regression from T3 to T4. However, the stable rate of regression across all time interval comparisons (T1–T3, T3–T4, T1–T4) makes this argument implausible.

Interview

All students received standard *Kohlberg* moral dilemmas at each of the four times, but not all of these dilemmas have been scored or reported. This section describes our reasoning about what and how to score. Readers not familiar with the technicalities of scoring may wish to skip ahead to the Results section.

In 1970, *Kohlberg* had two forms (A and B) of his moral judgment interview, and the pre- and posttesting at T1 and T2 followed a basic alternate-form design (A–B or B–A). This has been complicated by the fact that the stories of the three dilemmas that made up form A in 1970 have since expanded and become six dilemmas and two forms in the current usage, the new form A (Heinz, Officer Brown, and Joe) and form B (Mercy Killing, Dr. Rogers, and Louise). The original form B has also expanded into forms C and D, but only C is in current use. No revised manual has been created for the form D stories and in fact, at the time of the current data analysis, only one story from form C, Korea, had a new manual. Students at pretest were thus given either what is now scorable as forms A and B or form C and the opposite at posttest. 12 students were given forms AB, then C, and 10 took C, followed by AB; 2 were administered AB–AB and 2 C–C.

Unfortunately, comparison of scores from alternate form test administration rests on the assumption that scores on each form will be equivalent. This assumption is not met in our data, where mean scores on different dilemmas varied by as much as two-thirds of a stage. Because of this difference in mean scores and because our major question is whether individuals change over a longitudinal interval, the only analysis considered valid in this discussion is a comparison of scores on the same dilemma or dilemmas at different times. Since only 4 cases permit this kind of comparison from T1 to T2, T2 scores will not be reported here.

While most subjects did receive the T1 dilemmas again at T3 there is another problem with this comparison. The T1 to T3 comparisons are somewhat unequal due to the fact that T1 (and T2) interviews were administered in written form, which generally leads to shorter, unelaborated responses, while the T3 (and T4) interviews were given in oral form and thus were, in most cases, very thoroughly probed. The T1–T3 comparisons are also difficult because a number of subjects did not receive the same dilemmas at T3 that they had been given at T1. Since the noncomparability of alternative forms was not known at the time of the T3 interviews, a decision was made to use the form A dilemmas wherever possible, rather than the form B and C dilemmas, because the Heinz dilemma in particuliar is the most conducive to the elicitation of higher-stage reasoning.

25 subjects were given the Heinz dilemma at T3, and 21 of these received Officer Brown as well. Unfortunately, this left many of the subjects who had received form C at T1 without comparable data at T3. Some of the T3 interviewers did make an effort to give at least one form C dilemma again at T3 to those who had had it at T1. Thus, in all, there are only 20 complete T1–T3 comparisons: 12 form A–form A comparisons, and 8 form C–form C.

The final problem to be mentioned here is the lack of full (3 dilemma) forms in many cases. First of all, since the only form C dilemma with a revised manual was Korea, the form C–C comparisons reported in this paper are based on a single dilemma. Secondly, when form A was used at T3, the Joe dilemma was not used since it so rarely led to higher-stage reasoning. It must therefore be deleted from the calculation of the T1 (when it was given) scores for comparison with T3 (when it was not given). In 8 form A cases, the T1–T3 comparison is between averages of the Heinz and Officer Brown scores. In the 4 cases without Officer Brown, the T1–T3 comparison is between scores on the Heinz dilemma.

Intercoder reliability was calculated on a subsample of 5 subjects' T1 and T3 interviews. These interviews were again scored blind by a different one of the three scorers who had originally coded forms A, B, and C. Exact stage agreement as found on 5 of the 10 cases and 4 others were only one-third of a stage different, e.g., a score of 4 is counted as agreeing with a score of 4 with some 3 $[4 = 4(3)]$ or 4 with some 5 $[4 = 4(5)]$. The tenth interview was a two-thirds of a stage disagreement. Overall intercoder agreement is thus 90%. The Pearson correlation between the two sets of scores is 0.74. Reliability was also calculated on a dilemma-by-dilemma basis with the results being approximately the same. There was exact stage agreement on two-thirds of the 24 dilemmas and one-half stage disagreement on one-fourth of the dilemmas, giving a total of 0.92 agreement within one-half stage between coders. Coders were a full stage apart on two dilemmas. Pearson r on a dilemma-by-dilemma basis was 0.82. Although these findings are somewhat lower than the interrater correlations in the 0.90 range reported on cross-sectional data with the revised manual (*Berkowitz et al.,* 1978) or on *Kohlberg*'s (1979) longitudinal sample, the current reliability coefficients are within the normally accepted range, despite the fact that the average stage score in this sample is a full stage higher than that of the cross-sectional sample cited above, perhaps the highest stage sample to date, and thus, according to our critique, more prone to scoring error.

Although the problems with these data are important they are not insurmountable. There are a number of reasons for claiming that the longitudinal comparisons between our subjects' scores are nonetheless quite valid. First of all, the coding was done by *Kohlberg*'s three most experienced scorers, the authors of the revised manuals for the three forms, with each scorer coding only those cases which were on his or her form. Intercoder reliability was as high in single dilemmas as it was on scores based on full forms. In other words, change on a single dilemma over time was just as meaningful as change on a full protocol, although probably more vulnerable to random error. Reliability was higher on the written protocols when subjects were 19 years old and had a mean stage score of 4 (conventional) than on the thoroughly-probed oral interviews when subjects were 21 and had an average score of 4(5) (postconventional), suggesting that the finding of regression may be due more to the advancing ages and stages of these subjects than to the quality of the data. The fact that the percentage of regression is virtually the same in the written to oral interview comparisons as it is in the oral to oral interview comparisons is further support of this point.

Results

Kohlberg Stage Scores

Table I presents the original manual scores for the 26 subjects, labeled A–Z, at time 1 and time 3 when most subjects were college sophomores and seniors, aged 19 (mean = 18.5) and 21 (mean = 21.2), respectively, Fall 1970 and Spring 1973. Table I also presents the same data rescored by *Kohlberg*'s most experienced coders by the revised (1978) manual (column 4). The T4 data were coded only by the revised manual since the original manual is no longer in use. Scores listed in the left-hand side of this column are from form A dilemmas while scores listed in the right side are from form C. Since almost all of these form C subjects received the form A dilemmas (Heinz and Officer Brown) at T3 and T4 and since these are the best worked-out higher-stage stories, these are the scores reported for the T3–T4 comparisons, in the subjects who have them.

When subjects had both A and C forms at T3, both scores are listed, permitting the two pairwise comparisons (T1–T3 and T3–T4) but not the T1–T4 comparison since this is between scores based on different dilemmas. 3 subjects did not have the form C dilemma at T3; for these subjects it is not possible to make longitudinal comparisons between T1–T3 or T1–T4. The subject who did not get the form A dilemmas at T3 does have fully comparable form C scores at T1, T3, and T4. The fifth column in table I lists the dilemmas analyzed in these comparisons.

Original Manual

Before being scored by the revised manual the T1 and T3 cases had been scored by *Kohlberg*'s original manual. In 1974, 66 of the 78 T1, T2, and T3 cases were scored according to the original global stage scoring system (*Kohlberg*, 1972) by a coder trained by *Kohlberg*. 11 of the 12 missing cases were in the possession of another investigator at the time of the coding and thus could not be scored. One interview was never recovered. Roughly one-third of the protocols were coded by a second experienced coder. Full agreement or agreement within one-third of a stage [i.e., stage 3(4) = 3(4); stage 3(4) = 3] was found in 25 out of 29 cases (0.86). Since neither coder is currently available, the two scores were simply averaged into a single global score per case for the purpose of the current analysis. An examination of the original manual scores in table I shows that there are 12 instances of progression, 4 of no change, and 6 of regression (noted by an asterisk in the table) in the 22 cases for which we have full T1 and T3 data. Six of these regressions are of two-thirds of a stage or more. All but one of the regressors move from a postconventional

Table I. Kohlberg stage scores from adolescence to adulthood

Subject		Kohlberg original manual	Kohlberg revised manual form A/C		Dilemmas analyzed	
time	age					
A–1	18	4(5)		3		k
A–3	21	4(5)	4		h+o	k
A–4	26	–	4		h+o	
B–1	19	4	4(3)		h+o	
B–3	22	5	5		h+o	
B–4	27	–	4*		h+o	
C–1	19	4(5)	5		h+o	
C–3	22	5	5		h+o	
C–4	25	–	5(4)**		h+o	
D–1	18	4(5)	4		h+o	
D–3	22	4(5)	5(4)		h+o	
D–4	25	–	4*		h+o	
E–1	19	4(3)		4		k
E–3	22	5	4(5)	5(4)	h+o	k
E–4	27	–	4(5)		h+o	
F–1	19	4	4		h+o	
F–3	22	4(5)	4		h+o	
F–4	27	–	4		h+o	
G–1	18	5(4)	5(4)		h+o	
G–3	20	5	4(5)*		h+o	
G–4	25	–	4**		h+o	
H–1	18	4	4		h+o	
H–3	20	5	4(5)		h+o	
H–4	25	–	5(4)		h+o	
I–1	18	4	4(3)		h	
I–3	21	4(5)	4(3)		h	
I–4	25	–	5(4)		h	
J–1	19	na		4		k
J–3	21	4(5)	5(4)	3(4)*	h+o	k
J–4	26	–	4(5)*		h+o	
K–1	18	5(4)		3(4)		k
K–3	21	5	5(4)	5	h+o	k
K–4	26	–	5(4)		h+o	
L–1	18	5		4		k
L–3	21	5(4)*	4(3)	na	h+o	na
L–4	26	–	4		h+o	
M–1	19	5(4)		4(3)		k
M–3	22	5	4(3)	na	h+o	na
M–4	27	–	4		h+o	

Table I (cont.)

Subject		Kohlberg original manual	Kohlberg revised manual form A/C		Dilemmas analyzed	
time	age					
N–1	19	5		3		k
N–3	22	4*		4(5)		k
N–4	27	–		4(5)		k
O–1	18	5	4			h
O–3	20	5	4			h
O–4	27	–	4(5)			h
P–1	19	4(3)		4		k
P–3	21	5	4(5)	3*	h+o	k
P–4	26	–	4*		h+o	
Q–1	17	5		5(4)		k
Q–3	20	na	5(4)	5	h+o	k
Q–4	25	–	5(4)		h+o	
R–1	18	5		4		k
R–3	21	5		5		k
R–4	–	–		–		
S–1	19	4(5)		4(3)		k
S–3	22	3(4)*	4	4	h+o	k
S–4	27	–	4		h+o	
T–1	18	4(5)		4		k
T–3	21	3(4)*	4	5(4)	h+o	k
T–4	26	–	4		h+o	
U–1	19	4(5)		4(5)		k
U–3	22	3(4)*	4	na	h	na
U–4	27	–	5(4)		h	
V–1	19	na		4(3)		k
V–3	22	4(5)	5(4)	4	h+o	k
V–4	27	–	5		h+o	
W–1	19	na	5		h	
W–3	21	4(5)	5(4)*		h	
W–4	26	–	4(5)**		h	
X–1	18	4(3)	4(5)		h+o	
X–3	21	4(5)	4(3)*		h+o	
X–4	26	–	4(5)		h+o	
Y–1	19	5	4(5)		h	
Y–3	21	4*	4*		h	
Y–4	26	–	5		h	
Z–1	19	4	4		h+o	
Z–3	21	4(5)	5(4)		h+o	
Z–4	26	–	4*		h+o	

Italic type = Female subjects (A, F, S, T and U); k = Korea dilemma; h+o = Heinz + Officer Brown dilemmas; na = not available; * = 2- or 5-year longitudinal interval regressor; ** = 7-year longitudinal interval regressor.

score [4(5) or 5(4)] to a conventional score (no stage 5 present). There were 7 other postconventional scores at T1 in this initial coding which either progressed or did not change. Thus, roughly one-half of the subjects who scored as postconventional at T1 regress over the $2^1/_2$-year interval while only one of those scored as conventional did so. 1 subject seems to skip a stage, but his T2 score would supply the missing stage. The distribution of the regressors supports our claim that there were problems with the higher stages according to the original manual.

Sex differences are also present in the scoring by the original manual. Women and men started out approximately equal at T1 with an average score of 4(5). At T3, the average women's score had dropped two-thirds of a stage, with 4 out of 5 women regressing from 4/5 to 4(3) or 3(4), while the men's average score increased to 5(4). Although *Kohlberg* (1969) has suggested that sex differences in moral judgment might be attributable to differences in experience, the current data cast some doubt on that hypothesis. Since the women are approximately equal to the men in educational and occupational goals, achievement, and experience, the presence of sex differences in this sample is problematic. Although these differences by sex (and by group, later in this paper) are not significant (F[2, 18] = 0.1192, p < 0.89) statistically, they are in the same direction as previously reported sex differences in moral judgment (*Gilligan,* 1977). Failure to find significance is at least partially due to the small number of subjects in this study and does not preclude qualitative analyses of group means to see whether they are in the predicted directions.

Revised Manual

In the rescoring by the revised manual, from T1 to T3 there are 6 cases of regression (asterisk) out of the 22 comparable instances (table I). Of the 22 subjects, 6 can be considered postconventional while 16 are conventional (stage 4 or lower). Four of the regressions are from the postconventional level while only two are from subjects who score as conventional, suggesting again that the postconventional scores are more vulnerable to regression than the conventional scores.

Although half of the regressions are of only one-third of a stage, three regressions are of two-thirds of a stage or more (14%). In order to check on the validity of these regressions we included three regressors in our reliability sample of five complete T1–T3 intervals. In addition to the high overall reliability correlation between the two coders' scores already reported, the second coder confirmed two of the original coders' regressions, both of them one-third of a stage regressions. Thus, it is possible that even the one-third of a stage regressions are meaningful. At any rate, whether we are conservative as to what constitutes regression or how much confirmation to demand, the percentage of regression from T1–T3 is still in the 14–28% range, closer to the 20% regression rate originally noted by *Kohlberg and Kramer* (1969) than to the random error rate of 7% recently suggested by *Kohlberg* (1979). Sex differences persist in the rescoring by the new manual with mean scores for men roughly one-third of a stage higher than for the women at both T1 and T3 [4 vs. 4(3), and 4(5) vs. 4, respectively]. The male and female averages are given later in table II.

Looking next at the T3 to T4 interval, we find the same patterns repeated. This is especially important since these are our strongest cases. In fact, a subset of 18 cases can actually be considered optimal rather than suboptimal data. These subjects have comparable moral judgment interviews both times, the two most reliable stories (Heinz and Officer

Brown) from *Kohlberg*'s best worked-out form (A). The thoroughly probed oral interviews were given by doctoral students well versed in the theory (at T4 by the second author). The transcripts of these interviews were scored by one of *Kohlberg*'s most experienced coders, the author of the form A manual.

Of these 18 cases, 4 are scored as progressors, 7 as nonchangers, and 7 as regressors (asterisk). Again requiring more than one-third of a stage change for a case to be considered a regression, there are 3 subjects whose scores show regressions of two-thirds of a stage or more – 14%. It is quite possible that there is some ceiling effect at work here. Since stage 6 is no longer in the manual, it is difficult for a stage 5 subject to progress; the coder could however indicate guess points at the highest stage (and did so in 2 cases). At any rate, the fact that two-thirds of the regressions were from stage 4(5) or 5(4) rather than 5 makes a ceiling effect seem less likely.

Turning now to the full set of 24 cases (including form C as well as form A) for which we have comparable T3 and T4 dilemmas, the patterns persist. 8 subjects progress, 8 remain the same, and 8 regress. 5 of the regressors lose one-third of a stage, while 3 are coded as two-thirds of a stage or more (13%). All 8 regressions are in cases scored as postconventional and again this represents more than 50% regression in postconventional cases, as opposed to the lack of any regression in the cases scored as conventional. The T3 sex difference persists at T4 with men again scored as one-third of a stage higher than women, 4(5) and 4, respectively.

Finally, in the 13 cases for which we have a full comparable set of cases (either all form A or all form C) at T1, T3, and T4, *Kohlberg*'s hypotheses are again disconfirmed in about 15% of the subjects. 3 individuals (C, G, and W, double asterisk) end up with a lower score at age 26 than they had at age 19, 2 of these two-thirds of a stage lower (15%). Thus, these data show that *Kohlberg and Kramer*'s (1969) finding of regression in moral development from adolescence to adulthood is replicated but extended in the current sample. In the data reported here, whether the comparison is between age 19 and age 21, 21 and 26, or 19 and 26, whether we accept one-third of a stage regression as meaningful or require two-thirds for significance, whether we accept a single coder's judgment or demand a second coder's opinion, whether the scores considered are based on single dilemmas or full protocols, whether the interviews are written or oral, the finding comes out the same: a significant proportion of a higher stage sample regresses in moral judgment between adolescence and adulthood when scored by *Kohlberg*'s standards of moral development.

Reconstruction

Having established the persistence of the phenomenon of late adolescent regression in higher-stage interviews scored by the manual revised to solve precisely this problem, we will turn our attention to interpretation and the promised reconstruction. The simplest explanation of our findings is that the regressions are a function of scoring error. The general finding that in many of the comparisons, approximately one-third of the subjects progress, one-third regress, and one-third stay the same, might be adduced as support of that view. While both *Kohlberg*'s critics and his supporters may agree with slightly different versions of this explanation, we do not. Advocates of *Kohlberg*'s theory may claim that the manual is still new and therefore some slight random error is to be expected. They might also claim that the lack of full form scores increases the possibility of scoring error. Those opposed to the theory may view our data as further confirmation of their belief that it is impossible to code moral reasoning reliably, especially that of adults. In our opinion, the only way to answer these critics is to proceed as *Kohlberg* has in trying to demonstrate empirically that individuals progress longitudinally through a sequence of stages – but that will require an expansion of the definitions of the higher stages.

Support for our position comes from a recoding of the same interview data according to our own scoring manual (*Murphy*, 1978) which was based on a reconstruction of *Kohlberg*'s theory around the adult cognitive stage hypothesis outlined earlier. Our finding of developmental progression, where the *Kohlberg* manual found regression, is our answer to both the claim that it is impossible to code these data and the claim that it is only the scoring manual and not the theory itself which needs revision.

Hypothetical Moral Dilemmas Scored by a Perry Manual

The T1, T3 and T4 dilemmas were also coded blind to identity and time by another scorer (the second author) according to a manual based on *Perry*'s (1968) theory of intellectual and ethical development. Briefly, this process involves coding each statement in the standard moral judgment interview to determine which of *Perry*'s epistemological positions seems to underlie it, with scores ranging from 1 to 6. *Perry*'s scheme has nine positions, but since 6 through 9 are positions of mature commitment, everything in this range was coded simply as position 6. Thus, for example, the statement in response to the Heinz dilemma that one should not say whether Heinz should or should not steal the drug because there is no way of asserting objectively that one answer to a moral problem is better than another, would (depending on context) probably be coded position 3 or 4 (multiplicity subordinate or coordinate), or some combination of the two. As in the *Kohlberg* scoring, guess scores are weighted less than those which match the manual.

The score per dilemma is essentially a numerical average of the position scores of every statement in the dilemma (following the older, less complex method originally used by *Kohlberg* in 1972). This comes out as a number between 0 and 6.00 (in our data, between 2.67 and 5.95 at T1 and T4), which is then rounded off into a global position score using the same third of stage steps used by the *Kohlberg* scorers (3.19 = 3; 3.20 = 3(4); 3.50 = 4(3); 3.81 = 4, etc.). It must be stressed that this coding is of the same normative moral judgments that the *Kohlberg* scorers code; and just as they try to infer the underlying structure of the reasoning and compare it to a model based on *Piaget*'s cognitive stages, this coding attempts the same process of analysis but used a different comparison, the structural sequence of intellectual and ethical development described by *Perry*. In other words, this is moral judgment coding, albeit based on a different model of moral development.

Moral Development: Perry Position Scores

This rescoring of the same reasoning serves as a check on the reliability of the *Kohlberg* stage regressions. In the 22 cases which permit T1 to T3 comparisons, a similar blind coding of the same moral judgment interviews at T1 and T3, but according to the *Perry* (1968) model, shows 18 cases progressing, 3 not changing, and 1 regressing (one-third of a stage). These scores are presented in table II beside the same original manual scores reported in table I but with both *Perry* position and *Kohlberg* stage scores converted to their decimal equivalents [4(5) = 4.33] and then multiplied by 100 to permit averaging and correlation. Although regressions are permissible within *Perry*'s theory, the general upward progression is as required for a developmental theory.

The *Perry* model scores for both men and women at T1 are position 4(3) (367) and at T3 they are 4. At T4 the women are coded an average of one-third of a position lower than the men [4(5) and 5, respectively]. Although this is counter to the predictions of this study, an inspection of the unrounded-off average scores for males and females at the bottom of table II shows that the addition of 3/100 of a position score to the female average at T4 would result in a rounded-off score of 5(4), the same as the males'. It seems reasonable that the difference could be the result of scoring error.

From T3 to T4, 15 subjects are coded as progressing, 6 as stable, and 4 as regressing. Only one of these regressions (4%) is of two-thirds of a stage, the standard we adopted for validity in the *Kohlberg* score regressions. Over the full 7-year interval, from T1 to T4 there are 13 cases which permit longitudinal comparisons; 12 of these are coded as progressing, 1 as not changing and none as regressing. Thus the finding of 92% progression and 0% regression from age 19 to age 26 provides strong support for the developmental claims of the Perry model.

Looking at the *Perry* position scores of the *Kohlberg* regressors, we find that they are taken from the full range of *Perry* scores in this sample. Three of the regressors are from the mid-range of *Perry* position scores, progressing from 3(4) or 4(3) to 4 on the *Perry* scale, two of the *Kohlberg* regressors are at the top of our group of *Perry* scores, moving from position 4(3) to 5(4), and one is at the bottom of the distribution with *Perry* scores of 3(4) and 4(3) at times 1 and 3, respectively. From T3 to T4 the pattern is similar. Here again, 3 of the 8 regressors are at the top of the *Perry* distribution, moving from a mixture of positions 4 and 5 to a mixture of 5 and 6 or pure 6. One of the regressors is in the mid-range, progressing from 4(3) to 4(5), and 2 are from the lowest with stable scores of either 4 or 4(3). The other 2 cases are coded as also regressing according to the *Perry* manual, moving from positions 5 to 4 and 4 to 4(3). Since all of the *Kohlberg* regressors are in some form of relativism on *Perry*'s scale – positions 4(3) and beyond – they conform to our interpretation that it is the relativizing of their moral reasoning that is problematic for *Kohlberg*'s scheme. Overall, however, there does seem to be some relationship between the *Kohlberg* scores and those based on *Perry* with small positive correlations at each of the three times of 0.38, 0.13, and 0.26, respectively.

Illustration

Our data indicate that while *Kohlberg*'s analysis of moral judgment provides clear evidence of development in some undergraduates, for others it offers no explanation for the apparent changes which have taken place. This finding is consistent with our contention that there may be another form of postconventional moral judgment that previously has been mistaken for regression or developmental failure, given the constraints of the *Kohlberg* scoring system. Our

Table II. Perry position scores from adolescence to adulthood

Postconventional contextual

Subject time	Kohlberg form A	Kohlberg form C	Perry form A	Perry form C	Dilemma of fact
A–1		300		400	–
A–3	400		400		type I
A–4	400		400		–
B–1	367		333		–
B–3	500		433		type I
B–4	400*		600		–
C–1	500		400		–
C–3	500		467		type I
C–4	467**			533	type II
D–1	400		333		–
D–3	467		500		–
D–4	400*		400*		–
E–1		400		367	–
E–3	433	467	400	400	type I
E–4	433		400		–

Postconventional contextual group means

Subject time	Kohlberg form A	Kohlberg form C	Perry form A	Perry form C	Dilemma of fact
T1	393		367		–
T3	460		440		–
T4	420		467		–

Transitional

Subject time	Kohlberg form A	Kohlberg form C	Perry form A	Perry form C	Dilemma of fact
F–1	400		300		–
F–3	400		400		type I
F–4	400		433		–
G–1	467		400		–
G–3	433*		433		type I
G–4	400**		600		type II

Subject time	Kohlberg form A	Kohlberg form C	Perry form A	Perry form C	Dilemma of fact
H–1	400		367		–
H–3	433		400		–
H–4	467		467		–
I–1	367		300		–
I–3	367		367		–
I–4	467		500		–
J–1		400		367	–
J–3	467	333*	400	467	–
J–4	433*		367*		–
K–1		333		400	–
K–3	467	500	400	400	–
K–4	467		567		type I
L–1		400		367	–
L–3	367		467		–
L–4	400		433*		–
M–1		367		333	–
M–3	367		400		–
M–4	400		400		–
N–1		300		367	–
N–3	433		500		–
N–4	433		467*		–

Transitional group means

Subject time	Kohlberg form A	Kohlberg form C	Perry form A	Perry form C	Dilemma of fact
T1	382		356		–
T3	415		426		–
T4	433		470		–

Postconventional formal

Subject time	Kohlberg form A	Kohlberg form C	Perry form A	Perry form C	Dilemma of fact
O–1	400		300		–
O–3	400		400		–
O–4	433		533		–

Kohlberg form A/C = *Kohlberg* hypothetical moral dilemmas scored by the *Kohlberg et al.* (1978) revised manual – form A dilemma scores in left-hand side of column, form C scores in right-hand side; Perry form A/C = the same *Kohlberg* hypothetical moral dilemmas reported in column 2, rescored by a manual based

Table II (cont.)

Subject time	Kohlberg form A/C		Perry form A/C		Dilemma of fact
P–1		400		367	–
P–3	433	300*	367	433	–
P–4	400*		367		–
Q–1		467		400	–
Q–3	467	500	400	467	–
Q–4	467		467		
R–1		400		333	–
R–3		500		400	–
R–4		–		–	–

Postconventional formal group means

	Kohlberg form A/C	Perry form A/C	Dilemma of fact
T1	417	350	–
T3	450	392	–
T4	433	456	–

Subject time	Kohlberg form A/C		Perry form A/C		Dilemma of fact
X–1	433		333		
X–3	367*		367		
X–4	433		367		
Y–1	433		367		
Y–3	400*		400		
Y–4	500		500		type I
Z–1	400		400		
Z–3	467		367*		
Z–4	400*		433		

Conventional group means

	Kohlberg form A/C	Perry form A/C	Dilemma of fact
T1	417	371	–
T3	415	388	–
T4	442	442	–

Conventional

Subject time	Kohlberg form A/C		Perry form A/C		Dilemma of fact
S–1		367		367	–
S–3	400	400	400	367	–
S–4	400		467		type I
T–1		400		367	–
T–3	400	467	333	367	type I
T–4	400		433		–
U–1		433		400	–
U–3	400	na	433	na	–
U–4	467		500		–
V–1		367		367	–
V–3	467	400	400	467	–
V–4	500		433		–
W–1	500		367		–
W–3	467*		400		–
W–4	433**			400	

Grand means[1]

full sample

	Kohlberg form A/C		Perry form A/C		Dilemma of fact
T1	400	[4]	362	[4(5)]	–
T3	429	[4(5)]	412	[4]	–
T4	433	[4(5)]	460	[5(4)]	–

female sample

	Kohlberg form A/C		Perry form A/C		Dilemma of fact
T1	373	[4(3)]	360	[4(3)]	–
T3	404	[4]	396	[4]	–
T4	410	[4]	447	[4(5)]	–

male sample

	Kohlberg form A/C		Perry form A/C		Dilemma of fact
T1	410	[4]	359	[4(3)]	–
T3	444	[4(5)]	412	[4]	–
T4	437	[4(5)]	460	[5(4)]	–

on *Perry* (*Murphy*, 1978); *italic* type = female subjects; * = 2- or 5-year longitudinal interval regressor; ** = 7-year longitudinal interval regressor.

[1] For subjects with both form A and form C scores at T3, only the form A scores were used to calculate the T3 means.

93

alternative conception applies particularly to those groups (women and relativists) whose judgments have been most problematic for *Kohlberg*'s developmental analysis. While the central problem in late adolescent moral development was considered by *Kohlberg* to be metaethical relativism (and thus as outside his domain of normative judgment), the persistence of relativism in the face of the principles that were originally considered to provide its solution suggests the need for a new approach. We have shown that the findings of *Perry* provide the basis for an alternative conception of postconventional moral judgment that can explain the occurrence of moral development in adulthood while retaining the basic cognitive-developmental assumptions about the process of stage change. This approach relates moral development to ego development in late adolescence by positing experiences of commitment and responsibility as critical to both developmental processes. At the same time, it considers that the changes which occur in moral judgment during late adolescence and adulthood may qualify as structural transformation in a strict Piagetian sense of cognitive restructuring.

To illustrate the way in which the move toward contextual relativism leads to changes in moral judgment which are mistaken for regression within the *Kohlberg* system, we consider the responses of two 'regressors' to demonstrate how the apparent regression in moral judgment can better be construed as a progression toward a more inclusive, and in that sense more adequate, form of judgment. From sophomore to senior year, subject J's moral judgment scores go from *Kohlberg* stage 4 to stage 3(4) on the Korea dilemma. In that interval, his *Perry* scores on the same dilemma progress from 4(3) to 5(4) signifying a move toward contextual relativism. The *Kohlberg* regression centers around the senior year qualification of a judgment which was, in sophomore year, absolute. Asked to judge whether a marine captain should send a man back to his probable death to blow up a bridge in order to save a company in retreat, this student argues at T1 from a clear stage 4 societal perspective that the maintenance of social order overrides the cost of the life lost. He states that the captain should order one of his soldiers to blow up the bridge rather than going himself (since only he is capable of leading the retreat) because 'without his leadership, the entire company could perish. One life lost is less a blow to his company, the army it belongs to and the ideas the army represents.' He believes the captain clearly 'has the right' to order the demolitions expert to go on this mission because:

'By being on that field every soldier has potentially agreed to die for his country and to follow the rules of the army game, to the hilt if necessary. He has given up the absolute power of the will, *voluntarily* or why else would he be there? Thus the captain is ordering him to fulfill his contract and to play the game to the hilt.'

These responses receive two match-point stage 4 scores, according to *Kohlberg*'s new manual.

At the T3 interview, however, subject J's judgment clearly has changed. Now, he believes that instead of ordering the expert demolition man to go, the captain should hold a lottery 'because you never know what is *really* going to happen'. The relativism that has begun to pervade his judgment is apparent when, after he states that a lottery is better because 'you should at least make it as fair as possible', his answer to a question as to whether fairness should have a place in military strategy is that:

> 'It depends. [*ON WHAT?*] On what you want to do. If you want to win, if you want to demolish the country, if you just want to defeat your enemy, the other soldiers, what sort of a victory do you want? What sort of aim do you have in mind ... I'll talk about Israel. They should try to win a battle if they are invaded at any cost, in other words, burn up their own houses, burn the countryside to roust the enemy if necessary, kill as many as possible to make them desist. I don't mean if they have the atomic bomb developed to drop it on Baghdad or something. So I don't know.'

The contextual relativism seems to have reached its limits even as he talks. He can see the potential validity of both of the frames of reference he supplies, but not the way of ultimately choosing between them. His judgment now illustrates perfectly what *Perry* means by 'the realization of Relativism' (position 5) and the *Perry* score of 5(4) as an average of the reasoning he used throughout the dilemma is indicative of the pervasiveness of this position in his reasoning.

While we are not arguing that uncertainty is 'higher' than certainty or that contextual theories of philosophy are better than formalistic ones, we are claiming that our subject's reasoning is both more differentiated and more integrated at T3 than at T1, because it takes into account aspects of the dilemma that previously were not considered. While the explicit use of the concept of fairness, rather than the preservation of social order, might seem to indicate a move toward principled moral judgment in *Kohlberg*'s scheme, the relativisitic nature of subject J's responses leads them to be scored only as less adequate in *Kohlberg*'s terms. The discovery that 'it depends' renders his judgment more relativistic, but also more inclusive and more adaptive.

A second illustration of our claim that it is contextual relativism that is mistaken for regression according to the *Kohlberg* revised manual is provided by subject B, one of the highest *Perry* position subjects in the sample. Some of his reasoning, coded at position 6 (or higher) according to *Perry*'s standards of development, indicates the way in which contextual relativism changes normative moral judgments in a manner scored as regression according to *Kohlberg*'s manual.

At T3 subject B is no longer plagued by the kinds of uncertainty that afflicted our earlier relativist, and B's first few judgments about the Heinz dilemma are coded as match points for stage 5 in the new *Kohlberg* manual and as position 4 or higher on *Perry*. Subject B has no trouble solving the Heinz dilemma in terms of the logical priority of the right to life over the right to property, but there is more to his reasoning than this hierarchy of rights. As he considers other aspects of the dilemma his thinking becomes more attuned to its contexts: While he thinks that 'everyone has the obligation to relieve human misery and suffering if possible ... I do think you have certain obligations to your wife or your friends or relatives that are just deeper'. This is precisely the kind of statement that slips through *Kohlberg*'s manual, and in its appeal to the personal is coded as a guess 4. Asked whether Heinz should steal for a complete stranger, subject B thinks that depends too, 'if it were just a question of if the drug would make the guy feel better, may be it is not so clear there, how deep is the obligation. You can't go around and crusade for everybody. It is just impossible.' We argue that this kind of contextual consideration is not simply a metaethical reflection upon conventional judgment but that it has transformed the subject's normative judgment.

Asked whether the wife has a right to expect Heinz to steal, he offers two contexts in which this question can be answered and claims that both are legitimate: 'Yes, I think so. First of all because she is a person and second of all, because she is his wife.' In other words, Heinz has both universal obligations to his wife as a person and a special obligation to her as his wife. If he does not love his wife at all, then 'the obligation is the same as if she were just another person, he has the obligation'. If he does love her, then 'when people are in love and get married, that is a new set of obligations and then your life essentially becomes that person, and it becomes so close to that person's that you really can't separate the two ... I think she had the right to expect it.' The lack of a single clear principle and the talk of love lead the *Kohlberg* scorer to guess 4/5. On the *Perry* coding, this statement and the next are guessed as high as 6.

Is our subject's talk of two contexts really significant? Does the addition of a context of personal, special obligations to a construction based on a universal hierarchy of rights signal a change and a progression in moral judgment? Asked whether his moral beliefs had changed since he came to Harvard, subject B answers that as a result of experiences in 'trying to get [my beliefs] into practice' he has become

'... more considerate, taking into account other people's feelings and other people's opinions and other people's lives and how you as a person affect their lives. And seeing whether your effect is a good effect or a bad effect. And before, I didn't really care about [that] too much. My first responsibility was mainly to myself, and the other just went along.'

In other words, subject B tells us that his beliefs have expanded to take into account the actual consequences of his actions. He has, in fact, learned from experience. Although he has not lost his ability to justify his judgments according to logical systems (the first context) he tells us that he now tries to consider much more and to take responsibility for the actual effects of his actions on the other people involved (the second context).

We have outlined three points illustrating a progression in reasoning along a continuum from adolescent certainty (subject J, T1), to the kind of relativism which *Perry* calls multiplicity (subject J, T3), to a contextual relativism that permits commitments in relativism and responsibility for choice (subject B, T3). By the new manual, the second and third of these forms of reasoning are coded as regressive. We argue instead that they demonstrate a clear understanding of principles of justice (the notions of fairness and reciprocity that underlie postconventional formal reasoning in our PCF designation) but that these principles constitute only one among several legitimate contexts in which the dilemma can be construed and resolved (our PCC category).

Validity of the Reconstructed Scores

The distinction between PCC and PCF reasoning was one of the concepts that guided the current data analysis and provides the link between *Perry*'s relativism and *Kohlberg*'s. If *Kohlberg and Kramer*'s (1969) finding of relativistic regression was an indication that the original scoring system was unable to measure the actual development of a certain type of individual's reasoning, and if this finding was replicated in the current data with the new manual, we could then argue that the problem lay in the basic theory, not its operationalization in the manuals. And if we could show that the group that was scored PCC on the basis of the contextual relativism of their reasoning about real life was essentially the same group of individuals whose relativistic hypothetical moral reasoning had been so problematic for the theory, we would have replicated in a different sample the finding that the theory is an inadequate representation of the development of a certain group of individuals. According to *Kohlberg* (1976) these data in longitudinal cases would argue strongly against the universality of his theory.

In addition to the hypothetical moral reasoning scores, table II also contains additional data. The cases are categorized into four groups according to a coding of the subject's reasoning about real-life situations. This basic structural-developmental coding also included the categories of conventional and transitional into PCC. PCF was conceived of as an early form of postconventional development which preceded the transitional category. In 1975, the senior author sorted the 26 cases into these categories on the basis of one-page summary sheets which outlined the transcripts of the subjects' T3 interviews, excluding their hypothetical moral reasoning. The summary sheets included short descriptions of subjects' real-life dilemmas, identity statements, and commitments. The sorting was done blind to moral judgment stage score and was thus totally independent of it. All hypothetical moral judgment coding was done by other scorers.

A kind of construct validity for *Gilligan*'s global PCC-PCF sorting is provided when we return our attention to the *Perry* position scores on the hypothetical dilemmas (column 3). Although the group means are tightly clustered at T1, at T3 the group ranking is in the predicted order, with the PCC group almost half of a position higher than the PCF group and more than half of a position higher than the conventional group. This order is basically preserved at T4 although the gap has shrunk to 0.11 and 0.25 of a stage, respectively, and although the transitional group is now 3 points higher than the PCC group. Returning to the *Kohlberg* manual scores on the hypothetical dilemmas (column 2), we see that there is a different ranking and that the PCC group replicates the *Kohlberg and Kramer* findings. Like their regressors, this group has the second lowest mean score at age 19 (T1) and the highest at age 21 (T3).

One final finding is of note. In the course of our early drafts of this paper, we were struck by the importance of the real-life dilemmas in precipitating the transformation of moral judgment reported by our PCC subjects. In the transition from PCF to PCC reasoning, one subject referred to the actual dilemma he faced as 'a dilemma of the fact', that his principles of justice did not enable him to solve the moral problem. Instead, the confrontation with the actual dilemma appeared to initiate a new kind of moral questioning which seemed to have a clear stage-transitional quality. We found this very suggestive, and eventually went back through our data to see whether any of our other subjects spontaneously reported similar experiences. We found 11 incidents in which the students spoke in explicitly structural terminology about the destruction of old structures of reasoning in actual life situations that had revealed their limitations ('and then my whole world fell apart') – type I dilemmas. 3 students also described a process of reconstructing their ways of making sense of the world ('and what came out was not just a different set of rules but a whole other way of looking at it') — type II dilemmas. Some details of this process are evident in the cases discussed above and a more complete description is presented in *Gilligan and Murphy* (in press).

Table II also lists the students who mention a dilemma of the fact which leads to transition. The results are again strongly suggestive. At T3, 4 of our 5 PCC candidates report an actual life dilemma that leads to questioning of former principles, and 1 also reports a kind of reconstruction of moral judgment. 2 of the transitional subjects report dilemmas leading to disequilibrium while none of the PCF and only 1 of the conventional subjects reports such experiences. At T4, 4 other subjects report type I dilemmas of the fact. There are two additional type II reconstructions, one each in both the PCC and the transitional groups, from subjects who report having dilemmas of the first kind. The actual dilemmas which led our subjects to experience the limitations of their own previous moral judgments include the inability to communicate with a lover, the realization by one lawyer that he had unwittingly prosecuted an innocent man, the decision about how to react to a spouse's infidelity, a couple's choice to have an abortion, the inability to live up to a principle of absolute truth for one subject, and for another, the inability to live up to a principle of forgiveness.

Conclusions

The present paper has demonstrated that in some subjects, at least, *Kohlberg*'s theory cannot distinguish between the absolutism of adolescent logic and adult principled thinking. This group of bright adolescents can talk impressively about principles but falters when it comes to solving 'the dilemma of the fact'. Scored by *Kohlberg*'s original and revised standards for moral maturity, these individuals show up initially in late adolescence as false positives and seem to regress longitudinally as real-life experiences of 'responsibility and irreversible choice' lead them to appreciate 'shades of gray' and 'become much less absolutistic' in their judgments. We claim that these individuals are capable of full formal operations even in their early absolutism, and that its relativizing has many of the characteristics of structural stage change. Since the *Kohlberg* stages do not take this cognitive shift into account, they cannot reliably code moral development after adolescence in many higher stage subjects because they mistake contextual relativizing for moral regression.

The research reported here brings us a step closer to integrating childhood and adult development into a single life-span developmental perspective. This perspective builds on *Kohlberg*'s basic three level structural model but is based on a redefinition of the higher stages that takes into account the transformations in reasoning that result from actual adult experiences of moral conflict and choice, experiences that *Kohlberg* acknowledged in 1973 as necessary for mature moral judgment. This redefinition has reversed, in a select sample in the 19–26 age range, the problem of higher-stage regression and the findings of sex bias against women. Research in progress should shed further light on the applicability of this method of coding to moral reasoning in more representative samples of older adults, in cross-cultural data, and in other historical times.

Acknowledgement

This research was supported by grants from the Spencer Foundation and the Milton Fund of Harvard University. The authors wish to thank *Michael Basseches, Robert Kegan,* and *Steven Ries* for their collaboration in the inverview design and the collection of the 1973 data. We also wish to thank *Susan Benak, John Gibbs, Lawrence Kohlberg, Roger Landrum, William Perry,* and *Sheldon White* for their suggestions and comments on an earlier draft of this paper, *Andre Guerrero, Dennis Norman, Lydia O'Donnell,* and *Carol Taylor* for their reading of this draft, and *Donna Hulsizer* for her continuing collaboration. Our deepest thanks must go to the 26 men and women who participated in this study. Its success is due in large part to their willingness to risk sharing details of their lives that were often intensely personal. The generosity with which they shared many hours of their time and their hospitality during the 1978 interviews has made them collaborators with us in this research. The opinions presented in this article, however, are those of the authors alone.

References

Arlin, P.K.: Cognitive development in adulthood: a fifth stage? Devl Psychol. *11:* 602–606 (1975).
Berkowitz, M.W.; Gibbs, J.C. and Broughton, J.M.: The relation of moral judgment stage disparity to developmental effects of peer dialogues; Harvard University (1978; unpublished).
Brown, R. and Hernstein, R.J.: Psychology (Little, Brown, Boston 1975).
Chandler, M.: Relativism and the problem of epistemological loneliness. Hum. Dev. *18:* 171–180 (1975).
Edwards, C.P.: Societal complexity and moral development: a Kenyan study. Ethos *3:* 505–527 (1975).

Fishkin, J.S.: Metaethical reasoning, ideology, and political commitment: empirical applications of a proposed theory; Yale University (1975; unpublished).

Gibbs, J.C.: Kohlberg's stages of moral judgment: a constructive critique. Harv. Educ. Rev. 47: 42–61 (1977).

Gibbs, J.C.: Kohlberg's moral stage theory: a Piagetian revision. Hum. Dev. 22: 89–112 (1979).

Gilligan, C.: In a different voice: Women's conceptions of self and of morality. Harv. Educ. Rev. 47: 481–517 (1977).

Gilligan, C.: Moral development in the college years; in Chickering, The future American college (Jossey-Bass, San Francisco, in press).

Gilligan, C. and Kohlberg, L.: From adolescence to adulthood: the rediscovery of reality in a postconventional world; in Appel and Preseissen, Topics in cognitive development (Plenum Press, New York 1977).

Gilligan, C. and Murphy, J.M.: The philosopher and the dilemma of the fact: evidence for continuing development from adolescence to adulthood; in Kuhn, Intellectual development beyond childhood (Jossey-Bass, San Francisco, in press).

Guindon, A.: Moral development: form, content, and self – a critique of Kohlberg's sequence; St. Paul University, Ottawa (1978; unpublished).

Holstein, C.: Development of moral judgment: a longitudinal study of males and females. Child Dev. 47: 51–61 (1976).

Inhelder, B. and Piaget, J.: The growth of logical thinking from childhood to adolescence (Basic Books, New York 1958).

Kohlberg, L.: Stage and sequence: the cognitive-developmental approach to socialization; in Goslin, Handbook of socialization theory and research (Rand McNally, Chicago 1969).

Kohlberg, L.: Issue scoring guide; Harvard University (1972; unpublished).

Kohlberg, L.: Continuities in childhood and adult moral development revisited; in Baltes and Schaie, Life-span developmental psychology; 2nd ed. (Academic Press, New York 1973).

Kohlberg, L.: Moral stages and moralization: the cognitive-developmental approach; in Lickona, Moral development and behavior (Holt, Rinehart & Winston, New York 1976).

Kohlberg, L.: The meaning and measurement of moral development. Heinz Werner lecture, Clark University, Worcester, Mass., April 1979.

Kohlberg, L.; Colby, A.; Gibbs, J.; Speicher-Dubin, B., and Power, C.: Assessing moral stages: a manual; Harvard University (1978; unpublished).

Kohlberg, L. and Gilligan, C.: The adolescent as a philosopher: the discovery of the self in a post conventional world. Daedalus 100: 1051–1086 (1971).

Kohlberg, L. and Kramer, R.: Continuities and discontinuities in childhood and adult moral development. Hum. Dev. 12: 93–120 (1969).

Kurtines, W. and Grief, E.: The development of moral thought: review and evaluation of Kohlberg's approach. Psychol. Bull. 81: 453–470 (1974).

Meacham, J.A.: A dialectical approach to moral judgment and self-esteem. Hum. Dev. 18: 159–170 (1975).

Murphy, J.M.: Moral judgment coding based on Perry; Harvard University (1978; unpublished).

Perry, W.B.: Forms of intellectual and ethical development in the college years: a scheme (Holt, Rinehart & Winston, New York 1968).

Piaget, J.: The moral judgment of the child (Free Press, New York 1965; 1st ed. 1932).

Piaget, J.: Intellectual evolution from adolescence to adulthood. Hum. Dev. *15:* 1–12 (1972).

Puka, B.: Moral education and its cure; in Meyer, Reflections on values education (Wilfred Laurier University Press, Waterloo, Ont. 1976).

Reid, H. and Yanarella, E.J.: Critical political theory and moral development: on Kohlberg, Hampden-Turner, and Habermas. Theory Society *4:* 479–500 (1977).

Riegel, K.: Dialectical operations: The final period of cognitive development. Hum. Dev. *16:* 345–376 (1973).

Riegel, K.: The development of dialectical operations. Hum. Dev. *18:* No. 1–3 (1975; also Karger, Basel 1975).

Schwab, J.J.: Review of 'Education and the education of teachers', by R.S. Peters. Harv. Educ. Rev. *48:* 408–410 (1978).

Simpson, E.L.: Moral development research: a case study of scientific cultural bias. Hum. Dev. *17:* 81–106 (1974).

Sullivan, E.: A study of Kohlberg's structural theory of moral development: a critique of liberal social science ideology. Hum. Dev. *20:* 325–376 (1977).

Vygotsky, L.S.: Thought and language (MIT Press, Cambridge 1962; 1st ed. 1934).

Michael Murphy, Graduate School of Education, Harvard University, Larsen Hall 309, Appian Way, Cambridge, MA 02138 (USA)

Cognitive Stages or Developmental Phases? A Critique of Kohlberg's Stage-Structural Theory of Moral Reasoning

Don Locke

Abstract

After some preliminary doubts about Kohlberg's method of assessing moral reasoning, his 'stage-structural' theory is criticized under six heads. (1) The claim that the stages constitute *structural wholes*, representing unified and differentiated patterns of thought: it is argued that the available evidence, and Kohlberg's own methodology, unambiguously implies a developmental continuum, not discrete stage structures. (2) *Invariance*, which, after counter-evidence led to a revision in the theory, has yet to be demonstrated. (3) *Cultural Universality*: it is argued that, because of an ambiguity in the notion of a universal principle, Kohlberg's arguments against cultural relativism tend, if anything, to support it. (4) *Logical Necessity*: it is argued that Kohlberg shows at most that the sequence forms a hierarchy, from which neither its logical nor even its psychological necessity follows. (5) *Increasing Cognitive Adequacy*, with the associated claim that it is cognitive conflict which produces movement from one stage to another: it is argued that the empirical evidence conflicts with the theoretical claims, and that the theoretical arguments establish, at most, an increase in moral understanding, which could well increase, rather than decrease, cognitive conflict. (6) *Increasing Moral Adequacy*: this claim is as yet unjustified in any of its three possible interpretations. Finally it is suggested that Kohlbergian theory is in danger of becoming, in Lakatos's terms, a degenerating research programme.

Over the last two decades Lawrence Kohlberg has elaborated a cognitive-developmental theory of moralization which increasingly dominates both the academic study of moral development, and the theory and practice of moral education. As is well known, Kohlberg has identified six stages of moral reasoning, for which I give a recent formulation (Kohlberg *et al.*, 1977, I, pp. 24–8) together with their more familiar labels:

(1) *The Heteronomous Stage* (punishment and obedience orientation): right is blind obedience to rules and authority, avoiding punishment, and not doing physical harm.
(2) *The Stage of Individualism and Instrumental Purpose and Exchange* (instrumental relativist orientation): right is serving one's own or others' needs and making fair deals in terms of concrete exchange.

Mr. Don Locke is Reader in Philosophy, Department of Philosophy, University of Warwick, Coventry, CV4 7AL.

(3) *The Stage of Mutual Interpersonal Expectations, Relationships, and Interpersonal Conformity* ('good boy — nice girl' orientation): right is playing a good (nice) role, being concerned about other people and their feelings, keeping loyalty and trust with partners, and being motivated to follow rules and expectations.

(4) *The Social System and Conscience Stage* ('law and order' orientation): right is doing one's duty in society, upholding the social order, and the welfare of the society or group.

(5) *The Stage of Social Contract or Utility and of Individual Rights* (social-contract legalistic orientation): right is upholding the basic rights, values and legal contracts of a society, even when they conflict with the concrete rules and laws of a group.

(6) *The Stage of Universal Ethical Principles* (universal ethical principle orientation): guidance by universal ethical principles which all humanity should follow.

At its broadest, Kohlberg's theory is that moral development crucially involves and depends on a cognitive development through each of these six 'moral stages'.

Perhaps it is only to be expected that moral reasoning, as such, should involve a cognitive component, but it is less obvious that moral development in general is primarily a cognitive matter, and even if we restrict ourselves to moral thinking in particular, it seems likely that such things as feelings, imagination and personality must enter in as well. Indeed this emphasis on cognition seems but one indication of Kohlberg's general bias towards the rational aspects of morality as against the emotional. Nevertheless it is not entirely clear how far Kohlberg does regard moral development as specifically cognitive. At times he rightly rejects any rigid distinction between the cognitive and the emotional, insisting that both derive from a common basis (Kohlberg, 1969, p. 389–91; 1971a, p. 188–90; 1971b, p. 44). But this, it emerges, is, because the emotional element is itself determined by the cognitive, and the thesis is still that 'cognitive–structural features are the core of moral development' (1971b, p. 44).

However the special feature of Kohlberg's theory is not so much the claim that moral development involves a cognitive development, as the claim that it incorporates a sequence of distinct cognitive structures which represent not just different styles of thinking, typical phases through which any normal individual can usually be expected to pass, but qualitatively different patterns of thought and understanding which must inevitably occur in the order that they do. It is this 'stage-structural' theory of moral reasoning in particular, as opposed to other possible cognitive-developmental accounts, or theories of moral development generally, which I wish to examine. I shall argue that despite the undeniable interest and importance of Kohlberg's findings, and the originality and fruitfulness of his analysis of moral thinking, his insights and evidence cannot begin to support the enormous theoretical weight he wishes to place on them.

Kohlberg has suggested that only this stage-structural theory can account for the actual evolution of moral thinking, since this must depend on an interaction between the individual and his environment such as the stage-structural theory postulates, 'rather than being the direct result of maturation or the direct result of learning' (1969, p. 348). But although some such interactionist explanation will undoubtedly be more plausible than any theory which appeals solely to inborn factors, or solely to environment, that provides no reason for preferring the stage-structural account to any other theory which allows for an interaction of the two. Similarly the theory has been supported by the repeated finding that whereas individuals can readily grasp and repeat reasoning at their own and lower stages, they have difficulty in understanding and recapitulating reasoning at higher stages, and especially reasoning more than one stage above their own (Rest, Turiel and Kohlberg, 1969; Rest, 1973). But while this may show that the level of moral reasoning does depend crucially on cognitive capacities, it does not by itself establish that the different stages involve distinct cognitive structures, or distinctively moral cognitive structures, as opposed to depending on more general cognitive abilities. The stage-structural theory must rely on more specific evidence about the nature and sequence of the stages themselves.

Kohlberg himself has offered four criteria for the existence of distinct cognitive structures — qualitative differences, invariant sequence, structural unity, and hierarchical integration (1969,

p. 352–3) — but I will state and evaluate the theory in terms of six fundamental theses:

(1) The different stages constitute *structural wholes*, which unite a variety of different responses to different moral situations, and reveal quantitative rather than qualitative differences in the mode of response.

(2) The sequence is *invariant*, always occurring in the same order and with no stages omitted, though individuals do not always develop at the same rate or reach the same final stage.

(3) The sequence is *culturally universal*, with the same stages occurring in the same order in every society.

(4) The sequence is *logically necessary*, in that the inner logic of moral concepts is such that the order could not, logically, be other than it is.

(5) The sequence represents an increasing *cognitive adequacy*, in that each new stage enables the individual to resolve and reconcile moral claims and conflicts arising at earlier stages.

(6) The stages also represent an increasing *moral adequacy* so that progression through the six stages to a final stage of universal moral principles provides an appropriate and justifiable goal for moral education.

Measurement and methodology

Some of these claims are so striking and contentious that the natural reaction is to question the evidence on which they are based, especially in view of the obvious dangers of accidental distortion, prejudice and pre-conception when assessing the moral reasoning of others. There is, for example, an amusing tendency to assume that all who discuss the theory must have reached the highest possible stage; and a rather more suspect tendency to downgrade the reasoning of those whose conduct or values we happen not to approve of. Thus one commentary (Brown and Herrnstein, 1975, p. 335) dismiss as 'surely' Stage One a family who systematically rob a parked car, when their behaviour shows clearly that they must be at least at Stage Two: they are not deterred by punishment or authority; they post a guard to maximize the satisfaction of their individual needs. Similarly Kohlberg himself presents a series of remarks of Adolf Eichmann (1969, p. 383) which were ranked 'with good inter-judge agreement' as exhibiting moral reasoning primarily at Stage One and only once rising as high as Stage Three, even though several remarks to the effect that he was only obeying orders seem transparently to involve a Stage Four respect for authority rather than a Stage One fear of authority (Kohlberg elsewhere assesses 'the traditional Army world' as Stage Four), and some might even be ranked at Stage Six. For example,

> Adolf Hitler may have been wrong all down the line, but one thing is beyond dispute: the man was able to work his way up from lance corporal in the German Army to Fuhrer of a people of almost eighty million. I never met him personally, but his success alone proves to me that I should subordinate myself to this man. He was somehow so supremely capable that people recognized him

could well be the expression of some neo-Nietzschean universal principle concerning which individuals are worthy of universal respect. It is surely only moral prejudice — morally admirable but scientifically reprehensible — which allows Kohlberg's researchers to rank it at Stage One (!).

But this and many cases like it are but informal examples on which nothing of importance turns. It is more serious when the 'criterion judgments' by which Kohlberg's preliminary and as yet unpublished scoring manual (Kohlberg *et al.*, 1977) measures an individual's stage of moral reasoning exhibits a similar value bias. Yet if someone defends a judge's decision to punish, in a situation where Kohlberg himself believes the breach of the law was justified, by arguing that 'social order will be undermined if individuals begin to decide for themselves what are "good" reasons to break the law', or that 'exceptions to punishing law-breakers can lead to totally subjective and inequitable decisions in administering punishment', he will be ranked at Stage Four, despite palpably appealing to social utility rather than mere respect for the established law. Even more significant is the systematic downgrading of emotion, so that appeals to love and sympathy, even to a universal love for all mankind, are ranked as Stage Three, which may well account for the sex-bias that some have suspected in Kohlberg's scoring (see Modgil and Modgil, 1976, pp. 98, 193).

Yet what is most puzzling is the apparent arbitrariness in assigning certain criterion judgments to the various stages. To take some scattered examples, it is hard to see why 'It is important to keep a promise because if you don't you'll lose your friends' should count as Stage Two rather than Stage Three, why 'If you break the law then you have to pay the penalty' should count as Stage Three rather than Stage Four, why 'The effect of jailing a good citizen can only be detrimental to society' should count as Stage Four rather than Stage Five, or why 'Human life is the highest value we have. It is sacred' should count as Stage Four rather than Stage Six. Nor is it obvious why 'If he doesn't try to help and she dies he won't be able to live with himself for the rest of his life' counts as Stage Three, when 'If you don't have the integrity to keep your word you will lose respect for yourself' counts as Stage Four.

Of course it is open to Kohlberg to reply that insofar as empirical evidence confirms that these judgments are characteristic of the stages to which they are assigned, it is our intuitive understanding or preliminary formulation of those stages which is at fault, not the ranking of the criterion judgments. But we then run the danger that in scoring subject's responses we are not measuring what we think we're measuring, that the development we are charting is not a sequence through those six stages of reasoning but something else instead. Indeed it is obvious that much of the difference between the criterion judgments for different stages has little to do with those stages as originally specified, but is rather a matter of complexity of reasoning, if not mere verbal fluency. For example, the Stage Three responses 'Human life is precious' or 'Life is more important than greed' seem to differ from the Stage Five 'Any human life has an intrinsic value of its own, regardless of whose it is' or 'The right to life transcends the right to property' only in lack of sophistication, not in the form of the reasoning involved.

But in what follows I shall put such doubts behind me. As befits a philosopher my concern is not with the factual accuracy of Kohlberg's findings, but with their interpretations and implications, supposing them to be correct. For although his six theses together constitute one of the most stimulating and interesting theories ever to emerge in the little-explored borderlands between philosophy and psychology, I am in the end extremely dubious about them all.

Structural unity

If the six stages of moral reasoning do incorporate distinct cognitive structures then individual styles of reasoning can be expected to form structural wholes, exhibiting a particular form or stage of thinking to the exclusion of other types: 'the implication is that various aspects of stage structures should appear as a consistent cluster of responses in development' (Kohlberg, 1973b, p. 181). This in turn will have two aspects: stage-consistency — an individual should tend to use same-stage reasoning in all his moral thinking; and stage-separation — there should be discernible discontinuities in his style of reasoning, as he moves from one stage to the other. Yet the available evidence seems to count against both.

As regards stage-consistency, it appears that no-one ever exhibits reasoning belonging solely at a single stage. Indeed only 12 per cent of Kohlberg's original subjects, and 29 per cent in a replication, had more than half their responses scored at their predominant stage, with the rest of their responses distributing in a normal curve over a number of stages (Kohlberg, 1969, p. 387; Weinreich, 1977b, p. 37). Kohlberg has recently claimed that 'almost all subjects manifest more than 50 per cent of their responses at a single stage, with the rest at adjacent stages' (1976, p. 47), but the evidence for this striking new finding has not yet been made available. Moreover subjects tend to be at different stages of reasoning on different topics: although they tend to reason in the same way about the same issues (life, law, property, etc.) in different contexts, they tend to reason differently about different issues even in the same context (Kohlberg *et al.*, 1977, I, p. 41—2).

As regards stage-separation, longitudinal studies do not seem to have produced any evidence of sudden shifts in an individual's style of thinking. Indeed it would be difficult for them to do so, since responses normally range across several stages at once, and in fact most individuals are assigned not to pure stages but to 'transitional' or 'consolidating' stages which involve a mixture of forms of reasoning (Kohlberg *et al.*, 1977, II, p. 22). Most striking of all, something like a third of the criterion judgments used to measure the stages are themselves classified as between stages. The fact that most individuals are between stages would seem to count against the hypothesis of separate cognitive structures; the suggestion that particular instances of reasoning themselves fall between stages seems frankly inconsistent with it.

Against this it may be urged that individuals can be expected to function at different stages simultaneously, as they gradually come to apply a new pattern of reasoning to new problem areas; or it may be maintained that some degree of stage mixture is necessary to provide for movement from stage to stage, a point to which we will return. But to argue that

> usage of various stages does not contradict the idea that development is to be described in terms of stages that meet the structured whole criterion. Stages are structured wholes not so much because they reflect a unitary form of individual functioning but because they refer to qualitatively different forms of thought. Consequently, the stages define 'ideal types' which are representative of forms of thought rather than people (Turiel, 1969, p. 115).

is precisely to concede that we are dealing not with particular cognitive structures which individuals actually possess, but with general patterns of thought which can be abstracted from particular cases.

The question at issue is whether the six stages represent fundamental changes in cognitive functioning, or merely identify recurrent phases in a continuously evolving process, like the stages in a game of chess or an electoral campaign. The evidence is unambiguously for a developmental continuum, not discrete structures (see Rest, 1976, p. 207ff.): it seems clear that we are dealing not with different cognitive structures, but with a gradual improvement and refinement of cognitive abilities, and no doubt other abilities as well.

Invariance

Kohlberg's original confident claims to have discovered an invariant sequence in the development of moral reasoning rested largely on cross-sectional studies which showed that the older children are, the higher their stage of reasoning tends to be. But strict invariance can be established only by following individuals through time, and a series of longitudinal studies have provided ample evidence of both stage-skipping and stage-regression (Kohlberg and Kramer, 1969; Blatt and Kohlberg, 1975; for a summary of independent studies see Modgil and Modgil, 1976, pp. 80, 86, 92, 121—2). Of course, stage-skipping followed by stage-regression can always be explained away as the result of scoring-error (Blatt and Kohlberg, 1975, p. 141), though equally it may be evidence that for some individuals the stage-sequence is reversed; and apparent stage-skipping may be due to movement through the intervening stage(s) in the interval between testings. But apparent regression from higher stages to lower ones is more difficult to deal with, and people in prisons and universities, in particular, reveal a disconcerting tendency to slip from Stage Four or Five to a sort of anarchic, every man his own morality at Stage Two.

At first Kohlberg seemed prepared to accept this and other regressions as an unfortunate fact of life consistent with the general principle that you can attain higher stages only by passing through lower ones (cf. the culturally-induced regression in the dream concept among the Atayal, 1969, p. 358). But he has since recognized that inasmuch as higher stages are held to be cognitively superior to lower, such regression should occur only in cases of cognitive disturbance or deterioration, and he has accordingly had to modify both the interpretation and the assessment of the stages, most notably by introducing an intervening transitional stage, moral relativism rather than moral egoism, dubbed Stage Four and a half. Apparent regression generally is to be understood as a destabilizing, a 'dedifferentiation and disorganization', of the existing stage prior to movement to a higher stage, rather than a return to earlier stages (see Turiel, 1974).

Accordingly Kohlberg's scoring system is being revised and his data reworked in an attempt to reconcile them with the invariance thesis. Indeed insofar as he explicitly defines the (construct) validity of his measures by the one criterion of whether they reveal an invariant sequence (1976, p. 46), it will be impossible for a valid Kohlbergian measure to refute the invariance thesis! Presumably it will be refuted only by the eventual failure ever to find a valid measure, so defined. In the meantime the verdict on the claim to have discovered an invariant sequence, as opposed to a general regularity, will have to be Not Proven, until such time as both the scoring system and the empirical data are more readily available for independent scrutiny.

Cultural universality

Clearly the danger of imposing our own moral values on the moral reasoning of others becomes that much greater when we turn to study communities other than our own. But I am concerned here not with Kohlberg's claim to have discovered the same sequence of development in widely differing communities, but with an important conclusion he wishes to draw from that finding: that it constitutes a refutation of ethical relativism, the doctrine that morality can vary from community to community, even from individual to individual. For although the points that Kohlberg makes against ethical relativism (1971a, p. 155–63, p. 174–80) are both interesting and important, his theory does not, as he believes, show that there is a universal morality underlying cultural differences. If anything it establishes exactly the opposite.

Notice first that Kohlberg is explicitly concerned with the form of moral reasoning, not its content: his six stages are specified in terms of the sort of consideration to which the individual appeals in making moral judgments, not the content of the particular moral judgments that he makes. Similarly Kohlberg's various lists of some 30 'universal aspects of morality' — notions of right or duty, values of life and truth, attitudes of love and respect — are also formulated entirely in general terms, leaving it open what particular rights or duties there might be, or what particular value life or truth might have. So the most that Kohlberg can claim to have shown is that moralities share a common form, not that they share a common content. And that hardly needs to be shown, for it is conceptually guaranteed: if there is to be any coherent sense in the notion of a morality at all, then there must be some feature or set of features or range of overlapping similarities in virtue of which different moralities with their differing contents can all of them qualify as moralities in the first place. This common form, being essential, will accordingly be universal: no morality can be without it, for without it it would not be a morality.

But on the other hand, if Kohlberg is right about the six stages of moral reasoning, it seems that moralities will differ in content, depending on the stage of reasoning which their adherents have reached. Indeed Kohlberg concedes that 'our findings lead us to conclude that there are differences in fundamental moral principles between individuals, differences in stage'. But what is universal, he goes on, is not the principles but the stages, though even this cannot be strictly accurate since, as he also says, 'our two highest stages are absent in pre-literature or semi-literate village cultures'. So the most that he can claim, as he does, is that Stage Six principles 'would in fact be universal to all mankind if the conditions for socio-moral development were optimal for all individuals in all cultures' (1971a, p. 177–8). But until we reach that happy day, moral principles will presumably differ from culture to culture, and from individual to individual, depending both on the level of reasoning and its particular content.

Moreover, even if everyone were to attain Stage Six it would not necessarily follow that they would share the same moral principles. A phrase like 'a universal set of moral principles held by men in various cultures, our Stage 6' (1971a, p. 178) is ambiguous between principles which are universal in the sense of being held by everyone, and principles which are universal in the sense of being regarded as universally binding. A principle might be shared by everyone without being regarded as universally binding: like 'Thou shalt not kill' it might admit of exceptions, such as self-defence and war, not to mention plants and animals. Alternatively a principle might be regarded as universally binding, without everyone accepting it: 'Abortion on social grounds is never justified' is meant to be universally binding, but is not universally held. Clearly, since not everyone reaches Stage Six, Stage Six principles will be universally held only in the sense that those who do hold them apply them universally, not in the sense that everyone holds them. Indeed it does not even follow that individuals arriving at Stage Six, and accordingly adopting principles that are meant to be universally binding, will always adopt the same principles: it seems perfectly possible for people to hold different, incompatible, sets of universally binding principles (Locke, forthcoming).

Logical necessity

Why does moral reasoning develop in this particular order? Why should the sequence be invariant, or culturally universal? Kohlberg's answer is that it does because it must: the sequence is logically necessary in that it 'represents a universal inner logical order of moral concepts . . . the order or differentiations could not logically be other than it is' (1971a, p. 187; 1971b, p. 48). Now if this were so there would, of course, be no need for the research data that Kohlberg and his associates have gathered so laboriously these two decades past: we would no more need psychology to demonstrate that individuals go through just these stages in just this order than we need sociology to demonstrate that bachelors are unmarried. But by the same token it would be a mistake to move too readily from an observed sequence to a claim of logical necessity.

Somewhat surprisingly Kohlberg nowhere attempts to elucidate the way in which the sequence of stages is logically necessary. Instead he illustrates the claim by a discussion of children's understanding of their dream experiences (1969, p. 356—61), a discussion which is an illuminating example of the dangers and difficulties that lie hidden here. Apparently the development of children's understanding of the nature and status of dreams follows the same order both among the American middle classes and among the Atayal, a Malaysian tribe living on Formosa, who believe that dreams are real experiences. This makes it unlikely that the development is a result of social learning, though that may account for the regression of the Atayal to earlier stages after the age of 11. Instead, Kohlberg suggests, we have here 'progressive differentiations of the subjective and objective which logically could not have had a different order'. Nevertheless it emerges that some 20 per cent of Kohlberg's American subjects, and an unstated number of Atayal, manage to diverge from this 'logically necessary' order. It is surprising enough when Kohlberg claims this 80 per cent fit as 'acceptable evidence for the existence of an invariant sequence' (1966, p. 11). But even a single exception would be enough to show that the sequence cannot be logically necessary.

What has gone wrong? The first thing to notice is that the question is not whether one concept logically presupposes another, in the sense that it could not apply unless the other did. Rather the question is whether *possession* of one concept logically presupposes possession of another, in the sense that someone who possessed the one concept must necessarily possess the other. The concept of cat, for example, logically presupposes that of animal, in that nothing could be a cat unless it were an animal. But possession of the concept of cat does not logically presuppose possession of the concept of animal: a child might possess the concept of cat without possessing that of animal, i.e. be able to differentiate cats from other things without being able to differentiate animals from other things. This, presumably, is why Kohlberg speaks of an order not of concepts but of differentiations, abilities to differentiate. Nevertheless, his argument moves fallaciously, and from false premises, from one point to the other:

It is apparent that the differentiation of the immaterial from the material presupposes the inside—outside distinction since all immaterial events are inside the body (but not vice versa). It is also apparent that internality (location of the dream experience inside the body) presupposes unreality (recognition that the dream is not a real object) since a real object could hardly be in the body. The observed sequence, then, is one which corresponds to the inner logic of the concept of reality itself (1969, p. 359).

But for a start 'immaterial' does not presuppose 'internal', nor does 'internal' presuppose 'unreal': rainbows and shadows are immaterial items occurring outside the body, and pains — not to mention hearts and livers — are internal items which are nonetheless real. And even if this were so, it still would not follow that the ability to differentiate material from immaterial presupposes the ability to differentiate internal from external, or that it in turn presupposes the ability to differentiate real from unreal. That is to make precisely the mistake of passing from one concept's presupposing another, to the possession of one concept presupposing possession of the other.

With this for a warning we can return to the claim that the sequential development of moral reasoning is logically necessary, in that 'each new basic differentiation made at each stage logically depends upon the differentiation before it' (1971a, p. 187). This can hardly mean, as Alston seems to suggest (1971, p. 274–5), that because differentiation of A from B presupposes possession of the concept of A, the concept of A must therefore be possessed before the concept of B: it is equally possible that the concept of B is possessed first, or that both are acquired together. Rather, the argument seems to be that if distinguishing A from B requires the ability to distinguish B from C, but not vice versa, the differentiation of B from C must therefore precede the differentiation of A from B. So what needs to be shown, in order to establish that Stage Four reasoning, for example, logically must come before Stage Five, is that the ability to distinguish what is required by society at large from what is acceptable to particular individuals (i.e. the ability to distinguish Stage Four considerations from Stage Three) must come before the ability to distinguish what is actually for the good of society from what is required by society (i.e. the ability to distinguish Stage Five considerations from Stage Four).

Now for all I know it may indeed be that while some people can distinguish between what is acceptable to others and what is required by society, but not between what is required by society and what is for the good of society, everyone who can make the latter distinction can also make the former. But this empirical fact, supposing it to be a fact, is a long way from establishing any logical necessity. To do that we would have to show that it is inconceivable, even self-contradictory, to suggest that someone should be able to distinguish between what is good for society and what is required by society, without being able to distinguish between what society requires and what particular individuals approve of. It is, perhaps, unlikely, but I can see no reason to think it impossible, much less logically impossible. Nor, so far as I can see, does Kohlberg make any attempt to argue that it is.

It seems likely, therefore, that when Kohlberg speaks of 'logical necessity' he understands the expression in something other than its standard philosophical sense. What he has in mind, I suspect, is that the sequence of stages is psychologically necessary, thanks to the nature of the concepts involved. For the stages are, he claims, hierarchical integrations, in that each stage incorporates, modifies and extends, the distinctions and discriminations made at previous stages. This will not make the sequence logically necessary — it remains conceivable that people might begin with a complete set of discriminations and then gradually lose them, though we would then be dealing with a phenomenon of human regression rather than human development — but there is an obvious sense in which each later stage presupposes the earlier ones.

Even so, when Kohlberg comes to give details of this hierarchical integration (1971a, p. 195–213) he in fact argues merely that at each stage the subject makes differentiations which he previously did not. But this shows only that the different stages involve different differentiations; it does not show that those differentiations have to occur in this particular order. There is nothing to rule out the possibility that new differentiations might be acquired in a different order, thus producing a different hierarchy of integrations, nor even the possibility that individuals might skip several stages, acquiring several new differentiations simultaneously rather than successively. This particular hierarchical sequence may be the one which we actually find, but no reason has yet been given to conclude that it is necessary, either logically or psychologically.

When Kohlberg speaks of 'hierarchical integration', however, he sometimes seems to have in mind a separate thesis, the thesis of increasing cognitive adequacy (e.g. 1969, p. 353). And although this too does not show that the sequence is in any way necessary, it does offer a different, more satisfactory and more informative, account of why the stages should occur in the particular order that they do.

Cognitive adequacy

This thesis forms the core of the stage-structural theory. It offers an explanation not only of why the sequence of stages is as it is, but of why people move from stage to stage at all; it provides support both for the thesis of distinct cognitive structures, and for the thesis of increasing moral adequacy; and without it, or the thesis of logical necessity, there is no reason to expect the sequence to be either invariant or culturally universal. It is a thesis sometimes obscured by Piagetian jargon: the increasing differentiation and integration of the higher stages ensures the maintenance of an equilibrium, defined as a balance of assimilation and accommodation, between organism and environment. More simply, the claim is that the different stages of reasoning provide increasingly more satisfactory ways of dealing with the moral environment. At any particular stage the individual will have a certain way of handling his moral experience, the claims and conflicts which the society of other people imposes on him. But new experiences, more complex social interactions, or a more sophisticated perception of what those interactions involve, may generate claims and conflicts which he cannot handle in the usual way, and he will be forced to develop a more sophisticated and effective method of handling his moral environment, and so move to a higher stage of moral reasoning. Thus the greater cognitive adequacy of the higher stages explains not only why moral reasoning develops in the order that it does, but why it develops at all.

There are two sources of empirical evidence for this thesis of increasing cognitive adequacy. The first is that people tend to prefer higher stage reasoning to lower, even to the extent of preferring reasoning at stages above their own (Turiel, 1969, p. 102–5; Rest, 1973; Rest, 1976, p. 202). But since they tend to prefer reasoning at stages higher than those they properly understand (of those with a consistent preference 83 per cent preferred Stage Six, a stage which hardly anyone either uses or understands (Rest, 1973, p. 103–4)!), the explanation cannot be that they perceive those higher stages as cognitively superior. Nor, for the same reason, do people actually use the stages which they most prefer. Indeed it is not even the case that they prefer to use the highest stage which they do understand: subjects can ' "thoroughly" comprehend' and show a substantial (at least 20 per cent) use of a higher stage, and yet not use it in the majority of their judgments (Rest, 1973, p. 105). The thesis of increasing cognitive adequacy would predict that (except in transitional cases) stage-usage would peak at the highest stage understood. In fact it follows a normal distribution around the most favoured stage, which shows precisely that people tend not to use the highest stage of which they are capable.

The second source of evidence comes from intervention studies. If people move from stage to stage to resolve conflicts in their moral thinking, then cognitive conflict ought to be the major source of stage change, and a number of studies (e.g. Turiel, 1969; Blatt and Kohlberg, 1975) have shown that moral discussions and exposure to conflicting reasoning can promote movement from stage to stage. But the exact form of this cognitive conflict remains unanalysed. Turiel has suggested that a mixture of stages is necessary to produce cognitive conflict in the individual, and therefore that a mixture of stages is needed to produce movement from stage to stage

(Turiel, 1969, p. 129–30). Yet the theory seems clearly to require that the conflicts be within the individual's own stage of reasoning, and that he move up a stage in order to escape them. Conflicts between one stage and the next would be expected to inhibit stage-movement rather than promoting it, confirming the individual to his own level of reasoning. Even more curiously, Turiel attempted to assess the cognitive–conflict model by exposing subjects to conflicting arguments at the stage above their own, although any evidence that this produced movement to that stage would actually be evidence *against* the thesis that individuals move from stage to stage in order to escape cognitive conflict!

No doubt this is why Turiel found that subjects exposed to conflicting reasoning at the next higher stage showed less movement upwards than subjects exposed to the next lower stage showed movement downwards (this was obscured by the fact that the control group also showed more tendency to move down than up: only by comparing the experimental group with the control group, rather than with each other, could Turiel claim that the +1 treatment was more effective than the −1 (Turiel 1966)). But the fact that subjects exposed to conflicting arguments at a lower stage did move downwards, instead of being confirmed in their higher stage, is itself further evidence against the theory. The obvious explanation, rather, is some form of modelling or social learning.

The most striking support for the theory would be if individuals exposed to conflicting arguments at their own stage moved to a higher stage even without exposure to higher stage reasoning, but evidence for this is, so far, indefinite and conflicting (Keasey, 1973; Kohlberg, 1976, p. 52). More effective, presumably, would be exposure to conflicting arguments at the existing stage, combined with exposure to higher stage reasoning which actually resolved the conflicts thus produced. But the difficulty here is that, apart from a purely philosophical argument for the supreme adequacy of Stage Six, which I will discuss elsewhere (Locke, forthcoming), there is as yet no indication of exactly how higher stage reasoning does enable the individual to resolve and reconcile moral claims and conflicts arising at lower stages! Thus when Kohlberg examines in detail the differences between the stages (1971a, p. 195–213) he shows only that the lower stages involve an inadequate conception of the nature and scope of morality: the Stage Two moral reasoner cannot properly understand the Golden Rule, the Stage Three reasoner is unable to make the step from personal relationships to society as a whole, and so on. So the higher stages represent a heightened moral awareness, a growing moral sophistication, and to that extent might well be said to involve a cognitive advance on lower stages. Yet as Kohlberg himself seems well aware (1971a, p. 182) an improvement in an individual's understanding of morality and moral reasoning is not at all the same thing as an increased ability to handle the moral environment or solve moral problems. Indeed it might prove the very reverse: the more sophisticated our moral understanding, the more difficult it may be to resolve conflicting moral claims. Certainly someone resting secure in the ethical egoism of Stage Two may find it easier to decide what to do, than someone agonizing over the individual rights and social utilities of Stage Five.

It seems to be the Piagetian jargon of differentiation and integration, and the associated ambiguity of 'hierarchical integration', which conceals this crucial gap in the argument, the gap between moral sophistication and cognitive superiority. As Kohlberg introduces this terminology, increasing differentiation and integration seem to be the means by which assimilation and accommodation occur, and equilibrium is maintained in the face of new and discordant experiences. But as he actually uses it, they have nothing to do with assimilation, accomodation and equilibrium at all. Sometimes it refers to the way in which the discriminations made at one stage allegedly presuppose those made at others, but more frequently 'increasing differentiation and integration' turns out, once again, to involve a greater understanding of the nature of morality and moral discourse. For example, Kohlberg tells us that by differentiation he means the differentiation of moral values and judgments from other values and judgments, or the differentiation of 'ought' from 'is', which crucially involves a recognition of prescriptivity and universalizability as the distinctive formal features of moral judgments (1971a, p. 184–5, p. 214–8; 1971b, p. 46). Or again,

discussing rights in particular, differentiation involves distinguishing rights from other considerations, while integration involves the recognition that rights and duties are correlative, that if I
have rights others will have corresponding duties, and vice versa (1973, p. 637–8). These claims
are extremely contentious — there has been much discussion as to whether moral judgments are
universalizable in any useful sense, or whether rights and duties are correlative — but the important point here is that none of this provides any support for, or throws any light on, the claim
that higher stages of moral reasoning are better equipped to resolve and reconcile moral claims
and conflicts. If there is cognitive development here, it consists solely in an improved understanding of the nature of morality and of moral language.

Moral adequacy

Inasmuch as he believes that the one depends on the other Kohlberg himself tends to run together the thesis of cognitive adequacy and the thesis of moral adequacy. But the two must be
distinguished if we are properly to evaluate his claim to derive moral 'ought's' from the facts of
human development. Of course Kohlberg does not claim that the later stages are morally superior
just because they are later, much less that prescriptive moral judgments can somehow be reduced
to descriptive psychological ones. But he does believe that once we recognize why one form of
moral reasoning is developmentally later than another we will also see that it is morally superior.
For if one form of reasoning is psychologically more adequate it will be morally preferable as well,
and whatever else moral education might be concerned with it should at least be concerned with
the development of moral reasoning, with bringing as many people as possible as quickly as possible to as high a stage of moral reasoning as possible. In this way, Kohlberg suggests, we can
'commit the Naturalistic Fallacy and get away with it'; we can, after all, move from an 'is' to an
'ought' (1971a).

We need to be clear, however, exactly what this alleged moral superiority consists in. Kohlberg's own justification for moral development as the goal of moral education appears to be that
it will eventually lead everyone to adopt the same basic set of universal principles:

> The problem of offering a non-indoctrinative education which is based on ethical and
> epistemological principles is partially resolved by a conception that these principles represent
> developmentally advanced or mature stages of reasoning, judgment and action. Because there
> are culturally universal stages or sequences in moral development . . . stimulation of the
> child's development to the next stage in a natural direction is equivalent to the long range
> goal of teaching ethical principles (Kohlberg and Mayer, 1972, p. 475).

But there is no reason to expect that moral development will result in any particular set of principles. The argument against ethical relativism showed only that moralities share a common form,
common because it is essential to their qualifying as moralities in the first place, not that they
share, or even will ideally come to share, some common content. There is a further argument,
which I criticize elsewhere (Locke, forthcoming), that Stage Six reasoning requires certain absolute
principles of justice, equality and respect for persons. But even if that argument is accepted, it
shows only that Stage Six reasoning is superior to others: it does nothing to show that Stage Four
reasoning is morally preferable to Stage Three, or Stage Three to Stage Two. And in a world where
so very few ever get beyond Stage Four it would, to put it mildly, be optimistic to base moral
education on the ultimate superiority of Stage Six!

Alternatively this moral superiority might be held to consist in the greater cognitive adequacy
of the higher stages of moral reasoning. For if the higher stages did provide the individual with
more satisfactory ways of handling his moral environment and solving his moral problems, that
would suffice to show that they are also morally preferable. But we failed to find any evidence
of this: there was only the claim that the higher stages are more advanced, not in their ability to
solve moral problems, but in their understanding of the nature and scope of morality itself. And
just as there is no reason to think that more sophisticated moral reasoning is better equipped to

solve moral problems, so there is no reason to think it morally preferable. The Stage Three moral reasoner, relying on the approval of his fellows, may well be preferable to the Stage Four advocate of law and order, or even the Stage Five social utilitarian (Weinreich, 1977a, p. 13—14).

Finally, the moral superiority of the higher stages might be held to consist in the fact that it is more likely to lead to moral conduct. Since this presupposes some judgment as to which conduct is moral and which not, it cannot support the claim to derive an 'ought' from an 'is', nor the claim to have found a non-indoctrinative or value-fair basis for moral education, but it would support the claim that higher stage reasoning is morally preferable to lower stage reasoning. But the evidence here is sketchy and conflicting. Some studies have found a correlation between moral reasoning and moral conduct (see Broughton, 1978, p. 87), but another found that subjects who moved up a stage were more likely to cheat than those who did not, though perhaps for extraneous reasons (Blatt and Kohlberg 1975, p. 149), while the oft-cited study of the Berkeley Free Speech Movement showed that Stage Two reasoners were more likely to do the 'right' thing than either Stage Threes or Stage Fours (Haan *et al.*, 1968). Broughton has replied to this that acting for Stage Two reasons is not the same behaviour, morally speaking, as acting for Stage Five or Six reasons (1978, p. 87). But if acting morally is identified with acting on Stage Five or Six reasons the argument that higher stage reasoning produces more moral action becomes circular — and, moreover, moral action becomes extremely rare, given the paucity of Stage Five and Six reasoners!

There is a fundamental problem here. As Kohlberg is well aware in rejecting any behavioural test for the validity of his measurement of moral reasoning, there need be no direct connection between moral thought and moral action, though the difference between the two is regularly obscured by ambiguous talk of 'moral development' and 'moral stages'. Hence there is no theoretical guarantee that improvement in one will lead to an improvement in the other. Indeed the cynical will expect the very reverse: that the more sophisticated our moral thinking, the more sophistical it is liable to be; that given man's enormous capacity for hypocrisy, self-deception and special pleading, the more adept he will be at finding some way of avoiding those claims and duties which happen not to suit him. Tolstoy, for one, thought that a simple moral consciousness is more likely to be pure and holy than a cerebral one, and who is to say he was wrong?

What we need is some account of the connection, or lack of it, between moral thought and action, perhaps the most difficult and most interesting problem in this area. It would be unfair to complain that Kohlberg has not provided one (for an interesting discussion and some useful suggestions, see Brown and Herrnstein, 1975, Ch. 6), but it is appropriate to point out that there are special difficulties for the stage-structural account. For on the one hand there are six stages of moral reasoning but, reduced to its simplest, only two courses of conduct available in any concrete situation: either to do it, or not. Hence the same piece of behaviour might be the result of reasoning at quite different stages. On the other hand the various stages are identified by the form of reasoning, not its content, so reasoning at the same stage might result in quite different decisions about what to do (this point is missed by Brown and Herrnstein, despite their earlier recognition that the different stages can provide reasons both pro and con any particular course of action). So even if we had some general theory of the relationship between moral thought and moral action, there would still be no direct connection between an individual's stage of moral reasoning and his actual conduct: the form of reasoning will not determine even what he thinks he ought to do, much less whether he will actually do it.

This difficulty could be avoided if we were prepared to identify the stages of moral reasoning by content as well as by form, or to allow that the form of reasoning can, in part, determine its content. Indeed the ways in which the stages were originally specified, together with the evidence of some correlation between stage of reasoning and actual conduct, would seem to suggest that there is some such interaction between form and content. Among other advantages, identifying stages by content as well as by form would force us to lay bare the hidden value assumptions which underly the stage-structural theory. But although this seems to me one of the most promising ways in which the theory might be developed and modified, Kohlberg himself has found it necessary to put more, rather than less, emphasis on the form/content distinction, from the need to discover an invariant sequence in the development of moral reasoning (1976, p. 43; 1977, I, p. 33—5).

Postscript

We have examined the six fundamental theses of the stage-structural theory of moral reasoning, and found reason to doubt them all. Nevertheless I would not want to minimize the importance of Kohlberg's contributions to the study of moral development. What is mistaken, I believe, is not his original insights but the immense weight of theory he wishes to place upon them. Perhaps those insights would never have occurred without the theory to inspire them, but the danger now is that the theory is allowed to dominate the empirical data, rather than allowing the data to determine a theory as, for example, in the need to make the distinction between form and content more rigid than ever, in the hope of discovering the desired invariance. In particular it seems a mistake to insist on a theory of distinct cognitive structures when the evidence is both for a developmental continuum and for a less rigidly cognitive explanation of moral thinking.

The late Imre Lakatos proposed a distinction between what he termed 'progressive' and 'degenerating' research programmes in science, and there are unfortunate signs that the Kohlbergian programme is in danger of falling into the latter category. Any theory is liable to empirical refutation — indeed Lakatos says that 'all theories are born refuted' (1968, p. 163)! — but the crucial question is how these refutations are handled, whether by adjustments to the theory which increase its content and explanatory power, or by adjustments which serve only to eliminate the anomaly:

> If we put forward a theory to resolve a contradiction between a previous theory and a counter-example in such a way that the new theory, instead of offering a — content-increasing — scientific *explanation*, only offers a — content-decreasing — linguistic *reinterpretation*, the contradiction is resolved in a merely semantical, unscientific way (1968, p. 164).

One clear example of just such a linguistic reinterpretation is in the 'elimination' of the regression to Stage Two found among college students, by reclassifying it as Stage Four and a half. It is no answer to point out that Four and a half does differ significantly from the original Stage Two: this will have to be true of any regression if, as is claimed, earlier stages are not retained in their original form, but are restructured, reintegrated, at higher stages. Other examples of manoeuvres which serve merely to protect the theory are the revision of the scoring method (in Lakatos's terms, a modification of the interpretative, as opposed to the explanatory, theory) in the hope of preserving the invariance thesis; the explanation of stage structures as ideal types which, properly understood, conflicts with the claim that they are distinct cognitive structures; and the claim that actions performed for Stage Two reasons or Stage Six reasons are not the same behaviour, which makes it impossible even to discuss the relationship between some particular form of behaviour and a particular stage of reasoning.

Kohlberg has done us the inestimable service of identifying certain fundamental and evolving patterns of moral reasoning. But what those patterns represent, how they are to be explained and analysed, ought to be a discovery, not an assumption, of future research. What the study of moral development needs at this stage of its own development is not the elaboration of an extremely specific and highly speculative theory, be it stage-structural, cognitive-developmental, or any other sort, but a wide-ranging approach to the facts which, for the moment, leaves their theoretical explanation open. But, to repeat, without the pioneering work of Lawrence Kohlberg, we would not even have the facts to explain.

References

ALSTON, W.P. (1971). 'Comments on Kohlberg's "From is to ought" '. In: MISCHEL, T. (Ed), *Cognitive Development and Epistemology*. New York: Academic Press, 269—84.

BLATT, M. and KOHLBERG, L. (1975). 'The effects of classroom discussion upon children's level of moral judgment', *J. Moral Educ.*, 4, 129—61.

BROUGHTON, J. (1978). 'The cognitive—developmental approach to morality: a reply to Kurtines and Greif., *J. Moral Educ.*, 7, 81--96.

BROWN, R. and HERRNSTEIN, R.J. (1975). *Psychology*. New York: Little, Brown and Co.

HAAN, N., SMITH, M.B. and BLOCK. J. (1968). 'Moral reasoning of young adults: political—social behaviour, family background, and personality correlates', *J. Personal. Soc. Psychol.*, 10, 183—201.

KEASEY, C.B. (1973). 'Experimentally induced change in moral opinions and reasoning', *J. Personal. Soc. Psychol.*, 26, 30—38.

KOHLBERG, L. (1966). 'Cognitive stages and preschool education', *Human Devel.*, 9, 5—17.

KOHLBERG, L. (1969). 'Stage and sequence: the cognitive—developmental approach to socialisation.' In: GOSLIN, D.A. (Ed), *Handbook of Socialisation Theory and Research*. Chicago: Rand McNally, 347—480.

KOHLBERG, L. (1971a). 'From is to ought: how to commit the Naturalistic Fallacy and get away with it in the study of moral development.' In: MISCHEL, T. (Ed), *Cognitive Development and Epistemology*. New York: Academic Press, 151—235.

KOHLBERG, L. (1971b). 'Stages of moral development as a basis for moral education.' In: BECK, C.M., CRITTENDEN, B.S. and SULLIVAN, E.V. (Eds), *Moral Education: Interdisciplinary Approaches*. Toronto: University of Toronto Press, 23—92.

KOHLBERG, L. (1973a). 'The claim to moral adequacy of a highest stage of moral judgment'. *J. Philos.*, 70, 630—46.

KOHLBERG, L. (1973b). 'Continuities in childhood and adult moral development revisited.' In: BALTES, P.B. and SCHAIE, K.W. (Eds), *Lifespan Developmental Psychology: Personality and Socialisation*. New York: Academic Press, 180—204.

KOHLBERG, L. (1976). 'Moral stages and moralization: the cognitive—developmental approach.' In: LICKONA, T. (Ed), *Moral Development and Behaviour: Theory, Research and Social Issues*. New York: Holt, Rinehart and Winston, 31—53.

KOHLBERG, L., COLBY, A., GIBBS, J., SPEICHER-DUBIN, B. and POWER, C. (1977). Assessing moral stages: a manual. Unpublished. Harvard University.

KOHLBERG, L. and KRAMER, R. (1969). 'Continuities and discontinuities in childhood and adult moral development', *Human Devel.*, 12, 93—120.

KOHLBERG, L. and MAYER, R. (1972). 'Development as the aim of education', *Havard Educ. Rev.*, 42, 449—96.

LAKATOS, I. (1968). 'Criticism and the methodology of scientific research programmes', *Proceedings of the Aristotelian Society*, 69, 149—86.

LOCKE. D. (Forthcoming). 'The illusion of Stage 6', *Journal of Moral Education*, 9.

MODGIL, S. and MODGIL, C. (1976). *Piagetian Research: Compilation and Commentary*, Vol. 6 Windsor: NFER Publishing Company.

REST, J.R. (1973). 'Patterns of preference and comprehension in moral judgment', *J. Personal.*, 41, 86—109.

REST, J.R. (1976). 'New approaches in the assessment of moral judgment.' In: LICKONA, T. (Ed), *Moral Development and Behaviour: Theory, Research and Social Issues*. New York: Holt, Rinehart and Winston, 198—218.

REST, J.R., TURIEL, E. and KOHLBERG, L. (1969). 'Relations between level of moral judgment and preference and comprehension of the moral judgment of others', *J. Personal.*, 37, 225—52.

TURIEL, E. (1966). 'An Experimental test of the Sequentiality of developmental stages in the child's moral judgments', *J. Personal. Soc. Psychol.*, 3, 611—18.

TURIEL, E. (1969). 'Developmental processes in the child's moral thinking.' In: MUSSEN. P., LANGER, J. and COVINGTON, M. (Eds), *Trends and Issues in Developmental Psychology*. New York: Holt, Rinehart and Winston, 92—133.

TURIEL, E. (1974). 'Conflict and transition in adolescent moral development', *Child Devel.*, 45, 14—29.

WEINREICH, H. (1977a). 'Some questions for Professor Kohlberg'. Unpublished paper. Presented at conference on Moral Education and Moral Development, University of Leicester.

WEINREICH, H. (1977b). 'Some consequences of replicating Kohlberg's original moral development study on a British sample'. *J. Moral Educ.*, 7, 1, 32—9.

The Majesty and Mystery of Kohlberg's Stage 6

Bill Puka

The deepest secrets in Kohlberg's vision of moral development lie hidden at Stage 6, the highest stage of moral reasoning in his system. Here rest the great soul and Achilles heel of Kohlberg's overall approach. As Kohlberg sees it, the soul of the stage sequence is reciprocal justice, universal egalitarian justice. It threads each stage to the next and ties a firm knot at the top, but for many critics and supporters (including myself) Kohlberg's justice focus is a flaw in theoretic character. A more balanced combination of fair and kindly rationales in stage structure sustain development better. The very notion of tying a knot at the end of development, at Stage 6, seems arbitrary. Certainly there is no empirical basis for it in Kohlberg's system.

Unlike some critics, however, I believe that the more kindly and embracing spirit of respect in Kohlberg's stages can be saved while exorcising "demon" justice. Nevertheless, this salvaging process must begin at the roots of Stage 6 difficulties and move forward step by step. Stage 6 cannot adequately recant and reaffirm itself piecemeal, as had been Kohlberg's way most recently (Kohlberg, Levine, and Hewer, 1983).

I begin this process by recounting the extraordinary claims Kohlberg has made for Stage 6, and then take a somewhat lighthearted stroll through the "empirical caveats" of Stage 6, harkening to "the call of care" that depicts the deficits of justice relative to benevolence. These deficits are pictured at a deep logical level, underlying the largely symptomatic complaints made by critics such as Gilligan (1982). I contrast the moralities of individual respect and group concern along Kohlberg's stage sequence, observing that Stage 6 alone fails to integrate them fairly. In a subsequent section, I consider problems with Kohlberg's equilibration model, with its implication that Stage 6 justice can solve all moral problems in principle. Cases of individual merit and responsibility are posed that liberal-egalitarian principles at Stage 6 cannot accommodate. Finally, I challenge Kohlberg's claim that rights and duties are fully symmetrical at Stage 6 and that this symmetry accounts for problem-solving adequacy. (Some loose ends of Stage 6 are exposed.) Kohlberg's correlativity criterion of adequacy itself is linked to the improbabilities of Stage 6 decision-making. The essay ends with suggestions for overcoming the difficulties posed.

This panoply of problems, I believe, requires that we first prune Stage 6 greatly, then eventually weed it out of the stage sequence entirely. Stage 6 seems neither a natural nor most adequate stage of moral reasoning. Nor does it seem even a promising candidate for these positions. The need for Stage 6 even as a hypothetical end point in Kohlberg's system has never been demonstrated. In fact, it has never been argued. There is little reason to believe that the stage sequence cannot stand much as it does now when its Stage 6 supports are pulled away.

I believe that Kohlberg's empirical accomplishments can withstand the expulsion of almost all his controversial claims in ethics, metaethics, and structuralism. His stages would be much unburdened by banishing them. (See Puka, 1990.) Of course, there may be some reason to speculate about whether there are higher stages of development yet to be uncovered. There are surely good reasons to consider what forms of reasoning would improve on naturally developing ones by extrapolating current stages beyond Stage 5. However, such metatheoretic speculations should not be included directly in a social scientific theory of cognitive development. Neither should they be its guiding psychological or philosophical light.

Setting the Stage

Clearly, for Kohlberg, Stage 6 is not simply the stage after Stage 5. Neither is it merely the most elevated stage in his sequence, as regal as this position may be. Accounts of Stage 6 powers are far more extravagant.

On the psychological side, Stage 6 is portrayed as the most adequate moral stage possible. It is *maximally* integrated and differentiated, reversible and equilibrated. This means that every key moral concept is distinguished from its quasi-moral correlates. (Prudential or conventional "oughts" are distinguished from moral ones.) Each concept also bears a fully symmetrical relationship to its reciprocal—for each duty there is a right and all rights and duties are equal. Moreover, Stage 6 principles of justice are universal, covering the entire range of fundamental moral concepts and able to solve all morally relevant problems in principle. Any morally relevant stage structure that was more inclusive, equilibrated, integrated, or differentiated would transcend the moral domain. It would encompass cosmological and ethical questions about the meaning and ultimate value of life. Thus it could not oversee Stage 6 on its own turf.

Kohlberg maintains, moreover, that not a single stage can be defined or rated without using a prior definition of Stage 6. It is through Stage 6 structure that we identify the moral constituents and adequacy of any stage as opposed to its role-taking or pragmatic acuity. Since Stage 6 is defined by the concept of justice, all stages are forms of justice: moral stages are *justice* stages. One stage is judged higher than another insofar as it approaches the particular sort of justice Stage 6 prefers—general, abstract, formal, principled, egalitarian, and rights-oriented. Kohlberg even credits his use of Stage 6 presumptions in research design with his uncovering stage structures in reality (Kohlberg, 1984, p. 305).

On the philosophical side, the role of Stage 6 is even more grandiose. It is pictured as the logical core of the ultimately valid moral theory. By conceptual inspection, Kohlberg concludes that moral philosophic theories simply elaborate stage structures. They merely refine the inherent rationales of moral common sense. Since Stage 6 is as far as moral logic can go without waxing cosmic—without questioning the meaning of life—the best moral theories can only vary its theme.

In addition, since Stage 6 is structured by a certain brand of justice, its claim to ultimate validity decides many age-old philosophical disputes. Stage 6 validates moral views that focus on right and wield the logic of right/wrong; it undermines views that look to the good and direct us to approach it on a continuum of worse to better. Stage 6 favors universal principles over pragmatic rules, or situational habits, or particular intuitions. It even favors Kantian respect for persons—equal regard for individual autonomy—over utilitarian concern for group welfare. Kohlberg has gone so far as to claim that the most sophisticated forms of utilitarianism, chief rivals to justice for the moral philosophic crown, are not even on a cognitive par. (Their inner core and fundamental foundation are a whole stage lower, a whole stage less cognitively mature than egalitarian justice.)

Stage 6 in Instructive Caricature

As Kohlberg sees it, then, our natural evolution in moral awareness leads "inexorably" toward Stage 6, morality's crowning glory. Each ethic, spontaneously fashioned to face life's dilemmas, is but a closer approximation of the ultimate ethic Stage 6 affords. Each approximation of Stage 6 is more fit to reality itself, Stage 6 most of all. Looking over the invariant sequence of stages with their unitary end-in-view, it is as if nature itself had written Stage 6 into our hearts, into our first tacit promises and shared rituals.

Yet despite this royal mandate from nature and our steadfast progress along the stage sequence, one after another of us mysteriously fails to realize our ordained, Stage 6 destiny. So Kohlberg's data show. Even the most sensitive of us barely scale the summits of Stage 5. Most of us lie marooned in the moral conventionalism of Stage 4, despite generous servings of morally stimulating social life in highly complex democracies. This is the great mystery of Stage 6 universalism. It is a paradox born of the occasionally transcendent relation Stage 6 bears to social science. For while Stage 6 is the only stage of moral reasoning that is truly adequate and principled, that does justice to justice, it is also the only stage that really does not exist.

Kohlberg has been quite frank about this reality (or lack of it) recently (Kohlberg, 1984, p. 240). Stage 6 is not included in the Colby-Kohlberg scoring system (Colby, Kohlberg, and collaborators, 1987) because, admittedly, it does not have adequate data behind it to be termed an "empirical stage." (An empirical stage theory should contain only empirical stages.)

Yet as with most magical things, Stage 6 seems able to pop in and out of reality. Under the stage scheme presented by Kohlberg for over twenty years, Stage 6 was vividly present. Supporting data and samples of Stage 6 reasoning appeared in all classic Kohlberg essays. Then, as new and empirically improved stage descriptions appeared, transforming Stages 1–5, Stage 6 slipped off, disappeared altogether. All stages supposedly rest on Stage 6; yet when it vanished, none noticed. Still, even as Stage 6 became a nonissue for Kohlberg's new science, it reappeared again as a hypothetical stage. As such, it defined the sequence conceptually, awaiting empirical confirmation in future. Moreover, after Kohlberg reanalyzed the most evolved and structurally distinct portions of current Stage 5 reasoning, the dim profile of Stage 6 again became visible. At least Kohlberg claimed to see it. Thus the search has resumed for the rest of its noble features.

Given this envisioned place in nature, it is no wonder that Stage 6 has a majestic aura about it. Given its unpredictable reluctance to take its place, or to stay in its place, it is no wonder that Stage 6 mystifies. No doubt it is the combination of these qualities that makes Stage 6 so unbelievable for many.

Rumblings Offstage: Empirical Caveats

The empirical status of Stage 6 always should have been in question since the data for Stage 6 have always been thin and anomalous, even when they supposedly existed. Kohlberg has never offered readers more than a few anecdotal responses from a handful of Stage 6 cases to illustrate its existence (Kohlberg, 1981, pp. 160–166, 205–214, 217–218). None at all were cited from the longitudinal sample that gave birth to his other stages. Rather, citations came from the unprobed writings of moral exemplars and philosophers and from the ruminations of conscientious objectors. Often Stage 6 responses were credited explicitly to "Philosopher 3" in Kohlberg's writings. The views of these especially reflective or committed individuals are likely to be influenced by special training and insight. They are least likely to be naturally developing and generalizable, the stuff of universal Piagetian stages.

Kohlberg's latest sample of Stage 6—the case of Joan, cited in this volume—is at least as puzzling as past cases.[1] Joan's way of thinking about interpersonal problems suggests that she is extremely reflective and especially experienced in this area. She is *personally* mature and insightful in this sense. However, Kohlberg provides no grounds at all for evaluating the *structure* of her moral reasoning at the principled level, much less at Stage 6. This is very disconcerting given the thrust of Kohlberg's theoretical renaissance over the last decade. Here differentiating style and structure, personal maturity and cognitive adequacy, has been central to redefining Kohlberg's stages. The new rigor of his qualitative data has been achieved by moving away from an intuitive sense of maturity in reasoning to an explicitly structural analysis. In replying to critics, Kohlberg makes much of this distinction between his "hard" structural stages and "soft-stage" reasoning found by researchers such as Fowler, Perry, or Gilligan (Kohlberg, 1984, pp. 236–249). Moreover, when discussing the religious and cosmological thinking characteristic of development in later life, Kohlberg drives a sharp wedge between the obvious wisdom often shown in such thinking and the surprisingly low structure of its moral stage.

Why then is Kohlberg so impressed with what Joan has to say in her moral interview? Why should *we* be? In fact, it is precisely the degree of Joan's reflectiveness and experience that should give us pause in evaluating her natural stage. Whatever spontaneous form her moral reasoning once took, it now seems to have been reworked as she thought through issues in a concentrated, self-conscious way. The so-called dialogical approach Joan takes in conflict resolution bears a striking resemblance to the interpersonal styles of political and personal-growth movements popular among American college students in recent decades. Of course, only research would show whether this resemblance is coincidental—whether Joan is an interpersonal ideologue and expert in some sense. But without such research, and given Joan's response profile, Kohlberg cannot assume a naturally arising universal structure; in particular, he cannot assume a dialogical structure such as that posited by Habermas (see Kohlberg, 1984, ch. 4).

Indeed, Joan makes explicit reference to Immanuel Kant's philosophical ethics. She not only studied this ethical theory but appears to have integrated it into her style of moral reasoning. This can be seen by her use of commonsense terms like "dignity" or "integrity" in the technical sense formulated by Kant. Normally "dignity" is used to mean an elevated quality of demeanor or a quality of life sufficiently free of "animal needs." "Integrity" normally refers to a virtue akin to honesty, or to the intactness of one's physical or psychological systems. Joan uses these terms as near synonyms, however, to refer to the Kantian moral self as a self-determined or autonomous unity. She also makes explicit reference to "special obligations" and "moral claims" in this connection, using these terms in the technical sense current among philosophers. The same tendencies are found in "Philosopher 3."

Kohlberg's a priori definition of Stage 6 and its use in designing research and theory raises some question about how empirically based the stages are. This suspicion is exacerbated when Kohlberg clings to Stage 6 and its "big brother" role in defining stages even as the data desert. The structural approach to moral judgment is somewhat interpretive or reconstructive by nature, even as it is descriptive in intent. It does not merely recount and organize the general rationales we ourselves identify and consciously use in making moral judgments. Rather it makes explicit the implicit logic embodied in the way we coordinate our piecemeal reasons, beliefs, and rules of thumb. In so doing, structuralism aims to describe. That is, it aims to go below the surface to show the organization of our intellect, whereby our reasoning processes unfold as they do. Structuralists claim that stages are empirical phenomena, a claim based on the capacity of formalization to provide a more profoundly accurate description of what the data show.

At the same time, this "description" is a posit, a stab at the best explanations for what causes moral judgments to take certain shapes. To be credible, the structuralist must be vigilant in assuring that empirical findings are not predetermined by conceptual assumptions. Kohlberg's approach, however, reverses the role of form and fact here, explicitly using Stage 6 as a formal hypothesis in search of formal, structural data. Yet if form is to be read into the data as it is found, where is the protection here against the hypothesis itself providing it? Surely such a biasing outcome is likely, despite Kohlberg's so-called "bootstrapping" reconstruction of his method.[2]

Ideologically Speaking

Many observers are struck by the ideological tone of Kohlberg's claims for the centrality in moral development of justice and equal rights. They are bothered especially by the alleged cross-cultural supremacy of liberal justice. This Stage 6 claim still haunts the stages even as Stage 6 disappears from Kohlberg's scoring system. So long as the structure of Stage 6 remains in the wings, helping to guide research and theory, it may be criticized. The announcement of its return, in the present volume, can only rekindle ideological criticism even though critics must now speak mysteriously (I shall) as if Stage 6 both existed and did not exist.

As just noted, Kohlberg explicitly designed his research dilemmas to pull for just resolutions. These dilemmas pose conflicting individual claims of rights and duty. Moreover, Kohlberg himself claims to interpret responses to these dilemmas via a particular intellectual tradition in the West: the liberal, social contract tradition in its peculiarly Kantian form. Notably, Kohlberg never has cited a putative case of Stage 6 reasoning that occurs outside of western industrialized nations or the direct influence of their educational curricula. (Mohandas Gandhi's alleged Stage 6 reasoning was preceded by rigorous training in British conceptions of justice and equality at law school in London.) These sorts of observations have spawned two main criticisms. In the first, Stage 6 justice is portrayed as the favored ideology of particular socioeconomic systems and social historical conditions. Its rights are the tools of western individualism (of capitalist entrepreneurialism per-

Morality and Cognitive Development

haps) and the bane of more communal, joint-responsibility traditions found in eastern or "third world" cultures. (Obviously there are many more and less reasonable variations on this theme; see Simpson, 1974; Sullivan, 1977.) In the second criticism, Stage 6 reflects particular sorts of social perspectives, roles, and relations, certain types of needs and ego-developmental processes related to gender and status. It is the typical logic of the demanding, alienated male, primarily, in a contentious and sexist society (Gilligan, 1982).

The first sort of criticism has not caught on, perhaps because its dialectical approach to social science seems more ideologically bent than Kohlberg's liberalism. Such views normally have two major problems. The dramatic correlations they draw between certain practices or interests in a society and the logic of its favored moral concepts are highly selective and incomplete. Moreover, the road they travel from correlation to causal dependency is breathtakingly short. (For example, since rights appear to occur most in western culture and sometimes to dramatically serve individualism, therefore they are the tools of western individualism and cannot be otherwise grounded.)

Since Kohlberg (1984, ch. 4) has recounted and responded to prominent versions of this critique, I will forego further detail here. However, if we take this sort of critique in moderate doses, as a view that apportions burdens of proofs, its challenge to Kohlberg cannot be denied. A system of moral reasoning that supposedly is universal must explain its failures to appear. This is especially so when its schedule of appearances breaks down along cultural or socioeconomic lines. There are plausible excuses for cognitive underdevelopment in individual cases. However, they do not seem applicable on so vast a social scale. Consider two.

On Kohlberg's equilibration model, cognitive structure adapts progressively to universals of social structure. We can imagine historical circumstances in which the basic structure of society was still in evolution or had been broken down due to war or natural catastrophe. Here even full adaptation to actual structure would not be full adaptation to social structure in a universal sense. Many third-world and eastern cultures, however, have been evolving in their way far longer than western ones have. Their basic social form is surely in place. Thus this first sort of dodge will not do. At the same time, extreme political repression, authoritarian customs, and religious ideologies can stunt development. They can keep members of certain cultures from the role-taking and critical thinking opportunities they need to view society from "all" points of view. But surely in some nonwestern societies, many members of privileged classes are free to think flexibly and critically. Surely they do not spend most of their time being oppressed or oppressing others, even ideologically. Such comparable conditions from the East to the West are ripe for Stage 6 liberal justice as Kohlberg describes it. Why did it not seem to appear in the East when it seemed to appear in the West? The second dodge falters also.

Ideological charges become compelling here if only because it would be so difficult for Kohlberg to explain them away. Imagine the scrupulous comparisons that would have to be made between the structures of different societies, and between societies in different cultures, to show their fundamental similarities. Only in this way can we depict social universals. Imagine the scrupulous distinctions that would be needed between morally essential social structures and culturally contingent ones. These distinctions would be all the more difficult and dangerous to make if we tried a third dodge, that of assuming that cultural universals are still evolving and so happen to arise in the complex secondary institutions of "western-style" nation states. These are the institutions that only Stage 6, supposedly, can negotiate adequately.

An objective theoretical justification of Stage 6 would help in this process. However, it could not stand its own ground against ideological charges unless it could demonstrate its own independence from cultural bias. By contrast, most justice theorists such as Rawls base their conceptions on so-called intuitions or considered judgments. These consist of moral beliefs that are commonly agreed upon in a society and built into the logic or ordinary moral discourse there. What better way is there to play into ideological hands?

Note again, however, that mere correlations between cultural mores and liberal justice are not the key to Stage 6 troubles

here. The burdens of proof become unbearable when we combine: (1) the ultimacy of Kohlberg's adequacy claims for Stage
6, (2) the "thinness" of cross-cultural data, (3) the lack of standard "arrested development" explanations for Stage 6 no-
shows, and (4) Kohlberg's own explicit association of Stage 6
reasoning with highly specific intellectual traditions in western
philosophy. Normally claims for the universal supremacy of
any commonsense system of belief would need overwhelming
cross-cultural evidence. Instead, Kohlberg seemingly offers us
none whatsoever.

Even though the first type of ideological criticism failed to
attract a crowd, the second has created a sensation under Gilligan's banner of response ethics and relational care. In some
circles, Gilligan's observations are believed to spell the demise
of Kohlberg's stage theory. (Again, I believe this general sort
of response is understandable given Kohlberg's attempt to define the whole stage sequence as relative to Stage 6 justice.) A
large audience in and out of psychology seems to feel, at least,
that Gilligan's levels of care seriously challenge the ethic of
justice and Kohlberg's ultimacy claims for Stage 6.

With other critics, Gilligan notes that in most interpersonal
situations of daily life, judgments of justice seem judgmental
(in the negative sense) and often out of place. They have a
formality and abstractness about them, a legalistic adherence
to general principle even in the face of individual pain or
frustration. As such they are often unresponsive to the lively
dynamics of situational conflict or opportunity, to the differing
aspirations and vulnerabilities of particular individuals. Worse
yet, they willingly leave us hurt and resentful once morality
has spoken, so long as the calculus of rights and equality has
been served. Once we get our fair share, any further complaints are our own personal problem. In deciding that these
lingering burdens of justice are not "legitimate claims," just
judgment can often seem hegemonic and downright punitive.

Justice tends to overlook special loyalties stemming from
"special" ties. (In fact it calls our natural, most intimate ties
"special," and the institutional ties of institutional rights "natural.") Rather than orienting to people in relation, and in need
of each other, justice presumes and sanctions the autonomy of

each individual above all. It then depicts the morally salient aspects of these relationships as expressions of autonomy, as implicit contracts or agreements. At the least, this orientation is one-sided.

Moreover, this sort of slant can be attributed to various biases that infect Kohlberg's research methodology and theoretical reconstruction of findings. Among these are male gender bias in Kohlberg's original research sample and the use of abstract, hypothetical issues in moral judgment interviews. These issues pose potentially violent conflicts between individual interests that pull for regularized and explicit principles of conflict resolution. Such an individualistic slant at the methodological level seemingly mirrors the western cultural bias seen by some critics in Kohlberg's approach. It is reflected further in Kohlberg's theoretical assumption that morality, by nature, is a form of conflict resolution among individuals; it is a form of "unnatural" cooperative relationship through contractual rules. This slant also seems to correlate with the characteristic male sense of identity and self-other relation (uncovered by Gilligan's "self-description" interview) that conceives society as relatively isolated individuals in potential conflict. In this respect, Kohlberg's emphasis at the higher stages on "rights to noninterference" also extends apparent gender bias to the theoretical level.

In discussing concrete (and nonconflictual) moral issues with respondents, Gilligan finds an alternative moral theme in common sense reasoning, a theme that overcomes these moral deficits of justice. This theme orients to persons in a highly caring, empathetic, and personalized way. It attends and responds to their particular needs in particular contexts. It recognizes that their networks of interpersonal relationships are the most morally salient features of these contexts. The care theme seeks to engage others in flexible and cooperative struggle with moral dilemmas. It seeks to nurture interpersonal bonds, avoid hurt, and pursue what is "best for all concerned." These moral aims stem from a female sense of society as webs of intimate relationship, rather than as sets of strangers in isolation and conflict. Developmentally, the "different voice" of care passes through a level of self-protection (self-absorption) and of conventional altruism (self-abnegation) on the way to a fair and responsible balancing of self-care with care for others.

A Voice Too Soon

Gilligan's approach holds great promise, if only because it stands within two venerable traditions. One is the tradition of critical theory, which exposes and excoriates the competitive and possessive egoism lurking behind individual rights (Marx, 1843/1972; MacPherson, 1962). The other is the even longer benevolence tradition, which extends from the virtue conceptions of Aristotle, the Confucians, and (Christian) agapeism, through utilitarianism and the "self-actualization" conceptions of Fromm and Maslow.

Yet to bring out the promise of Gilligan's critical and constructive positions requires a great deal more theoretical analysis than she provides. It also requires supporting empirical research of a seemingly different sort than has been offered so far (e.g., Langdale, 1983; Johnston, 1985; Attanucci, 1984). Gilligan (1977) originally offered her "different voice" conception as an "interpretive hypothesis" and has reiterated this characterization more recently (1986). After ten years of first being heard, the "different voice" remains a hypothesis as far as moral development is concerned. Virtually no theoretical work has been done on Gilligan's justice critique, nor on the alternative theme of care as a developmental track. For example, Gilligan has never extended her piecemeal criticisms of Kohlberg's hypothetical dilemmas or forced-choice interview format with a rigorous and thoroughgoing analysis of Kohlberg's research methodology. Nor has Gilligan offered a standard review of the literature substantiating bias claims in Kohlberg research. To the contrary, Gilligan (1986) has failed to offer any serious response to Walker's (1984) review of Kohlberg studies, challenging charges of gender bias. Gilligan's recent writings (e.g., Gilligan and Wiggans, 1987) speculate broadly on care and its developmental origins. Smatterings of data from various areas of research are cited in these narratives. Yet such writings do not engage in the standard data-based form of theory-building where theoretical claims are derived exclusively and parsimoniously from the empirical results of case studies. (Gilligan seems to be aiming at a different sort of account, one that has its own sorts of assets.)

While empirical research has gone forward on care "focus" or "orientation," virtually no research has been reported in support of care *levels*, i.e., care *development*. Yet only care levels have clear relevance to Kohlberg's developmental stage theory. (Kohlberg has explicated themes of justice, and of other moral concepts, that do not appear to develop. These are explicitly left out of his stage descriptions. Themes of "moral honor" that have been prominent in "macho" cultures are a notable example.) As yet, no standardized or reliable scoring system for care levels has been developed. Lyons's (1983) system for scoring care does not code for levels. Thus it is not surprising that virtually no developmental theory of care has arisen. Moreover, Walker (Walker, de Vries, and Trevethan, 1987) has been unable to replicate the sort of findings that allegedly support a theory of care focus or orientation.

The urgent need for a comparative, moral philosophic analysis of care and justice themes also remains unfulfilled. Only through such an account can one demonstrate the "equal credibility" or "adequacy" of care relative to justice. Only through such an account can Gilligan show that Kohlberg's emphasis on justice constitutes bias. After all, if justice is a highly adequate moral theme, or at least more adequate than care, then it should be emphasized along the stage sequence. It should be especially prominent at higher stages.

As matters now stand, Gilligan's original critique of justice might be said to observe certain symptoms without diagnosing the disease. Importantly, this critique does not offer any distinction between the uses and abuses of justice reasoning in moral judgment. Moreover, it does not correlate care and justice at any developmental level to evaluate their comparative pros and cons. Is justice reasoning, with its legalistic Stage 4 rules or its individualistic Stage 5 rights, clearly less adequate than the pervasive selfishness of care at Level 1, or the utterly demeaning and disempowering self-abnegation of care at Level 2? (See Gilligan, 1982, chs. 3 and 4.) How is it determined that care at its mature Level 3 is more helpful or benevolent overall than Stage 5 justice with its utilitarian orientation and "ideal or harmony serving" orientation? (See Kohlberg, 1984, pp. 406, 631–536.)

In addition, Gilligan's original account fails to draw a clear relation between the "justice focus" and "justice orientation" she observes and criticizes, and "justice reasoning" at any Kohlberg stage. Indeed, Gilligan basically ignores Kohlberg's fundamental distinction between holistic, structural systems of cognitive-moral reasoning and cognitive orientations, styles, and types. The latter phenomena are explicitly recognized and excluded from Kohlberg's developmental stage theory. (In Kohlberg's theory, justice does not occur as a global orientation that exists outside, and in addition to, the different justice structures of particular stages.)

This apparent omission compounds with a far more serious one in Gilligan's account. This is the failure to address Kohlberg's crucial distinction between a type morality and a general one (Kohlberg, 1981, ch. 4). A type morality or moral theme expresses the sensibilities and interests of certain (broad or narrow) types of people or groups. It supports certain favored values and serves circumscribed purposes. The theme Gilligan terms "justice focus" is characterized as a type morality that favors the characteristic outlooks and interests of males. As such it promotes the values of individualism, free competition, and the like. The theme Gilligan terms "care focus" is characterized as a type morality as well; it reflects the characteristic female sense of relatedness to others and promotes values of intimacy, security, and so on, as Gilligan notes.

A general morality, by contrast, is explicitly designed to recognize and accommodate the range of type moralities or circumscribed moral themes. It is designed to render them compatible where they diverge. Kohlberg's higher-stage notion of "egalitarian justice" or "unconditional respect" is a general morality in this sense, designed to foster general cooperation amid various forms of divergence. And it is perfectly possible for "justice focus" and "care focus" to function compatibly with "justice reasoning" in Kohlberg's sense. They can function at different levels, serving different ends. Gilligan's account does not consider this option.

According to Gilligan, Kohlberg's justice theme is biased because it favors the characteristic outlooks and values of males over those of females or relational types. This could mean: (1) Kohlberg's justice theme is a type morality that is biased only when it is represented as a general morality; (2) Kohlberg's justice theme not only represents an overgeneralized type morality but is a biased and inadequate morality per se, malfunctionally rigid, impersonal, and overly individualistic; (3) Kohlberg's justice theme is a general morality that places undue emphasis on certain outlooks and values that happen to correlate with a certain type morality. This emphasis causes justice to be limited and skewed in the performance of its functions. This correlation also makes justice partisan and unfair. It prevents justice from accommodating divergent type moralities evenhandedly.

By contrast, adequate and mature moral judgment, according to Gilligan, combines or balances the equally credible themes of care and justice (Gilligan, 1982, p. 100).

Yet if (1) is the problem, then it is unclear how adding care to justice would help. Two type moralities do not add up to a general morality. And this is so even if characteristic male types and female types exhausted human types (or moral types), which they do not. (There are uncharacteristic types, for instance gay and lesbian types, bisexual and androgenous types.) Typing also occurs in the values and functions and purposes of type moralities, as well as in the features of those who typically hold and pursue them. Indeed, type moralities are, by nature, primarily in-group moralities. The aim of fostering cooperation amid diversity often is secondary to them. Thorny issues of cooperation occur primarily in regard to a dissident fringe who are pressured, tolerated, or cast out. General moralities are melting-pot moralities by nature. Dealing with divergence is a central and ongoing task in which every type has a comparable say.

If (2) is the problem, then we must wonder why care would aspire to be "comparably credible" to justice. What does the "different voice" announce, after all: that justice is not the only highly problematic theme in morality? That there is an alternative, caring way to think poorly?

If (3) is the problem, then Gilligan must show why this is so by comparing option (3) with a further option that goes as follows: (4) Kohlberg's justice theme places proper emphasis on issues of equal respect, individual rights, principles of fairness, and the like. This is because these issues serve the purposes of a general morality best, given the existence and strength of divergent type moralities and human interests. While key features of this general theme correlate with some features of a particular type morality (justice focus), this does not render justice reasoning partisan or inadequate. The functions and purposes of this type morality may be more inherently like those of a proper general morality than existing alternatives. (Males may be well socialized to occupy positions of broad social authority.) Alternatively, these type features may be more inadvertently like general ones, since the social and conceptual mechanisms that serve individual egoism, self-protection, and competition may be serviceable also for broad and varied forms of social cooperation. After all, many forms of human cooperation occur indirectly, at a great distance. They occur among varied individuals and (ethnic) groups with little knowledge of each other and a history of mistrust and prejudice. Here self-concern and protection may make great sense. (We may not like this, and may want to change it, but it is a recalcitrant fact.)

It is easy to scoff at option (4) as a not-so-subtle expression of patriarchy, or as merely liberal (rather than radical) feminism. But "scoffing," like "claiming," is not theoretical analysis. It is notable also, in this context, that the gentle and highly personal ethic of caring has exerted powerful political force, historically, in the hands of social and religious reformers. In the same way, a certain economic system seemingly spawned by individual greed and ruling-class interest has typically fostered general economic efficiency, enhanced human productivity, and the spreading of literacy, opportunity, and even culture among the general populace. Justice may not be well-intentioned enough, but it may serve best. Only exhaustive theoretical analysis will tell. And only such analysis can dispel the mystery of how moral themes portrayed as conflicting with one another can simply be balanced or combined in one's

mature judgment. How does one amiably combine the punitiveness and aloof judgmentalism of justice with the dialogical
struggle and "not hurting" of care? (See Puka [in press-a; in
press-b; in press-c] for detailed discussions of Gilligan's "different voice" hypothesis in relation to Kohlberg's theory.)

Given how much is missing from Gilligan's original account
of moral development—as one would expect of a *hypothesis*—it
is remarkable that the Kohlberg-Gilligan debate is still taken
seriously. It is surprising that Kohlberg (in Kohlberg, Levine,
and Hewer, 1983) replied to Gilligan's critical remarks in such
detail, making concessions to care that might seem unwarranted. Perhaps this testifies to the obvious weakness of the
Stage 6 ideal, as well as the obvious need for "something more"
alongside "mere" justice. But it is a sad commentary on the
field otherwise, as I think Gilligan would agree. For she has
not even attempted to fill in the gaps I have cited here: she
has not sought to create a theoretical alternative to Kohlberg's
stage theory or to promote a Kohlberg-Gilligan debate.

Nevertheless, Gilligan's original account has merit and potential. To empower it, and to render it more clearly relevant
to Kohlberg's, we must go deeper into the heart of justice and
care. The critique of justice should address the core structure
and defining logic of Kohlberg's moral stage reasoning. (Alternatively, it must present an elaborate theoretical account of
why logic or a structural emphasis is inherently inadequate
[i.e., less adequate than something else] in moral cognition.)
Gilligan's alternative theme of care also should show its alternative structure or logic. (Alternatively, it must demonstrate
equally credible "ways of knowing" at the levels of moral perception, dialogue, response, and the like. Again, this must be
accomplished explicitly, in a thoroughgoing way, to transform
hypothesis into theory.)

For example, the account of care might note that we (west-
erners?) tend to identify primarily with our individuality, with
our unique personality features, talents, motivations, and
friendships with others. By contrast, some of us (non-western-
ers?) tend to identify our selves with groups, with the family,
tribe, or clan. Caring attends to both. Yet justice supposedly
respects us as persons by respecting our essential personhood,

Morality and Cognitive Development

our shared and equal personhood. This is the part of us that does not distinguish us from others as unique personalities, but does distinguish us from groups and relationships. (Essential moral personhood resides in psychological capacities primarily.) Moreover, justice advocates claim that to do otherwise would mean injustice, inequality, tyranny. Supporters of care may wonder, then, if justice truly can respect us as persons, either as the unique persons we now are or as those we will be when it respects us fairly and equally. Correlatively, can justice truly be fair when it respects us as us? Here justice may seem morally inadequate as a matter of principle, its own principle. It seems troubled not merely by being cold and callous, not caring enough, but by a basic contradiction in its own moral logic. In this context, *caring* seems the best way to *respect* persons.

These are the sorts of questions and problems that Kohlberg's theory cannot ignore. They not only attend and show responsiveness to Kohlberg's basic moral assumptions in their own terms, but they base their alternative suggestions on those very assumptions. I believe that this sort of account can be developed for benevolence. Let us consider how to begin.

The Call of Care

As with the previous ideological critique, we can pare back the extent of Gilligan's critical claims and focus on apportioning Kohlberg's burden of proof. Any strengths of care (or a like ethic) that justice overlooks or overrides can be used philosophically to question the ultimacy of Stage 6. Ironically, the empirical likelihood and moral theoretic adequacy of Stage 6 justice is challenged most strongly when we combine the best insights of caring critics with the caring components of Kohlberg's own (empirical) Stages 3–5.

Starting with Stage 3, each stage in Kohlberg's sequence has two main components. One deals with respect and toleration for individual life and liberty and the other with group stability and welfare. These concerns are most integrated at Stage 3, where rights are accorded relative to our loyalty to the group and our empathy toward others. By Stage 5, the orientations of individual respect and concern for group welfare are highly differentiated into two orientations, namely individual rights and social utilitarianism. Even here, the respect accorded individuals is based on their accepting the principle of mutually beneficial cooperation.

At Stage 6, however, a radical transformation occurs. The Stage 5 rights orientation is carried forward in refurbished components of new and more universal rights, but individual rights nonetheless. However, the social utilitarian orientation is recast in the logic of positive rights or rights of aid. This transformation signifies that our concern for the welfare of others and our valuing of relations or the group are now assimilated under the logic of respect—respect for people's free pursuit of welfare and cooperation. Group welfare is only to have moral impact (in defining obligations) where it is freely pursued by individuals who may form groups or relations, but need not do so. Group welfare counts only to the degree that individuals actually count it by choosing it, not in the sense that it morally *should* be chosen or pursued.

The problems caused by this Stage 6 anomaly are twofold. Cognitively, Stage 6 seemingly reverses structural trends preceding it in the stage sequence. It integrates respect and concern *at the expense of* higher-stage differentiation between them. This structural distortion engenders a second problem of moral reductionism. Stage 6 logic assumes that morally valid portions of concern for the *quality* of *experience* and for *relations* or *groups* can be captured by respect for individual autonomy. It assumes that the logic of promoting good on a continuum can be captured by the disjunctive, all-or-none logic of just/ unjust, permissible/intolerable. But it clearly cannot. (This is why the deontology-teleology debate between Kantians and utilitarians still rages, despite Kohlberg's claim to have resolved it.) Concern and respect are different moral attitudes. They are directed at very different features of persons and in very different ways. My concern for your welfare should cause me sometimes to enhance it, and sometimes to pursue your best interests over your actual desires. It also should lead me to weigh the value of relationships and the welfare of groups more heavily than the value of individuals; considerations of welfare and good are aggregative. Concern leads me to do what is *best* for *all* concerned. Empathy pulls toward the greatest amount of suffering. By contrast, my respect for your autonomy applies to you primarily as an individual. Our (free) wills are metaphysically individualized even if they can be influenced strongly by others or used cooperatively to create joint decisions. To respect your choice as an individual means not to infringe on it, or to help you fend off infringements (natural or otherwise). All additional aid toward you merely broadens your options—the scope and force of your will—or increases your welfare. It does not accord you autonomy as a person. I need not violate your rights to hurt you, nor do you have a right that I attend to you, befriend you, or cooperate in your pursuits.

Considerations of respect and concern, rights and utility may often accompany and complement each other. Yet they orient differently even when they overlap, and they must sometimes conflict. Indeed, if rights and utility did not conflict, we would not need rights, and Kohlberg would not set himself up as a deontologist. A major function of individual rights in deontological justice is to protect the individual against overwhelming social interest.

Gilligan's critique of justice actually focuses on negative features of this particular antisocial role that rights play. As noted, she couches them in attitudinal terms—callousness and unresponsiveness, formality and impersonality, legalism and punitiveness. Yet these deficiencies of an equal-rights orientation can be tied to the very logic of rights and hence to the central strengths of Stage 6 justice. Regardless of how compassionately or flexibly one attempts to apply rights or justice, basic features of care must be ruled out on principle. This is required by the tolerationist implications of respect and the all-or-none, liberty-versus-coercion logic of rights as conveyers of toleration. Thus in order to guarantee individual autonomy, rights must be indifferent to how autonomy is used, to what values our freedoms embody or pursue. In putting rights first (as Kantian deontologists do) we therefore provide a protected haven for any value pursuits or forms of life that do not violate others' rights. Through equal protection we place morality in the impossible position of being indifferent on principle to the selfish greed of one and the altruism of others. After all, you cannot grant me a (near-absolute) right of way *as a person* and then constrain me to go a certain way. At the least you cannot interfere with whatever way I choose to go—even by competing—so long as I do not tread on you or (at Stage 6) neglect your basic needs.

Worse yet, since rights are correlative to duties at Stage 6, my duties of justice themselves constrain you from intervening for good. They prohibit you from benefiting others by utilizing *some* of my *unneeded* goods or "pressing" (obliging) me into (some) service. In fact, the morality of equal rights requires you to stand by while I willfully or whimsically destroy resources—burn my property, blow my brains out—regardless of what good my life or resources could do others. It would give my claim to destroy goods the right of way over your claim to benefit others or society with them. Even highest-stage liberal justice prefers, as a matter of course, any activity that can be performed self-sufficiently (without violating rights) over any pursuit that requires cooperation but cannot attract it sufficiently. Moral quality cannot matter.

At this level of ultimate duties, we can see why the justice/care dichotomy is not one of obligation versus supererogation (i.e., going beyond). It is not one of rights and duties versus virtues and ideals. Morally misconceived duties of respect threaten and restrict our liberty and responsibility to care as surely as threats or wrongful coercion do—at least for the morally conscientious.

I do not mean to imply that we should force people to relate to each other or cooperate toward benevolent ends. (Still, in some instances where needed infringements are few and slight and the ends at stake are great and pervasive, such coercion may be preferable.) Rather I am claiming that basic moral differences between certain uses of autonomy should be accorded basic moral place. So should the good-enhancing rationales we should adopt toward them. The point is not to override rights and respect with care and welfare. Rather it is to formulate moral concepts, orientations, and obligations that build in the proper relation of respect and concern in the first place. Stage 6 individual rights do not. Utilitarian maximization rules may not either. But at least a rule-utilitarian, rights principle can give rights stronger standing (utility) when they are directed to good ends. It illustrates that equal respect need not imply liberty toward the good in a way rights cannot countervene.

In principle, Stage 6 justice is indifferent among these values. In effect, it favors selfish possibilities over joint ones and restricts our basic liberty in defense of perverse value priorities. Therefore, it is logically and morally deficient—deficient on principle and to the core. Stage 6 justice is also silent on our responsibilities to *increase* the good, and to nurture virtue in ourselves and others. (These are not matters of "*more* just" or "*un*just" behavior.) Thus it is morally negligent as well. Structurally, Stage 6 is distortive and reductionistic, ineptly differentiated and integrated.

Bad Prospects

Thus far we have considered four major problems with Stage 6.

1. Apparent data for Stage 6 always have been too thin and confounded to support a natural and highest moral stage.

2. New alleged cases of Stage 6 reasoning are not structurally defined by Kohlberg. The case of Joan, like previous cases, seems confounded by special training and reflection.

3. Kohlberg's use of such cases to support Stage 6, and the continued use of stage 6 in defining the stage sequence, raises suspicions that his stages are somewhat unempirical and biased.

4. Burdens of proof have not been borne regarding the empirical universality and scientific neutrality of Stage 6, that seem at odds with its apparent biases toward liberal ideology, patriarchy, individualism, and rights. Similar burdens of proof have not been borne in justifying the universalizability of justice and its capacity to practice what it preaches on respect for persons.

Such problems in Stage 6 not only impugn its reputed existence and adequacy at present, but also reduce its prospects of arising in the future. If the stage sequence were to proceed beyond Stage 5, it would not move toward Kohlberg's universal rights. At least such an outcome is unlikely if later stages properly integrate previous structural differentiations of respect and concern. Additional considerations not only strengthen this doubt, but increase the unlikelihood that any brand of Stage 6 would ever arise—just, caring, or otherwise.

The first consideration is that Stage 5, as a high-level, post-conventional structure, is extremely well equilibrated. It is well adapted to its environment and internally stable. Thus it is not likely to be unsettled by any new dilemmas that the basic universals of our social environment can devise. Stage 5 is especially unlikely to yield to a liberal-egalitarian form of Stage 6 justice since it already has an equal-rights orientation. Its rule-utilitarian orientation also has an egalitarian focus. (The rule for this orientation is to protect equal rights as preferred means to utilitarian social good.) Importantly, Kohlberg's own research methods seem based on these beliefs and doubts. He found it necessary to devise special, sophisticated dilemmas to uncover differences in higher-stage reasoning, differences between the egalitarianism of Stages 5 and 6. His lifeboat and Korea dilemmas pull for either Stage 6 egalitarian reasoning based on equal rights alone, or Stage 5 egalitarian reasoning that includes social utilities. (Stage 5 considers the value of our actions and abilities in calculating our equal claims; Stage 6 committedly ignores these values.)

For such differences in our egalitarian reasoning to develop naturally in the first place—for some of us to forsake Stage 5 equality for Stage 6—our basic social environment would have to exert even more refined and subtle pulls on our cognition than these special dilemmas do. And these pulls would have to take the same direction. Universals of our environment would have to grip our consciousness with vivid but subtle forms of inegalitarianism. Yet in this venture they would not have the luxury of morally focused hypotheticals. Nor could they use Kohlberg's unrelenting probe questions to keep our moral perception and deliberation to the point. Rather our social world would have to catch and hold our egalitarian attention with whatever real-life dilemmas it could muster and press forward amid the complexity and confusion that make up daily life. Its press would have to be so strong or prolonged—it would have to make so much trouble for Stage 5 egalitarianism—as to pull this preeminently integrated structure apart. Moreover, the damage would have to take a form that only Stage 6 might remedy.

Suppose this disintegration were to happen. Then the ultimately arduous process of constructing an even more evolved and reintegrated Stage 6 replacement would have to begin. Is there really enough social support among the bare universals of our complex and often unjust world to support this process? Consider that moral development through Stage 4 had a range of existing social conventions to adapt to, to help guide structural construction. Even Stage 5 had certain constitutional ideologies to help guide its evolution—Bills of Rights from many nations, always balanced with principles "providing for the common good." But where in the world can Stage 6 look for constructive help to carve out its fully universal rights and fully egalitarian principles? Where would it look for the even more balanced mix of universal benevolence and justice that it needs? There seems no model for Stage 6 to grapple with, no model to suggest the feasibility of such a seemingly utopian and speculative cognitive enterprise.

As things stand, not even the concerted (often hypothetical) reasoning of philosophers has been able to solve the problems that Stage 5 faces in trying to balance individual rights and social welfare. Moral theory has been locked in this controversy for a full century. Most important, its contestants see much of their task as theoretical: is a utilitarian reduction of rights to social welfare or a Kantian reduction of social utility to equal rights more theoretically elegant? Each of these reductionist "Stage 6" structures can *simulate* the workings and results of the other if it is rigged to do so, but not in a refined, tidy, or honest way. While either version may improve on Stage 5, as current Stage 6 logic may, it is not clear that these improvements are required by everyday problem-solving. Yet only in this way, according to Kohlberg's view, could any Stage 6 naturally arise.

Stage 6 as Moral Philosophy

Let us conclude our consideration of Stage 6 with a closer look at its moral philosophy. Kohlberg's case for the ultimate moral adequacy of Stage 6 combines structural with moral philosophic considerations. The ultimate structural adequacy of Stage 6 rests ultimately on two features of the equilibration model. The first is adaptivity, the capacity of Stage 6 to solve all moral problems in principle. The second is reciprocity or reversibility, the complete correlativity of individual rights and duties at Stage 6. Presumably it is the functional struggle to solve problems, to deal with society effectively, that leads to the complete internal symmetry of Stage 6. Likewise, this internal symmetry affords Stage 6 its functional effectiveness. Such an interrelation of functional and logical virtues affords the sort of stability and efficiency, as well as the consistency, completeness, and elegance that an adequate prescriptive theory requires.

Unfortunately, Kohlberg has never really shown how well Stage 6 solves the broad range of moral problems. Rather, he has offered alleged Stage 6 solutions to a dozen or so unusual problems, most involving life and death. Only one study reported by Kohlberg even purports to show that Stage 6 subjects agree on solutions to moral problems, a crucial feature of *ultimate* problem-solving adequacy. In this study (Erdynast, 1973) only two moral problems are confronted by only a handful of Stage 6 respondents. Moreover, it is now clear from Kohlberg's standard scoring manual that these respondents should have been scored at Stages 4 or 5.

Kohlberg derives the moral adequacy of Stage 6 from a philosophical evaluation of reputed Stage 6 problem-solving. Stage 6 judgments meet criteria of adequacy set by Kantian, formalistic, deontological justice theorists. Moreover, Kohlberg claims, these criteria are the best around. My previous criticisms of justice logic, framed from the perspective of benevolence, were meant to cast doubt on this claim. Even more primal doubt can be cast on Stage 6 by *using* this claim, by arguing from Kantian assumptions in just the way Kohlberg does against care, to fault liberal egalitarianism itself. Consider the following.

The recent Rawls-Nozick debate within Kantian justice theory revived perennial questions of whether individual merit or equality should determine just due or property rights (Rawls, 1971; Nozick, 1974). Which basis for rights truly respects our persons? Kohlberg tries to skirt this dispute by claiming that Stage 6 is neutral between such options. At the level of basic moral structure they are both egalitarian—equality by merit, equality by person. He views the dispute as a matter of theoretical detail rather than basic logical structure. This will not do, however, since, among other things, it is inconsistent with Kohlberg's own position. Meritocratic justice (just desert reasoning) is characteristic of Stage 4 reasoning. But it does not figure into the defining criteria of Stage 5 or 6 judgment at all. Moreover, tying merit considerations to the sorts of rights Kohlberg describes at Stages 5 and 6 consistently yields judgments that oppose those proposed by Kohlberg at Stage 6.

This is seen clearly in the central Heinz dilemma. According to Kohlberg, Stage 6 directs a husband (Heinz) to steal a drug that can save his wife's life (even a stranger's life) if its owner-inventor (the druggist) will not sell it at a feasible price. This is because life takes precedence over property as a universalizable principle of moral preference. Moreover, the need to respect rights overrides any bad consequences of doing so. (These consequences would include financial loss for the druggist, arrest, trial, and likely incarceration for Heinz, and judicial costs to the taxpaying community.) Put in ideal role-taking terms, anyone would be willing to suffer great costs or take great risks to save another's life assuming, ideally, that he or she would be willing to do likewise for me (or anyone).

However, once individual right claims become meritorious, the druggist's claims to withhold his drug *must* or *might* be put first. (Either alternative is unacceptable at Stage 6.) Here we might not be willing to slide back and forth between roles, playing "just anyone," playing simply "a person" in need or a person with property, regardless of how that need or property arose.

The first alternative might be posed by a libertarian version of meritocracy. As Nozick might argue, Heinz's wife is dying of a disease, of cancer, not of the druggist's greed. The druggist has not caused her disease nor stolen the remedy from her. He is not even withholding the remedy from her; this would imply that the drug is a free good (like air) or that she has stronger claims to it than he. Actually, however, her claim to the remedy is need, and need alone obviously does not produce remedies, goods, or *holdings*.

The druggist, by contrast, has a merit claim to the drug as an expression of his effort and choice. The drug is his autonomous self expressed or objectified, his free labor congealed in a product. It should be respected as such from the Kantian point of view. The moral conflict here is not between life and property. It is a question of whether we can violate a (meritorious) right claim in order to promote a good consequence or uphold a value. From Nozick's point of view, Kohlberg's Stage 6 solution is utilitarian (perhaps caring), not Kantian or just. It uses the druggist's choice and free activity (autonomy) as mere means to good ends—to prevent evil or loss, not to prevent wrong. (Dying of disease is not being murdered.)

Just as Heinz's wife could not have obliged the druggist to produce the drug in the first place, even to save her life, she cannot now oblige him to sell it at a price she and Heinz have "set." (You and I are not obliged to become biochemists or physicians just because people are gravely ill.) It is through his choices and efforts that the very possibility of her cure has come to exist at all. The druggist chose to research and produce this drug as a part of his occupation, as a product he might sell for a fee. A primary and legitimate aim in taking on this extra work was to increase his (family's) standard of living. Admittedly, his material costs of production were far lower than the price he set for the good, but undertaking this research meant foregoing other activities, experiences, and possible accomplishments that he may have found more gratifying. The druggist could not be sure his efforts would come to anything. His risky investment of labor and effort would not have been compensated by Heinz or other potential consumers had he failed to produce a cure.

In all these ways the druggist's pricing policy seems reasonable and fair. Indeed, it may reflect proper Kantian self-respect rather than selfishness. At the least it is within the druggist's rights to set prices based on a reasonable estimation of his sacrifices and the worth of his labor or self-investment. Moreover, pursuing even a high standard of living through special effort, free trade, and fair pricing certainly seems permissible if it harms no one else in itself. (Not lowering a fair price is not a harm in itself.) Even when motivated by greed, such a pursuit does not seem to violate or commit an injustice toward others.

This brand of justice, of respect for persons, will satisfy some of us but outrage most. While it captures our relations to products well enough, it all but ignores our relations and responsibilities to each other. (Holdings should be mere instruments for carrying on such relations.) Note, however, that we need not accept the libertarian line holistically or even substantially in order to question Stage 6 liberalism. If there is anything significant to this meritocratic rationale, even as a subsidiary component of justice, the ultimate adequacy of Stage 6 begins to crumble. It is important to note, also, that even Nozick as libertarian would find Heinz's druggist callous and cruel, unfeeling and inhumane. Faced directly with the desperate couple, the druggist should have acted with compassion, at least letting Heinz pay for the drug on time, perhaps simply giving it to him for nothing in this exceptional case. Even where there is no personal involvement, we should create charities or even government programs to handle such emergencies (so long as no one is forced to contribute). But, crucially, such aid would not be an individual's right (for the libertarian). It would either be an ideal, or a primarily social responsibility. It would express joint concern or care for our human "neighbors," but not mere respect or just treatment. As such, the need for aid could not override or violate rights; it could not be enforced.

The caring perspective may accommodate part of this argument, the part that distinguishes obligations of justice from those of concern. But it may balk at having rights override care as the libertarian prefers. Still, there are less libertarian versions of meritocratic justice that may satisfy care and justice perspectives outside of Stage 6. Their emphasis would fall more strongly on the relation between our responsibility for a situation and the duties others bear to us in that situation.

Suppose the drowning man (in Kohlberg's dilemma of the same name) were a daredevilish and vicious hoodlum. Suppose he jumped into dangerous water on a whim, or to avoid enemies, or to make new ones. Let us assume, by contrast, that you, a passerby and his potential savior, are an Oxfam (hunger-relief) fund raiser and a very safety-conscious individual. According to Stage 6, you would be obliged to assume a grave and near equal risk of drowning to rescue this villain. He would have a basic right that you do so that overrides your noble commitments. After all, a life is at stake. To neglect your duty here is either (1) to confuse an unconditional right to life with the quality of a person's character; (2) to advance the greater good at the illegitimate expense of that right; (3) to "punish" someone (cosmically?) for being careless or ill-intentioned; or (4) to allow your moral choice to be determined by the morally arbitrary accident that he, and not you, is in trouble. (Stage 6 reminds us that "there but for the grace of God go I.")

But actually the hoodlum is not at grave risk by accident. Rather it is largely his own choice and negligence that landed him in the soup. (He is not a hoodlum purely by accident either.) The same can be said, in part, for why you are safe and dry. Whether or not you desire that the bad "get theirs" or that "the greater good be served," it is unclear why you should take on the *full consequences* of the hoodlum's irresponsibility and viciousness (or even of those who helped make him so) out of mere respect for his person. The threat to his life is not merely there in his being. It did not simply happen to him. Rather, he put it there, and thereby imposed on you the duty to aid him. To "refuse" a daring rescue is not to neglect his rights or even to claim that his rights have been altered by his actions. It is merely to note that our duty to him and his claims on it have been lessened by his actions, by his voluntarily assuming the foreseeable burdens of them. (It is *Kohlberg's* task to show that rights and duties are correlative.) When we assume the other person's role as an equal person we can then discount these burdens, for the most part, as his own special affair. In

the same way that toleration need only respect the choosing
person, not the particular *values* chosen, so my duty to the
hoodlum (or to anyone) need not put me equally in his *place*,
especially the place he has made for himself. Kohlberg's roles
and duties at Stage 6 cannot accommodate these distinctions.

Consider a more difficult and heart-rending case. Suppose
a group of destitute villagers refuse to move out of an area
perennially plagued by drought, flood, disease, and war. They
have fervent, culturally defining beliefs about the importance
of ancestral traditions and homelands. Need we who can aid
them (or steal for them) do so, and do so often, out of mere
respect for their persons? Would this not amount to subsidizing
their traditions and beliefs, their cultural interests, at a significant threat to our own? Their choice to stay put, as important
as it is, renders their destitution an unfair burden on us to a
large extent. But Stage 6 cannot see this to any extent. (And
if our villagers' problems were largely the doing of economic
imperialists in our society, do we violate rights by not paying
victims the compensation that these victimizers owe them?)

Of course we owe the destitute or endangered *something* just
because they are people, no matter what they have done. And
surely they can never be wholly responsible for their plight,
far from it. Kohlberg trades on this by posing our most ultimate
moral claims in his dilemmas. But Stage 6 must show that this
is all there is to it, that (basic) duties cannot be altered in degree
by changes and inequalities in responsibility. It must show that
our ultimate regard for the irresponsible or vicious is not primarily compassion rather than respect.

Even when people's plight is beyond their control and is no
one's fault but nature's, we need not take on the full burdens
of their tragedies and misfortunes. At least it is not their right
that we do so. The liberal-egalitarian prescription to so do at
Stage 6 is more a form of cosmic (Stage 7?) justice than moral
(stage) justice. This is because it attempts to compensate for,
rather than merely ignore, nature's indifference to our moral
systems. Stage 6 tries to right tragedies and misfortunes as if
they were wrongs or injustices, by redistributing their burdens
equally to each. This is what ideal role-taking requires of us.
It has us *take on* others' problems as if they happened to us, as

if they were our fair share of obligation. Here responsibility is thrust on us as if we assumed it.

Cosmic justice translates into supererogation when seen from the noncosmic justice perspective. Consider Stage 6 directives to attempt daring rescues and to steal for the poor or afflicted. Are these not the heroic and exemplary ideals of the very good Samaritan rather than the normal duties of the merely fair individual? While we may applaud Stage 6 for going beyond the call of justice, should its justice not own up to caring?

The life and death focus of many Kohlberg dilemmas obscures the power of responsibility and merit, as well as the tendency of Stage 6 egalitarianism to overstep individual rights. The need to preserve life seems to override every other moral consideration, including the ever-partial degree to which we are responsible for our plights. It seems to demand heroic effort. But consider other, wholly different ranges of cases that Stage 6 must solve, cases posing trade-offs among less ultimate interests. Suppose Heinz's wife is ill but not dying. Suppose she and Heinz are spendthrifts and well-known "party animals," facts that account in part for her ill health and Heinz's inability to buy medicines. (Of course we will assume, by contrast, that the druggist has always scrimped and saved except when charities came to call or friends were in need.) Must the druggist now sell a $2,000 drug for $1,500 if this is all Heinz can raise? Can Heinz steal the drug now?

Similar questions can be raised about other Kohlberg dilemmas. For instance, in Kohlberg's Stage 6 judgment we must transport someone to an appointment so long as the cost of doing so does not outweigh (or equal?) the cost of not showing up. (We would normally call this doing someone a favor. But not doing this "favor," for Kohlberg, constitutes a violation of rights.) Does it make a difference if the person needing the ride often makes appointments with no idea of how to keep them, perhaps assuming that some sucker will give him a ride? Does his irresponsibility in the matter not decrease one's own?

Again, if there is any strength to these "meritocratic" rationales, even as components of liberal justice, the ultimate adequacy of Stage 6 justice is in serious doubt. And this doubt merely compounds the doubts that care raised earlier. I believe the strengths of these rationales are clear.

Kohlberg has not appreciated the demands for adequacy taken on by touting Stage 6 as the ultimate structure of moral theory. It will take its shape only by dealing well with the sorts of everyday problems social universals can generate. How could this process generate the necessary logical finesse to handle the sorts of philosophic hypotheticals hurled at moral theories? The adequacy demonstrated by problem-solving, by equilibration to the environment at Stage 6 concerns only one feature of moral theoretic adequacy, namely, prescriptivity. At best, universal problem-solving adequacy would qualify Stage 6 justice as a champion applied ethic. Yet this still leaves open the question of how well Stage 6 structure can explain and justify moral judgments, as any adequate moral theory must. Most philosophical theories focus on a certain territory in the moral domain—rights, distributive justice, virtue. And they do so to a limited theoretic extent—justification, prescription, or application.[3] By contrast, Kohlberg touts Stage 6 structure and principles as the ultimately adequate basis for performing all these theoretical tasks—social, political, and interpersonal; justificatory, explanatory, and prescriptive. Running Stage 6 through this gauntlet is all the more amazing when one considers that its developmental training program is focused on solving problems, not on explaining solutions. While Kohlberg searches for stages, and characterizes them in the modes of explanation, or justification, their adaptive developmental logic is supposedly applied. If Stage 6 is to approach criteria of adequacy for moral philosophical theories, then it should address the differences between the theoretical tasks of justification, explanation, prescription, and application. From the research point of view, this might mean testing them more explicitly in the mode of choice or deliberation for choice than Kohlberg does. It might mean describing them in that mode as well in theory. At the least, differences between practical utility and logical or theoretical impeccability must be acknowledged.

Reversibility and Correlativity

The more specifically logical and theoretically relevant side of equilibration is reversibility. At Stage 6 every right in every role has a correlative duty to respect it, and vice-versa. There are no loose ends. Thus we can advance claims or judgments at Stage 6 consistently as we change or reverse points of view on a moral conflict. This operational balance accounts for the functional stability and efficiency of Stage 6, and for its decisiveness when making judgments. This full symmetry of conceptual relations also affords Stage 6 structure a logical unity and elegance that the more philosophically elaborated portions of moral theory can only envy. Conceptual elegance is key to *theoretical* adequacy in particular. Perhaps then when we view these internal virtues of Stage 6 *at their junction* with problem-solving acuity, Kohlberg's Stage 6 boasts will seem sensible.

Unfortunately, there are at least three critical problems with Kohlberg's reversibility criterion that he has not addressed. I can only touch on these here. The first concerns how we decide which moral concepts, rationales, and perspectives to correlate with each other in the first place, and which possible match-ups to ignore. How do we determine the correct correlations to draw, and know when they are complete? Starting at Stage 3, Kohlberg speaks of there being social roles and social perspectives, individual rights and duties, and general principles of justice. If at Stage 6 individual rights and duties match within individual roles, what happens to social perspectives and general principles? How are they related to these individual matches? Consider briefly the serious consequences of how we answer or fail to answer the question. As Stage 6 presently stands, each individual is bound to aid others, even to risk death (in the drowning man dilemma) or jail (in the Heinz dilemma) in order to fend off dire threats and deprivations. Clearly this leads to a seriously arbitrary and unfair distribution of the burdens and benefits of justice itself across society. The burdens fall unfairly on those who are close by, on those who happen by, and on the more morally conscious or kindly. The typical way a just society handles this problem is through institutional arrangements—fire departments and rescue squads to save those in danger, public health and welfare programs for the destitute and gravely ill. This assures justice from the "social perspective." Yet, crucially, a Stage 6 logic that simply matches individual rights and duties cannot prefer this "more just" alternative. It cannot handle these inequities caused by justice itself. (Nowhere in Kohlberg's Stage 6 solutions are provisions made to compensate the druggist *in any amount* for the illegal theft of his drug, or to compensate Heinz on any level for having to become a thief and risk jail.) Yet if we add a distributional principle of justice at the social level—to handle inequities, to complement Stage 6 rights and duties—how can we maintain full logical symmetry and correlativity?

One possibility is to maintain that for each individual right there is both an individual duty (to each other) and a single general duty at the social level. For each individual duty there are individual rights and a general social right. Likewise, individual perspectives correlate with each other and with "the social perspective." Though this does not preserve a one-to-one symmetry of rights and duties between roles and persons, it does yield a neat set of matched triangles. It relates each person to each other directly and indirectly through social principles of justice, leaving no rights or duties dangling. The problem is, however, that there can be no Stage 6 social rights per se (except explicitly delegated special rights to enforce individual rights). Society has no actual will of its own, it is not a person. And to sanctify the "social interest" through rights is to "outlaw" dissent and insure majority tyranny. Thus full symmetry breaks down and we must either drop the social perspective or correlate individual rights and duties to a general social duty of justice alone. Both of these options and the ambiguity between them violate Kohlberg's reversibility criterion. Moreover, the moral consequences of choosing the social duty option are implausibly onerous at Stage 6. Greater obligations would be placed on us through this correlativity of duties than the logic of mere fairness or respect toward persons should require.[4]

A second problem with the reversibility criterion concerns role-taking. Unlike philosophical theories of justice that use hypothetical models of decision making—Rawls's original position, utilitarianism's ideal observer—Kohlberg's stage structures evolve and function through *actual* role-taking. This is a *competence* that could only evolve from prolonged *performance*. Two questions arise in this context. First, is it *possible* in practice for us to fully differentiate and integrate all the roles needed to make the kind of large-scale, cross-cultural moral judgments that most distinguish Stage 6 from Stage 5? Second, are the moral and logical prerequisites in place at Stage 6 to determine what considerations we can claim legitimately from each reciprocal role? Kohlberg assumes that because we can take and reverse roles in some manageable cases we can therefore handle unmanageable cases *in principle* at Stage 6. Yet we would need *some* evidence of actual decision-making in unwieldy cases to know that Stage 6 solves all problems *adequately* in principle. Maximum adequacy is the key.

Of course, we can reduce the size of the role-taking problem in these large-scale cases by putting whole sets of roles in the same class. "They are all the same in position," we might say, "so they will all have the same legitimate claims." Our final resolution of the dilemma then merely involves taking the roles of these larger classes or "representative persons." The problem is, however, that this is precisely the maneuver to be justified. A crucial part of how we find out that claims are legitimate in each role is by seeing whether we can advance them from *all* roles. This is the key to Kohlberg's argument for the inadequacy of utilitarianism as a moral theory; it is why Stage 5 balancing of rights and utility cannot work. We could not advance these sorts of principles reversibly, Kohlberg maintains, if we *really* put ourselves in the place of people locked in moral dilemma. In some of these actual roles, supposedly, we would sense a strong cognitive conflict and imbalance rather than feeling conceptually equilibrated and content.

As things stand, Kohlberg has never been able to specify what counts as a Stage 6 claim that one could advance in any role, much less all roles. More important, his Stage 6 principle cannot specify relevant claims as a logical class or component of cognitive structure. Do we advance *interests* in each role, or *needs* only? Do we advance both, but only after deciding in advance which ones are legitimate or just claims? (And how do we decide this?) Before we can fully integrate roles, rights, and duties, we must know what sorts of claims we are to feel equilibrated about. These typical problems of ethical reasoning are damning to Stage 6 adequacy, as anyone who seriously uses Kohlberg's Stage 6 ideal role-taking procedure will find. (And the ideal role-taking procedure is the intellectually *refined* version of Stage 6 role-taking.)

Finally, when we relate the internal criterion of reversibility to the external criterion of adaptivity or problem-solving, we find that reversibility itself is largely responsible for the implausible solutions that Stage 6 generates. (Full correlativity of *liberal* rights and duties, at least, leads to inadequacies in Stage 6 judgment.) As noted, the logic of Stage 6 implies that we each must take on extreme risks or deprivation out of (mere) respect for any other individual. Supposedly, to allow someone to suffer destitution, illness, or death for lack of our aid is to do them an injustice. Previously I noted that these implications seem to violate crucial distinctions between cosmic and moral justice, between duties of justice and benevolence (or care), and between obligation and supererogation. The correlativity of rights and duties fosters these abuses in two ways. First, it does not allow us to adjust our degree of duty or responsibility to others so as to reflect the degrees of responsibility they have assumed themselves. Thus refusing to satisfy needs that others have irresponsibly created for themselves looks like a failure to fully respect rights of aid. To discount our duty to them is to reduce our correlative rights. Second, correlativity does not allow us to conceive certain needs and claims as primarily social problems that invoke primarily joint responsibilities. Correlative rights and duties can only portray any individual's full need or claim as any other individual's full or near-equal burden. This is so whether or not the individuals concerned choose to bear it cooperatively. In all sorts of cases such a logic seems blatantly implausible.

To sum up once more, the much-touted reversibility and correlativity criteria actually undermine Stage 6 rather than clinching the case for its adequacy. Fully correlated rights and duties seem to leave out, or even violate, general principles of justice. In addition, fully reversible role-taking seems infeasible in those very cases that distinguish Stage 6 judgment. It may be psychologically impossible to integrate all roles reversibly in large-scale or cross-cultural decision-making. It seems conceptually problematic to determine what goes into the roles one should take. Neither the criterion of reversibility nor the principles of Stage 6 justice can guide us sufficiently here. Moreover, correlating rights and duties makes it impossible to adjust our degree of responsibility toward others without seeming to deny their rights. Yet a failure to recognize that the responsibilities that others take on diminish our duties toward them causes Stage 6 to push us too far.

What Is to Be Done?

When we add these structural and philosophical problems to those noted previously, the magic of Stage 6 seems more mystery than allure. I believe that these challenges to Stage 6 recommend certain steps that researchers influenced by Kohlberg might take.

1. Drop Stage 6 justice completely from the stage sequence as an emerging structure, as a hypothetical structure, or as a formal end point for defining structural evolution.

2. Drop the notion of a most adequate structural end point of moral development (above Stage 5 or elsewhere) as well as the claim that it is needed to define a developmental sequence of moral judgment or conduct a nonindoctrinative program of moral education.

3. Search for solid data (from longitudinal samples especially) regarding the possible existence of higher *natural* stages. Interpret these findings in their own terms as the *data* best dictate.

4. If necessary, hypothesize a variety of possible Stage 6 structures for interpreting moral judgment data that seems to transcend Stage 5. At least one of these hypothetical structures should *extrapolate* from Stage 5. Another should extrapolate from Stages 3 and 4, or from possible mixtures of the two. (This would counter methodological biases in describing higher stages.) Another hypothetical structure might form a mixture of just and benevolent logics at higher stages and levels.

5. Redescribe all stages in their own terms, and relative to each other, rather than in relation to Stage 6. (Differences between moral rights, social justice, and legal justice should be observed.) Piecemeal comparative criteria of adequacy may be used for these purposes, rather than a presumed end point of development. (Most evaluations of adequacy are performed in this comparative way.) Alternatively, morally neutral or bipartisan end stages might be used, along with the various hypothetical structures posed above. Or both types of criteria might be used in combination.

6. While continuing the moral discussion and just-community approach to moral education, do not place special emphasis in discussion on reasoning that approaches the peculiarities of Stage 6. (I doubt that this kind of higher-stage stimulation currently occurs very often in Kohlbergian education.)

7. Analyze current data and extend research on the structure of value judgments. Include also those judgments of character, merit, and virtue that are most closely related to fulfilling principles of justice and benevolence. This might fill out the structure of these principles and of their structural relations to each other.

8. Drop all claims about the superiority of Kantian, formalist, deontological, Rawlsian, or Habermasian justice in ethics and the support moral psychology may seem to offer for these claims. Adopt a more nonpartisan view toward the logics of right, justice, benevolence, virtue, and value, and rethink their possible interrelations at the levels of strict, special, and imperfect obligation.

I believe that if these steps were followed, surprisingly few changes would be needed in Kohlberg's stage sequence (1–5), and that these changes would bring out and extend the logic of benevolence. In my opinion, Kohlberg's theory is much more morally and empirically adequate than the flawed structure of Stage 6 makes it seem. Most of the criticisms of Kohlberg's theory can be swept aside by merely eliminating Stage 6 in all its forms and reputed influences in the theory. The mystery is how legions of Kohlberg supporters and critics were taken in by the dubious magic of this dubious stage for so long.

Notes

1. Kohlberg's coauthored chapter in the present volume now contains two alleged cases of Stage 6 reasoning. My commentary on the case of Joan is based on a previous draft by Kohlberg that presented her case alone and in greater detail.

2. Kohlberg has offered a reconstruction of his method (Colby et al., 1983) that may seem to contradict my criticisms here. As I see it, however, Kohlberg's bootstrapping model is a post hoc remedy for the dangers I cite, and a partial one at that. When it works, it shows that some initial biases can later be justified with data.

3. Rawls's theory focuses on justice only, and on social justice in particular. In addition it primarily considers the role of social justice in specifying the principled basis for enacting a federal constitution within a large-scale nation state. This involves the problem of which moral precepts we can legitimately enforce, rather than merely that of which precepts are morally legitimate. To approach even this circumscribed problem, Rawls makes the ideal assumption that the citizenry will comply with the constitution once it is enacted. His principles are designed solely to specify and justify certain general obligations; they all but ignore the question of what rights we might have and whether they are correlative to our duties. In addition, Rawls explicitly distinguishes his constitutional principles from those that would prescribe or justify particular public policies. He also distinguishes his theory of social and political justice from a moral theory of right that would handle interpersonal problems. Yet even such a theory would concentrate on explanation and justification, to parallel Rawls's effort, not on decision-making as Kohlberg's does. In order to decide cases and render particular prescriptions, general principles would need specific rules of application. Explanatory principles are not decision strategies as they stand. The whole field of applied ethics testifies to the difficulty of trying to move from such general principles to cases. In fact, many philosophers have abandoned the attempt as misguided and hopeless. Instead they try to generate applied or prescriptive theories by generalizing from the circumscribed rules of thumb we use to solve particular cases.

4. At Stage 6 all rights and duties are universal, not merely social (societal). They apply to all persons as persons all over the world. Thus whatever general duties we have, they cannot be tailored to our particular society or nation state. They cannot presume a particular social grouping as their framework or target in the first instance. (In this regard, Kohlberg's Stage 6 solution to the Korea dilemma should not take the side of American soldiers first and ask which of them should blow up a bridge to "stop the enemy." On principle, both sides should have equal claims—including civilians and the military—and separate accounts should be given of special obligations to one's country.) Thus our reversible social duty of justice must be, first, to form social aid organizations when they exist (and support them when they do) and, second, to do so on a worldwide scale. Consider further what such correlativity means. Out of mere respect for each other as autonomous beings, each of us would be obliged to help establish and maintain international (or multinational) institutions to deal with deprivation, danger, illness, and so forth. You would have a duty to each other person to do such things, and if you did not fulfill it, you would have helped perpetuate injustice among us. You would have violated individual rights insofar as they are correlated with the general duty of social justice. I assume that many readers may find this consequence outlandish, believing that we have gotten moral correlations confused. Such altruism cannot be owed each other merely as persons, merely out of fairness. But how does *reversibility* help us allay this confusion or modify these consequences?

References

Attanucci, J. (1984). *Mothers in their own terms: A developmental perspective on self and role.* Doctoral dissertation, Harvard University Graduate School of Education, Cambridge, MA.

Colby, A., Kohlberg, L., Gibbs, J., and Lieberman, M. (1983). A longitudinal study of moral judgment. *Society for Research in Child Development: Monograph Series, 48.*

Colby, A., Kohlberg, L., and collaborators. (1987). *The measurement of moral judgment* (2 vols.). New York: Cambridge University Press.

Erdynast, A. (1973). *Improving the adequacy of moral reasoning.* Doctoral dissertation, Harvard University Graduate School of Education, Cambridge, MA.

Gilligan, C. (1977). In a different voice: Women's conceptions of the self and of morality. *Harvard Educational Review,* 47:481–517.

Gilligan, C. (1982). *In a different voice: Psychological theory and women's development.* Cambridge, MA: Harvard University Press.

Gilligan, C. (1986). Response to critics. *Signs,* 11:324–333.

Gilligan, C., and Wiggans, G. (1987). The origins of morality in early childhood relationships. In J. Kagan and S. Lamb (Eds.), *The emergence of morality in young children.* Chicago: University of Chicago Press.

Johnston, K. (1985). *Two moral orientations—Two problem-solving strategies: Adolescents' solutions to dilemmas in fables.* Doctoral dissertation, Harvard University Graduate School of Education, Cambridge, MA.

Kohlberg, L. (1981). *Essays on moral development. Vol 1: The philosophy of moral development.* San Francisco: Harper and Row.

Kohlberg, L. (1984). *Essays on moral development. Vol. 2: The psychology of moral development.* San Francisco: Harper and Row.

Kohlberg, L., Levine, C., and Hewer, A. (1983). *Moral stages: A current formulation and a response to critics.* Basel: Karger.

Langdale, S. (1983). *Moral observations and moral development: The analysis of care and justice reasoning across different dilemmas in females and males from childhood through adulthood.* Doctoral dissertation, Harvard University Graduate School of Education, Cambridge, MA.

Lyons, N. (1983). Two perspectives: On self, relationships, and morality. *Harvard Educational Review.* 53:125–145.

MacPherson, C. (1962). *Political theory of possessive individualism: Hobbes to Locke.* Oxford: Oxford University Press.

Marx, K. (1972). On the Jewish question. In R. Tucker (Ed.), *Marx-Engels Reader.* New York: Norton. (Original work published 1843)

Nozick, R. (1974). *Anarchy, state, and utopia.* New York: Basic Books.

Puka, B. (1990). Reconstructing Kohlberg's theory: Preserving essential structure, removing controversial content. In J. Gewirtz and W. Kurtines (Eds.), *Moral development: Advances in theory, research, and applications* (Vol. 1). Hillsdale, NJ: Earlbaum.

Puka, B. (in press-a). Care—in an interpretive voice. *New Ideas in Psychology.*

Puka, B. (in press-b). Interpretative experiments: Caring and justice, in many "different voices." *Human Development.*

Puka, B. (in press-c). The liberation of caring. *Hypatia: A Feminist Journal of Philosophy.*

Rawls, J. (1971). *A theory of justice.* Cambridge, MA: Harvard University Press.

Simpson, E. (1974). Moral development research: A case study of scientific cultural bias. *Human Development*, 17:81–106.

Sullivan, E. V. (1977). A study of Kohlberg's structural theory of moral development: A critique of liberal social science ideology. *Human Development*, 20:352–376.

Walker, L. (1984). Sex differences in the development of moral reasoning: A critical review. *Child Development*, 55:667–691.

Walker, L., de Vries, B., and Trevethan, S. (1987). Moral stages and moral orientations in real-life and hypothetical dilemmas. *Child Development*, 58:842–858.

The Illusion of Stage Six

Don Locke

Abstract

Kohlberg's developmental theory of moral reasoning postulates a supremely adequate form of moral thinking to which all other stages are tending, labelled Stage Six. Kohlberg identifies this with a principle of justice, though without adequately justifying the elimination of other autonomous universal principles. The claim that this principle provides consistent, reversible and universalizable moral judgements is criticized: by itself a purely formal principle of justice can provide no particular moral judgements at all; for that we need independent values, such as the value of life which Kohlberg appeals to, but does not justify, in his discussions of the Heinz dilemma. More generally there is no reason to expect that any form of moral reasoning will be supremely adequate in Kohlberg's sense, providing a solution to all moral problems and dilemmas. The principle of justice is merely one among the many specifically moral principles which Kohlberg locats at Stage Five, albeit the one which he personally happens to favour.

Perhaps the most striking feature of Lawrence Kohlberg's many accounts of his cognitive-developmental theory of moral reasoning is the crucial importance which he attaches to the form of reasoning labelled Stage Six, when it is a stage of development that only a tiny minority of individuals actually attain. Indeed it appears that even that number has had to be revised downward in the light of changes to the theory and scoring system, until it begins to seem that only a handful of saints and heroes, such as Socrates or Martin Luther King, remain. In fact so slender is the empirical evidence for a separate form of Stage Six reasoning that the official scoring manual (Kohlberg *et al.*, 1977) prefers to ignore it altogether. Clearly, then, the case for Stage Six must be almost wholly theoretical, not to say philosophical, as the supremely adequate form of moral thinking to which all other stages are tending. And by the same token it may seem that criticisms of Kohlberg's claims for Stage Six will leave the rest of the theory untouched. But that, I think, is to underestimate the significance of Stage Six. It is the apogee of his system, providing both a focus and a rationale for the stage-development that allegedly leads to it; it is as crucial to the theory as Kohlberg's own writings make it. Without Stage Six the cognitive-developmental account stands in need of radical re-thinking, to put it no higher.

The interpretation of Stage Six

Kohlberg's own characterization of Stage Six in terms of self-chosen universal ethical principles, together with his insistence that the different stages are to be identified by the form of moral reasoning, rather than by its content, naturally suggests that Stage Six reasoning consists in adopting some set of moral principles — any set of moral principles — whose application is not limited by time, place, person, or circumstance. This would, in effect, amount to Hare's 'universal

Don Locke is Professor of Philosophy, Department of Philosophy, University of Warwick, Coventry CV4 7AL.

prescriptivism' (1952, 1963) which construes a morality as a system of universal principles, though which particular principles we happen to endorse remains a matter for individual decision. But it is immediately obvious that, understood in this way, Stage Six fails to identify a distinct form of moral reasoning, since the principles invoked may themselves be characteristic of other, 'lower' forms of reasoning: the Ten Commandments, for example, could be construed as universal principles at a Stage One level; the Ethical Egoist's principle, always to pursue your own self-interest, would be a Stage Two universal principle; and so on. Instead of providing a distinct stage of moral development, Stage Six would appear to be a refinement or sophistication, or as Gibbs has suggested (1977) a 'reflective extension', of earlier stages.

But it soon emerges that this is not at all how Kohlberg intends his Stage Six to be interpreted, for he explicitly denies that the Ten Commandments are principles, in his sense of the term. A principle is 'something more abstract than a general rule'; it is 'a general guide to choice rather than a rule of action', 'something like "a consideration in choosing" rather than a definite rule prescribing a class of acts' (1971b, p. 58). Thus 'Don't spit' is a rule proscribing a particular course of action, and so too, more generally, is 'Don't be rude'; but 'Respect the dignity of other persons' is more like a principle, by which such concrete rules might themselves be validated. Moreover rules can come into conflict, whereas principles are absolute and universal; they are, if you like, the meta-rules whereby specific rules of conduct are assessed, and conflicts between them resolved. But finally, and most crucially, although several different considerations might offer themselves as possible universal principles, there is in the end only one such principle, variously described as the principle of justice, equality, or respect for persons (see 1971a, pp. 218–20). Thus 'our conception of moral principle implies that one cannot ultimately separate form and content in moral analysis' (1971b, p. 60).

Nevertheless it is not all clear why Kohlberg thinks that justice provides the only possible principle, even in his specialized sense of the word. Ayn Rand, for example, has developed an ethic in which values of individuality, self-sufficiency and self-realization take precedence over justice and equality, which are merely devices for holding the few exceptional individuals down to the level of the rest, to the ultimate detriment of all (1964); Kohlberg himself recognizes that Hitler regarded racial destiny, and the Bolshevics regarded 'humanity', as higher moral values, or absolutes, which take precedence over the particular claims of particular people (1971b, p. 61); and the Utilitarians are not the only ones to adopt the good of the whole as the ultimate moral arbiter, taking precedence even over justice and respect for persons. But Kohlberg refuses to classify these as instances of principled reasoning in his sense: even the appeal to benevolence is rejected on the arbitrary and unargued grounds that 'benevolence in the sense of "love, empathy, sympathy, human concern, humanism" and so on can never be a principle of choice. It is primarily another stage-3 virtue label, not a guide to action' (1971b, p. 63).

It is, I suspect, an ambiguity of 'universal principle' which accounts for Kohlberg's belief that there can be only one such principle, in his sense. For principles might be universal in the sense that they are held by everybody, or in the sense that they are applicable to everybody: clearly Stage Six principles will be universal only in the latter, not the former sense. But if we fail to notice the difference it can easily seem that universal principles must be the same for everyone, for if different people hold different principles, how can they be universal? Then, having assumed that there can be only one set of universal principles, the most obvious candidate, perhaps the only plausible candidate, for principles which everyone might agree on will be principles which treat everyone alike, i.e. principles of justice, equality, and respect for persons. So when Alston protested that 'a judgement based on a principle of racial destiny . . . can be seen as just as prescriptive' (and, we might add, just as universal) 'as a judgement based on an application of Kohlberg's principle of justice' (Alston, 1971, p. 277), Kohlberg found it difficult to take the objection seriously:

For most of us, it is counter-intuitive to believe that racial destiny could be held as a universal prescriptive principle. This is because no human being held it or similar beliefs as such a principle at least none in our research studies (1971a, p. 221).

The obvious counter-example, Adolph Hitler, is then dismissed on the grounds that his judgements were not prescriptive because he believed that might makes right (!?), and not universal because they were not intended to cover the decisions of Jews and others. Yet clearly the principle 'Everyone and everything must be subordinated to the purification of the Aryan race, is both prescriptive and universal, laying down a requirement intended to apply equally to the blue-eyed blonde and the unfortunate Jew, not to mention Hitler himself. What Kohlberg cannot accept, of course, is that it is a principle which everyone might *adopt*, the Jew included. Thus the ambiguity of 'universal principle' makes it seem as though the only possible universal principles will be such things as justice, equality, and respect for persons.

So what is distinctive about Kohlberg's Stage Six is not the appeal to universal principles as such, but the appeal to a principle of justice in particular. The moral philosophy appropriate to Stage Six is not Hare's Universal Prescriptivism, but Kant's Categorical Imperative and Kingdom of Ends. Indeed to call it the 'universal principle orientation' is highly misleading, for these are not principles which are universally held, and other, quite different principles might — perhaps mis-guidedly — be regarded as universally binding. Stage Six moral reasoning is universal only in the sense that it involves treating all men alike, according everyone the same respect and value, regardless of status, regardless of situation. It would be less misleading to adopt some different label, and call it, e.g., the 'justice and equality orientation'. Yet Nietzsche, for one, claimed to have seen through the morality of justice and equality, and to have progressed beyond it, perhaps to a Stage Seven 'individual supremacy orientation' which those of us stuck at Stage Six, Kohlberg perhaps included, cannot properly comprehend, and systematically misinterpret in terms that we do understand, as if it were some form of regression to Stage Two. So is there any way in which Kohlberg can demonstrate that Kant is superior, not merely to Nietzsche but to all other moralities?

The principle of justice

The superiority of Stage Six is supposed to consist in the fact that it is only at this level that moral reasoning becomes 'ultimately equilibrated'. According to the cognitive-developmental theory it is cognitive conflict which drives the individual from one stage of reasoning to the next; it is the need to reconcile moral claims and resolve moral conflicts which oblige us to restructure our moral thinking, and so arrive at higher and more adequate stages of moral development. So if Stage Six is the ultimate stage of moral reasoning then, at that level, there ought to be no moral claims and conflicts left unresolved. Indeed that is precisely why Kohlberg believes that there must be a Stage Six, even if so very few individuals ever actually attain it. So to show that the appeal to the principle of justice does constitute this highest stage of moral reasoning, it is necessary only to show that it (and it alone?) provides us with unique and universal solutions to all moral problems.

This is ensured, apparently, because the principle of justice provides us with judgements which are completely consistent, reversible, and universalizable (1973a). By 'consistent' Kohlberg evidently means that judgments do not conflict with one another: Stage Six moral reasoners will arrive at a single unanimous opinion as to what is right or wrong in any particular situation. By 'reversible' he means judgments which will be acceptable no matter what your particular role in the situation: Stage Six moral reasoners will arrive at judgments which they are prepared to accept, however they might affect them personally. And by 'universalisable' he means judgments which are, as he also puts it, 'universal across actors' (1971a, p. 208), making the same demands of all parties: Stage Six moral reasoners will arrive at judgments which accord everyone the same rights and duties, without distinction of person. It is important to note here that what philosophers, following Hare (1963), commonly call 'universalizability', i.e. the applicability of the same judgment to anyone, yourself included, who might find themselves in the same situation, is closer to what Kohlberg terms 'reversibility'. His 'universalizability', on the other hand, goes well beyond

Hare's requirement that moral principles be universal in form, to the claim that genuine moral principles must be applicable to everyone — so that 'Be loyal to your family', for example, is held not to be universal, since not everyone has a family (1971b, p. 58)!

However, in order to arrive at judgments which are thus consistent, reversible and universalisable, we have to engage in a process of what Kohlberg calls 'ideal role-taking', in which we look at the particular situation from the point of view of each individual in turn. If we do this, Kohlberg believes, we will discover that the only reversible judgment, acceptable regardless of which position we happen to occupy, will be one which invokes the principle(s) of justice, equality and respect for persons, by taking equal account of the interests of all parties. Moreover any such reversible judgment will also be universalizable: 'If something is fair or right to do from the conflicting points of view of all those involved in the situation, it is something we can wish all men to do in all similar situations' (1973a, p. 642). And since the solution is both reversible and universalisable, it will also be consistent, a single unanimous judgment as to what, in that particular situation, ought to be done.

Now all this would be extremely exciting if only it were true, but I can see no reason to think that it is. Indeed the difficulties are obvious enough in Kohlberg's own preferred example, the celebrated Heinz dilemma. This concerns a man whose wife is dying of a cancer that can be cured only by a drug which is being sold at ten times its cost, much more than Heinz can afford. He tries to buy the drug for as much as he can find, but the druggist refuses. So should Heinz steal the drug? According to Kohlberg, only a Stage Six moral reasoner, relying on ideal role-taking and the principle of justice, will arrrive at a unique and universal solution to this problem, a judgment which is consistent, reversible and universalizable.

Yet for a start it seems entirely possible that different ideal role-takers might start from different values, and so arrive at different, conflicting judgments as to what Heinz should do. Kohlberg tells us that:

> Heinz must imagine whether the druggist could put himself in the wife's position and still maintain his claim, and whether the wife could put herself in the druggist's positon and still maintain her claim. Intuitively we feel that the wife could, the druggist could not. As a result, it is fair for the husband to act on the basis of the wife's claim (1973a, p. 643).

But this is merely a reflection of Kohlberg's personal belief that 'anyone who understands the values of life and property will recognize that life is morally more valuable than property' (1971a, p. 174; 1971b, p. 39). Yet there have been those prepared to lay down life, both their own and other people's, for property, both their own and other people's, and more generally for the right of each to do as he will with his own. Such a person might well feel that the druggist can maintain his claim even when he puts himself in the wife's position, and not vice versa. In that case ideal role-taking would indeed resolve the conflict in accordance with a principle of justice which gives each party his due; but it would provide a *different* solution. It is a merit of Hare's account of universalizability that he recognizes, as Kohlberg does not, that different universalizers might be prepared to universalize different moral judgments, and so arrive at different, conflicting solutions to the same moral problem.

Nor is there any guarantee that ideal roletaking and the principle of justice will produce a solution which is reversible, in the sense of acceptable no matter which party you might happen to be. Of course if you firmly believe that the right to life takes precedence over the right to private property — or vice versa — then you will arrive at a verdict which will seem valid no matter which position you imagine yourself into. But if, instead, you find it difficult to decide between the two in a case such as this, then the result of thinking yourself first into the wife's position and then into the druggist's might be to provide you with two equally persuasive claims, neither of which is reversible. Indeed that is precisely what you would expect of a genuine moral dilemma. True, this is unlikely to happen with the Heinz dilemma as it stands, but it is obviously a highly loaded example, specifically designed to bolster Kohlberg's personal belief in the supreme value of human life. Alter the example somewhat, turn it into a genuine dilemma (as I have been forced to do, in order to get profitable discussions among groups of philosophy students): suppose that the druggist is not trying to make an exorbitant profit but merely wants a sum sufficient to support his own wife and family, and to continue his researches into an improved version of the drug; or, to confront Kohlberg's own beliefs more directly, suppose that the only way in which Heinz can get his hands on the drug is by actually killing the druggist. There is no reason to think that ideal role-taking and the principle of justice will provide reversible solutions in such cases as these. Justice may require that we give equal weight to the legitimate claims of all parties; but where the conflicting claims are equally legitimate, how can justice decide between them?

Finally, there can be no guarantee that any solution will be universalisable in Kohlberg's idiosyncratic sense of 'universal across actors', making the same demands of everyone involved. Certainly it does not follow, as he imagines, that if a solution is just it will treat all parties in the same way. For the result of imaginatively thinking oneself into the position of all the parties involved may be a recognition that some have special rights and duties which others do not: that, for example, a wife has a claim against her husband, and he has obligations towards her, which would not arise if they were complete strangers. It is entirely possible that a just and fair solution will discriminate between individuals, that the appeal to justice might reveal that Heinz, and Heinz alone, has a duty to do all he can to protect his wife, even at considerable cost to himself.

But underlying all this is a fundamental misconception on Kohlberg's part, concerning the nature of justice. For justice itself is a purely formal principle which 'dictates that we consider every man's moral claims equally' (1971b, p. 64). But which claims are moral, which claims we ought to consider, justice as such does not say; it tells us to give each man his due, but it does not tell us what that due is. For that we need some substantive values, independent of justice itself. Indeed without some such independent value, the principle of justice is entirely empty: there is no 'due' for justice to see that every man gets.

In Kohlberg's discussions of the Heinz dilemma this independent value is provided by the special status of human life, and it is obvious enough that his own solution to the problem rests entirely on that, and not on any appeal to justice as such. Indeed this almost seems to be a situation where some other value *does* take precedence over justice: is it fair to steal the druggist's invention, even in such dire circumstances as these; it may be justified, but is it just? Moreover Kohlberg offers no justification for this preference, beyond the fact that those who read his writings will feel, 'intuitively', that life is more valuable than property, at least in this particular, heavily-biased example. Certainly there is no way of getting from an abstract formal principle of justice or equality to the specific value of human life, or to any specific value at all. So far from the principle of justice being the only principle capable of providing the unique and universal solutions to all moral problems which we need if Stage Six moral reasoning is indeed to be 'ultimately equilibrated', the principle of justice, by itself, is totally incapable of providing any solution, not merely to the Heinz dilemma, but to any moral problem whatsoever!

The status of Stage Six

At this point we might begin to wonder whether some other principle might not meet the requirements of Stage Six, by providing some universal principle which can be relied on to resolve and reconcile all moral claims and conflicts. But that requirement seems to me thoroughly misconceived.

There is, first of all, no reason to believe that any such ultimate resolution of all moral problems is in principle possible. Kohlberg believes that the Heinz dilemma can be resolved, though we have seen that this is due partly to the way in which he incorporates his own personal values into his principle of justice, and partly to the tendentious way in which the dilemma is formulated, so that the sophisticated, liberal and humane audience to which he addresses himself can be expected to agree with his particular solution. But as we have also seen, other dilemmas may not be so easily resolved, a point on which Kohlberg is himself somewhat ambiguous. Thus in discussing the problem of whether a man whose wife refuses to sleep with him, might be justified in sleeping with someone else, Kohlberg writes:

> . . . while universal moral principles apply to the situation, they do not lead to a definite unambiguous decision or solution. The dilemma about sex is different from the dilemma about life. The real problem is that nothing has been specified in this situation. There really is nothing in the act of sex, per se, which is right or wrong. We haven't been given what we need to determine rightness or wrongness of a choice from a moral point of view. We're not clear what the implications of this act are in terms of respect for persons, equity or human welfare in these situations. As a result we can't define clear obligations or rights or wrongs though the situation isn't morally neutral (1973b, p. 21)

Here Kohlberg appears to be saying that there would be a definite unambiguous decision or solution, if only the morally-relevant features of the situation were adequately specified. But, ironically, the features which he dismisses as morally irrelevant (e.g. sex with someone to whom you are not married) are precisely those which some others, no less principled than he, would see as determining a definite unambiguous solution. Nor is it clear how Kohlberg can justify his solution, if he has one, against their's, except by insisting on his principles, while they insist on their's.

But secondly, and more crucially, there seems no reason to insist that moral reasoning will reach its highest, most advanced stage when it is able to provide unique and universal solutions to moral problems. Indeed, so far from its being characteristic of more developed or more sophisticated moral thinking that it enables us to resolve and reconcile all claims and conflicts, this seems rather to be characteristic of more simplistic moral thought. Someone who adopts a 'law and order' orientation, for example, will have a clear and unambiguous solution to the Heinz dilemma, one which is consistent, reversible and universalizable: the druggist is quite within his rights, stealing is against the law, so the wife cannot be saved. But instead of being evidence for the superiority of Stage Four reasoning, this seems rather to demonstrate its inadequacy. There are moral problems which lack a unique and universal solution; there are moral problems — the true dilemmas — which lack any non-arbitrary solution at all. To prefer a form of reasoning because it leaves no claims or conflicts unresolved, or because it demands the same conduct of everyone, seems a mark of moral simplicity, not moral sophistication.

Moreover this criticism cuts to the very core of the cognitive-developmental theory. It is an essential claim of that theory that the higher stages are cognitively superior to the lower, and this cognitive superiority consists in the greater adequacy of higher stages in resolving moral problems. It is this which explains not only why the various stages form the hierarchy they do, but why and how individuals move from stage to stage — in order to escape cognitive conflict, and arrive at some form of cognitive moral equilibrium. I have argued elsewhere that the empirical evidence does not support this claim (1979); I am arguing now that it is not theoretically justified either. If Kohlberg's claims for the principle of justice, or for Stage Six more generally, were correct, that would be proof not of their cognitive superiority but of their cognitive inadequacy, their inability to deal properly with the real variety and complexity of moral problems.

None of this is to deny that there is a form of moral thinking which answers to Kohlberg's description of ideal role-taking. But ironically the philosopher whose own account comes closest to Kohlberg's is not Rawls but Hare (1963), and Hare sees it not as an appeal to justice but as a form of Utilitarianism, which Kohlberg writes off as merely Stage Five! This in turn suggests that Kohlberg's Stage Six does not identify a form of moral reasoning which can be systematically distinguished from the appeals to utility, social contract, or individual rights which he ranks as Stage Five. Indeed these are themselves such a thoroughly mixed bag that it is difficult not to see Kohlberg's principles of justice, equality, and respect for persons as simply one among the many alternative, and no doubt inter-related, forms of 'principled' or 'post-conventional' morality. What distinguishes them is not their superiority, cognitive or moral, over the various forms of Stage Five moral thinking, but simply the fact that they are the principles to which Kohlberg personally subscribes. And no doubt there are others: the 'principled individualism' of Nietzche or Ayn Rand, for example, which Kohlberg would presumably write off as merely a transitional Stage Four and a half; or the mysterious, mystical sense of unity with the cosmos to which Kohlberg has himself developed, and which he accordingly identifies, albeit tentatively, as a possible Stage Seven (1974).

But there is no justification, either philosophical or psychological, for seeing any of these as distinct developmental stages, or as involving structurally dissimilar forms of moral reasoning. They share the features of autonomy, universalisability and prescriptivity which a number of writers have seen as essential to morality, properly so-called. As Baier has pointed out (1974), genuine moral reasoning, on Kohlberg's criteria, does not emerge until Stage Five — the earlier stages are not, strictly, stages of *moral* reasoning at all — so in that sense Stage Five can be seen as the highest, and final, stage in the evolution of distinctively moral reasoning. But there is no reason to regard any one system of principle or post-conventional morality as going beyond the others, except as an expression of one's own personal moral convictions. Let justice rule the world, by all means, if that is your preference. But Stage Six is an illusion.

References

ALSTON, W. P. (1971). 'Comments on Kohlberg's "From is to ought".' In: MISCHEL, T. *Cognitive Development and Epistemology*. New York: Academic Press.

BAIER, K. (1974). 'Moral development', *Monist*, 58, 601–15.

GIBBS, J. C. (1977). 'Kohlberg's stages of moral judgment: a constructive critique', *Harv. Educ. Rev.* 47, 43–61.

HARE, R. M. (1952). *The Language of Morals*. Oxford: Clarendon Press.

HARE, R. M. (1963). *Freedom and Reason*. Oxford: Clarendon Press.

KOHLBERG, L. (1971a). 'From is to ought: How to commit the Naturalistic Fallacy and get away with it in the study of moral development.' In: MISCHEL, T. *Cognitive Development and Epistemology*. New York: Academic Press.

KOHLBERG, L. (1971b). 'Stages of moral development as a basis for moral education.' In: BECK, C. M., CRITTENDEN, B. S., and SULLIVAN, E. V. *Moral Education: Interdisciplinary Approaches*. Toronto: University of Toronto Press.

KOHLBERG, L. (1973a). 'The claim to moral adequacy of a highest stage of moral judgment', *Journal of Philosophy*, 70, 630–46.

KOHLBERG, L. (1973b). 'The implications of moral stages for problems in sex education.' In: KOHLBERG, L. *Collected Papers on Moral Development and Moral Education*. Harvard University: Center for Moral Education.

KOHLBERG, L. (1974). 'Education, moral development and faith', *J. Moral Educ.* 4, 15–16.

KOHLBERG, L., COLBY, A., GIBBS, J., SPEICHER-DUBIN, B., and POWER, C. (1977). *Assessing Moral Stages: A Manual*. Harvard University: Center for Moral Education.

LOCKE, D. B. (1979). 'How to improve your moral thinking? A critique of the stage-structural theory of moral reasoning', *J. Moral Educ.* 8, 3, 168–81.

RAND, A. (1964). *The Virtue of Selfishness: A New Concept of Egoism*. New York: Signet Books.

9. Why Act on Kohlberg's Moral Judgments? (Or How to Reach Stage 6 and Remain a Bastard)

ROGER STRAUGHAN

The subtitle is not my own invention. At a conference on moral development held at Leicester several years ago and attended by Lawrence Kohlberg and a number of his associates, an informal discussion group met one afternoon to consider precisely that topic. The wording has ever since summed up for me one of the most fascinating and neglected areas of Kohlbergian theory, which I shall attempt to explore further in this chapter.

What is commonly known as 'the judgment/action issue' is not really a single, unified 'issue' at all, but a rather messy collection of loosely linked problems with which philosophers, psychologists and others have long been concerned—ever since Socrates' provocative claim that to know the Good is to do it. Philosophers have busied themselves with questions about the logical relationship between moral judgment and moral action; the emotive, prescriptive and conative features of moral judgments; and the analysis of 'moral weakness' and 'bad faith'. More recently psychologists have tried to study the empirical relationship between 'moral cognition' and moral behaviour, and to propose theoretical interpretations of that relationship.

These general concerns have given rise to a host of more specific problems, some of them highlighted by the design of the various psychological research studies and the assumptions lying behind them. Considerable difficulties have arisen in trying to reach agreement over what is to count as a moral judgment and how one is to know whether or not a subject has made one, and over what is to count as a moral action and how one is to know whether or not a subject has performed one.

The conceptual and methodological questions here are closely intertwined, but the logical priority of the former over the latter has not always been realized—we have to be reasonably clear about what it is we are trying to study before we try to

169

study it. Misleading conclusions can easily be drawn by researchers who fail to respect this logical priority.

'The judgment/action issue' thus becomes an exceedingly complex matter, in that it is constituted by a variety of different problems of logically different kinds. All of these, however, stem from an apparently obvious feature of human life—namely that we all at times fail to do what we think we ought to do. This feature can be expressed in all sorts of ways; for example, by saying that human beings often fail to act upon their principles or to live up to their ideals, or that they are prone to moral weakness or weakness of will, or that they can at times reveal an inconsistency or gap between their moral reasoning and their behaviour. Various explanatory concepts have been used to account for this phenomenon, ranging from the theologian's 'original sin' through the commonsense notions of 'conscience' and 'character' to the psychologist's 'ego strength'. Attempts to define and explain the relationship between moral judgment and action, then, inevitably lead us into a conceptual minefield. It will be the contention of this chapter that Lawrence Kohlberg has not picked his way with sufficient care in this perilous area.

What has Kohlberg's contribution been here? It is an all-too-common criticism of Kohlberg that he is 'interested only in moral reasoning' and that his theory has nothing to say about moral *action*. A study of his extensive writings shows that this charge is not justified, yet the fact that it is so frequently levelled is perhaps not without significance. Kohlberg's predominant concern clearly *is* with moral reasoning, and it is certainly arguable that he has not said *enough* about moral action. Morality is by definition a practical business, for it is about what ought and ought not to be *done*. Of course, a person's reasons and justifications why it ought or ought not to be done are of great moral significance and interest, yet the very concept of morality becomes distorted, even incomprehensible, if undue emphasis is placed upon its 'judgmental' or 'theoretical' aspects. This fundamental point about the nature and function of morality is well underlined by Hare's comment: 'If we were to ask of a person, "What are his moral principles?" the way in which we could be most sure of a true answer would be by studying what he *did*' (italics in original).[1]

Kohlberg's basic approach to the study of morality, however, is in radical disagreement with Hare in this respect. According to Kohlberg, one finds out what a person's moral principles are (or whether he really has anything which Kohlberg would count as moral principles), not by studying how he actually behaves, but by analyzing and interpreting his verbal responses to a hypothetical dilemma. Yet, as I have argued elsewhere,[2] this hypothetical approach has important logical limitations, which make it an unreliable guide to what happens in 'real-life morality'. For example:

1   moral conflict comes to be construed exclusively as conflict between rival moral principles (such as truth-telling versus promise-keeping, or respect for property versus respect for life). This kind of moral conflict, however, is probably less common empirically and less central logically than is the clash between principle and inclination (when I judge that I *ought* to do *x*, but do not feel that I *want* to do *x*);

2   hypothetical dilemmas necessarily lack that first-hand immediacy which is an essential ingredient of genuine moral experience. In making a real-life moral decision, my motives, feelings, wants and emotions may run counter

to my hypothetical reasoning and judgments, which will often need to be modified if I actually find myself in such a situation. Direct emotional experience of a situation is a necessary condition of participating in it as a moral agent—and such participation is a very different activity from engaging in a hypothetical ethical debate about the Heinz dilemma.

Kohlberg's methodology, by its very nature, virtually equates moral agency with the making of judgments about hypothetical ethical dilemmas, and this orientation must impose severe limitations on what he can say about morality proper and the real-life business of moral decision-making. In this respect at least Kohlberg simply by-passes 'the judgment/action issue'. However, it would be unfair to suggest that Kohlberg totally ignores the problematic relationship between moral judgment and moral action, for he does occasionally in his voluminous writings address himself to this question. The remainder of this chapter will be devoted to a critical appraisal of this portion of his work.

Kohlberg's claim in brief is that the higher the stage of reasoning a subject is at, the more likely is he to act in accordance with his moral judgments, and that consequently 'maturity of moral thought should predict to maturity of moral action.'[3] This is because 'moral judgment determines action by way of concrete definitions of rights and duties in a situation.'[4] The evidence usually cited by Kohlberg to support this conclusion comes from experimental cheating tests, Milgram's obedience studies and an analysis of the Berkeley University sit-in.[5]

This account of 'moral action' is extremely scanty in comparison with the elaborate exposition and interpretation which characterizes Kohlberg's work on moral judgment. It is in my view inadequate and obscure in a number of respects; by examining these we may be able to clarify more precisely what is at stake in 'the judgment/action issue'.

(1) Drawing Conclusions from the Evidence

My first set of objections concerns the sort of evidence to which Kohlberg refers and the conclusions he tries to derive from it. The range of 'moral behaviour' on which he bases his generalizations is very restricted and hardly representative of our everyday experience. Decisions about whether or not to cheat or inflict electric shocks during psychological experiments or to join a university sit-in protest do not represent typical dilemmas with which most moral agents are faced. Indeed, it is doubtful whether the cheating test raises a *moral* issue involving *moral* behaviour in any significant sense at all. As Kohlberg himself says, '... the experimental situation is Mickey Mouse (it does not matter much whether one cheats or not), and ... it is fishy (the experimenter explicitly leaves the child unsupervised in a situation where one would expect supervision).'[6] This point is underlined by Hersh, Paolitto and Reimer: 'Experimental cheating tests ... are one step removed from real-life decisions. Subjects may not know that they are being observed for their cheating behaviour, but they do know they are involved in an experiment and may not attribute much importance to their actions.'[7] But the whole point about moral actions and situations is that importance *is* attributed to them and that they are *not* 'Mickey Mouse,' so why should Kohlberg think that he is investigating *moral* behaviour in such experiments?

To draw general conclusions about 'moral action' from such dubious examples, then, is quite unjustifiable. The moral domain covers a vast area, and it is a complex task to attempt to map out its main contours in terms of its characteristic form and content.[8] The meagre data on which Kohlberg bases his account of 'moral action' cannot begin to do justice to this complexity.

Furthermore, the data as presented cannot for the most part illuminate what Kohlberg appears to think they do, for in order to study the relationship between moral judgment and action we need to know (a) what the subject believed he ought to do, and (b) what he actually did do. Yet in the cheating tests it is *assumed* that subjects always think it wrong to cheat, and in the Milgram study it is *assumed* that subjects always think it wrong to inflict the electric shock; so the percentages which Kohlberg quotes are always of how many Stage X subjects *actually* cheated or gave the shock. But it is perfectly possible that many subjects do *not* believe they ought not to cheat or to give the shock, and are thus showing 'consistency' or 'strength of will' in acting upon their beliefs by cheating or giving the shock; this is particularly likely in the Milgram experiment, where many may believe they ought to keep to the terms of their contract and do what the experimenter asks them to do. Equally it is possible that some non-cheaters and non-shockers are showing 'inconsistency' or 'weakness of will' in *not* acting (because of some counter-inclination) upon their belief that it is morally *right* to cheat or give the shock in that situation. Kohlberg's percentages tell us nothing about all this, yet that is the information we need in order to clarify the relationship between judgment and action.

Kohlberg, then, fails to distinguish clearly enough between 'consistent action' (where subjects do what *they* judge is the right thing to do) and 'virtuous action' (where subjects do what is *generally considered* to be the right thing to do—by the experimenter at least). It is only studies of 'consistent action' which can help us unravel 'the judgment/action issue,' but unfortunately such studies seem to be conspicuous by their absence. Even the Berkeley sit-in analysis was based on *post-hoc* interviews, and asking students a year after the event why they acted as they did, and how they *now* think they perceived the situation *then*, is a very different procedure from trying to establish whether or not they acted as they believed *at the time* they ought to act.

As Kohlberg's data, therefore, can tell us little about either genuine moral action or consistency between judgment and action, his conclusion cannot be relied upon to throw much light upon the issue he claims to be tackling.

(2)   Choices and Reasons for Action

My second set of objections concerns a further failure on Kohlberg's part to draw essential distinctions and to specify precisely which aspect of 'the judgment/action issue' he is dealing with. This confusion is well illustrated in his article 'From Is to Ought', which concludes with a subsection entitled 'From Thought to Action'.[9] Kohlberg begins this subsection, as the title suggests, by discussing how to 'relate moral judgment to moral action' (pp. 226–8), placing his customary reliance upon cheating tests in arguing that 'maturity of moral thought should predict to maturity of moral action' (pp. 228–9). There are immediate problems here over how 'should' should be interpreted, and more seriously over what is meant by 'maturity of moral action' (other than that Kohlberg presumably approves of it); for as Blasi has commented, '. . . at present nobody seems to know the parameters by which to evaluate the degree of maturity specifically in moral action, independently of cognition'.[10] It is difficult to know what Kohlberg is talking about here, particularly as he has in the preceding paragraph stated that there is 'no valid psychological definition of moral behaviour', and that the only differentiating criterion is 'what the people involved think they are doing' (p. 228).

Leaving this difficulty aside, however, we soon find that Kohlberg is not really concerned with moral *action* at all but with moral *choice*, sliding into a discussion of the latter without appearing to realize that there is a crucial distinction to be drawn here, which lies at the very heart of the issue he is supposed to be analyzing. He writes, 'Prediction to *action* thus requires that the alternatives are ordered by a hierarchy related to the individual's basic structures. In the case of Stage 4, we could only predict how a subject would *choose* when social order stands clearly on one side and other values on the other, as in civil disobedience' (p. 230, my italics). As another example of how 'stage defines choice', he then refers to 'the principled subject's sensitivity to justice which gives him a reason to not cheat when "law and order" reasons have become ambiguous or lost their force.' The conclusion drawn in the following sentence is that 'moral judgment dispositions influence *action* through being stable cognitive dispositions' (p. 230, my italics).

This passage reveals serious confusion. There is one question about whether 'stage defines *choice*' (for example, does being at Stage 5 rather than 3 affect whether one decides that it is right or wrong to cheat, steal drugs for one's wife, etc.), and another question about whether 'moral judgment determines *action*' (for example, does being at Stage 5 rather than 3 affect whether one actually behaves as one believes one ought in cheating, stealing drugs for one's wife, etc.). These questions are logically distinct, and to blur that distinction is to miss the main point of 'the judgment/action issue'.

The confusion arises from the ambiguity of the notions of 'moral choice' and 'moral decision'. These can refer either to:

1 'judgmental', 'propositional' choices and decisions *that* it is right or wrong to cheat, steal drugs, etc., or to
2 'behavioural', 'action' choices and decisions *to* or *not to* cheat, steal drugs, etc.

It is this distinction which produces the possibility of 'weak-willed' behaviour, which in turn lies at the heart of 'the judgment/action issue', for it is normally considered a not uncommon feature of our moral experience to decide *that* we ought to do *x*, but to want for various reasons to do *y* rather than *x*, and consequently to decide *to* do *y* rather than *x*.

Why does Kohlberg ignore this distinction and say so little about the topic he claims to be investigating in this passage—'behaviour which is consistent with an individual's moral principles' (p. 228)? The explanation seems to lie in his failure to probe sufficiently deeply the concept of 'reasons for action'. Yet again there are crucial distinctions to be drawn here. In cases of 'weak-willed' behaviour what appears to be happening is that two different kinds of 'reason for action' are in conflict. The agent accepts that there are good reasons why he ought to do *x*, yet other reasons are operative upon him in the actual situation which lead him to do *y* instead. In other words he sees that factors *A*, *B*, *C*, constitute reasons which *justify* or *require* the doing of *x*, yet he fails to do *x* because factors *D*, *E*, *F*, constitute reasons which *motivate* or *incline* him to do *y*—or to put it more simply, we do not always want to do what we believe we ought to do. Reasons for action of a justifying kind, therefore, do not always provide us with reasons for action of a motivating kind.[11]

Kohlberg does not appear to recognize that these different kinds of reason for action can or should be distinguished. In the passage already quoted, in discussing how 'stage defines choice' he states, 'It is the principled subject's sensitivity to justice which gives him a reason to not cheat when "law and order" reasons have become ambiguous or lost their force', and immediately continues, 'We are arguing that moral judgment dispositions influence action . . .' (p. 230). But justice and law and order are *justificatory* considerations, and while these may well define the subject's 'judgmental' choice *that* it is wrong to cheat, they will not necessarily provide a *motivational* 'reason to not cheat' in the actual situation, where counter-inclinations may weigh more heavily when the chips are down.

This confusion between motivation and justification is evident elsewhere in Kohlberg's work. At one point he writes mysteriously of 'the motivational aspect of morality (as) defined by the motive mentioned by the subject in justifying moral action.'[12] At another he produces a table of 'motives for moral action' corresponding to each of the six stages.[13] Yet in none of these cases is Kohlberg really describing *motives* for *action*—that is, reasons which motivate a person actually to *act* in a certain way; what he is describing are verbal justifications of moral judgments—that is, reasons which a person gives to justify why he thinks that it is right to act in a certain way. Again we must conclude that it is Kohlberg's overwhelming methodological emphasis upon moral *judgment* which leads him to equate these fundamentally distinct kinds of 'reason for action'.

(3) Rules and Principles

'Reasons for action' are also connected with a further oddity in Kohlberg's account, which concerns his view of rules and principles. Higher-stage subjects, who are allegedly more likely to act in accordance with their judgments than lower-stage ones, are said to reason in terms of principles rather than rules: 'morally mature men are governed by the principle of justice rather than by a set of rules'.[14] So principles appear to have a stronger, more reliable 'motivational power' than rules:

> The motivational power of principled morality does not come from rigid commitment to a concept or a phrase. Rather, it is motivated by awareness of the feelings and claims of the other people in the moral situation. What principles do is to sort out these claims, without distorting them or cancelling them out, so as (to) leave personal inclination as the arbiter of action.[15]

What precisely distinguishes a rule from a principle in Kohlberg's view? We are told:

> Justice is not a rule or a set of rules, it is a moral principle. By a moral principle we mean a mode of choosing which is universal, a rule of choosing which we want all people to adopt in all situations. We know it is all right to be dishonest and steal to save a life because it is just . . . We know it is sometimes right to kill, because it is sometimes just . . . There are exceptions to rules, then, but no exception to principles . . . A moral principle is not only a rule of action but a reason for action.[16]

This passage raises a host of questions, many of which fall strictly outside the scope of this chapter. Does Kohlberg, for example, grant too high and exclusive a status to 'the principle of justice', placing it at the apex of a Platonic hierarchy, where 'there are not many virtues but one', because 'the good is justice'?[17] Why can we not describe Stage 4 reasons as based on *principles* concerning the maintenance of law, authority and social order? Does Kohlberg really mean that moral principles are *universal* ('rules of choosing which we want all people to adopt in all situations') rather than *universalizable* in Hare's much more sophisticated sense? Who are the 'we' who all 'know' that it is sometimes all right to be dishonest, steal and even kill? Considerable strength of will is required to drop the pursuit of these tempting quarries.

There are, however, quite enough problems lurking in the principle/rule distinction as Kohlberg propounds it, and in the relevance he implies that it has for 'the judgment/action issue'. Kohlberg's distinction is obscurely expressed and is made no clearer by his description of a moral principle as a *rule* of choosing and also a *rule* of action; the distinction between a rule of action and a reason for action goes unexplained; and the ambiguity of 'choosing' and of 'a reason for action' is again ignored.

Let us try to dispel some of this conceptual murk. What characterizes a principle and distinguishes it from a rule (as we normally understand these terms) is not its content or its 'universality', but its function. Principles represent sets of highly general considerations which we *appeal to* in order to *justify* a particular course of action in a particular situation.[18] Rules on the other hand prescribe more specifically what is or is not to be done in that situation. In terms of content, therefore, there is room for possible overlap between rules and principles: truth-telling or promise-keeping, for instance, could count either as rules in situations where they function simply as prescriptions (as in the rules for witnesses in a court of law, summarized in the oath), or as principles if they are appealed to as a source of justification (as in an argument about the rights and wrongs of gazumping).

If principles, then, are essentially justificatory in nature, they do not have any *necessary* 'motivational power', for the reasons given in the previous subsection, and when Kohlberg claims that 'a moral principle is not only a rule of action but a reason for action', he can be referring only to a *justifying* 'reason for action' of the kind that is involved in the making of 'judgmental', 'propositional' choices and decisions. Principles cannot therefore be relied upon to bridge the judgment/action gap. We understand what is meant by expressions like 'he acted against his principles', and do not feel that we are talking logical or psychological nonsense when we use them. 'Having principles' is no guaranteed defence against succumbing to counter-inclinations. As Neil Cooper puts it, 'There is no necessary one-one correlation between the order of priority of a man's moral principles and the order of strength of his desires'.[19] This is because moral principles have a 'cool-hour' quality: 'a man's moral principles are those of his principles of action which in a cool hour he is least prepared to abandon belief in, however much he may be tempted to deviate from them in the heat of the moment'.[20] These important conceptual points show clearly why principles are an appropriate medium through which to describe some central features of Kohlberg's theory, for the discussion of *hypothetical* moral dilemmas is very much a 'cool-hour' activity. But it is in the heat of the moment that one has to choose or decide *to* act or *not to* act upon one's judgments, and here at the heart of 'the judgment/action issue' the role of principles becomes much more problematic than Kohlberg appears to realize.

CONCLUSION

My aim in this chapter has not been to show that Kohlberg is wrong in his claim that higher-stage subjects are more likely to act in accordance with their judgments than lower-stage subjects. Indeed, I have argued elsewhere that there are logical considerations which support this claim.[21] Kohlberg's suggestion that 'attention' correlates with 'strength of will'[22] could also be a fruitful one, and is again in accord with my own attempts at a logical analysis of 'weakness of will'.[23] (I have not referred to this aspect of Kohlberg's work in this chapter, as it appears unrelated to his basic, cognitive-developmental interpretation of 'the judgment/action issue'.)

What this chapter has shown is that Kohlberg pays scant attention to the complex relationship between moral judgment and moral action. He is prevented from getting to grips with these complexities, partly by the constraints of his 'hypothetical' research method and partly by the inadequacy and undifferentiated nature of his conceptual armoury. Whether or not 'cognitive definitions determine behaviour' as Kohlberg maintains, his own 'cognitive definitions' of moral agency, choices, decisions and principles have certainly determined and restricted his behaviour as an investigator of the moral domain.

REFERENCES

1 Hare, R. M. (1952) *The Language of Morals*, London, OUP, p. 1.
2 Straughan, R. (1975) 'Hypothetical moral situations', *Journal of Moral Education*, 4, 3, pp. 183–9. Also (1982a) *I Ought to, But . . .; A Philosophical Approach to the Problem of Weakness of Will in Education*, Windsor, NFER-Nelson, pp. 173–6
3 Kohlberg, L. (1971) 'From is to ought: How to commit the naturalistic fallacy and get away with it in the study of moral development', in Mischel, T. (Ed.) *Cognitive Development and Epistemology*, New York, Academic Press, p. 228.
4 *Ibid.*, p. 229.
5 See, e.g., Kohlberg, L. (1969) 'Stage and sequence: The cognitive-developmental approach to socialization', in Goslin, D. A. (Ed.) *Handbook of Socialization Theory and Research*, Chicago, Ill., Rand McNally, pp. 395–6. Also (1970) 'Education for justice: A modern statement of the Platonic view', in Sizer, N. F. and T. R. (Eds.) *Moral Education: Five Lectures*, Cambridge, Mass., Harvard University Press, pp. 77–9.
6 Kohlberg (1971), *op. cit.*, p. 229.
7 Hersh, R. H., Paolitto, D. P. and Reimer, J. (1979) *Promoting Moral Growth*, New York, Longman, p. 96.
8 See Straughan, R. (1982b) *Can We Teach Children to be Good?* London, Allen and Unwin.
9 Kohlberg (1971), *op. cit.*, pp. 226–32.
10 Blasi, A. (1980) 'Bridging moral cognition and moral action: A critical review of the literature', *Psychological Bulletin*, 88, 1, p. 8.
11 See Straughan (1982a), *op. cit.*, esp. Chs. 3 and 5.
12 Kohlberg, L. (1963) 'The development of children's orientation toward a moral order', *Vita Humana*, 6, p. 13.
13 Kohlberg (1969), *op. cit.*, pp. 381–2.
14 Kohlberg (1970), *op. cit.*, p. 70.
15 Kohlberg (1971), *op. cit.*, p. 231.
16 Kohlberg (1970), *op. cit.*, pp. 69–70.
17 *Ibid.*, p. 70.
18 See Peters, R. S. (1981) *Moral Development and Moral Education*, London, Allen and Unwin.
19 Cooper, N. (1971) 'Oughts and wants', in Mortimore, G. W. (Ed.) *Weakness of Will*, London, Macmillan, p. 197.

20 *Ibid.*
21 Straughan, R. (1983) 'From moral judgment to moral action', in Weinreich-Haste, H. and Locke D. (Eds.) *Morality in the Making*, Chichester, Wiley, pp. 125–40.
22 Kohlberg (1969), *op cit.*, pp. 396–7.
23 Straughan (1982a), *op. cit.*, esp. Ch. 6.

Journal of Personality and Social Psychology
1975, Vol. 32, No. 2, 255-270

Hypothetical and Actual Moral Reasoning in a Situation of Civil Disobedience

Norma Haan
Institute of Human Development, University of California, Berkeley

The nature of the correspondence between stages of moral reasoning about hypothetical dilemmas and stages of moral reasoning about an actual situation of civil disobedience was analyzed in terms of choice of action, ideology, and personal-social constructions for 310 Berkeley students. Two thirds of the students used a different stage of reasoning—46% higher and 20% lower—for the actual situation than they did for the hypothetical dilemmas. The patterns of gain accorded with the cognitive-moral theory's propositions concerning developmental readiness in young adults within a disequilibrating situation; action that supported ideology was also associated with gain. Loss, not predicted by the theory, characterized students whose action and ideology were inconsistent and whose personal constructions suggested special sensitivity to authority conflict. An argument is made that cognitive-moral research needs to recognize that structures are often filtered through a variety of functions before they become manifest in either thought or action.

Although the number of significant studies recently generated by the cognitive theory of moral development is impressive, almost all this work is based on subjects' reasoning in regard to hypothetical dilemmas, those designed by Kohlberg (1969). A question important to the further development and refinement of the theory needs to be kept in mind: What are the patterns of correspondence between reasoning, deciding, and acting in actual situations of moral conflict and reasoning about hypothetical situations? This question is more than a matter of "good" design or of validating an instrument by behavioral criteria; it is rather a consideration of the conditions under which people actualize their structural capacities in both thought and action. Most work has assumed that the stage used in hypothetical reasoning is the same as the stages used in situational reasoning and action—or at least that the two are as-

sociated—whereas instances of moral courage might be described as cases in which the stages of situational reasoning and action are higher than the stage of hypothetical reasoning, and moral default as cases in which they are lower than the stage of hypothetical reasoning. Moreover, the circumstances that support or diminish the accuracy of equating actual reasoning with action are not known. These issues concern the interregulation of cognition and action and are addressed in this report with a variety of information, which includes actual moral reasoning and the action choices of Berkeley students in regard to the sit-in of the Free Speech Movement (FSM) at the campus administration building in 1964.

These issues are also addressed in the work by Turiel and Rothman (1972), which employed an experimental paradigm wherein children were confronted with immediate but relatively mild, contrived moral dilemmas and were asked to make both cognitive and behavioral choices. This procedure and its variants (see Turiel, 1966, 1974) have yielded critical understandings of normative stage development and transition for the conventional moral level. The focus here, however, is not primarily on development, but rather on the implications of intense situational involvement as it affects young adults' inter-

The original research was funded by grants to Brewster Smith, Jeanne Block, and Norma Haan from the Rosenberg Foundation of San Francisco and the Foundations' Fund for Research in Psychiatry. The present work was supported by U.S. Public Health Service Grant HD 1650, directed by Paul Mussen.

Requests for reprints should be sent to Norma Haan, Institute of Human Development, University of California, Berkeley, 1203 Edward Chace Tolman Hall, Berkeley, California 94720.

regulation of hypothetical and actual moral thinking and action choice. It is expected that systematic discrepancies sometimes occur among the moral levels that people use when they think about what a hypothetical person should do, when they think about what *they* should do, and when they act. Further, it is assumed that these discrepancies will not only be associated with people's moral capacity but also with their more general ability to cope with the complexity, intensity, and content of particular situations.

Since civil disobedience is used in this study as the action criterion, and it is not one that reasonable people can immediately accept as a moral action, more needs to be said about it and activism generally. Although moral protest must always be activist in the sense of intervening in an ongoing course of events, activism is not necessarily a moral behavior. It may be undertaken for nonmoral reasons that are merely personally preferred or capricious. However, as reported (Haan, Smith, & Block, 1968), activism was a statistically frequent choice of Bay Area principled students as compared to conventionally moral students during the 1960's.[1] The previously published findings were based on subjects whose moral reasoning was stage homogeneous (approximately one half of a sample of 900); later study (Haan & Block, Note 1) that included all subjects with moral scores sharpened the contrast. Roughly 70% of a number of different activist groups, but only 46% to 26% of various nonactivist groups, used principled thinking as a major or minor way of deciding hypothetical moral issues. Fishkin, Keniston, and MacKinnon (1973) recently reported a replication of this general finding in a study of activism arising from the bombing of Cambodia.

Nevertheless, the nature of student activism during the 1960's was group protest, and not all persons are disposed to join or to act in groups. In fact, further examination of the original data (Haan & Block, Note 1) indicated that morally conventional activists differed from conventional nonactivists in seeing

themselves as impulsive, socially skillful, and indulged by their parents. Both were group affiliative, but the nonactivists joined social rather than political groups. Principled nonactivists differed from principled activists in regarding themselves as more tender, reserved, and sensitive, and in comparison they were not group affiliative.

These findings indicated that nonmoral, personal predispositions affect and thereby confound the criterion of activism as moral action. At the same time common social logic dictates that the principled person should protest in a situation of clear violation of his principles if he is to maintain self-consistency (integrity); however, group action is not required. Moreover, in the judgment of citizens, legal systems, and wise men, ultimate moral responsibility rests with the individual.

Nevertheless, the criterion of activism, and here the civil disobedience of the Free Speech Movement, had methodological and substantive advantages: the FSM crisis was local, particular, and vivid in its impact on a large number of people. The act was the climax of a campus situation that had endured for 4 months in great complexity and heat (after new campus regulations were announced that would sharply restrict political activity), and almost all those arrested must have expected that they would be. Consequently, it can be expected that most students were informed and deliberate in their choice. Few were able to be nonpartisan as the situation became one of "no exit." Moreover, there was considerable campus consensus about the rightness of the act. Campus polls (Lyons, 1965) showed that about 70% of the students became pro-FSM, and in the end the University of California Academic Senate voted 824 to 115 to support a series of resolutions that were widely regarded as affirming the arguments of the Free Speech Movement. Although a majority consensus neither decides the rightness of an act nor the moral level of any individual's action, all matters considered and for the purposes of this empirical study of group trends, it appeared reasonable to work with the assumption that in general few doubted that a distinctively moral action of objective and personal expense had been taken, whether they agreed on its value or

---

[1] The term *principled* refers to Stages 5 and 6 as they are described in the Kohlberg (1969) system; *conventional* refers to Stages 3 and 4.

not. The polarization of this issue meant that those who did not sit in had probably also examined the moral grounds of their positions. The task here is to understand how students of various persuasions structured their moral thinking and their action decisions as these relate to their hypothetical thinking, which is taken as the baseline.

HYPOTHESES AND QUESTIONS

Features of the Situation

The public debate of the student leaders, faculty, and administrators from September to December was often couched in morally principled terms; however, the majority (68%) of the students were not morally principled. Thus the speakers' and listeners' structuring of the situation did not often match. This is a naturalistic instance of disequilibrium, the vehicle of development conceptualized and investigated by Langer (1969) for cognitive progress and by Turiel (1969) for moral progress. It was expected, then, that gains from hypothetical to actual moral reasoning might occur, irrespective of the students' ideological position.

Second, since the moral theory is concerned with the evolution of increasingly differentiated structures, little attention has been given to the possible effects of ideological disagreement on the development of moral forms (see Alker & Poppen, 1973; Keasey, 1973, for exceptions). It seems possible, however, that an action taken for reasons of ideological stance could subsequently stimulate more adequate forms of moral justification. This would be most likely if the person is in developmental flux and/or in an inescapable situation where no choice is in essence a choice, since the conflict might be more adequately resolved by the emergence of more differentiated moral forms. On this count, too, gain might be generally expected, especially among those students who had taken a clear position.

Finally, the situational stress needs to be considered. Stress is commonly expected to result in decrement in function; however, moral action, even when personally expensive, can also represent a move to greater clarity and calm. Thus stress could work to produce either decrements or increments in the students' moral levels.

Developmental Status of the Subjects as Young Adults

Given the situational necessity of moral self-examination, it was expected that students who reasoned at the same stage for the hypothetical and FSM situations would be those who had stably consummated their moral development. Presumably, two different states could account for such stability: (a) a defensive closedness to further disequilibrium and termination at a lower stage or (b) the capacity to integrate moral decision and action so as to structure the authority-affronting situation in principled terms.

Some students could be expected to be in developmental flux. Kohlberg and Kramer (1969) report that progress continued until the late twenties with a longitudinal sample, and Haan (1974) found like changes in a follow-up study of Peace Corps Volunteers. The disquieting situational features should then lead the developmentally ready students to use higher stage forms in reasoning about the FSM, but according to the theory this readiness should be prefigured in their hypothetical reasoning by some minor use of higher stage forms.

The use of a lower stage to structure the FSM situation is not an instance of regression, since hypothetical reasoning, as an indicant of capacity, is maintained. In this context, loss is likely to be an encapsulated structural disorganization related to personal reactions that results in manifest dysfunctioning specific to this real-life, stressful situation. Blatt (1970) reports that black adolescents use lower stages in reasoning about conflicts involving society than they do in thinking about interpersonal relations, and Kohlberg, Scharf, and Hickey (1973) report that lower stages are used by prisoners when they reason about prisons. Thus the loss phenomenon probably cannot be understood solely in moral terms. The stressed person may remain latently at his achieved moral stage and may use it again in less complex, trying situations. Presumably, unresolved moral stress would be evidenced by a failure to complement one's convictions with action or by continuing indecision.

METHOD

Subjects

The present sample was drawn from a larger one of 394 Berkeley undergraduates who were enrolled during the FSM crisis and who participated several months later in a study of student activism. Various reports of analyses that included additional subjects from San Francisco State University and the Peace Corps have been made (for the most general descriptions see Block, Haan, & Smith, 1969; Haan et al., 1968; Smith, Haan, & Block, 1970). The subsample of 310 Berkeley students chosen here met several criteria: Their answers to the FSM questions were in sufficient detail to be scored, and either the same score was given to each subject by two judges working independently ($n = 290$) or both judges' designations resulted in a clear classification of the subject as having maintained parity, gained, or lost in relationship to his hypothetical reasoning ($n = 20$). Subjects were contacted from the following groups: the FSM arrestees, the California Conservatives for Political Action (an activist, Ayn Rand group), Young Democrats, Young Republicans, and a cross-sample randomly drawn from the registration files (ns for the various groups can be seen in Table 2). Although personal contact was made with the leaders of each group—except for the randomly drawn sample—letters were written to almost all potential subjects, and data collection forms were sent and returned in the mail. As a result, response rate was not high (roughly 50%), so neither Berkeley students nor particular subsamples are well represented.

Data

Data included five of the moral interview stories designed by Kohlberg (1969), the FSM moral questions, biographical information, reports of political-social beliefs of self and family, Q-sorted descriptions of self and ideal self, and the Child Rearing Practices Report (Block, Note 2), a retrospective Q-sorted description of mothers' and fathers' techniques. Five questions were asked about the Free Speech Movement (e.g., "Do you think it was right or wrong for the students to sit in? Why or why not?" "Suppose an authority doesn't keep his agreement; what then is the extent and nature of one's own obligation? Explain your position.").

A condensed scoring guide defining the pro and con ideological positions for each stage is shown in Table 1. Reliability of scoring, based on the weighted modal stage scores of two judges, was .82 for the hypothetical stories and .72 for the FSM questions. The protocols were masked for sample membership. To increase the number of subjects, those who used mixed stages of moral reasoning were classified according to their major, predominant stage and grouped with those whose reasoning was more

stage homogeneous. Subjects who used the same stage of reasoning for the hypothetical and FSM situations will be called the equal group; those who used higher stages for the Free Speech Movement, the gain group; and those who used lower stages for the Movement, the loss group.

RESULTS

Sex Differences

Sex differences in moral change patterns were analyzed within each stage of hypothetical reasoning and for all stages combined. Although more women gained (45%) compared to men (36%), none of the differences were significant; consequently, most subsequent analyses were done with men and women combined.

Moral Change Groups' Variations in Use of Minor Stages

The extent of variation in stage use across the five hypothetical stories was calculated for each moral change group considered as an entity. Although the assigned stage accounted for approximately 45% of the reasoning for the entire sample, the gain subjects did use a greater proportion of higher stage reasoning than the other two (a total of 43% compared to the equal group's 24% and the loss group's 33%). Consequently, higher stage FSM reasoning for the gain group may reflect a readiness to develop, prefigured in their hypothetical thought and then energized by the crucial nature of the situation. Note, however, that the reverse was not true for the loss group, which actually used more higher stage as well as less lower stage thinking than the equal group (lower stage thinking was 24% for the loss group, 28% for the equal, and 14% for the gain group). Consequently, the FSM reasoning of the loss subjects appears to be a disjunctive response to the situation, not predictable from their hypothetical thinking. The results for the gain subjects accord with the theory, whereas those for the loss subjects do not.

General Patterns of Moral Change by Stages of Hypothetical Reasoning

More students (46%) reasoned about the FSM situation in higher stage terms than maintained parity (34%) or used lower stage

TABLE 1

EXAMPLES OF SCORING GUIDES FOR MORAL REASONING ABOUT THE FREE SPEECH MOVEMENT
(FSM) SIT-IN: PRO AND CON POSITIONS

Pro	Con
	Stage 2	
Focuses on the students' needs, denies sit-in harmed the University; says it worked; needs to retaliate against manipulative authorites.	Sit-in was a tool that didn't make sense since power lay with the authorities.
	Stage 3	
Sit-in was both right and wrong, but the motives were good; necessary because authorities were unfeeling about students' needs.	Other, more peaceful means could have been used; authorities knew students' best interests and would have responded if they were approached reasonably.
	Stage 4	
Sit-in was instrumental to the pursuit of social values and goals which form a coherent unit; new authorities were needed.	FSM's violation of rules made the sit-in wrong; the system provides orderly means for redress that should not be disrupted.
	Stage 5	
Authorities broke social contracts with the students, making it mandatory that the students sit in as a dialogue for establishing new understandings.	Concern that FSM didn't use legitimate means to attain objectives; students could leave; their enrollment was an agreement to live by the University's rules.
	Stage 6	
Focuses on the objective values of civil rights; differentiates moral and legal obligations to justify this civil disobedience.	Trust is always conditional even in an ideal society; an individual authority revoked agreements, so that disobedience to the institution was neither logical nor ideal.

forms (20%), as can be seen in Table 2. This difference significantly departs from a chance split ($\chi^2 = 40.97$, $p \leq .01$). The predominance of the gain pattern is consistent with assumptions discussed earlier that certain aspects of the situation and the participants should generally stimulate moral progress.

Consideration of the change patterns for each stage shown in Table 2 indicates that (a) no student used Stage 1 for structuring the FSM situation, which is not unexpected for a university population; (b) gain was the predominant trend for those who used Stage 2 and 3. However, some users of Stages 2 and 3 may have been in flux and confused and thereby misidentified by the standard scoring system, but may then have resolved their confusions to reveal their latent capacity

in the FSM questions (see Haan, 1971; Haan, Stroud, & Holstein, 1973; and Turiel, 1974, for empirical examinations of young adults who are probably transitional between the conventional and principled levels and who temporarily use relativistic thinking that has superficial similarity to Stage 2 thinking; similar phenomena may occur with Stage 3); (c) the majority of Stage 4 users maintained equality between their hypothetical and actual reasoning; and (d) students representing both principled stages split fairly evenly between the equality and loss patterns.

Although the more specific meanings of these results are yet to be explicated, they do suggest that students of different moral stages structured this authority-defying situation in divergent ways. The results could be thought to represent a regression toward the mean,

TABLE 2

DISTRIBUTION OF MORAL CHANGE PATTERNS BY CONTACT SAMPLE
AND MORAL STAGES (HYPOTHETICAL REASONING)

Stage (Hypothetical)	Loss		Equal		Gain		Total	% Stage (Hypothetical) within subsample
	n	%	n	%	n	%	n	
Total sample								
2	0	0	5	13	33	87	38	12
3	2	3	26	28	63	69	91	29
4	27	29	43	46	24	26	94	30
5	30	43	26	38	13	19	69	22
6	(10)	(55)	(8)	(45)	—	—	(18)	6
Total[a,b]	59	20	100	34	133	46	292	100
FSM arrestees								
2	0	0	3	18	14	82	17	21
3	2	8	6	23	18	69	26	32
4	3	25	0	0	9	75	12	15
5	8	31	8	31	10	38	26	32
6	(4)	(33)	(8)	(66)	—	—	(12)	—
Total[b]	13	16	17	21	51	63	81	100
Cross-sample								
2	0	0	2	14	12	86	14	9
3	0	0	17	32	37	68	54	36
4	17	29	29	50	12	21	58	38
5	14	56	9	36	2	8	25	17
6	(4)	(100)	(0)	(0)	—	—	(4)	—
Total[b]	31	21	57	38	63	42	151	100
Conservatives/Republicans								
2	0	0	0	0	5	100	5	11
3	0	0	2	29	5	71	7	16
4	5	25	13	45	2	10	20	44
5	5	38	7	54	1	8	13	29
6	(1)	(100)	(0)	(0)	—	—	(1)	
Total[b]	10	22	22	49	13	29	45	100

Note. Numbers in boldface represent the highest values obtained.
[a] Democrats ($n = 16$) are included in these calculations.
[b] Stage 6 users are excluded from all summary calculations.

but the main findings of moral stage research with regard to the developmental status of young adults, as well as other more controlled analyses to be reported in this article, make this statistical explanation untenable.

Patterns of Moral Changes by Stages of Hypothetical Reasoning Within Contact Samples

The moral change patterns for the four main contact groups are also shown in Table 2. (15 Democrats are not included; many of them were civilly disobedient and thus became members of the FSM sample.) The differences in moral change patterns were significant when the FSM arrestees were compared with the cross-sample, $\chi^2(2) = 9.63$, $p \leq .10$, and with the Conservatives/Republicans, $\chi^2(2) = 12.91$, $p \leq .05$, but the comparison between the cross-sample and Conservatives/Republicans was not.

Attention to the individual stages shows that gain was the predominant trend for FSM arrestees of all stages, while only Stage 2 and

3 users gained in every sample. The Stage 4 patterns are markedly different from one sample to the next: None of the 12 FSM subjects reasoned about the Free Speech Movement in Stage 4 terms; 75% gained and 25% lost, whereas approximately half of the cross-sample and Conservatives/Republicans Stage 4 users maintained parity. Stage 5 also shows contrasting patterns: the FSM subjects are approximately equally divided between loss, equality, and gain, most cross-sample subjects lost, and Conservatives/Republicans maintained parity. As for the few users of Stage 6, 8 of the 12 FSM arrestees maintained parity, whereas none of the other 6 subjects using Stage 6 forms did. The loss rate is approximately equal across samples.

From these findings we can conclude that Stage 2 and 3 forms of reasoning in university students are apparently not consolidated, since both were frequently abandoned for higher stage reasoning irrespective of their holders' group membership, and that changes to higher stages are specific to sample membership, whereas loss occurred in all samples.

Patterns of Moral Change with Action or Attitude Controlled

Although the Free Speech Movement was primarily supported by liberals and radicals, its civil libertarian issues drew support from persons of other persuasions. For instance, support for the Movement was indicated by 18% of the Conservatives/Republicans group and 49% of the cross-sample. Moreover a sizable proportion of the pro-FSM students (54%) did not become civilly disobedient. In view of these anomalies, four new groups representing combinations of attitude and action were constituted: (a) the FSM arrestees, (b) pro-FSM students who were not civilly disobedient, (c) con-FSM students, and (d) students neutral to the Movement.

Acting or not acting among pro-FSM students. Table 3 shows the differences in moral change patterns associated with the pro-FSM students' decision to sit in or not. A highly significant difference occurred, indicating that arrested students more often used mature forms in reasoning about the Free Speech Movement. This finding counters the explanation that the results are an artifact of a regression to the mean, since generally the arrestees also used higher stages of hypothetical reasoning: 41% of the arrestees were principled compared to 32% of the nonacting students.

The moral change patterns for all the users of Stage 2 and 3 forms are virtually indistinguishable; substantial majorities of both gained. However, action choice did have divergent effects for the Stage 4 users. Significantly more of those acting did structure the Free Speech Movement as a principled moral issue, whereas considerably more of the nonacting group formulated the FSM situation as they had the hypothetical dilemmas, as a formal question of law and order. Their loss rates are the same. The Stage 5 comparison indicates that significantly more students who did not integrate reasoning, action, and ideology were members of the loss group, compared to the substantial gain for those who did. This pattern is replicated with the Stage 6 users, although the small numbers of subjects makes the observation tenuous when considered for this stage alone. Noteworthy, however, is the stability of the 8 out of 12 civilly disobedient subjects.

Altogether, the results suggest that (a) the situational reasoning of Stage 2 and 3 subjects was not influenced by their action choice, (b) Stage 4 subjects who integrated their ideology and action moved to explaining the situation in principled terms, and (c) the situational reasoning of the Stage 5 and 6 subjects was most reactive to an inconsistency between commitment and action. Thus, even though the stage designations for the two situations do not often correspond, the students' baseline capacity appears to exert an important influence on their ex post facto cognitive construction of the FSM crisis when their action choice is taken into account. This may suggest that the nonacting, principled students needed to evoke various defenses—rationalizing, denial, compartmentalization—to explain themselves to themselves during the aftermath of the sit-in. The consequence appears to have been a deterioration in their cognitive moral constructions of the situation impelled by a continuing need to reconcile their action with their pro-FSM ideology.

185

TABLE 3

Patterns of Moral Change with Action or Attitude Controlled

	Action among pro-FSM students					Attitude of non-civilly disobedient students				
	Moral change patterns			n	x^2		Moral change patterns			n	x^2
	Loss	Equal	Gain				Loss	Equal	Gain		
					All Stages[a]						
Sitting in	16%	21%	**63%**	81	31.29***	Pro FSM	**45%**	32%	23%	97	ns
Not sitting in	**45**	32	23	97		Neither	29	**46**	26	35	
						Con FSM	35	**47**	18	78	
					Stage 2						
Sitting in	0	18	**82**	17	ns	Pro FSM	0	8	**92**	13	ns
Not sitting in	0	8	**92**	13		Neither	0	20	**80**	5	
						Con FSM	0	0	**100**	3	
					Stage 3						
Sitting in	8	23	**69**	26	ns	Pro FSM	0	29	**71**	28	6.94**
Not sitting in	0	29	**71**	28		Neither	0	**64**	36	11	
						Con FSM	0	20	**80**	25	
					Stage 4						
Sitting in	25	0	**75**	12	6.90**	Pro FSM	26	**37**	**37**	27	12.43***
Not sitting in	26	**37**	**37**	27		Neither	**46**	**46**	8	13	
						Con FSM	24	**67**	10	42	
					Stage 5						
Sitting in	31	31	**39**	26	8.12**	Pro FSM	**52**	41	7	29	ns
Not sitting in	**52**	41	7	29		Neither	**50**	33	17	6	
						Con FSM	**50**	**50**	0	8	
					Stage 6						
Sitting in	33	**67**	—	12	.08*[b]	Pro FSM	**100**	0	—	3	ns
Not sitting in	**100**	0	—	3		Neither	0	0	—	0	
						Con FSM	**100**	0	—	3	

Note. Stage numbers refer to hypothetical reasoning. FSM = Free Speech Movement. Numbers in boldface represent the highest values obtained.
[a] Excludes Stage 6 users.
[b] Probability of Fisher's exact test.
* $p < .10$.
** $p < .05$.
*** $p < .01$.

FSM attitudes among the non-civilly disobedient. Ideological differences toward the movement relate only to the moral change patterns for the two conventional stages. The pattern of differences for the Stage 3 users indicates that those who took either pro or con positions made substantial gains, whereas the uncommited had a high rate of parity. Considering the insufficiency of Stage 3 forms

with their emphasis on harmony vis-à-vis the moral complexity of civil disobedience, I suggest that the neutral students may have reacted with defensive withdrawal and denial. Haan et al. (1973) have previously shown that Stage 3 hippies generally tend to be more defensive than either Stage 2 or 4 users. It is of some importance to underscore the finding that the anti-FSM Stage 3 users improved their reasoning, an indication that a pro ideology in itself does not explain the gain pattern.

Turning to Stage 4, as a more differentiated construction of authority's moral relationships to followers, we find highly significant differences. The most salient trend is that 67% of the con Stage 4 users were stable, unlike their ideological companions at Stage 3. An anti-FSM attitude could be well supported by Stage 4 thinking in ideological alliance with the university authorities. However, a sizable proportion (46%) of the neutral Stage 4 users lost. A main concern of Stage 4 reasoning is the formal regulation and order of society. Since this situation was neither ordered nor regulated, apolitical Stage 4 users may not have known where to turn. At the same time their sophisticated forms would have kept them concerned with the problem of civil disobedience.

It is congruent with the special nature of conventional moral structures that ideological position relates to the change patterns, since conventional formulations depend heavily on external guidance. For the Stage 3 individual the ultimate locus of his responsibility is his loyalty to others; for the Stage 4 the locus is his commitment to extant social systems. This is not to say that principled persons are disloyal or uncommitted to systems; rather, the hierarchical organization of principled reasoning is more differentiated, and moral responsibility lies in the moral principles of the self.

Personal–Social Constructions of Self and Parents

Analyses of the personal–social data permit further evaluation of the likelihood that the change patterns can be attributed to three different phenomena—developmental readiness, developmental stabilization, and the defensive compartmentalization of the self. Analyses of variance were done following adjustments to remove the effects of two covariates: the moral stage of hypothetical reasoning and the degree of political conservatism–radicalism. The stages of hypothetical reasoning were controlled because the subsamples had varying distributions as well as unequal change patterns. Political stance was controlled so that the results would not simply reflect relationships between personality and politics. Thus the intent was to consider the personal–social conditions of movement in the most general sense. It should be noted that the young people's task of describing themselves and their parents by means of Q sorts produces personal constructions that do not necessarily or accurately represent their social realities. (Block et al., 1969, reported modest correlations of .37 and .40 between young people's descriptions of their parents and their parents' own self-descriptions.) All of these measures, like other self-reports (or any other behavior for that matter, as discussed in Haan, 1965), are determined by the individual's immediate motivations and his ego strategies of task engagement and self-disclosure. Q sorting is a process that involves the construction of social formulations, just as moral reasoning involves the construction of prescriptive, ideal formulations.

Equivalence compared with change (gain or loss). No significant demographic differences were found between the equal and change groups of either sex. Both equal groups report greater political–social compatibility with their parents: The men agreed with them about student demonstrations (whether pro or con), and the women attributed personal and ethical influence to their mothers as well as political influence to their teachers (see Table 4). The few self and ideal qualities that differentiate the groups suggest that equals of both sexes generally saw themselves as relatively judicious and autonomous and less reactive to interpersonal situations than the change groups. A variation of this theme distinguished their contrasting constructions of their parents. Both equal groups described their parents' child-rearing postion and attitudes as not only clear and well defined but also as relatively detached. In contrast, both change groups saw their parents as being emotionally entangled with them—warm and intimate but intrusive and ambivalently disciplinary. Thus the subjects' constructions of self and parents are consistent both with the equal group's maintenance of moral stability at all stages and with the changers' situa-

TABLE 4

PERSONAL-SOCIAL DIFFERENCES BETWEEN EQUAL AND CHANGE GROUPS

Male equal group higher ($n = 43$)	All male changers higher ($n = 100$)[a]	Female equal group higher ($n = 44$)	All female changers higher ($n = 78$)[a]
Parental agreement / **Source of influence**			
Agree with mother** and father** about student demonstrations		Personal influence: mother** Political influence: teachers** Ethical influence: mother*	Personal influence: older friends*
Self			
Idealistic*	Conventional** Calm** Foresighted* Considerate** Tolerant* Sensitive*	Considerate**** Fair, just**	Talkative*
Ideal			
Courageous** Guilty*	Self-confident*** Responsive* Dominating** Masculine*	Generous** Reserved** Fair, just* Orderly*	Independent*** Self-confident** Dominating*
Mother			
Let me know she was angry with me** Encouraged me to do my best*	Expected gratitude from me*** Expected me to control my feelings*** Thought children should be seen, not heard** Helped me when I was teased* Thought bad things could happen to me*	Children should be seen, not heard* Believed in early toilet training* Taught me not to cry at an early age* Enjoyed seeing me eat* Children shouldn't play without supervision*	Found it difficult to punish me** Great deal of conflict between us** Let me make my own decisions* Gave me family duties*
Father			
Let me take chances, try new things*** Believed competitive games were good*** Withheld sexual information until I could understand** Let me know when he was angry* Children shouldn't keep secrets*	Tended to spoil me**** Didn't want me to play rough games*** Shared warm, intimate times with me** Too wrapped up in his children** Worried about my health** Gave me comfort when I was upset* Kept me away from different values*	Liked time for himself*** Always knew where I was*** Important for me to play outdoors** Placed my mother's wishes ahead of my own* Punishment would find me if I were bad* Kept me away from different values*	Shared warm, intimate times with me* Was sorry to see me grow** Threat punishment more giving it** Greatest satisfactions from children* Let me make my own decisions* Bad things could happen to me* Had family duties to perform*

[a] Gain and loss groups combined.
* p < .10.
** p < .05.
*** p < .01.
**** p < .001.

tional reactivity and consequent readiness to shift their forms of their reasoning and choice of action.

Gain and loss groups compared. The members of the male gain group, compared to the loss group, saw themselves as interpersonally critical and unforgiving as well as guilty and disjointed (see Table 5). They rejected, even on an ideal basis, interpersonal warmth and commitment and wanted to be more *individualistic* and *foresightful.* They described their parental relationships as containing some conflict. Difficulties with their mothers centered on social–political issues, whereas their paternal relations lacked warmth and were defined by anger and contentiousness in regard to discipline and control. Men in the loss group, on the other hand, described themselves most positively, particularly in the interpersonal realm. Their ideal-self characteristics reiterate this regard but also suggest a degree of social vulnerability: *needs approval, talkative, reserved, competitive,* and *masculine.* They described their parents, particularly their fathers, as unusually protective, involved, and demonstrably loving, perhaps even cloying.

Altogether, then, the male students' personal–social constructions clearly contrast: The gain group took an adversary role with their parents and the world, particularly in regard to matters of authority and intellectual difference, whereas the loss group saw themselves in a remarkably open, even exposed, interpersonal position, regarding themselves and their parents as particularly intimate, considerate, and loving. The gain group's constructions are consistent with their developmental readiness; they appear ready to question authority and conventional regulation (the level of their anger is not absolutely great; the result is due more to the loss group's low scores). The loss group's constructions appear not to be anticipated by the moral theory. If anything, their personal description seems compatible with Stage 3 morality, but this effect was controlled, and there were only two Stage 3 subjects in the loss group. An interpretation based on an interaction of ego capacity and stress suggests that their loss may have resulted from a disrupted expectancy that the world of authority

was in loco parentis and as responsive to their openhanded ingratiation as they felt their parents to be. During the crisis, suppositions of harmony with authority became patently unsupportable, if for no other reason than the necessity of choosing which authority to follow.

Turning now to the results for the women, we can see that those who gained saw themselves as open, interpersonally reactive, sensitive personalities. This theme was repeated in their ideal-self descriptions along with several other virtues that seem necessary self-views for wishing oneself to be moral: *empathic, idealistic, genuine, fair,* and *just.* They described their mothers as supportive and willing to consider their preferences, although they believed their fathers often exerted more disciplinary force. Neither parent was seen as having urged their daughters to be competitive. The loss group members saw themselves as controlled and proud, and they idealized self-denial. Their mothers were more educated and viewed as ethically influential, disciplining, and powerful. Both parents urged their daughters to compete.

Unlike the men's, the women's gains are associated with a positive view of their parents. Thus the possibility presents itself that the women's gains were energized by the situational challenge rather than by the opportunity to resolve a developmentally transitional need to criticize authority, as appeared to be the case with the men. The women's loss, associated as it was with a self-denying, controlled view of self and a description of their mothers as influential, authoritative, and prodding, seems to suggest that their daughters may not have been able to conceive of themselves as having either individual responsibility or the need to make comprehensive moral decisions in an authority-defying situation.

Altogether then, gain for both men and women seems to be based on a latent but evocable capacity consistent with the theory's view of developmental readiness in this age group. However, the use of less mature forms in reasoning about the Free Speech Movement represents a shift that is not expected by the theory. Loss in men was related to an unrealistic denial of social complexities and conflict; loss in women is evidently associated with dependency and lack of separation from their families. Both loss groups seem ill prepared to cope with an authority-defying, confused, intense situation. It seems possible that these personal constructions evoked defensive structuring with a resulting logical lacuna about the FSM crisis, whether or not these students sat in, as approximately 25% of the loss group did.

DISCUSSION

The general finding that two thirds of this large sample used a different stage in thinking about this situation of civil disobedience than they did when they responded to the hypothetical dilemmas needs to be considered first. There were various aspects of the data collection that could have skewed the results toward gain but probably do not apply to the observations of loss or to those of equality. The moral data were written responses to the dilemmas and the probe questions; consequently, there was no way to ascertain whether the students' higher stage FSM reasoning reflected a superficial modeling of the moral rhetoric of the leaders. An open-ended interview would have permitted more rigorous probing to test the solidity of their formulations about the movement and the hypothetical dilemmas. However, if modeling was the basis for the observed gain, it would

TABLE 5

PERSONAL–SOCIAL DIFFERENCES BETWEEN GAIN AND LOSS GROUPS

Male gain group higher ($n = 60$)	Male loss group higher ($n = 40$)	
Self		
Critical***	Genuine***	Free, not hung up***
Guilty*	Tolerant**	Calm**
	Impulsive*	Sympathetic*
	Considerate*	
Ideal		
Individualistic*	Impulsive***	Reserved**
Foresightful*	Sympathetic**	Amusing**
	Talkative**	Need approval*
	Generous*	Competitive*
	Masculine*	Tolerant*
Mother		
(none)	Had firm rules for me***	
	Comforted me when I was upset**	
Index of general disagreement	Expressed affection by kissing, hugging**	
(politics, social issues and personal conflict)***	Joked and played with me**	
	Thought children should be supervised**	
	Didn't allow me to be angry with her*	
Father		
Good deal of conflict between us****	Comforted me when I was upset****	
Often felt angry with me****	Was easy going with me***	
Felt too much affection weakens a child***	Joked and played with me***	
Didn't permit me to question decisions***	Shared intimate times with me***	
Scoldings and criticism would help me**	Encouraged me to talk about troubles***	
Thought children should be seen, not heard**	Expressed affection by kissing, hugging**	
Physical punishment best discipline*	Was too wrapped up in his children**	
Thought I should always control my feelings*	Enjoyed a houseful of children**	
Dreaded my questions about sex*	Didn't want me to be different**	
	Children shouldn't have secrets*	

TABLE 5 (continued)

Female gain group higher ($n = 52$)		Female loss group higher ($n = 26$)
Personal influence: close friends**		Mother's education** Ethical influence: mother**

Self

Genuine***	Sensitive**	Self-controlled*
Sympathetic**	Adventurous*	Proud*
Impulsive*	Empathic*	

Ideal

Curious***	Genuine***	Self-denying**
Idealistic**	Empathic*	Playful*
Fair, just*		Doubting*

Mother

Helped me when I was teased***	Thought competitive games good**
My preferences considered in family plans**	Punished me by isolation*
Found it difficult to punish me**	Thought criticism would improve me*
Worried about my health**	Mother had more authority than father*
Didn't allow me to tease others*	

Father

Expected me not to get dirty*	Thought competitive games good*
Taught me that punishment would find me*	Encouraged me to do better than others*
Believed in early toilet training*	

* $p < .10.$
** $p < .05.$
*** $p < .01.$
**** $p < .001.$

be necessary to assume that differential exposure, modeling, and reinforcement occurred for the gainers within each sample as well as between various samples; for example, anti-FSM Stage 3 users who gained (80%) were exposed to and reinforced to model the administration's point of view, but the anti-FSM Stage 4 users (10% gained) were generally not. The moral–cognitive theory would acknowledge differential exposure and effects, but would stipulate that only some students would be affected by leaders' speeches and would then assimilate certain aspects to their own constructions. Specifically, these subjects would be those who were developmentally ready, a supposition supported here by the total gain group's somewhat more frequent, minor usage of higher stages than their assigned stage. The latter interpretation seems to fit the results better.

Another extraneous source of gain needs to be considered. Undoubtedly, most subjects had a great investment in the FSM questions. Here again, one would have to assume, in order to account for the systematic differences, that motivation varied on a linear dimension according to the subjects' gain, equality, and loss within samples and between samples. It does seem likely that the greater gain of the arrested students and even that of the con-FSM students could be explained on the basis of motivational differences, since both needed to support their ideologies within the polarized context of the time. But how, then, are the overall loss rates of 16% for the arrested students, of 35% for the con-FSM students, and the rates of equality for both pro and con students to be explained?

Alternatively, it may be that stage gain is a frequent consequence of asking persons for the grounds and warrant of a moral action that they have already taken or decided not to take. The explication of this possibility and its conditions was the point of this study. Optimally, the person in moral conflict should be asked in the heat of the moment, before he acts or does not act, in order to know the formulation of his plan and understand his subsequent action. But research will not be able ethically to intrude at this opportune moment in very many real situations of intense moral conflict. After the fact most people will need to justify themselves. Nevertheless, this data collection did not sufficiently inquire into the students' intermediate constructions between thought and action. The FSM questions were worded impersonally, and no attempt was made to discover directly the degree of stress, doubt, and contradictory pressures that each person had experienced about his moral position and action. As a result, various extrapolations had to be made from the facts; for example, being pro-FSM and not sitting in (as facts) would lead to a sense of inconsistency (a loss of integrity, usually called guilt on different theoretical bases), and this internal circumstance would then lead to an encapsulated cognitive disorganization about the FSM situation, with consequent de-differentiation of moral reasoning.

Although there are deficiencies in this study—some reparable by future work and others endemic to moral research—they seem insufficient to account for the disproportionate rate of students using both higher stage and lower stage forms. This general finding is not evidence that the theory (Kohlberg's moral dilemmas) or the scoring system are invalid, since knowledge of the subjects' stage of hypothetical reasoning, taken as an index of capacity, was necessary to understand the results. It does imply, however, that the interaction of moral and nonmoral features within actual moral situations may have different sequelae than they do in hypothetical situations. In short, people are not always reliably true to themselves.

Turning to more specific aspects of the results, we can see that gain generally occurred (a) as expected, with developmentally ready students, (b) with all Stage 2 users,

who were probably actually of a higher stage irrespective of their ideology or action, (c) with pro and con Stage 3 users who were not civilly disobedient, and (d) most markedly for pro-FSM students of Stages 4 and 5 who were arrested. We see then that the theory's normative, genetic description of gain is approximately correct, that mere confrontation with moral conflict is sufficient to enable most university students of lower stages to use higher stage forms, and that action that is consistent with ideology apparently energizes moral thought. When the action is nontrivial, it may well be the first, rather than the last manifestation of an evolving comprehension of more sufficient moral structuring than can yet be articulated in a cognitive–hypothetical way. Nevertheless, it can be readily observed in moral interviews that hypothetical decision is not a pallid experience, since people struggle with the elegance of their suppositional resolutions. Still, moral action is not required, and therein lies the rub: Action actualizes, while thoughts can always be taken back. Moral situations of less consequence and duration probably produce more equivalence and less change, as Turiel (1966) first found in experimental study.

Three specific groups of equal students do fit the normative, prima facie equation of hypothetical reasoning, actual reasoning, and action: neutral Stage 3 users, con-FSM Stage 4 users, and the pro-FSM and arrested Stage 6 users. Since stability is not specific to any single stage, it may instead follow an interaction between moral capacity and other nonmoral features (as these were organized within the FSM situation) that obviates new accommodation. I propose that the following interactions occurred: (a) The moral forms of the uncommitted Stage 3 users were not only unsuited to grappling with disagreement among respected authorities, but their lack of ideology gave them no guidance; consequently, there was no necessity to and even good reason for them not to expose themselves to the hazards of moral accommodations. (b) Within this situation of law violation the con-FSM Stage 4 users committed themselves to an ideological position that was consistent with their moral structures, which emphasize law and maintenance of order; consequently, they had no need to accommodate. (c) Since the arrested Stage 6 users structured the situation as one of individual moral responsibility, it was consistent with their ideology and their decision to become civilly disobedient, so that they, too, maintained equality.

In effect, these equal subjects of different stages integrated their actual and hypothetical reasoning and their action choices as they saw the situation through the filter of their various ideological positions. Turiel and Rothman (1972) had suggested that the sufficiency of structural organization at higher stages should make for greater integration of reasoning with action. In fact, there is some evidence to support this supposition with the pro-FSM subjects if we assume that such a position led logically to civil disobedience. Among the pro-FSM students 54% of the principled ones sat in, whereas 60% of the nonprincipled did not (excluding the probably misidentified Stage 2 users: $\chi^2 = 2.89$, $p \leq .10$). However, the Turiel and Rothman study assumed all other nonmoral factors to be equal. In the FSM situation personal–social constructions and ideology appeared to function defensively to select information and action, with the consequence that the integration of action and thought occurred at lower stages as well.

Loss typified pro-FSM students who did not sit in, particularly Stage 5 and the few Stage 6 users, as well as the neutral Stage 4 users. The loss group was generally characterized by distinctive personal–social constructions, suggesting they had particular difficulties and hesitancies in dealing with authority conflict and disobedience. I suggest they were involved in dilemmas that were more affective and social than moral, with the result that they became inconsistent and disorganized in their moral thinking about the Free Speech movement.

The thrust of these analyses is that there are systematic differences—apparently attributable to nonmoral characteristics of the participants—between giving a story character fictitious moral advice and formulating and acting on advice for oneself. The hypothetical stage provided a baseline for understanding the presented form of FSM reasoning when the organization of action choice, the nonmoral aspects of ideology, and personal–social constructions were taken into account. It may eventually turn out that there are structural elements embedded in ideological and personality attributes that reciprocally interact with moral structures to achieve more comprehensive equilibrations than we are now able to see. However, people are not always equilibrated, particularly young adults and persons in the midst of social upheavals. Moreover, equilibration can be "artificial" and achieved at the cost of factual and logical distortion and the diminution of the self. Whatever the case, the present results make it clear that in nonhypothetical circumstances moral structures are more often qualified—attenuated or elaborated—than not.

It is not the main job of moral theory to account for nonmoral conditions that may be merely associated with various stages; there is ample work yet to be done in explicating the taxonomy of normative stage progression and transition. When nonmoral conditions alter moral constructions by selecting and filtering informational input, thereby affecting accommodation, the question becomes one of understanding function and not merely one of cataloging deviance. The FSM situation was most intense, but then, actual moral dilemmas of consequence often are. If function is so readily disturbed, moral theory, more than cognitive theory, will have to take this aspect of its subject matter into account.

REFERENCE NOTES

1. Haan, N., & Block, J. H. *Further examination of the relationship between activism and morality.* Unpublished manuscript, 1969. (Available from Norma Haan, Institute of Human Development, University of California, Berkeley, 1203 Edward Chace Tolman Hall, Berkeley, California 94720.)

2. Block, J. H. *The child-rearing practices report.* Institute of Human Development, University of California, Berkeley, 1965. (Mimeo)

REFERENCES

Alker, H. A., & Poppen, P. J. Personality and ideology in university students. *Journal of Personality,* 1973, *41*, 653–671.

Blatt, M. *The effects of classroom discussion upon children's moral judgment.* Unpublished doctoral dissertation, University of Chicago, 1970.

Block, J. H., Haan, N., & Smith, M. B. Socialization correlates of student activism. *Journal of Social Issues,* 1969, *25*, 143–178.

Fishkin, J., Keniston, K., & MacKinnon, C. Moral reasoning and political ideology. *Journal of Personality and Social Psychology*, 1973, *27*, 109–119.

Haan, N. Coping and defense mechanisms related to personality inventories. *Journal of Consulting Psychology*, 1965, *29*, 373–378.

Haan, N. Moral redefinition in the family as the fundamental aspect of the generational gap. *Youth and Society*, 1971, *2*, 259–284.

Haan, N. Changes in young adults after Peace Corps experiences: Political–social views, moral reasoning, and perceptions of self and parents. *Journal of Youth and Adolescence*, 1974, *3*, 177–194.

Haan, N., Smith, M. B., & Block, J. H. Moral reasoning of young adults: Political–social behavior, family background, and personality correlates. *Journal of Personality and Social Psychology*, 1968, *10*, 183–201.

Haan, N., Stroud, J., & Holstein, C. Moral and ego stages in relationship to ego processes: A study of "hippies." *Journal of Personality*, 1973, *41*, 596–612.

Keasey, C. B. Experimentally induced changes in moral opinions and reasoning. *Journal of Personality and Social Psychology*, 1973, *26*, 30–38.

Kohlberg, L. A cognitive–developmental approach to socialization. In D. Goslin (Ed.), *Handbook of socialization*. New York: Rand McNally, 1969.

Kohlberg, L., & Kramer, R. Continuities and discontinuities in childhood and adult moral development. *Human Development*, 1969, *12*, 93–120.

Kohlberg, L., Scharf, P., & Hickey, J. The justice structure of the prison: A theory and an intervention. *The Prison Journal*, 1973, *51*, 3–14.

Langer, J. Disequilibrium as a source of development. In P. Mussen, J. Langer, & M. Covington (Eds.), *Issues and trends in developmental psychology*. New York: Holt, Rinehart & Winston, 1969.

Lyons, G. The police car demonstrations: A survey of participants. In S. M. Lipset & S. S. Wolin (Eds.), *The Berkeley student revolt: Facts and interpretation*. Garden City, N.Y.: Arbor Books, 1965.

Smith, M. B., Haan, N., & Block, J. H. Social-psychological aspects of student activism. *Youth and Society*, 1970, *1*, 261–288.

Turiel, E. An experimental test of the sequentiality of developmental stages in the child's moral judgments. *Journal of Personality and Social Psychology*, 1966, *3*, 611–618.

Turiel, E. Developmental processes in the child's moral thinking. In P. Mussen, J. Langer, & M. Covington (Eds.), *Trends and issues in developmental psychology*. New York: Holt, Rinehart & Winston, 1969.

Turiel, E. Conflict and transition in adolescent moral development. *Child Development*, 1974, *45*, 17–29.

Turiel, E., & Rothman, G. The influence of reasoning on behavioral choices at different stages of moral development. *Child Development*, 1972, *43*, 741–756.

(Received April 17, 1974)

Hum. Dev. *22:* 89–112 (1979)

Kohlberg's Moral Stage Theory

A Piagetian Revision[1]

John C. Gibbs

Harvard University, Cambridge, Mass.

Key Words. Existential psychology · Formal operations · Level of discourse · Moral development · Social development · Two-phase model

Abstract. The purpose of this essay is to reconceptualize Kohlberg's theory and research on moral stages in the light of recent criticisms. In the early 1970s, Kohlberg extended his Piaget-based moral stages to apply to the philosophically oriented moral thinking associated with the adult years. This extension of his highest stages from the moral reasoning of 16-year-olds to the theory-defining perspective shown by some adults (mostly in the United States) has granted considerable ground for criticisms of the theory as elitist, ethnocentric, and excessively abstract. These criticisms underscore the need to reconsider the appropriateness of extending the Piagetian stage model to the adult years. The proposed revision describes moral development in adulthood as existential rather than Piagetian, and restricts moral judgment development in the standard stage sense to childhood and adolescence.

[1] An abbreviated version of this article was presented as a paper at the meeting of the Jean Piaget Society, Philadelphia, May 1978. I wish to thank *Marvin Berkowitz, Gus Blasi, John Broughton, Valerie Gibbs, Larry Kohlberg, Deanna Kuhn, Mike Murphy, Gil Noam, Bob Selman, John Sullivan, Helen Weinreich*, and an anonymous reviewer for their helpful comments on a preliminary version of the paper.

'There were not two kinds of moral
development, only one, and a theory of
adult moral development could not be
a theory of stabilization or ego
development, as opposed to being
a theory of moral-structural change'
(*Kohlberg*, 1973b, p. 198).

'If we should restrict the meaning of
"developmental" to those changes with age
that have childhood-type morphogenetic
features, then the application of the term to
the adult years reflects a hypothesis rather
than an established fact'
(*Flavell*, 1970, p. 249).

Kohlberg's stage theory of moral judgment development, we learn from many of his critics, is ethnocentric (*Simpson*, 1974), ideological (*Sullivan*, 1977), elitist (*Fraenkel*, 1978), restrictively abstract (*Aron*, 1977a, b; *Gilligan*, 1977; *Guindon*, 1978a, b), and perniciously individualistic (*Hogan*, 1975; *Reid and Yanarella*, 1977). My own critical opinion (*Gibbs*, 1977), which is among the more sympathetic (e.g., *Bereiter*, 1978; *Broughton*, 1978), is that although Kohlberg's theory is in fact ailing from these excesses, it will be fine once its proportions return to those of its proper constitutional frame. Kohlberg's traditional theoretical frame has been Piagetian, marked by the years of child-hood and adolescence. It is in the province of the preadult years that fairly uniform and cross-cultural qualitative changes in intellectual and ethical develop-ment do seem to exist. Kohlberg's stage sequence in recent years has expanded beyond this frame, however, Consequent to an effort in the early 1970s to resolve certain lacunae in his longitudinal data, Kohlberg encompassed within his structural stage sequence the metareflective ethics of some Western philosophers and lay adults. Kohlberg was right to identify philosophical reflection in the adult years as an important feature in human development. However, his assimilation of moral philosophical orientations to a Piagetian stage model (*Kohlberg*, 1973a, b) has served only to obscure the nature of both moral philosophies and Piagetian stages, as well as to effect a distorted picture of maturity in moral judgment. In this essay I will trace the history of Kohlberg's empirical and theoretical work, specifying with Monday-morning quarterback wisdom exactly how and why Kohlberg made his recent mistakes. I will then develop a Piagetian revision of Kohlberg's theory, arguing that such a revision largely cures the theory of its amply diagnosed ills and offers a more plausible understanding of moral judgment maturity.

Kohlberg's (1958) original dissertation did not involve the analysis of adult moral reflection; his dissertation sample included only children and adolescents as cross-sectional subjects. Even the inclusion of adolescents was an upward extension of age range from the 6- to 13-year-old sample studied in Piaget's seminal *Moral Judgment of the Child* (1965/1932). Following Piaget[2], Kohlberg sought to identify age trends in moral judgment that would prove to be general and uniform across social class, culture, sex, race, and social epoch, through the structural analysis of children's justifications and evaluations of their opinions as to the right action to take in hypothetical moral dilemmas. On the basis of the cross-sectional data he collected, Kohlberg hypothesized three levels – and within each level, two stages – of moral judgment development. A 'preconventional' level entailed stage 1 ('punishment and obedience') and stage 2 ('naive instrumental hedonism'). A 'conventional' level comprised stage 3 ('maintaining good relations, approval of others') and stage 4 ('social order and authority'). Finally, a 'postconventional' level of 'self-accepted moral principles' encompassed stage 5 ('contract and democratically accepted law') and stage 6 ('individual principles of conscience'). To assess whether this sequence of stages was in fact general and uniform, Kohlberg applied his stage typology in a 3-year interval tracking of his 10-, 13-, and 16-year-old sample. The longitudinal research also enabled Kohlberg to assess the typology in relation to certain additional Piagetian stage expectations, such as consecutive sequence (no stage-skipping in development) and nonregression (no stage reversals). It was the nonregression criterion, based on the Piagetian expectation of a naturally upward tendency in stage development (*Gibbs,* 1977), which was to pose a crucial and very consequential problem for the theory.

---

[2] In effect, Kohlberg has sought to be more 'Piagetian' than was Piaget himself regarding the development of moral judgment. *Piaget* (1965/1932) realized that at least his own moral judgment data did not support a 'stage sequence' claim in any strict sense, and contented himself with discussing 'phases' and age trends. *Kohlberg,* however, on the basis of his own (1958) dissertation research, concluded that moral judgment development did after all support a stage-sequence hypothesis, claiming that the moral stages as Kohlberg defined them satisfied stage-sequence criteria as discussed in Piaget's later writings (e.g., *Piaget,* 1960). Thus, Kohlberg has been more optimistic than was Piaget about the applicability of Piagetian stage-sequence criteria to moral judgment data. Yet, as I will argue, Kohlberg has revised his theory in ways which compromise the applicability of Piagetian stage criteria to his highest stages.

The Regression Problem and Kohlberg's 'Integrative' Solution

Over the past 20 years, Kohlberg has found through inspection of his longitudinal data that numerous aspects of his original 1958 definitions of the six stages did show nongenerality and irregularities (skipping, regression), and hence required deletion or revision. *Kohlberg* (1975) has discussed this revisional work in a favorable light as the progressive refinement and differentiation of the structural from the content features of moral thought. The most substantial revisions in the stage definitions have been prompted by a stage-regression problem discovered in the late 1960s. Kohlberg and his colleagues discovered that many of the longitudinal subjects who had shown stage 5 or stage 6 thinking as 16-year-old high school students apparently regressed to stage 2 during the college years (only to return to stage 5, however, after college). Kohlberg's initial reaction (*Kohlberg and Kramer,* 1969) was to interpret the anomalies as genuine functional regressions motivated by the turmoil from late-adolescent realizations of moral relativity. Subsequently, however, *Kohlberg* (1973b) renounced the idea that the college relativists had actually regressed to stage 2, and eliminated the apparent regression through certain revisions in his stage defnitions. Although Kohlberg's solution to the regression problem was an advance in some respects, it also created some grave new problems.

Kohlberg's revisions rested on a reinterpretation of the apparent regression from the highest stages to stage 2 as in fact a transition ('$4\frac{1}{2}$') from the conventional to the postconventional levels of moral judgment. The key to Kohlberg's reinterpretation was the argument that although the anomalous moral thinking of the 'regressed' college students resembled in content the naive hedonism and egoism of young stage 2 subjects, the college-student thought was far more abstract and philosophical than was that of the young subjects. To make this distinction, Kohlberg introduced the concept of 'level of discourse', i.e., the order of abstraction or reflection evident in subjects' modes of judgment. Whereas naive stage 2 thinking aimed at 'justifying moral judgment to an individual selfish actor', the college-student discourse was aimed at 'defining a *moral theory* and justifying basic moral terms or principles from a standpoint outside that of a member of a constituted society' (p. 192). The 'theory' emphatically 'defined' by the '$4\frac{1}{2}$' thinkers was a rather sophisticated meta-ethical subjectivist relativism (*Turiel,* 1974).

This level-of-discourse distinction provided Kohlberg with a tool for solving the regression problem. The discourse analysis had eliminated the notion that subjects principled in high school had really regressed to stage 2 by identifying a new transitional phase of sophisticated if self-serving relativism. Yet regression was still indicated to a certain extent, since it was still a regression to drop from stage 5 or 6 in high school to the transitional $4\frac{1}{2}$ in college. In order to eliminate this remaining 'regression', Kohlberg introduced truly substantial revisions in his stage definitions as well as stage theory.

Using the level-of-discourse concept, Kohlberg reexamined the supposedly principled moral judgments from the high school data, especially in relation to his subsequent postcollege versions of principled thinking. His question was this: if the new $4\frac{1}{2}$ thinking was at a philosophical level of discourse, then should not this also be at least the discourse level of principled-stage thinking (which presumably succeeded the $4\frac{1}{2}$ transition)? He concluded (*Kohlberg, 1973b*) that, whereas the level of discourse of the principled adult data was genuinely theory-defining, the discourse of the ostensibly principled high-school adolescent data was actually that of 'a generalized member of society' ('conventional' level). Specifically, whereas the principled adults proposed *a priori* theories in their discourse (natural rights, a universal value hierarchy, social contract), the idealizations of the adolescent discourse (appeals to moral law, love for all humanity, etc.) evidenced no such systematizations. Kohlberg therefore refined his postconventional stages into more philosophical constructs, and expanded his conventional-level stage definitions to include the formerly 'principled' idealizations as new 'B' substages. Correspondingly, the previous definitions of stage 3 and stage 4 became merely 'A' substage versions of the stages. Alongside concerns with others' approval and role-stereotypical good conduct (3A) were placed concerns for *mutual* good faith or understanding and for *universalized* caring (3B); alongside concerns with fixed responsibilities or authority and the givens of the law (4A) were placed concerns with *ideal* responsibility to contribute to a *better* society and with *moral* law (4B).

Kohlberg's principled stages, then — formerly locatable among the moral justifications of bright 16 year olds — were raised beyond the uncertain footing of late-adolescent relativism to the philosophical plateaus of some adults. Kohlberg realized that these revisions meant the conversion of his childhood-and-adolescence theory into what he called an 'integrative' life-span stage theory (*Kohlberg*, 1973b, p. 193). Kohlberg's 'integrative' aim was to extend the Piagetian ontogenetic stage model to encompass the processes distinctive of adult development. *Flavell* (1970, p. 250) commented: 'One could argue that adulthood is the nearest thing we have to a pure experiment-in-nature for assessing the change-making power of experience alone, that is, relatively unconfounded by significant and directional biological changes.' Expanding upon this idea, *Kohlberg* (1973b, p. 183) suggested that 'It falls upon the student of adult development to determine whether there are structural stages that arise through experience.' The tenor of the article was more assertion than whether-or-not speculation, however. 'There were not two kinds of moral development, only one' (p. 198), declared Kohlberg, and the one kind of development Kohlberg saw — in adulthood as well as childhood and adolescence — was Piagetian-structural. Nonetheless, Kohlberg was willing to found his adulthood structural stages upon the ego-developmental processes typically cited in postulations of adult psychosocial stages (e.g., *Schaie*, 1977). *Kohlberg* (1977b) suggested that whereas moral stage development in childhood entailed the general cognitive processes of social role-taking opportunities (which enter into some complex relation with maturation), moral stage development in adulthood presupposes experiences of meta-ethical reflection, personal choice, and commitment. Indeed, Kohlberg even proposed the relegation of the childhood stages to the realm of social cognition, reserving prescriptivity for the adult stages: whereas childhood moral judgment development involved 'an increasingly adequate comprehension of ... what the social system *is*', the emergence of stages 5 and 6 in adulthood entailed 'a postulation of principles to which the society and self ought to be *committed*' (p. 195). Clearly, this distinction was overdrawn, since in the very same article Kohlberg was reporting that the late childhood/ adolescent stages (3 and 4) were now to incorporate the prescriptive ideals which, after all, for 12 years had been considered principled. Yet some such distinction was valuable in Kohlberg's effort to 'integrate' adult development into the context of a model traditionally addressed only to child and adolescent development.

Was the Integrative Solution Successful?

The challenge to a structural-developmental model from the stage-regression discovery had been a serious one, and Kohlberg was bold enough to meet the challenge with pervasive revisions in his stage definitions and stage theory. In the upheaval of revision a new transitional phase ($4^1/_2$) was born, stages 3 and 4 gained A and B substages, and stages 5 and 6 became philosophically purified. Moreover, Kohlberg's revisions led him to become the first known *life-span* Piagetian stage theorist, gathering child social role-taking and adult meta-ethical crises under the same structural-developmental tent. In Kohlberg's neo-Kohlbergian theory, the stages of moral judgment development march right through the life span, with moral judgment maturity reserved for those adults showing the sophistication of ethical theory.

It can be seen that this theoretical turn of events, although an advance in certain respects, has come to be plagued with so many *new* problems that the whole idea of an 'integrative' solution must be called into question. The problems can be described in terms of four basic theoretical contradictions.

(1) The Contradiction between the New Principled Stages as Theory-Defining and the Piagetian Conception of Stages as Systems-in-Action

Kohlberg's level-of-discourse revisions were, in fact, a mixed blessing. Although lending new insight into the form of stage 3 and stage 4 thinking, the discourse analysis also in effect divorced the nature of 'principled' thinking from the usual sort of data of interest to a Piagetian psychologist. The meta-ethically reflective discourse identified by Kohlberg as critical to distinguishing the principled stages squares poorly with the Piagetian conception of ontogenetic stages as deep structures discovered through inferences as to organizations in subjects' problem-solving behavior (cf. *Karmiloff-Smith and Inhelder,* 1975). Whereas a subject's direct justification of a choice in a moral dilemma problem is not in principle different from a subject's justification of a choice in a transitivity or conservation problem, a subject's definition of a *theory* does in fact seem to be of a qualitatively distinct nature. To postulate that the articulation of a theory of natural rights and social contract (stage 5) signifies a higher natural stage in moral judgment would seem tantamount to postulating, in cognitive development, that subjects who articulate a theory of the scientific method (and not subjects who merely evidence such strategies in their problem-solving reasoning) are to be accorded the status of a higher natural stage. Although *Piaget* (1973/1970) has been willing to speculate that reflective philosophies may signify 'realizations' (p. 28) extending from natural stage origins (cf. *Gibbs,* 1977, p. 56), he does not consider those philosophies themselves to be natural stages.

(2) The Contradiction between Adult Ideology and the Piagetian Expectation that Structures Must Be Uncovered in the Spontaneous Mind

In the Piagetian approach, some of the richest treasures of structural significance are seen as residing in the spontaneous utterances of the young child. By the time the growing person is fully socialized, his or her thinking is considerably informed by the philosophies and ideologies which form the heritage of the given culture. Indeed, *Kohlberg* himself (1973a) has noted the isomorphism between his 'natural' adult moral structures and the formal ethical systems dominant in the history of Western professional philosophy. In view of the methodological problem of nonspontaneity or socialized ideology in the intellectual life of the adult, Kohlberg's claim of deep structure for adult ethical systems must be considered incautious.

(3) The Contradiction between the Rarity of the New Principled Stages and the Piagetian Expectation that a Structural-Developmental Stage Sequence Have Some Cross-Cultural Generality and Uniformity

As noted earlier, one of Kohlberg's original objectives was to assess the generality of the 1958 stage typology. Kohlberg himself in the ensuing years engaged in field interviewing in culturally diverse countries for the sake of establishing precisely such a generality (*Kohlberg,* 1969, pp. 282–285). With the new stringency in defining the principled stages, it is unlikely that previous findings of some principled thought in other cultures would be sustained. In fact, no cross-cultural study using the post-1973 scoring system has found any evidence of moral thinking in other cultures beyond that of the new stage 4B (see *Edwards,* in press). For that matter, stage 5 and stage 6 moral thinking is rare even among adults in this society (*Candee et al.,* 1978; *Gibbs et al.,* 1979).[3] Indeed, *Kohlberg,* in a recent invited address (1978a), even relinquished the claim that 'stage 6' represents an empirical construct. Thus, the principled stages fail to satisfy a criterion which has guided Kohlberg's endeavors since the outset.

(4) The Contradiction between the Isolation of the Adult Structural Stages and the Piagetian Expectation of a Cross-Developmental Parallelism

A final difficulty with Kohlberg's extension of the Piagetian model to the adult years pertains to Piagetian expectations of holism, a concept traditionally taken to apply not only within but also across structural-developmental domains (logical, social, moral, etc.). As *Kohlberg* (1973b) wrote, 'If moral stages are

[3] Corresponding criticisms, of course, have been made of Piaget's highest stage, formal operations. The correspondence is not a strong one. Whereas stage 5 is found virtually not at all in adolescent samples and in only 5–10% of adult samples, formal operations have been found in roughly 50% of *adolescent* samples (*Flavell,* 1977, p. 114). Hence, whereas formal operations is commonly enough in evidence to render reasonable the expectation of cross-cultural generality (cf. *Cowan,* 1978, pp. 273–279; *Flavell,* 1977, pp. 114–120), the same expectation cannot be held for Kohlberg's stages 5 and 6.

cognitive-structural, they must have some relationship to Piagetian logical stages' (p. 187). Yet in the same article, Kohlberg could find no parallel at all for stage 6 to a Piagetian logical stage, and had to relate stage 5 to a dubious third substage of formal operations. Thus, Kohlberg's relocation of stages 5 and 6 in adulthood more or less stranded those stages, i.e., disrupted the possibility of a formal correspondence between those stages and structural stages in other domains.

It is precisely these unresolved theoretical contradictions which have provided the primary fodder for the critical fire aimed at Kohlberg's theory in recent years. Kohlberg's restriction of mature moral thinking to the realm of abstract theory, for example, has invited criticism (e.g., *Guindon,* 1978a, b) to the effect that there is more to moral judgment than rarified abstraction. Second, the possibility of an ideological taint to the highest stages has led to *Simpson*'s (1974) branding of Kohlberg's theory as an ethnocentric foisting of certain Western philosophical traditions upon the ethical diversity of humanity, and to *Edel*'s (cit. *Edwards,* in press) milder question as to 'whether these stages (5 and 6) should not be regarded as cultural specializations under determinable conditions, and in fact, whether the criteria in the whole third (principled) level – with an emphasis on contract, individual rights, and democracy, culminating in individual conscience – does not have a strain characteristic of the intense individualism of Western European culture in the last two centuries.' Finally, other critics, concerned by the rarity of the highest stages, have attacked the elitism of a developmental theory in which the purportedly most mature stage is not 'reached' even by most moral educators (*Fraenkel,* 1978, pp. 254–255) and moral philosophers (*Aron,* 1977a, p. 201).

These criticisms, then, reflect at least partially upon Kohlberg's 1973 integrative 'solution' to the regression problem. Yet what alternative solutions would have worked better? One easy thought is that Kohlberg should perhaps have left the principled stages in their original form and place, located in the later adolescent years. Such a notion fails to cope with the regression problem and leaves unreconstructed the old content definitions of the conventional stages. A more serious tactic has been to sustain Kohlberg's effort to establish a successful integrative solution by searching for more suitable candidates for adult structural stages in moral and logical development. This is the tack taken by *Gilligan and Murphy* (1978) in their effort to define a 'contextualist' stage of adult moral and logical thought. It is possible that these researchers will, in fact, establish a cross-culturally general adult structural stage, although it must be noted that other proposals of adult structural stages (e.g.,

Arlin, 1975, 1977) have so far not fared well (*Cropper et al.,* 1977; *Fakouri,* 1976). After all, as *Cowan* (1978, p. 248) notes, formal operations or the application of 'equilibrated operations to both observed events and statements is a very flexible tool. The form can be applied over time to an incredibly vast number of content areas.' The challenge to find a more advanced 'form' would seem to be a difficult one.

A Two-Phase Model

My own approach to solving the regression problem follows the road *not* taken by Kohlberg in 1973. Reversing the Kohlberg declaration cited earlier, I would say that 'there are two kinds of development, not one'. In the following argument, I will propose a two-phase view of human development, such that a cross-culturally uniform or standard phase of growth eventually enables members of the human species to become existentially self-aware in such a profound sense that a uniquely human phase of consciousness and development comes to be initiated. Piaget's work has addressed *standard* development, up to and including achievement of the foundation for existential development in adulthood (cf. *Flavell,* 1970); and I see Kohlberg's work as quite parallel to Piaget's in this sense. My proposed revision of Kohlberg's theory is 'Piagetian' in that it gives to Piaget, so to speak, that which is Piaget's — or that which, among Kohlberg's stages, a Piagetian would want to claim. The term 'phase' seems most appropriate to refer to the two senses of development, since a temporal overlap between them is posited: in adolescence, not only does standard development come to fruition, but as well, the basis for existential development is established. Also, it should be noted that the sophistication, scope, and consistency of the standard developmental stages continue to develop over the course of the adult years (*Flavell,* 1971; *Kohlberg and Kramer,* 1969, pp. 106–109).

A fairly cogent argument for positing a fundamental qualitative distinction between child and adult development has been put forth by *Flavell* (1970). *Flavell's* argument for a two-phase model can be presented as follows. First, whereas basic cognitive change in childhood seems to be irreversible or virtually inevitable as well as uniform in direction and sequence, there is no evidence that such features characterize adult cognitive change (cf. *Labouvie-Vief,* 1977, p. 250). Second, the biological growth factors associated with maturation of the nervous system are evident primarily during childhood, consummating in late adolescence. Third (relating the first two points), the restriction of maturation to childhood, where it could contribute as an 'underlying presence' (p. 248) to cognitive change, may account for why general uniformity and inevitability in direction are found in child but not adult cognitive change. Fourth, although adult cognitive change does not seem to partake of the 'morphogenetic' features (p. 250) of child cognitive development (especially uniformity), it does have some interesting features in its own right. Adult thinking is notable, for example, for its 'theories regarding the self, others, and the human condition generally' (p. 250).

Although I endorse Flavell's argument in its essence, its features should be cast in the light of recent Piagetian writings in order to make clear what it does — and does not — contend. Piaget (1971) has probed the theme that human intelligence is heir to the classic mode of anticipation in animal life, instinct. Like instinct, intelligence is social. The social character of instinct becomes clear once one realizes that many instinctual patterns specify *different* and complementary activities for members of the species. Ethologists have highlighted many rather intricate heterosexual, familial, and worker-group interactions which seem to be largely determined by an epigenetic programming of some sort. The action of a participant in one of these instinctual patterns, then, finds meaning by virtue of its relation to the actions of other participants and more generally to the function served by the pattern. Although crucially different from the instincts, human intelligence does share this social character, whether the 'cooperations' one discerns are in children's games, social institutions, or scientific communities. Intelligence is heir to instinct; both are endogenous evolutionary products, both may actualize natural sequences in ontogenesis. *Piaget* writes that the formations of the cognitive stages are 'dependent on a sequential process comparable to a biological epigenesis' (1967/1971, p. 18).

Whereas the social interactions of instinct are programmed, however, the social interactions of intelligence are not. As the fundamental dynamics of organic life replace programming to become the 'method' (p. 366) for achieving knowledge, insight, invention, and reflective consciousness emerge in onto-genesis. The new method of intelligence relies for its operation not upon a hereditary apparatus but upon novel experience, achieving through equilibration successive structures and planes of consciousness (indeed, consciousness itself may furnish 'novel experience' at each level; *Piaget,* 1976). The greatest achievement of this method is formal operations, by which life becomes aware of itself and penetrates the universe through science. Formal operations and the cognitive structures which prepare the foundation for them evidence a sequence which is essentially uniform and consecutive, characteristics which testify to the role of 'biological factors'; but evidence for the indispensable role of experience is found in the age variations associated with the emergence of the successive levels in diverse environments (*Piaget,* 1966).

These recent writings of Piaget do much to clarify the spirit of Flavell's suggestion. Flavell is easily misinterpreted as saying that development in childhood is maturational, whereas development in adulthood is social and experiential. Such a misinterpretation, of course, does a serious disservice to Piaget's whole idea of 'maturation', which is profoundly social *and* experiential. I believe Flavell's suggestion is best understood in terms of Piaget's phylogenetic perspective. Thus, we say that the human species is unique in having not only one but two kinds of development. Like other species, the human species undergoes certain standard sequences of intellectual (including social-experiential) growth, although humanity surpasses other animal species in the method and flower of its intellectual development. This standard phase of development makes possible through formal operations a new, uniquely human phase of development, one which is founded upon the individual's emergent awareness of the conditions of his or her own existence. Because there is no epigenetic factor underlying existential development, one finds no necessarily standard sequence – but one does find new kinds of insight and wisdom expressed, for example, in philosophies of ethics, science, and life.

The Standard Phase

Human intelligence in the Piagetian view, then, is a holistic phenomenon which encompasses social and moral as well as nonsocial facets. Kohlberg's contribution to developmental psychology is therefore perhaps best appreciated in a context in which the relation of moral to social and logicophysical intellectual development is emphasized. In his effort to justify *moral* development as a distinct phenomenon, Kohlberg has underplayed the extent to which the moral stages relate to structural stages in other areas. The following is an admittedly over-simplified thumbnail sketch (for extensive reviews, see *Cowan,* 1978; *Flavell,* 1977; *Selman,* 1976) of four stages of standard development conceived in the broad structural sense: (1) centerings, (2) exchanges, (3) mutualities and (4) systems.

Stage 1: Centerings
The most consistently observed feature in early childhood is centration. The young child attends to one or another temporal state (past, immediately present,

future), spatial segment, or conceptual aspect of a situation, with little relating of these states, segments, or aspects to one another. Although there is a growing understanding that people may have different perspectives on a situation, there is little or no conceptual coordination of perspectives, e.g., no awareness that each person's perspective on a problem may be taking into account the perspectives (interpretations, claims, needs) of others. Probably because of such centerings, young children's thinking tends to be dominated by superficial appearances in physical, social, and moral realms of thinking; for example, the salient physical features of an authority (superior size or ability to punish) may be cited to justify the perspective of the authority as the morally right one.

Stage 2: Exchanges

The growing ability in mid-childhood to think interrelatively across the spatiotemporal and conceptual aspects of situations enables the child to penetrate superficial appearances and make inferences as to the underlying realities of his or her physical, social, and moral world. Coordinative thinking in physical tasks (such as detection of compensations and negations) enables the child to understand that some tasks call for a logical rather than a perceptual judgment. The child's social thinking shows an awareness that people's anticipations of others' perspectives can feed back to each respective perspective, thereby influencing the very formation of that perspective (*Selman,* 1976). The child's inferential and deductive activities, however, still 'hug the ground of detected empirical reality rather closely' (*Flavell,* 1977, p. 103). For example, the intangible values of a social relationship are understood in terms of 'empirical' or concrete considerations such as past or anticipated exchanges of favors, *quid pro quo* retaliations, and exactly compensatory restitutions.

Stage 3: Mutualities

The singular achievement of thinking associated with preadolescence or early adolescence is the ability to reason on a 'second-order' level, that is, to make inferences not simply on the basis of empirical reality (first-order thinking, stage 2), but instead, upon the *propositions* or *values* in effect furnished by such first-order thinking. It is probably the emergence of second-order thinking which gives rise to combinatorial and hypotheticodeductive problem-solving in logico-physical task situations. In the sociomoral realm, second-order thinking is probably manifested in the preadolescent's ability to disembed himself or herself from the ongoing exchanges of a two-person relationship, that is, to remove onself from one's immediate interests vis-à-vis another's and to view both perspectives from a third-person, impartial-spectator perspective (*Selman,* 1976). In other words, second-order thinking may make possible a progress from 'reciprocity as a fact' to 'reciprocity as an ideal' (*Piaget,* 1965/1932, p. 323), or to genuine mutuality in relationships. The preadolescent may show magnanimity or trust for the sake of a relationship, and appreciate 'punishment' for the sake of character reform rather than retaliation. It is this overall perspective which is expressed in *Baier's* (1965) articulation of what he terms 'the moral point of view', and which may constitute the empirical foundation for *Firth's* (1952, 1955) notion that an 'ideal observer' perspective is required for valid ethical decisions.

Stage 4: Systems

Evidence for a fourth stage is apparent primarily in the sociomoral realm, although such a distinction may also be helpful in the logicocognitive realm (e.g., *Wyatt and Geis,* 1978). Over the course of the adolescent years, there is a progressive ability to discern the systematic arrangements which are necessary to form a viable society, real or hypothetical (see *Adelson and O'Neil,* 1966; *Adelson et al.,* 1969). In their seminal studies, *Adelson et al.* found that the adolescent comes to appreciate law and the relation between the individual and society not simply in terms of prosocial intention and benevolent authority (stage 3), but more broadly in terms of social functions and practices. Thus, there is an 'expansion' (*Selman,* 1976, p. 307) in second-order thinking such that an overall perspective is applied not only to face-to-face relationships, but also to complex social systems as represented by modern society (cf. *Edwards,* 1975, in press).

The Existential Phase

The second-order thinking which may underlie the highest stages of standard development also provides the foundation for the existential phase of human development. In other words, the person engaged in second-order thinking can adopt a detached, 'meta' perspective not only on logicophysical problems, social relationships, and social systems; he or she may also apply such a perspective to more diffuse questions such as consciousness, ethics, reason, and life itself. The very conditions of personal existence, then, can become 'objects of contemplation' (*Flavell,* 1977, p. 123). Located at this level is Kohlberg's theory-defining discourse in which (as discussed earlier) moral terms are considered or justified 'from a standpoint outside that of a member of society' (*Kohlberg*, 1973b, p. 192; *Kohlberg and Gilligan*, 1971). This is probably also the frame of reference for professional meta-reflective treatments of ethics, science, mathematics, the fine arts, and so on. Thus, the individual (or the society in general) may enter a phase of development unknown to any other species. Because Piaget's primary perspective and developmental model have been biological, he has not investigated this existential sense of development (although one finds passing references, e.g., *Piaget*, 1967/1971, p. 37). The existential sense of human development is so fundamentally distinct from the standard sense that it is gratuitous and probably mistaken to assume, as Kohlberg has done, that the idea of stage in the standard-developmental sense can be extended to the existential realm of development.

For guidance in speculation about existential development one can turn to the early works of *Fromm* (1941, 1947, 1955). As was the case with Piaget, Fromm's conception of the person and human development is founded upon an evolutionary or phylogenetic perspective. In animal species where behavior is directed by instinctual drives, modes, and anticipations, there is an equilibrium between organism and ecology 'in the sense that the animal is equipped by nature to cope with the very conditions it is to meet' (*Fromm*, 1955, p. 29). At some point in human history, however, this natural equilibrium became progressively disturbed as persons on a large scale respectively came to confront the facts that they were essentially separate and limited, that their birth was at least partly happenstance, and their eventual death was inevitable. *Fromm* (1955, p. 30) considers this 'point of animal evolution' to be 'a unique break, comparable to the first emergence of matter, to the first emergence of life, and to the first emergence of animal existence'. In most individuals, realization of the human situation emerges as a concomitant to the achievement of objectivity in human development, since 'objectivity requires not only seeing the object as it is but also seeing oneself as one is, i.e., being aware of the ... constellation in which one finds oneself' (p. 113). Awareness of the disequilibrium inherent in the human situation generates uniquely human needs which require uniquely human solutions. The 'solutions', however, can represent either ultimately abortive attempts to return to the preexistential state of instinctual equilibrium, or affirmations of the human situation in terms of which one achieves existential development. *Fromm* (1955) differentiated five such existential needs and solutions. The person, confronting his or her discreteness and finitude, develops needs for a restoration of (a) identity, (b) relatedness, and (c) rootedness, and for some sense of (d) transcendence and (e) meaning (including devotion).

Coping with these needs can generate affirmative modes of being such as responsive individuality, mutual love, egalitarian community, productive creativity, and systems of reason and devotion. The social, economic, and cultural conditions of one's context in human history, however, may not permit the emergence of these affirmative solutions. Yet the existential problem does not thereupon die. *Some* response to existential needs must come forth. If the affirmative solutions are blocked, then negative pseudosolutions emerge: herd conformity, obsessions with power or submission, in-group chauvinism, wanton destructiveness, and rationalizing ideology.

Fromm's ideas of affirmative existential development seem to be reflected in the writings of a more recent life-span theorist, Erikson. Specifically, Fromm's articulation of existential needs for individuality, love or community, productivity, and rational philosophy finds its counterpart in Erikson's formulation of the adolescent and adult normative ideals of identity, intimacy, generativity, and integrity. There is also some correspondence between Erikson's normative failures and Fromm's development-thwarted negativities. For example, Erikson's themes of identity diffusion, isolation, and stagnation can be found in Fromm's writings. *Maier*'s (1978, p. 77) suggestion that Erikson's writings constitute a 'theoretical bridge' to existential thinking would thus seem to be essentially correct.

Much of the content for Erikson's conceptualization of adult 'normative crises', then, can be found in Fromm. Erikson, however, took a step which Fromm had not: he systematized these conflict polarities into a sequence of stages. Specifically, Erikson assimilated the latter four polarities to his eight 'stages of man', which extend throughout the human life span. Thus, like Kohlberg, Erikson has proposed an integrative stage theory for important aspects of human development. Moreover, *Erikson* (1968) seems to intend his stage progression to reflect a maturational or quasi-maturational significance:

'Whenever we try to understand growth, it is well to remember the *epigenetic principle* which is derived from the growth of organisms *in utero*. Somewhat generalized, this principle states that anything that grows has a ground plan, and that out of this ground plan the parts arise, each part having its time of special ascendancy, until all parts have arisen to form a functioning whole ... in the sequence of his most personal experience the healthy child, given a reasonable amount of proper guidance, can be trusted to obey inner laws of development, laws which create a succession of potentialities for significant interaction with those persons who tend and respond to him and those institutions which are ready for him. While such interaction varies from culture to culture it must remain within "the proper rate and the proper sequence" which governs all epigenesis. Personality, therefore, can be said to develop according to steps predetermined in the human organism's readiness to be driven toward, to be aware of, and to interact with a widening radius of significant individuals and institutions' (pp. 92–93).

The problem in Erikson's life-span theory bears some analogy to that which was detected in Kohlberg's. Erikson's 'inner laws', 'predetermined steps', and 'proper rate' presumably describe the dynamic of *all* of his life-span stages, and presumably correspond to the 'underlying presence' (*Flavell*, 1970) of maturational factors. Yet, as Flavell pointed out, physical and neural maturation is completed by late adolescence. The application of what we are calling a standard stage model for development to the adulthood years, therefore, is suspect. It is probably not an accident, for example, that Erikson can find bodily-maturation analogs for the first five – but not the last three – of his psychosocial stages (see *Maier*, 1978).

Perhaps the clearest way of expressing the point at hand is through a comparison of Erikson's with Piaget's use of the concept of stage. Establishing a stage sequence in the Piagetian sense necessitates investigation of empirical criteria such as underlying generality, upward directionality, consecutive sequence, and cross-cultural uniformity (*Gibbs*, 1977). The last two criteria are explicitly appealed to in the excerpt from Erikson ('While such interaction varies from culture to culture it must remain within "the proper rate and the proper sequence" '). Such criteria might be met by Erikson's infancy and childhood stages. In the case of the post-maturational adulthood stages, however, satisfaction of the criteria seems doubtful. It was in fact Kohlberg (*Kohlberg and Kramer*, 1969) who pointed out that

'sexual intimacy and marriage, vocational identity and achievement, parenthood, acceptance of life's completion and conclusion are matters of content, not form ... developmental tasks of content in themselves have no order, i.e., individuals can face vocational commitment or identity before or after sexual intimacy and parenthood. Psychologically it is possible to develop competent parental attitudes before developing capacity for sexual intimacy. Finally, the irreversibility of development defined in terms of developmental tasks is much in question. There are certainly many older adults, apparently mature and ready to face the tasks of integrity vs. despair, who suddenly seem to prefer regression to the tasks of establishing heterosexual intimacy' (p. 120).

It is not impossible that some standard stage-like shifts in adult life may yet be detected. For example, *Flavell* (1970; cf. *Neugarten*, 1966) suggested the possibility of 'a gradual reversal across adulthood in the way biological time is perceived, namely, from time-since-birth to time-left-to-live' (p. 252). *Inhelder and Piaget* (1958) suggested that there is a shift in the manner of formal operational behavior from adolescence to adulthood, i.e., from a certain idealistic naivete to a realistic understanding that theory must be equilibrated with reality (cf. *Gilligan and Murphy,* 1978). What are we to make of such 'shifts' in adult thinking? Clearly, they represent a nonrelative progression of some sort, and should be considered developmental. Development of this sort, however, is purely phenomenological and functional; what is missing is an identification of *structure.* It is presumably for this reason that Inhelder and Piaget avoided the temptation to assign a higher 'stage' to the functional advance toward wisdom and discretion in the adult years.

Role of Principled Thinking in Moral Judgment

The construction of principled thinking or of existential 'systems of reason', as Fromm would put it, is of clear value to normative moral decision-making. It is only through the use of philosophical principles that one can make systematic sense of the issues and priorities of difficult moral problems. Even when profound ethical dilemmas must be confronted, however, the contributions of principled reflection do not necessarily supersede the justifications stemming from the higher standard stages. This point can be illustrated with moral judgment data obtained in response to perhaps the most famous of the Kohlberg moral interview dilemmas, the Heinz dilemma. Here is the situation: Heinz's wife is dying of a cancer which only a newly discovered drug, which Heinz cannot afford, may cure. Heinz must decide whether to try to save his wife by stealing the drug, or to obey the law and let his wife die. What should Heinz do, and why? One subject's response, scored as transitional stage 3/4 in standard scoring (see *Kohlberg et al.,* 1978b), was that Heinz should steal the drug because 'it's more important that she (Heinz's wife) live than that some scientist make millions of dollars ... life is more important than making money.' This intuitive appreciation of the greater importance of life over money-making is essentially similar to the 'stage 5' and 'stage 6' responses to the Heinz dilemma frequently cited by Kohlberg. For example, one of Kohlberg's stage 5 longitudinal cases justified stealing the drug because the fact that 'there was a human life at stake transcends any right the druggist had to the drug'. The priority of life to property is also articulated by Kohlberg's classic 'stage 6' subject, who argued that 'Since all property has only relative value and only persons can have unconditional value, it would be irrational to act in such a manner as to make human life – or the loss of it – a means to the preservation of property rights (*Kohlberg*, 1971, p. 209).

Obviously, these philosophical justifications do improve the level of discourse of the naturalistic justification cited. The intuitive appreciation of life as 'more important' than someone's profit-making is refined into an articulation of the logical or rational *priority* of a life claim to a legal or societal (property rights) convention. Also, it is less clear in the naturalistic than in the metareflective material that Heinz's problem is a particular case requiring a general treatment of the relation between a life claim and a law or property claim. In general, then, these improvements do provide illumination as to the systematic basis for the naturalistic evaluation of life as 'more important' than 'making money'. One has only demonstrated, however, that principled reasoning can illuminate and refine normative reasoning – precisely the contribution which moral philosophers (e.g., *Brandt*, 1959; *Frankena*, 1973) for decades have told us that moral philosophy can make to the ordinary struggle with the most perplexing problems of human social life. Similarly, the systematizations offered by philosophies of number or language may help us resolve basic puzzles in mathematics or grammar – but we do not on that account hail those philosophies as representing a new standard stage. In other words, the emergence of philosophical reflection in human development is a valuable object of study in socio-historical, existential, and humanistic terms, but *not* in Piagetian stage-sequential terms.

Conclusion

In general, the view of moral development proposed here departs fundamentally from recent Kohlbergian theory. Over the past 20 years, Kohlberg has basically preserved the standard-stage model as his work has extended to the assessment of moral thinking in the adult years. He retained his 1958 trichotomy of preconventional (stages 1, 2), conventional (stages 3, 4), and postconventional (stages 5, 6) levels of moral judgment development, despite important revisions (A/B substages, the '4^1/$_2$' innovation, the rarification of 5 and 6). Kohlberg's 'integrative' view therefore reduces essentially to an extension of the standard stage sequence to encompass later segments of the human life span. My argument is that Kohlberg's revisions, although important, have not gone far enough. On the one hand, Kohlberg's basic insight in 1973 was correct: namely, that the relativistic subjectivism of some of his longitudinal subjects during late adolescence was not a structural regression but instead an epistemological advance to a new, theory-defining 'level of discourse'. On the other hand, Kohlberg's mistake (in this view) was to assimilate this theory-defining discourse to the traditional mold of his standard stages. Rather, Kohlberg should have recognized that the 'regression' problem called for a more fundamental revamping of his theory, one which would abolish his 1958 'levels' and place theory-defining perspectives beyond the reach of a standard stage sequence. How, for example, can Kohlberg justify continuing to characterize stages 3 and 4 as exclusively at a 'conventional' level given his revision of the stage definitions to include *idealized* mutualities and systems (substages 3B, 4B)? In the reconceptualization offered here, Stages 3 and 4 already evidence the workings of the very second-order thinking which, for many individuals, sooner or later gives rise to the need for development of a wholly new sort. Thus the adolescent may come to reflect not only upon social relationships and societies, but beyond that, upon life and personal existence. At this point, it is doubtful that we should still be in the stage-typing business ('$4^{1}/_{2}$', '5', '6'). Admittedly, the stage-typing temptation is understandable; we seek some way to represent the greater adequacy of rational-constructivist (e.g., priority-of-life) theories over subjectivist-relativistic theories of morality. If we elect to represent 'greater adequacy' of this sort simply by including the theories within a standard stage sequence, however, we generate a number of gratuitous problems. For example, ethical maturity becomes restricted to the philosophically sophisticated, and even within philosophical sophistication we imply the existence of a dubious 'natural' sequence (from '5' to '6').

Although the standard-sequence approach in the philosophical realm must be scrapped, the notion of development need not be. In Frommian terms, for example, we can relate interpretations of theoretical adequacy to the existential quest for *meaning*. According to *Fromm* (1955), reductionist ideologies are symptomatic of a retreat from existential problems, rather than a mastery of them through reason (defined by Fromm as 'a human faculty which must embrace the whole of the world with which man is confronted', p. 65). Although rational-constructivist theories cannot be said to represent a development beyond subjective-relativist theories in the standard-stage sense, they may nonetheless represent a looser sense of development, one which highlights constructivist ethical theories as functionally more adequate answers in the human quest for meaning. Perhaps Kohlberg could represent the distinctiveness of this latter sense of development by using letters rather than numbers. Beyond stage 3 or 4, then, Kohlberg could refer to 'S' (not '$4^{1}/_{2}$') for subjective-relativist theories and

'P' (not '5' or '6') for principled-constructivist theories. It could be argued that 'P' is more adequate than 'S', but the excess baggage symbolized by stage numbers could at last be discarded.

The posture of this essay has been constructive, or rather, reconstructive. Some basis was found for widespread criticisms of Kohlberg's theory as ethnocentric, overly abstract, and elitist; yet the chief generative source for these criticisms has entailed an aspect of Kohlberg's theory — his highest stages proposed in the context of an ostensible 'integration' of childhood and adulthood moral judgment development — which is amenable to revision. I argued that Kohlberg's integrative view only confounded and confused the mutually irreducible realities of child and adult moral judgment development, and I proposed instead a two-phase view which emphasizes the distinction between standard (child) and existential (adult) development. In this view, the highest stages are reconceptualized as reflective products of the human quest for meaning, rather than as natural standards for determining human moral maturity. The thrust of this essay, then, has been to reconstruct Kohlberg's theory so as to clarify its distinct conceptual underpinnings and in so doing to respond constructively to Kohlberg's recent critics.

References

Adelson, J.; Green, B., and O'Neil, R.: Growth of the idea of law in adolescence. Devl Psychol. *1:* 327–332 (1969).

Adelson, J. and O'Neil, R.: The growth of political ideas in adolescence. The sense of community. J. Pers. soc. Psychol. *4:* 295–306 (1966).

Arlin, P.K.: Cognitive development in adulthood. A fifth stage? Devl Psychol. *11:* 602–606 (1975).

Arlin, P.K.: Piagetian operations in problem-finding. Devl Psychol. *13:* 297–298 (1977).

Aron, I.E.: Moral philosophy and moral education. A critique of Kohlberg's theory. Schl. Rev. *85:* 197–217 (1977a).

Aron, I.E.: Moral philosophy and moral education. II. The formalist tradition and the Deweyan alternative. Schl. Rev. *85:* 513–534 (1977b).

Baier, K.: The moral point of view. A rational basis of ethics (Random House, New York 1965).

Bereiter, C.: The morality of moral education. Hastings Center Rep. *7:* 20–25 (1978).

Brandt, R.B.: Ethical theory. The problems of normative and critical ethics (Prentice-Hall, Englewood Cliffs 1959).

Broughton, J.: The cognitive-developmental approach to morality. A reply to Kurtines and Greif. J. mor. Educ. *7:* 81–96 (1978).

Candee, D.; Graham, R., and Kohlberg, L.: Moral development and life outcomes. Unpubl. paper (Harvard University, 1978).

Cowan, P.A.: Piaget with feeling. Cognitive, social and emotional dimensions (Holt, Rinehart & Winston, New York 1978).

Cropper, D.A.; Meck, D.S., and Ash, M.J.: The relation between formal operations and a possible fifth stage of cognitive development. Devl Psychol. 5: 517–518 (1977).

Edwards, C.P.: Societal complexity and moral development. A Kenyan study. Ethos 3: 505–527 (1975).

Edwards, C.P.: A comparative study of the development of moral judgment and reasoning; in Munroe, Munroe and Whiting, Handbook of cross-cultural research on human development (Garland, New York, in press).

Erikson, E.H.: Identity, youth, and crisis (Norton, New York 1978).

Fakouri, M.E.: Cognitive development in adulthood. A fifth stage? Devl Psychol. 12: 472 (1976).

Firth, R.: Ethical absolutism and the ideal observer. Philos. Phenomen. 12: 317–345 (1952).

Firth, R.: Discussion. Reply to Professor Brandt. Philos. Phenomen. 19: 414–421 (1955).

Flavell, J.P.: Cognitive change in adulthood; in Goulet and Baltes, Life-span developmental psychology. Research and theory (Academic Press, New York 1970).

Flavell, J.P.: Stage-related properties of cognitive development. Cogn. Psychol. 2: 421–453 (1971).

Flavell, J.P. Cognitive development (Prentice-Hall, Englewood Cliffs 1977).

Fraenkel, J.R.: The Kohlbergian paradigm. Some reservations; in Scharf, Readings in moral education (Winston Press, Minneapolis 1978).

Frankena, W.: Ethics; 2nd ed. (Prentice-Hall, Englewood Cliffs 1973).

Fromm, E.: The sane society (Holt, Rinehart & Winston, New York 1941).

Fromm, E.: Man for himself. An inquiry into the psychology of ethics (Holt, Rinehart & Winston, New York 1947).

Fromm, E.: Escape from freedom (Holt, Rinehart & Winston, New York 1955).

Gibbs, J.C.: Kohlberg's stages of moral judgment. A constructive critique. Harv. educ. Rev. 47: 43–61 (1977).

Gibbs, J.C.; Erickson, V.L., and Berkowitz, M.W.: Sex differences in moral judgment during adolescence and young adulthood. Unpubl. paper (Harvard University, 1979).

Gilligan, C.: In a different voice. Women's conceptions of self and morality. Harv. educ. Rev. 47: 481–517 (1977).

Gilligan, C. and Murphy, J.M.: The philosopher and the 'dilemma of the fact'. Moral development in late adolescence and adulthood. Unpubl. manuscript (Harvard University, 1978).

Guindon, A.: Kohlberg's post-conventional yogis. Unpubl. paper (St. Paul University, Ottawa 1978a).

Guindon, A.: Moral development. Form, content, and self – a critique of Kohlberg's sequence. Unpubl. paper (St. Paul University, Ottawa 1978b).

Hogan, R.: Theoretical egocentrism and the problem of compliance. Am. Psychol. 30: 533–540 (1975).

Inhelder, B. and Piaget, J.: The growth of logical thinking from childhood to adolescence (Basic Books, New York 1958).

Karmiloff-Smith, A. and Inhelder, B.: If you want to get ahead, get a theory. Cognition *3:* 196–212 (1975).

Kohlberg, L.: The development of modes of moral thinking and choice in the years ten to sixteen; unpubl. diss. Chicago (1958).

Kohlberg, L.: Stage and sequence. The cognitive-developmental approach to socialization; in Goslin, Handbook of socialization theory and research (Rand McNally, Chicago 1969).

Kohlberg, L.: From is to ought. How to commit the naturalistic fallacy and get away with it in the study of moral development; in Mischel, Cognitive development and epistemology (Academic Press, New York 1971).

Kohlberg, L.: The claim to moral adequacy of a highest stage of moral judgment. J. Phil. *70:* 630–646 (1973a).

Kohlberg, L.: Continuities in childhood and adult moral development revisited; in Baltes and Schaie, Life-span developmental psychology; 2nd ed. (Academic Press, New York 1973b).

Kohlberg, L.: The cognitive-development approach. New developments and a response to criticisms. Symp. Meet. Soc. Res. Child Development, Denver 1975).

Kohlberg, L.: The meaning and measurement of moral development. Invited Address Div. Educational Psychology Meet. Am. Psychol. Ass., Toronto (1978a).

Kohlberg, L.; Colby, A.; Gibbs, J.C.; Speicher-Dubin, B.; Power, C., and Candee, D.: Assessing moral stages. A manual. Unpubl. book manuscript (Harvard University 1978b).

Kohlberg, L. and Gilligan, C.: The adolescent as a philosopher. The discovery of the self in a postconventional world. Daedalus *100:* 1051–1086 (1971).

Kohlberg, L. and Kramer, R.: Continuities and discontinuities in childhood and adult moral development. Hum. Dev. *12:* 93–120 (1969).

Labouvie-Vief, G.: Adult cognitive development. In search of alternative explanations. Merrill-Palmer Q. *23:* 227–264 (1977).

Maier, H.W.: Three theories of child development; 3rd ed. (Harper & Row, New York 1978).

Neugarten, B.L.: Adult personality. A developmental view. Hum. Dev. *9:* 61–73 (1966).

Piaget, J.: The moral judgment of the child (New York, Free Press 1965/1932).

Piaget, J.: The general problems of the psychobiological development of the child; in Tanner and Inhelder, Discussions on child development. Proc. WHO Study group Psychobiological Development of the Child, vol. IV, pp. 3–27 (International Universities Press, New York 1960).

Piaget, J.: Need and significance of cross-cultural studies in genetic psychology. Int. J. Psychol. *1:* 3–13 (1966).

Piaget, J.: Biology and knowledge. An essay concerning the relations between organic regulations and cognitive processes (University of Chicago, Chicago 1967/1971).

Piaget, J.: Main trends in inter-disciplinary research (Harper & Row, New York 1973/1970).

Piaget, J.: Intellectual evolution from adolescence to adulthood. Hum. Dev. *15:* 1–12 (1972).

Piaget, J.: The grasp of consciousness. Action and concept in the young child (Harvard University Press, Cambridge 1976).

Reid, H. and Yanarella, E.J.: Critical political theory and moral development. On Kohlberg, Hampden-Turner, and Habermas. Theory Soc. *4:* 479–500 (1977).

Schaie, K.W.: Toward a stage theory of adult cognitive development. J. Aging Hum. Dev. *8:* 129–138 (1977).

Selman, R.L.: Social-cognitive understanding. A guide to educational and clinical practice; in Lickona, Moral development and moral behavior. Theory, research, and social issues (Holt, Rinehart & Winston, New York 1976).

Simpson, E.L.: Moral development research. A case study of scientific cultural bias. Hum. Dev. *17:* 81–106 (1974).

Sullivan, E.: A study of Kohlberg's structural theory of moral development. A critique of liberal social science ideology. Hum. Dev. *20:* 325–376 (1977).

Turiel, E.: Conflict and transition in adult moral development. Child Dev. *45:* 14–29 (1974).

Wyatt, K.B. and Geis, M.F.: Level of formal thought and organizational memory strategies. Devl. Psychol. *14:* 433–434 (1978).

John C. Gibbs, Graduate School of Education, Harvard University, Cambridge, MA 02138 (USA)

Irreversible, Stepwise Sequence in the Development of Moral Judgment: A Longitudinal Study of Males and Females

Constance Boucher Holstein

Pennsylvania State University, College of Human Development

HOLSTEIN, CONSTANCE BOUCHER. *Irreversible, Stepwise Sequence in the Development of Moral Judgment: A Longitudinal Study of Males and Females.* CHILD DEVELOPMENT, 1976, 47, 51–61. 2 issues central to the construct validity of Kohlberg's organismic 6-stage model of moral judgment development are empirically assessed: (*a*) stepwise, invariant sequence and (*b*) irreversibility of the stages in ontogeny. Individual developmental sequences for middle-class adolescents and adults over a 3-year period support the stepwise sequence requirement, but only in the movement from level to level rather than stage to stage, and only for the first 2 levels of the 3-level scheme. With respect to irreversibility, regression is found in the higher stages. Implications for the construct validity of Kohlberg's model of development are discussed.

This paper is designed to evaluate empirically the cognitive-developmental position (Kohlberg 1963, 1969, 1973; Kohlberg & Kramer 1969) that changes in moral judgment follow a stepwise, invariant sequence of six irreversible stages, structurally defined and content-free. While there are stronger and weaker versions of the developmental model, cognitive-developmentalists have opted for the strong organismic version: "The stage concept not only postulates irreversible qualitative structural change, but in addition postulates . . . that this change occurs in a pattern of universal stepwise invariant sequences" (Kohlberg & Kramer 1969, p. 99). Cross-sectional (Kohlberg 1963) and combined cross-sectional and longitudinal data (Kohlberg & Kramer 1969) showing age trends for grouped data have been offered as evidence for the devel-

opmental nature of the moral judgment sequence. To date, no longitudinal evidence has been presented to show that the stages as described and ordered are sequentially invariant and irreversible.

In view of the absence of such empirical evidence, a longitudinal study of 52 American adolescents and their parents was undertaken. Results of that study which deal with the issues of stepwise sequence and irreversibility are compared (by permission of the author) with the only other longitudinal study of moral judgment development yet available, that reported in Kramer's (1968) unpublished doctoral dissertation. A comparison of these two sets of data permits an evaluation of the generalizability of the results of the present study.

Revision of a paper presented at the meeting of the Society for Research in Child Development, March 30, 1973, Philadelphia. The first half of the research was supported by a dissertation research award from the Southwestern Region of the Soroptimists and was submitted in a dissertation to the Department of Sociology, University of California, Berkeley, in partial fulfillment of the requirements for a doctoral degree. The author would like to express appreciation of their guidance to her doctoral committee members, Professors John A. Clausen (chairman) and Norman W. Bell. The second half of the research was partially supported by small grant MH22159-01 from the National Institute of Mental Health, while the author was a research associate at Scientific Analysis Corporation, San Francisco, California. Gratitude is extended to Drs. Paul Baltes, Diana Baumrind, Roger Burton, Esther Greif, William Kurtines, and Robert Somers for their helpful criticisms of an earlier draft. Author's address: Pennsylvania State University, College of Human Development, Ogontz Campus, Abington, Pennsylvania 19001.

The Measurement and Ordering of Moral Judgment Stages

The stages can be described as ideal types, and they were so described in Kohlberg's (1963) first report of his cross-sectional study of 72 boys ranging in age from 10 to 16: "A careful consideration of individual cases eventually led us to define six developmental types of value-orientation. A Weberian ideal-typological procedure was used to achieve a combination of empirical consistency and logical consistency in defining the types" (p. 13). Each stage represented a qualitatively distinct type of justification for making a judgment of moral approbation or disapprobation on *another* person's action, whether completed or anticipated. These moral justifications were then ordered into a hierarchy on the basis of their successive approximation to the "formal" characteristics of a moral judgment as Kohlberg perceived them: "universal, inclusive, consistent, and grounded on objective, impersonal, or ideal grounds" (1971, p. 56). The stages were subsumed under three levels of moral thought and can be briefly described as follows (see Kohlberg [1969] for a complete presentation): *Level I, Preconventional:* Stage 1, Punishment and Obedience Orientation; Stage 2, Instrumental Relativist Orientation. *Level II, Conventional:* Stage 3, Interpersonal Concordance; Stage 4, Law and Order. *Level III, Principled* or *Postconventional:* Stage 5, Social Contract; Stage 6, Universal Ethical Principles.

The hypothetical stories of moral conflict developed to elicit moral judgments were limited to those in which the moral agent finds himself in conflict with constituted authority, vested in either a person or a set of rules relevant to the situation in question: "The ten situations used were ones in which acts of obedience to legal-social rules or to the commands of authority conflicted with the human needs or welfare of other individuals" (Kohlberg 1963, p. 12). The following story, without its probes, provides an example:

Situation III. Heinz Steals the Drug. In Europe, a woman was near death from cancer. One drug might save her, a form of radium that a druggist in the same town had recently discovered. The druggist was charging $2,000., ten times what the drug cost him to make. The sick woman's husband, Heinz, went to everyone he knew to borrow the money, but he could only get together about half of what it cost. He told the druggist that his wife was dying and asked him to sell it cheaper or let him pay later. But the druggist said, "No." The husband got desperate and broke into the man's store to steal the drug for his wife. Should the husband have done that? Why? [Kohlberg 1969, p. 379]

In addition, each situation was chosen for final inclusion in the set of dilemmas only if adults were divided over the morally right alternative action: "The story situations we used . . . placed in conflict two standards or values simultaneously accepted by large portions of the community" (Kohlberg 1963, p. 27). Morality so defined and measured follows a value-conflict model and has its most appropriate research application to such situations as the political realm, in which value consensus does not obtain, and resolution of conflict must be made.

One can distinguish philosophical, logical, and empirical grounds for ordering moral justifications into a hierarchy, and all three grounds have been used to justify the ordering of the six moral judgment stages (Kohlberg 1969, 1973). From the viewpoint of social science, the most important argument has been an empirical one, namely, that the scheme is developmental. Loevinger (1973) has suggested that stage theories can be reliable and useful dimensions of individual differences, but if they claim to be developmental, then age progression with respect to the stages must be demonstrated within some age range. The data to be reported will be used to assess the two central issues of stepwise, invariant sequence and irreversibility.

Method

Subjects.—Fifty-three upper-middle-class families, each with a 13-year-old son ($N = 24$) or daughter ($N = 29$), were studied in the first data collection wave (Time 1) during the winter and spring of the academic year 1967–1968. The names of all the families were drawn from the same eighth-grade class roster of the only junior high school in a wealthy, small (11,000 population) community in the urban San Francisco Bay area of California. Selection criteria for participation in the study included: (1) being Caucasian, (2) having an IQ over 100, as measured by the California Test of Mental Maturity (CTMM), and (3) constituting an intact family. Of 253 families, 174 fulfilled these characteristics, and each of the 174 was contacted by one letter identical for all, the only contact method permitted by the school district superintendent. A positive response was received from 30%. Characteristics of these self-selected 53 study families follow. Nearly all the fathers (mean age = 44) were college graduates (87%) with careers in business, management, or the professions. Median annual income for 1967, based only on father's income, was in the $20,000+ bracket. Most of the 53 mothers (mean age = 41) were college graduates (65%) or had attended college (30%), and only three worked. The children were very bright (mean IQ = 120), did well in school (the girls more so than the boys), and had no school record of behavior problems.

Examination of school records revealed that those children *not* participating in the study were significantly more likely to have been in the school system longer, $\chi^2(2) = 11.55$, $p < .01$, with a trend toward lower grades, $\chi^2(3) = 5.84$, $p < .20$. A slightly higher proportion of their fathers worked in blue-collar jobs or in business, and fewer worked in the professions, but the differences are not significant.

A 3-year interval, modeled after Kohlberg and Kramer (1969), was chosen for retest. Fifty-two of the original 53 families were located during the spring of the academic year 1970–1971 (Time 2), when adolescent subjects were high school juniors. All 52 adolescent subjects were retested. Forty-eight of the 52 fathers and 49 of the 52 mothers were retested, producing an overall attrition rate of 6%.

Procedure.—Five of Kohlberg's moral judgment dilemmas (Situations I, III, IV, VII, VIII) were chosen for use at both Time 1 and Time 2 because of their demonstrated utility in a previous study (Haan, Smith, & Block 1968). Home visits were made to all families at Time 1. Mothers were administered the test in interviews by the investigator, while fathers were interviewed separately by a male assistant. Children filled out a questionnaire form of the measure in a separate room at the same time their parents were being interviewed. At Time 2, 39 adolescents were given a questionnaire form of the measure by the investigator during a day of testing at the high school. The 13 subjects not in school were either interviewed in the next month by the investigator ($N = 6$) or, in the cases of those who had moved beyond a 200-mile radius of the researcher ($N = 7$), were sent a questionnaire form. During the same period of time, parents were sent a questionnaire form with instructions for self-administration. Those who had not responded after 2 months were interviewed by the investigator in their homes. As a result of these procedures, parents and children were not tested in the same order at both data collection periods. At Time 1, they were tested simultaneously; at Time 2, children were tested first.

Analysis of change in moral judgment from Time 1 to Time 2 by form of administration revealed no systematic differences. There was no more tendency ($p = $ N.S.) for adult subjects to score higher or lower if interviewed at Time 2 than if self-reporting. This may be attributable to the high level of education of the subjects, who were apparently comfortable either writing their own answers or verbalizing them in an interview. Kramer (1968) found that form of administration for eight working-class fathers studied appeared to make a difference with regard to their moral judgment profiles, with questionnaires producing more stage 1 responses than interviews.

Scoring methods.—The moral judgment protocols were scored in 1972, using the latest method of scoring (Issue Scoring) at the recommendation of Kohlberg (personal communication). This required all protocols from Time 1 ($N = 159$) to be rescored, since they had been originally coded (Holstein 1972) using the older Sentence Scoring method. In contrast to the older method, Issue Scoring uses the subject's orientation toward several socio-moral institutions or issues (e.g. the legal system, the "system of conscience") as the basis for determining moral judgment score, rather than sentence units. The major issue systems used in scoring can be outlined as follows (adapted from Kohlberg 1972):

1. The Legal System
   A. Rules of law (and rules of custom with quasi-legal force)
   E. Civil rights (basic rights to liberty and equity which the law must protect)
   G. Relations of punishment and legal judgment
2. The System of Conscience
   B. Guilt, fear, anxiety, and moral-character maintenance as motivating choice
   B_{II}. Personal blame and approbation
   B_{III}. Obligation and morality
   B_{IV}. Decision modes and responsibility
   B_V. Personal ethical theory
3. The Affectional System
   C. Relations of affection and concern for welfare
   C_{II}. Role stereotypes and norms of good family and friendship roles

K. Love, intimacy, and sex
4. The Leadership and Power System
    D. Relations of authority, respect, and leader-
       ship
    D_{II}. Civil stereotypes and norms of good
       authority and good citizen-follower roles
    E. Civil rights
5. The Economic System
    F. Relations of contract and reciprocity
    I. Property
    I_{II}. Work roles
    J. Truth and trust
6. The Body Integrity System
    H. Life

Briefly, a face sheet is prepared for each subject, showing stage orientation to the several
socio-moral issues found in the hypothetical
moral-conflict situations. In the present study
there were five such story situations. Rules
for assigning a Global Issue score (pure or
mixed score) for each issue are given in the
scoring manual. A final averaging across issues
gives each subject a Global-Global stage score
for the entire protocol. This may consist of a
pure stage score, ranging from 1 to 6, if 75%
of the Global Issue scores reflect one stage; or
it may consist of a mixed stage score. A mixed
moral judgment score of 5(4), for example,
would mean that between 50% and 75% of
the weighted Global Issue scores are at stage 5,
and at least 25% fall at stage 4.

Since 1971, Kohlberg has introduced into
his hierarchy a new stage which is beyond 4
and not yet 5 and defined as a "pragmatic
relativized stage 4" (1972). It has been labeled
4½ or 5T and will be referred to as 4½ in
this paper.

Rescoring of the moral judgment protocols
from Time 1 ($N = 159$) and scoring of Time 2
protocols ($N = 149$) were done blind by an
experienced coder who was originally trained
by Kohlberg. Protocols were identified only by
number, randomly grouped, and given for scoring in groups of 50. A second coder scored
a randomly selected 20% subsample of protocols for an estimate of interrater reliability.
With agreement defined as major and minor
code identical or reversed, interjudge reliability
is 79%. The Pearson product-moment correlation of judges 1 and 2 is .79. This level of
agreement is consistent with that found by
Kohlberg (1963). Only scores by the first coder
were retained for final analysis.

One other method of presenting moral
judgment is by means of a profile of percentage

of use of each of the six stages for each subject.
Since percentage of usage can be summed over
individuals and averaged, this method has been
used to show age trends in the use of each
stage for grouped data (Kohlberg & Kramer
1969). The stage profile generates a third
method of presenting individual moral judgment, the Moral Maturity Score (MMS). The
subject's percentage of use of each stage is
multiplied by that stage's numerical designation, summed across the stages, and multiplied
by 100. This produces a score ranging from a
theoretical low of 100 to a high of 600 for
each subject. Both moral judgment stage scores
and Moral Maturity Scores will be reported
in the Results section.

Reliability.—Since the moral issues listed
above are used as scoring units under the 1972
scoring method, each issue can be treated as
an item of a test. The Kuder-Richardson reliability formula (Ghiselli 1964) provides a
measure of interitem consistency. Treating each
issue as an item, then, the reliability coefficient
of the whole test at Time 1 is .89 and at Time
2 is .95.

Results and Discussion

Distribution of moral judgment.—Figures
1 through 4 show moral judgment stage change
from Time 1 to Time 2 for adolescents and
adults, sexes separated, in the form of grouped
data. Both major and minor stage scores are
given, since they provide information lost when
the major stage alone is reported. Rank is made
in accordance with the rule that the major code
will always take precedence in ranking a subject, regardless of the minor code. Comparisons
of mean MMS at Time 1 and Time 2 show that
scores are significantly higher at Time 2 for
girls, $t(27) = 5.96$, $p < .001$, two-tailed; for
women, $t(48) = 4.51$, $p < .001$, two-tailed;
and for boys, $t(23) = 7.40$, $p < .001$, two-
tailed; but no significant differences over time
were found for men.

While it is difficult to speak of a mode
for adolescent males (fig. 1), two peaks in the
data characterize them as modally stage 2 at
Time 1 and modally stage 4 at Time 2. For
girls (fig. 2), peaking occurs at stage 3 at
both testings, with the minor stage suggesting
some forward movement to stage 4 at Time 2.
Mean MMS for boys at Time 1 is 280.17 (SD
= 65.37) and for girls is 297.43 (SD =
37.25). The difference is not significant. Mean
MMS for boys at Time 2 is 371.25 (SD =

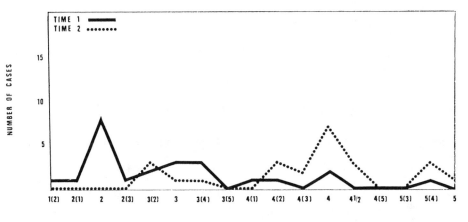

MORAL JUDGMENT SCORES

Fig. 1.—Frequency distribution of moral judgment scores for adolescent males over a 3-year test-retest interval.

59.06) and for girls is 350.50 (SD = 45.52), with boys showing a trend ($p < .20$) toward higher scores. These findings replicate those of Turiel (1972), who found a similar pattern for nearly identical age levels of a cross-sectional sample from a traditional (as opposed to a progressive) school.

Fathers (fig. 3) at both Time 1 and Time 2 are modally stage 4 or a mixture of 5 and 4 (the latter being more the case at Time 2),

with virtually no use of stage 3 thinking. The 12 middle- and eight working-class fathers studied by Kramer (1968) were also modally stage 4. On the other hand, stage 4 in combination with stage 3 accounts for the bulk of the mothers' scores at both Time 1 and Time 2 (fig. 4). Haan et al. (1968) found, in a study of several hundred university students, that the majority of females were modally stage 3, with 4 the next largest category of moral

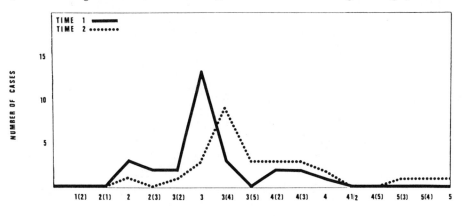

MORAL JUDGMENT SCORES

Fig. 2.—Frequency distribution of moral judgment scores for adolescent females over a 3-year test-retest interval.

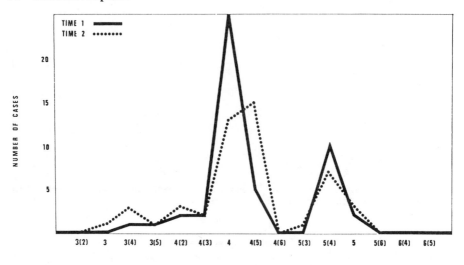

MORAL JUDGMENT SCORES

FIG. 3.—Frequency distribution of moral judgment scores for adult males over a 3-year test-retest interval.

reasoning employed. Mean MMS of fathers (408.65, SD = 43.86) is significantly higher than the mean score of mothers (366.06, SD = 35.40) at Time 1, $t(95) = 5.22$, $p < .001$. Mean MMS of fathers at Time 2 (409.67, SD = 39.52) is higher than that of mothers (393.82, SD = 42.29) but does not reach the level of significance ($p < .10$).

We cannot generalize our results because of the bias in our upper-middle-class, nonprobabilistic sample. However, the distribution of scores for our sample and the sex differences

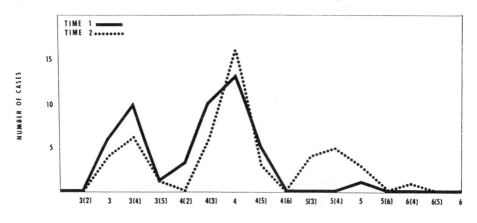

MORAL JUDGMENT SCORES

FIG. 4.—Frequency distribution of moral judgment scores for adult females over a 3-year test-retest interval.

found are consistent with those found in earlier studies (Haan et al. 1968; Hudgins & Prentice 1973; Kohlberg & Kramer 1969; Turiel 1972). In addition, the grouped data for adolescents suggest, as grouped data did to Kohlberg (1963), age trends in moral judgment.

IQ and moral maturity.—The mean IQ, as measured by the CTMM at Time 1, is 117.4 (SD = 12.6) for boys and 122.4 (SD = 10.2) for girls. IQ and moral maturity (MMS) are correlated for boys at both ages 13 ($r = +.42$) and 16 ($r = +.45$). This relationship is somewhat larger than that reported by Kohlberg (1964) for 72 young male subjects with age controlled ($r = +.31$). For girls, IQ and MMS are not related at age 13 ($r = .06$) but do show a relationship at age 16 ($r = .39$).

Stepwise invariant sequence.—Evidence of invariant sequence is a critical issue for Kohlberg's stage theory, because age trends based on grouped data, as presented in figures 1–4, do not imply individual sequence. If each higher stage requires a restructuring of the stage below it in order to emerge (Kohlberg & Kramer 1969), then it is not possible to skip a stage. Tables 1 through 3 present modal global stage movement over 3-year intervals in the form of transition matrixes for the young adolescent subjects of the present study (table 1), Kramer's late adolescents moving into young adulthood (table 2), and the parents of the present study (table 3).

To summarize briefly, movement for young males and females shown in tables 1 and 2 over 3-year intervals was from the preconventional level to conventional level, with stabilization at the conventional level. Young males in both the Holstein (table 1) and Kramer (table 2) studies tended to move directly to stage 4 from stages 1 or 2 by two- or three-stage jumps. Girls (table 1) were more likely to move one step, from stage 2 to stage 3.

Two-stage jumps from 3 to 5 were found for the Holstein adolescent and adult subjects (tables 1 and 3), with the proportion of stage 5s who moved directly from stage 3 more than twice as great for females (47%) than for males (19%).

Two methodological shortcomings of the present study make an evaluation of the stepwise, sequential requirement difficult. First, 21% of Holstein's adolescent subjects (table 1) skipped stages, in contrast to only 7% of the adults (table 3). Kramer (table 2) found

slightly less stage skipping (14%) in his longitudinal study of older adolescent subjects. From these trends we conclude that a 3-year testretest interval is too long when studying younger subjects, since they may have moved sequentially without its being observed. Second, short-term intraindividual fluctuation, in the sense of state as opposed to trait variability, might account for some stage movement over time. A better research design would have included short-term control groups in order to separate long-term change from short-term fluctuations.

Irreversibility.—The tendency of subjects from both the Holstein and Kramer studies to advance one stage, remain stable, or regress one stage or more is given in table 4. According to theoretical expectations of the organismic model (Kohlberg 1973), there should be no regressors. Moral judgment has been dichotomized into lower stage (stages 1–3) and higher stage (stages 4–6), based upon previous categorization by Kohlberg (1969). The proportion of higher-stage subjects who regress is similar across all age groups (20%, 33%, 21%, and 22%, respectively). There are virtually no lower-stage subjects who regress (2%, 0%, 0%, and 0%, respectively).

Because of the lack of short-term control groups in both studies, measurement error cannot be dismissed as an explanation for the regression found. An alternative interpretation, however, is that stages from the conventional level up are content-bound and used when and if preferred once certain cognitive prerequisites are met. The philosopher Alston (1971) has suggested that intelligent higherstage adults may simply prefer the stage they use for a variety of reasons rather than out of an inability to comprehend an even higher stage of moral reasoning. In support of this, he cites a number of instances in which moral philosophers would have to be ranked stage 4 rather than 5 or 6. That Alston's interpretation is not precluded by any substantive research findings can be shown in the following examples. Rest, Turiel, and Kohlberg (1969), using the old scoring system, have found that children are relatively incapable of paraphrasing higher-stage reasoning, but the ability of adults to do so has not yet been investigated. Kuhn, Langer, Kohlberg, and Haan (1972), using Kohlberg's scale, report that all morally principled adults (stages 5 or 6) in their study are capable of formal operational thinking but

TABLE 1

TRANSITION MATRIXES OF CHANGE IN MODAL GLOBAL STAGE FOR HOLSTEIN ADOLESCENT LONGITUDINAL SUBJECTS

MALES

Junior High (Time 1)	High School (Time 2)							N
	1	2	3	4	4½	5	6	
1	—		1					1
2		—	4	5		1		10
3			—	4	2	2		8
4				2	1	1		4
5				1		—		1
6							—	0
								24

FEMALES

Junior High (Time 1)	High School (Time 2)						N
	1	2	3	4	5	6	
1	—						0
2		—	4	1			5
3	1	11	4	2			18
4		1	3	1			5
5					—		0
6						—	0
							28

TABLE 2

TRANSITION MATRIXES OF CHANGE IN MODAL GLOBAL STAGE FOR KRAMER LONGITUDINAL SUBJECTS

HIGH SCHOOL	COLLEGE AGE						N
	1	2	3	4	5	6	
1	—		*1*	*2*			3
2	*2*	*1*	*2*				5
3			—	*4*			4
4		*1*		*4*			5
5		*1*	*1*	*1*	*4*		7
6						—	0
							24

COLLEGE AGE	YOUNG ADULT						N
	1	2	3	4	5	6	
1	—						0
2		*1*		*1*			2
3			*1*	*2*			3
4	*1*	*1*		*8*			10
5				*1*	*2*	*1*	4
6						—	0
							19

SOURCE.—Richard Kramer, "Changes in Moral Judgment Response Pattern during Late Adolescence and Young Adulthood: Retrogression in a Developmental Sequence" (Ph.D. diss., University of Chicago, 1968), p. 82 (by permission of the author).

TABLE 3

TRANSITION MATRIXES OF CHANGE IN MODAL GLOBAL STAGE FOR HOLSTEIN ADULT LONGITUDINAL SUBJECTS

FATHERS

Time 1	Time 2						N
	1	2	3	4	5	6	
1	—						0
2		—					0
3			—	*1*	*1*		2
4			*3*	*25*	*6*		34
5				*1*	*6*	*5*	12
6						—	0
							48

MOTHERS

Time 1	Time 2						N
	1	2	3	4	5	6	
1	—						0
2		—					0
3			*4*	*8*	*5*		17
4			*7*	*17*	*6*	*1*	31
5					*1*		1
6						—	0
							49

that some conventional-level (stage 4) adults are *also* capable of operating at the level of formal operations. Holstein (1974) finds that principled stage 5 and conventional stage 4 reasoning among the college-educated adult males in the present study varies as a function of types of occupation and levels of formal education from the baccalaureate up. Kohlberg (1973) reports that of his longitudinal male subjects now in their late twenties, only those who went to college became principled in moral reasoning. Adult socialization experiences relating to the development of moral preferences have yet to be investigated, especially

TABLE 4

PERCENTAGE OF LOWER AND HIGHER MORAL JUDGMENT STAGE SUBJECTS WHO REGRESS, REMAIN STABLE, OR ADVANCE OVER A 3-YEAR TEST-RETEST INTERVAL, SEXES COMBINED

MODAL GLOBAL MORAL JUDGMENT CHANGE OVER 3 YEARS	HOLSTEIN ADOLESCENTS		KRAMER ADOLESCENTS		KRAMER YOUNG ADULTS		HOLSTEIN ADULTS	
	Lower Stage $N = 42$	Higher Stage $N = 10$	Lower Stage $N = 12$	Higher Stage $N = 12$	Lower Stage $N = 5$	Higher Stage $N = 14$	Lower Stage $N = 19$	Higher Stage $N = 78$
Regress one stage or more	2	20	0	33	0	21	0	22
Remain stable	26	50	17	67	40	71	21	62
Advance one stage or more	71	30	83	0	60	7	79	17

NOTE.—Percentages may not add to 100 due to rounding.

those defining the college experience for young adults and those characterizing occupational commitment and involvement.

Possible sex bias in the scoring system.— The patterns in both the Holstein and Kramer samples of young males moving directly from stage 2 to 4 and in the Holstein study of females moving directly from stage 3 to 5 suggest possible sex bias in the scoring standards. As the stages are defined in the 1972 scoring manual, pure stage 3 reasoning is not compatible with the traditionally instrumental American male role, nor is pure stage 4 compatible with the traditionally expressive female role. This inference is supported by two additional analyses.

The first is an analysis of the relationship of moral judgment and political attitudes along a liberal-conservative dimension. These attitudes were assessed for subjects interviewed at home ($N = 111$) at Time 2 data collection. They were determined on the basis of attitudes, pro or con, toward six sociopolitical issues: (1) wiretapping, (2) fair housing, (3) gun control, (4) capital punishment, (5) medicare, and (6) abortion (see Holstein 1973 for a detailed description of the scale). If a subject adopted a liberal position on all six items, he was given a score of 100; if liberal on five of the six items, he was given a score of 83, and so on. All scores are proportions of items answered liberally.

All principled stage 5 subjects have higher liberalism scores than conventional stage 3 or 4 subjects, and this holds true for males and females, regardless of age. All stage 4 subjects are relatively conservative and no sex differences exist, regardless of age. But in the case of stage 3 subjects, females are significantly more liberal than males and nearly as liberal

as stage 5 females. This holds true for adolescents as well as adults. Stage 3 males are more conservative than either stage 4 or stage 5 males. A summary of findings for t tests of group means is given in table 5. Age groups have been combined due to their similarities with respect to results.

A positive correlation between liberalism and stage score for males is consistent with Kohlberg's (1971, 1972) argument that such a finding can be used as construct validation for his hypotheses concerning moral judgment levels. However, the female data fail to support this position. When reasons for attitudes on the six sociopolitical issues are examined, the stage 3 differences between males and females are instructive. Females often tended to cite compassion for another's suffering

TABLE 5

COMPARISON OF LIBERALISM-CONSERVATISM SCALES FOR MALES AND FEMALES

Modal Moral Judgment Stage	Males	Females
3:		
N	7	19
M	61.71	85.47
SD	18.45	16.30
4:[a]		
N	35	21
M	64.43	65.95
SD	23.36	24.16
5:[b]		
N	14	14
M	82.64	93.21
SD	24.15	12.04[c]

NOTE.—All t tests are two-tailed.
[a] Males, stage 4, include two males stage 4½.
[b] Females, stage 5, include one female stage 6.
[c] Summary of significant differences: males vs. females, stage 3: females > males (.01); within males, 3 vs. 5: 5 > 3 (.10), 4 vs. 5: 5 > 4 (.05); within females, 3 vs. 4: 3 > 3 (.01), 3 vs. 5: 5 > 3 (.10), 4 vs. 5: 5 > 4 (.002).

as a reason for being opposed to or in favor of a position. One of the hallmarks of stage 3 reasoning is a stress on compassion, sympathy, or love as a reason for moral action. Another hallmark of stage 3 is a concern for the approval of others, especially those in the primary group. This latter emphasis "catches" children's reasoning. But at the same time, the stage 3 emphasis on sympathy, so stereotypically part of the female role, is characteristic of much adult female moral reasoning in the present study. Many of the women are either predominantly stage 3 or, if stage 4, show so much stage 3 reasoning that their stage score is a mixed one (e.g., 4[3]).

An analysis of adult male and female mean differences on Kohlberg's moral issues A through K (described above) shows this difference clearly. Of the several moral issues which could differentiate men and women at either Time 1 or Time 2, it was found that mean scores on issue C in the affectional system were significantly different for the sexes at both data collection periods (Time 1: $t[84] = 4.71$, $p < .001$, two-tailed; Time 2: $t[80] = 3.50$, $p < .002$, two-tailed). Women were generally scored stage 3 on this issue, men generally stage 4. No other issue so consistently and strongly showed sex differences over time.

Conclusions

The limitations of this study should be clearly borne in mind while interpreting the results. First, the sample was self-selected, probably introducing a positive bias in the distribution of moral judgment scores. It was deliberately homogeneous with respect to socioeconomic background and geographic location, both factors tending to reduce the generality of our findings. In addition, generational similarities within sex were based on families rather than independent samples. Second, interpretation of stage movement over time is made difficult by virtue of two design defects: (a) a 3-year test-retest interval is too long when studying younger subjects, who may have passed through stages they appear to have skipped; (b) short-term intraindividual fluctuation, in the sense of state as opposed to trait variability, might account for some stage movement found during the 3-year test-retest period. A better research design would have included short-term control groups in order to separate long-term change from short-term fluctuations. With these limitations in mind, the results of this study, when compared with the one other longitudinal study available (Kramer 1968), have led to the following considerations:

The issue of stepwise invariant sequence. —The Holstein data for young adolescents support Kramer's data for older adolescents and young adults that movement is stepwise and sequential from level to level rather than stage to stage. There is stepwise movement from the preconventional level (represented mainly by stage 2) to the conventional level (stages 3 and 4). When individual stages are examined, progression is not stepwise.

Irreversibility. —At retest, higher-stage adolescents and adults in the Holstein study showed a significant tendency to regress, while lower-stage subjects were significantly more likely to have advanced. If the regression found in higher-stage subjects reflects real change in moral judgment maturity, then irreversibility, a major requirement of Kohlberg's stage theory, has not been met. However, the possibility of measurement error cannot be eliminated as an interpretation for these findings.

The sequential movement found for young people from the preconventional to conventional level, however, lends support to the proposition that the scheme is developmental up to this point. The normal, undeprived adolescents and young adults of these two studies tend to shed preconventional fear-oriented, morally egoistic justifications to become conventional, at least when they make moral judgments for other people. In addition, data for college-educated parents, in combination with the adolescent data, were reported as evidence that moral justifications tend to stay at the conventional level over time. Ironically, Kohlberg perhaps said it best himself when he wrote, "It is often assumed by psychologists that moral conflicts are conflicts between community standards and egoistic impulses. If this were true, it seems likely that the Type 3 and 4 moral orientations would persist throughout life" (1963, p. 27). This comment may be even more accurate when adults of lower educational level and income have been adequately sampled.

Sex bias in scoring standards. —The Kohlberg (1963) moral judgment stages were originally defined and empirically tested on a sample of young white males rather than across a representative sample of American society. The problem of what to do with such "irrational" sentiments as compassion or love in moral decision making is highlighted in a strongly cognitive scheme such as Kohlberg's (Hogan 1973; Mischel & Mischel 1975). Emotional response to moral conflict which is exemplified by females more than males results in adult female reasoning being categorized with children's. This is a problem, of course, because the moral judgment scale is defined as ordinal rather than nominal, since each stage is considered both cognitively and morally superior to the one preceding it (Kohlberg 1973). The problem of where to categorize irrational but morally relevant emotions such as compassion, sympathy, and love will remain a problem, especially in the light of consistent sex differences produced by scoring standards for these moral passions.

References

Alston, W. P. Comments on Kohlberg's "From is to ought." In T. Mischel (Ed.), *Cognitive development and epistemology.* New York: Academic Press, 1971.

Ghiselli, E. *Theory of psychological measurement.* New York: McGraw-Hill, 1964.

Haan, N.; Smith, M. B.; & Block, J. H. The moral reasoning of young adults: political-social behavior, family background, and personality correlates. *Journal of Personality and Social Psychology,* 1968, 10, 183–201.

Hogan, R. Moral conduct and moral character: a psychological perspective. *Psychological Bulletin,* 1973, 79, 217–232.

Holstein, C. B. The relation of children's moral judgment level to that of their parents and to communication patterns in the family. In R. D. Smart & M. S. Smart (Eds.), *Readings in child development and relationships.* New York: Macmillan, 1972.

Holstein, C. B. Moral judgment change in early adolescence and middle age: a longitudinal study. Paper presented at a meeting of the Society for Research in Child Development, Philadelphia, 1973.

Holstein, C. B. Developmental diversification, occupational specialization, and moral reasoning over the lifespan. Paper presented at a meeting of the American Psychological Association, New Orleans, 1974.

Hudgins, W., & Prentice, N. Moral judgment in delinquent and nondelinquent adolescents and their mothers. *Journal of Abnormal Psychology,* 1973, 82, 145–152.

Kohlberg, L. The development of children's orientations toward a moral order, I: Sequence in the development of moral thought. *Vita Humana,* 1963, 6, 11–33.

Kohlberg, L. Development of moral character and ideology. In M. L. Hoffman and L. W. Hoffman (Eds.), *Review of child development research.* Vol. 1. New York: Russell Sage, 1964.

Kohlberg, L. Stage and sequence: the cognitive-developmental approach to socialization. In D. A. Goslin (Ed.), *Handbook of socialization theory and research.* Chicago: Rand-McNally, 1969.

Kohlberg, L. Stages of moral development as a basis for moral education. In C. M. Beck, B. S. Crittendon, & E. V. Sullivan (Eds.), *Moral education: interdisciplinary approaches.* Toronto: University of Toronto Press, 1971.

Kohlberg, L. Issue Scoring guide. Unpublished manuscript, Harvard University, 1972.

Kohlberg, L. Continuities in childhood and adult moral development revisited. In P. B. Baltes and K. W. Schaie (Eds.), *Life-span developmental psychology: personality and socialization.* New York: Academic Press, 1973.

Kohlberg, L., & Kramer, R. Continuities and discontinuities in childhood and adult moral development. *Human Development,* 1969, 12, 93–120.

Kramer, R. Changes in moral judgment response pattern during late adolescence and young adulthood: retrogression in a developmental sequence. Unpublished doctoral dissertation, University of Chicago, 1968.

Kuhn, D.; Langer, L.; Kohlberg, L.; & Haan, N. The development of formal operations in logical and moral development. Unpublished manuscript, University of California, Berkeley, 1972.

Loevinger, J. Recent research on ego development. Paper presented at a meeting of the Society for Research in Child Development, Philadelphia, 1973.

Mischel, H., & Mischel, W. Moral behavior from a cognitive social learning viewpoint. Paper presented at a meeting of the Society for Research in Child Development, Denver, 1975.

Rest, J.; Turiel, E.; & Kohlberg, L. Level of moral development as a determinant of preference and comprehension of moral judgments made by others. *Journal of Personality,* 1969, 37, 225–252.

Turiel, E. A. A comparative analysis of moral knowledge and moral judgment in males and females. Unpublished manuscript, Harvard University, 1972.

The Cognitive-Developmental Approach to Morality: a Reply to Kurtines and Greif

John Broughton

Abstract

A recent critique of Kohlberg's cognitive-developmental approach to morality by Kurtines and Greif is examined in detail. It is found to contribute some useful indications of studies which were then needed, and many of which have been published since the critique appeared. A careful analysis of the literature on moral development, however, shows Kurtines and Greif's criticisms to be largely unfounded, and in several cases misrepresentative of research findings. As a result the empirical support for the 'stage' and 'sequence' components of Kohlberg's theory is under-estimated, as is the evidence in favour of a relationship between moral judgment and moral action. The misunderstandings largely reflect a common and mistaken attempt to reduce structural development in cognition to static psychometric traits, an attempt which confuses developmental theories with measurement instruments.

William Kurtines and Esther Blank Greif (1974) have brought our attention to some apparent weaknesses and anomalies in research on Kohlberg's account of moral development, and particularly to sins of omission on the part of Kohlberg himself. They correctly point to incompleteness in the data, especially with respect to the higher, or 'post-conventional' stages. They also point to a widely felt need for clarification of scoring procedures, which have themselves undergone a complicated stage—by—stage evolution (Kohlberg, 1975a). This response attempts to show that most of Kurtines and Greif's other criticisms are interesting queries deserving of answers which can already be given, rather than well-founded objections that might seriously undermine Kohlberg's claims. These queries turn out to be generated not only by lack of familiarity with the literature, but also by a broad misunderstanding of Kohlberg's theory, which derives from a research paradigm and a conception of science and the human mind quite at odds with Kohlberg's. This kind of difference has elsewhere been described as that between Aristotelian and Galileian modes of thought (Lewin, 1931; Elkind, 1969). In general, critical zeal in the application of this non-structural, non-developmental Aristotelian paradigm to a structural-developmental or Galileian theory appears to have encouraged pervasive misinterpretations of the research findings.

Specifically, Kurtines and Grief do not see that criticisms of Kohlberg's measurement procedure do not necessarily imply criticisms of Kohlberg's theory. The theory could be correct, and we

Dr. John Broughton is Asst. Professor of Developmental Psychology in the Department of Psychology, Teachers College, Columbia University, New York, 10027, USA.

could still debate the best way to bring a measurement instrument to bear on it (cf. Broughton and Zahaykevich, 1977). It is not possible to simultaneously evaluate the truth of the theory and the validity of an instrument designed to reflect and test the theory. In fact, to concentrate on a critique of validity and reliability of the instrument already presupposes that the theoretical ideas which the instrument is designed to test are true. Theories are true or false; measures are only good or bad. A poor measure can only be faulted relative to a theory presumed to be true (Kohlberg, 1975d). The result of Kurtines and Grief's misunderstanding is an ineffective criticism of a theory that needs and deserves a more thoughtful review, and which is susceptible to much more telling critiques. Kohlberg's case needs restating so that we are not distracted from these more fundamental problems. While some of Kurtines and Greif's legitimate questions have been answered by research reported since 1974 (see below), their spurious refutations have become seriously distracting by virtue of a growing tendency on the part of other authors to uncritically accept the Kurtines and Greif review (e.g. Gergen, 1976; Fraenkel, in press) and even to become active proponents of it (e.g. Hoffman, 1977).

More broadly, the misunderstanding reflects a not uncommon confusion about 'Piagetian' theory and research, and the claims that they make. It is therefore instructive to take this opportunity to clarify such general confusions, a task which Kohlberg has not taken seriously enough until recently (1975a, d). He could in fact be seen as contributing to this confusion by not making explicit his latent reconception of measurement, and by occasionally confusing his model with the more traditional psychometric one (Loevinger, 1974, pp. 59–60).

Focusing on the kinds of misinterpretations made by Kurtines and Greif, we should first draw attention to remarks seeming to indicate that Kohlberg has fulfilled neither of the two criteria most defining of a cognitive-developmental stage theory: 'stage' and 'sequence'. Although in Kurtines and Greif's critique these issues are disguised as test 'reliability' and 'validity', they are better dealt with in Kohlberg's original terms, so that questions about the developmental theory are not assimilated to the measurement issues.

Stages
Consistency

Stages are 'structured wholes' (*structures d'ensemble*), characterized by their internally consistent organization of categories and relations (Piaget, 1960; Pinard and Laurendeau, 1969). In discussing within-subject distributions of reasoning across different stages (p. 457), Kurtines and Greif state quite bluntly that 'a majority of an individual's responses are rarely at his modal stage'. On the same page, apropos of inter-item or inter-story homogeneity, they say that 'there are no estimates of internal consistency to be found anywhere in the research literature'. Although there are two intertwined issues (self-consistency of moral thought, and test homogeneity of moral situations), Kurtines and Greif's position on both appears to be directly in conflict with Kohlberg's major treatise on moral development theory (Kohlberg, 1969a), where (pp. 388–9) he clearly states that an average of 50 per cent of a subject's moral judgments fit a single stage, 'that the moral levels achieved in different stories show an average correlation of .51', and that in a factor analysis a 'general first moral factor accounts for most of the covariations from situation to situation'.[2]

It is true that in Kohlberg's (1958) dissertation, and the Porter and Taylor (1972) scoring system derived from it, consistency was lower than the 50 per cent mark. However, that rather crude measure was abandoned eight years ago in favour of a more 'structural' measure (Kohlberg, 1972, 1975d, Gibbs *et al.*, 1976), and it was this new measure that was used in several recent studies to which Kurtines and Greif refer (e.g., Holstein, 1973; Saltstein, Diamond, and Belenky, 1972). In a factor analysis of subject scores deriving from the new measure, Lieberman (personal communication) found that a first-level factor accounted for over 85 per cent of the variance, which is nearly three times as much as the variance accounted for in Kohlberg's original study.

Reliability

Kurtines and Greif are correct in raising the question of test—retest reliability, since Kohlberg has not been very vocal on the topic. However, they make the puzzling claim that 'evidence from experimental studies indicates that scores on the scale fluctuate greatly even over short periods of time' (p. 468). The claim is puzzling, since on page 465 the authors seem to be arguing that because Turiel was unable to obtain significant improvements in Kohlberg's score through training, we should conservatively treat the results as showing no change. There appears to be some conflict here, since either Turiel's results support Turiel's thesis, or else they at least provide us with inci-dental evidence of temporal stability. The issue of stability of reasoning over time is of course very important to the notion of structural stages, being in fact one of the main criteria of structural cognition (Smedslund, 1961), but Kurtines and Greif do not indicate when they are talking about structural stability and when they are talking about measurement stability.

The actual test—retest data, although preliminary, was scored blind, and showed no differences greater than one-third of a stage over a six-month interval (Colby, personal communication). This means that the biggest instabilities in score are of the order of a change from, for example '3(4)' to '4(3)' — a reversal of 'major stage' and 'minor stage'. These results correspond to the 90 per cent agreement on major stage reported by Kohlberg (1975d, Table 4). In addition, there are data on 'alternate form' reliability, since subjects are rated on two alternative and equivalent questionnaires, 'A' and 'B'. These data are exemplified in Table 1, where 66 per cent of instances are within one-third of a stage, and 100 per cent within two-thirds. (This estimate of alternate form reliability is conservative since each form was scored by a different rater. The differences then reflect unreliability due to inter-judge disagreements as well as alternate form differences.)

Table 1: Preliminary longitudinal data, scored blind. (These five cases, #s 5, 39, 41, 44, and 70, were rated on two equivalent questionnaire forms, A and B. The times of testing, O, A, B, C, D, E, represent respectively 1956/57, 1959/60, 1964, 1966/69, 1971 and 1974/75.)

	FORM A	*FORM B*	*TOTAL FORMS A&B*
5—0	2	2(1)	2(1)
5—A	2(3)	2(1)	2
5—B	2(3)	2	2
5—C	3	2(3)	3(2)
5—D	3	2(3)	3(2)
39—O	2(3)	2(3)	2(3)
39—A	4(3)	3	3(4)
39—B	4(3)	3	3(4)
39—C	4	4(3)	4(3)
41—O		2	2
41—A	3(2)	3(2)	3(2)
41—B	3	3	3
41—C	3	3	3
41—D	3	3(4)	3(4)
44—A	2(3)	3	3(2)
44—B	4(5)	4(3)	4
44—C	4	4	4
44—E	4(5)	4(5)	4(5)
70—O	3(2)	3(2)	3(2)
70—A	3(4)	3(4)	3(4)
70—B	3(4)	4(3)	4(3)
70—C	4(3)	4(3)	4(3)
70—D	4	4	4

Kurtines and Greif devote little space to the important form of reliability called inter-judge. Kohlberg (1975c, Part II, p. 84) tells us the degree of exact agreement is variously 70 per cent (Hickey, 1972) and 86 per cent (Saltzstein et al., 1972), the N being again 20 in both instances. In two other studies where the percentage agreement is reported (Edwards, 1975; White, 1975), it is at the 90 per cent level. Exactly what inter-rater reliability means is never discussed (Tomlinson, 1977). On this count, and many others, Kohlberg can be questioned for too uncritical an acceptance of standard social science methodology (cf. Morelli, 1978).

To conclude this section, while Kurtines and Greif point to interesting lacunae where more empirical work would be informative, they also confuse issues by failing to grasp the significance of the claim that moral judgments form a coherent and consistent network called a structural stage. This leads to a failure to distinguish measurement issues from developmental—theoretical ones (particularly confusing reliability with structural stability as well as structural wholeness), and to a failure to distinguish imperfections in scoring criteria from disconfirmations of empirical claims. Within-subject consistency is much greater than Kurtines and Greif assert, supporting the notion of stage intrinsic to Kohlberg's theory. As far as the measurement instrument is concerned, respectable levels of reliability are indicated by the data available.

Sequence

In order to show that Kurtines and Greif's discussion does not strongly challenge Kohlberg's claims for stages in moral development, we were obliged to focus several partial and often tangential suggestions in that discussion which were in danger of being seen as entirely disputes about scoring methods or reliability. When we come to consider the other major criterion of cognitive-developmental stage theories, that they describe invariant sequences, we have less focusing to do since the arguments are more explicit. However, we still find the assimilation of Kohlberg's theory to an inappropriate set of evaluative criteria, because questions of stage 'sequence' are addressed as though they were only questions of psychometric construct validity. It is not at all clear why the matter of sequence is considered by Kurtines and Greif to be an issue of construct validity, while the matter of stages is not. This preferential treatment seems to be quite at variance with Kohlberg's own claims in his 'Stage and Sequence' manifesto, (Kohlberg, 1969a), where he treats the two as correlative theoretical issues.[4]

The quasi-simplex correlation matrix

Kurtines and Greif attempt to undermine Kohlberg's use of the Guttman 'quasi-simplex' matrix of correlations as evidence for the sequential properties of stages. While this kind of evidence, presented early on by Kohlberg, is no longer necessary, since it is clearly pre-empted by longitudinal studies of sequence, it has considerably more validity than Kurtines and Greif admit. They argue that if we reverse the stages within levels of moral reasoning, (exchanging columns 1 and 2, 3, and 4, and 5 and 6), the matrix of correlations shows a very similar quasi-simplex pattern to the original ordered matrix.

First we might ask why the stages should be jumbled in this way. If Kurtines and Greif want to make a strong point against invariant sequence, why do they not simply randomly mix up the columns? The reason is presumably because there is *some* order here, perhaps the order between levels if not the order between stages. Thus their choice of transformation to apply to the matrix implicitly supports a weaker version of Kohlberg's claims. Kohlberg has pointed out anyway that the major transitions are between *levels* (1963a, p. 17).

Second, we might ask exactly what Kurtines and Greif expect us to see as 'similar' between the two matrices. The quasi-simplex pattern (correlations decreasing down columns) is violated by only two pairs of correlations (out of ten) in Kohlberg's matrix of actual data, whereas it is violated by *five* pairs in Kurtines and Greif's transformation.

Finally, it is a little unreasonable of Kurtines and Greif to chide Kohlberg for the lack of independence in the matrix, since the latter made this circularity quite clear (Kohlberg, 1958,

p. 101), and such non-vicious 'circularity' is a necessary part of the construction of ideal types (Weber, 1949; van den Daele, 1968; Broughton, 1974).

Longitudinal evidence

The form of evidence that Kohlberg prefers to adduce in support of the sequential ordering of his moral stages is from longitudinal research. Kohlberg's longitudinal findings appeared in print shortly after Kurtines and Greif's review (Kohlberg and Elfinbein, 1975, Table 3). Of 30 subjects followed at three-year intervals from age 10 to somewhere between aged 19 and 28, all are reported as either remaining at the same stage, or proceeding as much as three stages overall through the prescribed sequence. In only two cases was there more than one-stage advance in the interval between testings. Development appears to be gradual and stage-by-stage, transition from one to the next taking four to five years on average in adolescence, and tending (with some exceptions) to reach an apparent ceiling around age 20. Interesting and important as this evidence is, scoring of the longitudinal data was not uniformly blind with respect to age, and so vital sources of scorer bias have still to be dealt with before this evidence can be properly evaluated. Fortunately, some preliminary data have since become available (Colby, personal communication) which *have* been scored blind. These five longitudinal cases are shown in Table 1.

An earlier and controversial report of some specific longitudinal findings is Kohlberg and Kramer's (1969). These data were originally reported as evidence of anomalous 'sophomore regression', violating the principle of strict stage-by-stage development. This does not necessarily imply that the stage sequence is 'flexible' as Kramer (1968) originally hypothesized, and as Kurtines and Greif conclude, since all the 'regressors' were eventually found to advance to Stage 5. It is therefore unjust of Kurtines and Greif to say (p. 469) that 'longitudinal data demonstrated only that most males are at Stage 4 morality'. Furthermore, a detailed analysis of the actual profiles of these subjects shows that the 'return to Stage 2 reasoning' was only a partial one (Broughton, 1970).

Fortunately, however, we do not have to debate this issue, since the 'regression' turns out to be no regression at all! With a more adequate differentiation of form and content in the interpretation of late adolescent moral judgment, what was classified as 'regressive Stage 2 thinking' emerges as a new transitional form of judgment, colloquially referred to as 'Stage 4½' (Kohlberg, 1973a, 1975b; Gilligan and Kohlberg, 1974). Turiel (1974a) has argued that this is neither a stage nor a sub-stage but simply reflects a transitional reformulation of Stage 4 into Stage 5 [Turiel's own transitional subjects all progressed to Stage 5 within two years (Turiel, 1977)]. There is, however, general agreement between Turiel and Kohlberg that the moral outlook at this stage is egoistic in a new sense, bearing only a superficial similarity of content to the hedonism of Stage 2. It is a sophisticated meta-ethical individualism (Boyd, 1972), pre-supposing ethical relativism, a position that is clearly post-conventional, and not a form of naive pre-conventional hedonism like Stage 2. It was only poor probing of the original interview responses that permitted the occurrence of such a confusion of superficial content with deeper formal qualities of reasoning.[5]

Recently, Kuhn (1976) found evidence of regular slight advancements toward the next stage over a one year period in five- to eight-year-old children. Only five out of 50 subjects showed any decrement in stage score, and only one of these was more than a third of a stage. This independent data adds to our confidence about the sequentiality of moral stages, at least for Stages 1, 2 and 3.

Intervention studies

Under this third form of evidence for sequence, the deliberate acceleration of transition between stages, Kurtines and Greif confine their attention to Turiel's study (1966, expanded in 1969, 1972). It is important to realize that there is additional evidence. Blatt (1975) arranged classroom moral discussions in which judgments were constantly juxtaposed with arguments at the next highest stage. He found that reasoning at Stages 2, 3 and 4 regularly tended to move towards

Stages 3, 4 and 5 respectively. Hickey (1972) obtained similar results with the lower stages, through guided moral discussion in a prison setting. At a higher level, Boyd (1976) found educationally induced transitions, occurring in the direction specified by the theory of moral development.[6] Specifically at the principled level, Erdynast (1974; Kohlberg, 1973b) found progressive increments in the moral stages of businessmen following an intervention designed to encourage Stage 6 reasoning. Berkowitz, Broughton and Gibbs (1977) found that subjects averaged a third of a stage increment after moral discussions with a partner at the next highest stage of development. This kind of evidence from intervention studies is crucial not only to a confirmation of the sequence, but also to an elucidation of the dynamic mechanisms of the equilibration process (Berkowitz, 1976).

Turiel's Study

An important source of evidence considered in detail by Kurtines and Greif is Turiel's study, in which he tried to experimentally induce small upward and downward changes in stages of moral reasoning. Kurtines and Greif focus their energy on a refutation of Turiel's basic conclusion that the number of +1 scores of the +1 treatment group was higher than the number of +1 scores of any other treatment group. However, a careful reading of Turiel's paper reveals that this 'refutation' is erroneous, being based on misinterpretations of statistical significance.[7] Kurtines and Greif go on to point out that the change scores found in the study are very small. This is true, but it should come as no surprise if we accept the interactional basis of the structural explanation of developmental advance. The amount of logical conflict generated in the experimental situation must be minimal compared to the kind and enormity of conflicts that arise in the repeated everyday situations that are morally challenging. The changes in direct scores are only small relative to empiricist expectations that moral reasoning is impressed upon people through a process of social coercion. Turiel's loss is in this respect the rationalist's gain, since large changes would have been an indication of the predominance of accommodatory over assimilatory tendencies in moral judgment. The developmental interpretation is also supported by the very limited generalization reflected in the indirect scores.

Kurtines and Greif make a lot of the fact that the difference between +1 and −1 change scores is not significant at the standard .05 level. Their emphasis on strict adherence to significance levels is somewhat regressive in the face of the powerful critiques of such behaviour over the last 15 years (e.g. Levine, 1974; Cohen, 1962; and Bakan, 1966). The point is that changes in the +1 group were 50 per cent greater than changes in the −1 group, and so it is not strictly true for Kurtines and Greif to say that 'both seem equally effective' (p. 464). The existence of an effect, and its possible theoretical significance are warrant enough for holding judgment in abeyance here. The significance level does not measure the size of the effect. Kurtines and Greif are quick to run the risk of type II error, even though they present no argument that we should guard more carefully against type I error in this study (Cohen, 1966). At another point Kurtines and Greif switch horses, arguing that the general effectiveness of the +1 training is not demonstrable, *despite a significance level of p<·005*, simply because the actual *t* value is not given!

Their final objection is that instability in the moral judgment score, indicated by pre-test/post-test differences in the control group subjects, renders any change measures uninterpretable. However, since Turiel subtracts the appropriate control group changes from the measured effects in the experimental groups, 'instability' in the moral judgment score is already taken into account in the results. Furthermore, Turiel *does* justify this subtraction procedure, despite Kurtines and Greif's allegations to the contrary (p. 464). It is not clear anyway what their objections to this procedure could be. It makes more sense simply to inquire how the spontaneous regression is to be explained (Zinn, 1970). My own experience with repeated administration of the Kohlberg interview suggests that declining interest in the test leads to shorter and less careful answers, which in turn generate artificial lowering of ascribed scores.

In sum, although Kurtines and Greif are correct to point to a certain inconclusiveness in Turiel's results, their arguments are often misleading, and their statistical dogmatism obscures important information that may require explanation and further study. The critique seems particularly unjust, not solely because of its distortions, but on two further counts. First, it isolates issues from the context of the study as a whole. Thus the critical claim made, that the effects observed in the study are attributable to memory rather than structural change, is quite untenable in the face of the whole pattern of results we have just described. Second, the critique isolates the issues from a body of research which is consonant with Turiel's findings. For example, Rest *et al.*'s (1969) finding that 12- and 16-year-olds reject reasoning at the −1 level, and the analyses of change in studies already mentioned (e.g. Hickey, 1972), confirm Turiel's claims. Furthermore, Keasey (1973) and Tracey and Cross (1973) have succeeded in replicating Turiel's findings. A study by Sutton (1972), cited by Turiel (1974a), adds further support, despite starting out with radically different hypotheses. The only ambiguous findings are those of Arbuthnot (1975) which confirm only some of Turiel's hypotheses. Unfortunately, the apparent disconfirmation is not documented in Arbuthnot's paper. A fairer and more incisive critique of Turiel's work is presented in Zinn (1970), who points to the fact that the '+1/−1' nomenclature is based on the false premise of equal interval scaling of moral stages, and that it prevents the analysis of changes in the whole *profile* of moral reasoning.

In summarizing our findings so far, we see considerable cause to question Kurtines and Greif's criticisms, both insofar as they bear on the stage-like consistency of individual moral reasoning, and on the sequential ordering of these stages.

Relation of moral judgment and moral action

In general, much as Kurtines and Greif overestimate the evidence against 'stage' and 'sequence' claims, it seems that they underestimate the amount of empirical confirmation for the moral stages, and in particular the strong evidence of the relation of moral judgment to action. For example, they do not mention the fact that Kohlberg's stages are, to date, the best predictors found for the behaviour of the subjects in Milgram's 'shocking' experiment. Only subjects with principled moral reasoning questioned authority and quit the task (Kohlberg, 1970, 1969a, pp. 395–6; Milgram, 1974, p. 205). Moral stage predicted behaviour in this situation while standard measures of sympathy did not. Kurtines and Greif also selectively exclude the discriminant validity of the moral stage definitions in situations where cheating behaviour is assessed (Krebs, 1967). Kohlberg and Freundlich (in press) have found moral stage to predict recidivism in a study of post-release adjustment in delinquents. Finally, to counter Kurtines and Greif's suggestion that the research literature is insufficiently independent of Kohlberg's influence, an independent study by Krebs and Rosenwald (1973), which set out with some scepticism towards Kohlberg's theory, found that moral stage predicted subjects' fulfillment of a verbal commitment to return questionnaires with surprising discrimination. Another independent study (Gunzberger *et al.*, 1977) has demonstrated specific behavioural concomitants of the moral stages in a study of modes of distributing rewards. It seems therefore that we are justified in questioning Kurtines and Greif's conclusion (p. 468) that 'there is no clearly demonstrated connection between moral judgment, as measured by the Moral Judgment Scale, and moral action'.

One of the more interesting pieces of research on moral judgment and action is the Haan *et al.* study of political activism in the Berkeley Free Speech Movement. Kurtines and Greif argue that here Kohlberg's scale shows a lack of discriminant validity because subjects scored Stage 2 manifested the exact same 'sitting-in' behaviour as subjects scored Stage 6.[8] However, it is difficult to see how the activism of 'Stage 2 males' could in any way be described as *the same behaviour* as that of 'Stage 6 males', when its orientation is pragmatic, goal-orientated confrontation, rather than the taking of a moral stance on the principles of justice underlying civil liberties: These two behaviours are worlds apart. To try to argue that in some concrete, spatial sense their 'actual behaviour . . . was similar' is to resort to a primitive behaviourism that equates action with physical movement.[9] Kohlberg's stages are not accounts of behaviour, but rather describe *forms* of moral reasoning that can be used in support or rejection of a particular action. In addition, these forms are *logically interconnected* in a hierarchy of increasing moral adequacy; they are not pass/fail items. As Beilin (1971, p. 189) has pointed out, cognitive-developmental accounts stand and fall 'by the explanatory power of the entire theory'.

This is one reason that the stages of moral development do not depend upon prediction of action for their validity: they are stages of judgment. Another reason, according to Kohlberg, is that there is no coherent separate domain of 'moral behaviour'. Kohlberg's position is that moral behaviour does not develop (Kohlberg, 1963b), nor could it as long as it is defined behaviouristically apart from underlying reasoning (Kohlberg, 1975a). Correlatively, empirical findings show how situationally-specific moral behaviour is. Kohlberg's account of the relation of moral judgment to conduct is by no means complete (Smythe, 1974), but what Kurtines and Greif miss is that the relation between judgment and action within a cognitive-structural theory is quite unlike the relation traditionally described between traits of moral attitude and moral behaviour (cf. Taylor 1971). The structures of moral judgment determine action by defining how rights and duties are to be perceived in concrete situations (Kohlberg, 1969b). They are not 'values' predicting to greater or less incidence of pro-social behaviour.

'Counterevidence'

Under this heading Kurtines and Greif offer certain evidence meant to directly disconfirm Kohlberg's theory.

Modelling

Their main thrust here is to report studies reputedly showing that 'moral judgments are directly affected by social influence'. First, Kohlberg has not denied this. In fact he makes a stronger statement: that all moral disequilibration and re-equilibration is occasioned socially. If this were not the case, the intervention studies mentioned above would have no motivation or significance. Kohlberg denies, not that moral judgment is influenced socially, but that it is totally the product of social *learning* or copying via contingent or extrinsically imposed conditioning. Kurtines and Greif take Bandura and McDonald's data to demonstrate exactly that which Kohlberg denies. However, Bandura and McDonald were dealing with *Piaget's* stages of moral development, not Kohlberg's! 'Piaget's definitions of moral judgment responses do not meet the naturalistic criteria of structural stages, and hence social-learning manipulations of these responses do not indicate that moral judgment is not structural' (Kohlberg 1969a, p. 408). Even if we pass over this desideratum, Cowan *et al.* (1969) have shown via a replication study that Bandura and McDonald's results are equivocal, and in some cases 'the findings raise questions which cannot yet be answered within the social learning framework' (Cowan *et al.*, p. 261).[10] They object to the fact that atypical subjects were used who were already transitional between stages, that inferences about individual development were drawn from group means, and that choice data only rather than explanations were elicited in the post-test (although Bandura, 1969, appears to dispute this latter criticism). Turiel (1966), Kohlberg (1969a) and Cowan *et al.* point out that what Bandura and McDonald *have* demonstrated in concentrating on the reinforcement of moral response, is the learning of *the expected answer*, under social coercion.

Reversible changes in moral judgment under the control of experimenter and model have yet to be demonstrated. However, Kohlberg will continue to be vulnerable to objections of this ilk until he specifies exactly what the nature of moral experience is, and the precise relation of cognitive structures to his vaguely characterized 'structures of the environment' (Kuhn, in press; Riegel, 1975b; Sanders and Cone, 1975).

Sex differences

A second line of 'counterevidence' argues that, in a study by Holstein (1972), 'cross-sectional sex differences in modal response did not support the notion of an invariant sequence' (Kurtines and Greif, p. 467). Their argument is simply that the modal stage of reasoning for males was different from the modal stage for females. How this bears on the invariance of sequence at all is mysterious, to say the least. Differences in rate of development are expected, indeed predicted by the theory (Kohlberg, 1958; Smith and Firestone, 1973; Kohlberg and Gilligan, 1971). However, neither differences in rate nor differences in ceiling of development challenge the sequential nature of the stages.[11]

Personality correlates

A third line of 'counterevidence' appears to be lacking in relevance too. Hogan (1973) is reported as having developed a scale that distinguishes 'utilitarian, legal' (or rule-oriented) versus 'intuitive, principled' thinking. These types of thinking are found to be associated with particular personality characteristics. Finally we are told 'the more mature individuals tend to cluster in the center of this dimension'. We are supposed to infer that Stages 5 and 6 are therefore shown to be 'alternative, but equally valid, forms of moral thought'.

This argument does not bear on Kohlberg's theory because a) Kohlberg has clearly shown that morality is not reducible to personality dimensions such as more or less autonomy, more or less intuitiveness, or more or less rule-orientedness (Kohlberg, 1969a, 1971); b) the opposition of rule-oriented and principled morality is artificial (Unger, 1975); c) morality is not a quantitative matter (Kohlberg, 1958, p. 7); and d) Kurtines and Greif's statement (p. 469) that Hogan shows that 'personality differences are important determinants of an individual's style of moral reasoning', is untrue — he seeks only to research correlates (Hogan, 1973, p. 225).

In sum, Hogan (1973, 1974) asserts an ideological opposition to Kohlberg's view of morality, he does not seek an empirical test of it, or present evidence at variance with Kohlberg's theory. The explicit alignment of Hogan's moral traits or 'dispositions' with Kohlberg's Stages 5 and 6 appears to belong to Kurtines and Greif. In so doing, they in fact misinterpret Kohlberg, confusing Stage 5 with Stage 4, and Stage 6 with a version of 'Stage 4½'. Stage 5 reasoning does not imply the conventionality and resistance to change that Kurtines and Greif attribute to it, nor is there any evidence that it is the stage of moral reasoning characteristic of policeman or ROTC (Officer Training Corps) seniors. Neither can Stage 6 reasoning in any way incur an association with impulsiveness, intuitiveness, opportunism, and irresponsibility. Finally, the 'telos' or end-point of development in Hogan's model appears to comprise a form of 'natural law' ethics in which moral 'shoulds' are derivable from pre-existing laws of natural personality or human nature (p. 225). This is a version of the naturalistic fallacy that Kohlberg (1971) has so fully exposed.

In conclusion therefore, we find that none of the three lines of 'counter-evidence' is likely to bring the Kohlberg fish to shore, and we have reason to suspect that none of the three hooks is even properly baited.

Kohlberg's Theory of Moral Development

So far we have tackled the misinterpretation of research findings at their own level of analysis. There are however deeper misunderstandings of Kohlberg's theory that underlie these, a clarification of which helps us to read a certain unity into Kurtines and Greif's approach.

We find key symptoms in Kurtines and Greif's initial description of Kohlberg's theory. Along with a rather inexplicable reference to its being a projective test, they basically assimilate Kohlberg's work to the standard psychometric model. They call it the 'Moral Judgment Scale', whereas Kohlberg has explicitly distinguished cognitive-developmental stage theories from psychometric scales (Kohlberg, 1968; Kohlberg and de Vries, 1971).

Cognitive-developmental theories deal with fundamentally different phenomena. They are concerned with the structurally invariant sequential interactions of organism and environment that govern a sense of the logic of physical and social reality. They are not concerned with the assimilation of particular cultural information or conventional problem-solving strategies. This does not mean that Kohlberg's theory cannot give birth to a measuring instrument. It does mean that instead of assimilating that instrument to the psychometric model, the latter has to accommodate to a wholly emergent theoretical system, a variety of structuralism that defines measurement in a totally different way (Kohlberg 1975a; 1975d). Thus the usefulness of the moral judgment interview does not depend on the 'standardization' which Kurtines and Greif (p. 455) see lacking. (Incidentally the great majority of Kohlbergian research *has* used a standard questionnaire.) What Kohlberg's critics often appear to ignore is the fact that the instrument measures the *form* of moral reasoning (the *way* in which ethical issues are approached), not the specific content of the subject's response. As a result, variations in the content of administration and the effect they have on the content of answers are much less important. The use of Piaget's flexible 'clinical method' of questioning, where the interviewer encourages subjects to explain their original responses, is indispensable for elucidating the structural composition of the stages, and therefore 'standardization' of the interview would have prevented the development of the theory.

This is not the humanist's plea for 'freedom' or 'spontaneity'. It is the structuralist's plea against the logical positivism that exalts measurement and the strict methods of the natural sciences at the expense of a concern for *meaning*. Rigid standardization of questioning ignores the fact that meanings develop through inter-personal understanding in the test situation, and leads to a spurious 'objectivity' and to trivial results (Ryan, 1972; Hudson, 1972). It also leaves us with the possible problem that regularities in our results are entirely a function of specific factors associated with superficial characteristics of question form.

The alternative to 'objective' methods is not subjective chaos. As Cowan *et al.* have pointed out:

> We no longer have to assume that the 'unstandardized' approach works against the discovery of lawful relationships, since Piaget's method has led to some of the most replicable results in the field of psychology (1969, p. 272).

The same thing applies to Kurtines and Greif's criticism of the 'judgmental nature of the coding procedure' (p. 456). Coding that does not involve judgment is invalid, because it does not bear on the meaning of statements. Even scoring the WISC requires judgment. What do Kurtines and Greif's own criteria of objectivity consist of, if not particular judgments imbedded in the positivist tradition of psychometric inquiry? *Human intelligence* is the basic research instrument, not experimental design or psychometric technique. From Kurtines and Greif's point of view, human judgment is clearly to be equated with error, with bias. This is surely not the case when we have judgments that are ordered by generalizable, rational criteria, within explicitly defined categories, dictated by a clearly stated and self-consistent theory. However much effort it may require to obtain the scoring manual from Kohlberg, one finds that, although there is clearly room for improvement, it is fairly exemplary in the detailed constraints it places upon coding judgments, ensuring that they are as judgmental as possible in precisely the most theoretically justifiable way. To eliminate judgment from coding procedures brings with it the implication that we must eliminate judgment from research in general. It is not the presence, but the absence of a judgmental orientation that defines subjectivity (Cassirer, 1923). Kohlberg should therefore be exhorted to iron out the inadequacies of the scoring method, or develop a more sophisticated method, rather than to throw out the scoring method on the grounds that it requires human intelligence and understanding for its correct operation.[12]

It is precisely the development of such detailed judgmental criteria, elaborated and constantly revised in the light of longitudinal studies of natural moral development, and securely located in the context of a well-grounded and thoroughly argued philosophic ethical theory, that are perhaps responsible for the irritating delays in publication that Kurtines and Greif rightly point out. It is only when such construction of a theoretical-empirical edifice is reduced to a matter of reliability and validity in a psychometric scale that Kohlberg's programme of work as a whole becomes 'inexplicable'. Kurtines and Greif's criticisms, often bringing out problems that need to be dealt with, would only become forceful if they were directed at the same time towards Kohlberg's stages as a theory of moral development. One cannot attack such a theory without bravely standing astride the unfortunate gulf that has been opened between empirical technology and its theoretical focus (Kohlberg, 1975d). In our present instance, this would require paying some attention to at least three kinds of characteristics of Kohlberg's cognitive-developmental thesis. The first is its theoretical presuppositions: equilibration theory, structural psychology of cognition, subject—object interactionism, deontological view of morality as justice rather than welfare, etc. We must ask, are these justifiable, self-consistent, coherent and correctly interpreted within the theory? This has by no means gone undisputed (Alston, 1971; Peters, 1971; Siegal, 1975; Tomlinson, 1977). The second and related characteristic is the ideological foundation of the theory. Is it not true that the degree of intellectualism and individualism in the theory compromises its emancipatory potential? (Buck-Morss, 1975; Sullivan, in press; Broughton, in press). The third approximate focus for a critical examination is the internal logic of the theory, the conceptual organization of interview material through stage-by-stage differentiation and integration of categories and relations. The most fundamental question about a stage theory must be not the Aristotelian one of whether stages just reflect empirical regularities, but the Galileian one of whether or not their descriptions make sense as a lawful sequential ordering of progressively advancing and more adequate cognitive organizations. Several writers have found lacking the philosophical grounds of Kohlberg's treatment of post-conventional morality (Smythe, 1974; Siegel, 1974; Habermas, 1975; Buck-Morss, 1975, in press; Gibbs, 1975; Siegal, 1975; Baumrind, 1975; Tomlinson, 1977; Reid and Yanerella, 1977; Sullivan, in press; Morelli, in press). The paucity of data on the post-conventional stages has meant that such discussion has been confined to the level of philosophical presuppositions. Unfortunately, the question of the adequacy of the psychological theory cannot be answered without adding to this some empirical recourse to detailed interview material, since it is concrete moral judgments that such a hermeneutic system claims to interpret and evaluate as more or less adequate.[13]

Kurtines and Greif, on the other hand, exhibit the opposite shortcoming. Although they show some concern for the explanatory adequacy of the theory, when they do not take the theoretical logic and presuppositions of Kohlberg's framework into account, but interpret it merely as a psychometric scale, they confuse the following: values with morality, conformity with moral development, moral style with moral judgment, moral statements with moral structure, the content of moral choice with the form of the reasoning behind it, specific behaviours with moral action, psychometric scale with stage theory, scale types with stages, reliability/homogeneity with internal consistency of stages, standard error of measurement with horizontal decalage, measurement stability with structural stability, psychometric validity with stage sequence, and so on.

The result is, inadvertently, an expression of disappointment that Kohlberg is not in the projective test business. From this point of view it must seem sadly inexplicable that Kohlberg is weighed down with so much theory and so much laborious longitudinal research. A more helpful analysis would detail and criticize the ways in which the cognitive-developmental theory of morality succeeds or fails in the attempt to provide a radically different perspective on socialization, and a new paradigm for structural research, grounded in a structuralist rather than a logical positivist epistemology. The empirical utility of the cognitive-developmental approach has surely been demonstrated, but the question of its *truth* has yet to be seriously confronted. It is not, as Kurtines and Greif suggest, Kohlberg who discourages independent research, but the very conceptual and empirical difficulty of the task itself. To reject Kohlberg's theoretical perspective prematurely on the basis of criteria from another and more restricted orientation can only be a way of avoiding this important task.

Notes

1. A more extensive documentation of the critical points made here is available from the author. Thanks to the following for their suggestions: Augusto Blasi, Daniel Candee, John Gibbs, Alan Gordon, Lawrence

Kohlberg, Dennis Krebs, Marc Lieberman, Jane Loevinger, Robert Selman, and Elliot Turiel.

2. It could also be added here that the second factor (indicating situational specificity of response) was not significant. A more thorough factor analysis of story-item scores has been carried out by Lieberman (1973). Although a median correlation of .51 means that only about 25 per cent of the variance is accounted for, there is other support for Kohlberg's original consistency claim. Haan *et al.* (1968) found that over half of 957 subjects had a percentage of reasoning at their modal stage that was at least twice as great as the percentage found at any other stage. In Turiel's study (1966), the proportion of subjects with a mode this dominant was two-thirds. Also, Turiel (1969) and Rest *et al.* (1969) reported that, on average, the modal percentage is two and a half times as great as the percentage use of either adjacent stage. Finally, we have Kohlberg's own 'quasi-simplex' data (1963a), which show that only adjacent stages ever have positive correlations with each other. Of course, our interpretation of these findings is jaundiced by the indications that scorer bias might be partly responsible for the apparent consistency.

3. 'Structural' again means simply that the measure (like Piaget's logical tasks) taps the *form* of thought, or the way in which reasoning is organized, rather than the specific content of the response, a distinction which Kohlberg's critics do not take into account.

4. The issue of cross-cultural research is not reviewed here, since it will be dealt with fully in a forthcoming paper by Blasi and Broughton. Contrary to Kurtines and Greif's suppositions, there *is* considerable evidence available (five studies with cross-sectional, and three with longitudinal evidence), it *is* extremely relevant to verification of the moral development construct, and it *is* largely compatible with developmental theory.

5. When this revision is applied to the Haan *et al.* (1968) study, which Kurtines and Greif mention, that study no longer lends itself to a critique of the discriminant validity of the stages.

6. Boyd's study dealt with Stages 3, 4 and 5. Of the 11 subjects followed up one year after the 'moral acceleration course' and scored blind, five' maintained the same stage score, and five showed advance in the predicted direction. In an unpublished study, the present author found that 64 per cent of an experimental (educationally accelerated) undergraduate group showed upward change, compared to only 33 per cent of a control group over the same three month period. These subjects were also in the Stage 3 to 5 range. Boyd has suggested that the transition to post-conventional thought may be qualitatively different from other stage transitions, an opinion supported by Gibbs and Fedoruk's report (1975).

7. First, (p. 464) they argue in a bizarre fashion that Turiel's basic conclusion 'is at best ambiguous however, since the actual *t*s are unreported', even though the significance levels are! (For the curious, the *t* values are reported in the original dissertation.) Second, they state that 'Turiel claimed that the number of −1 scores of the −1 treatment group was not significantly higher than the −1 scores of any other treatment group.' This is not really true. Turiel (p. 616) *did* conclude that the −1 treatment had an effect in moving subjects down one stage. Kurtines and Greif arrived at this false impression by failing to notice that Turiel's *t*-test was a *Dunnett t*-test for the simultaneous comparison of one group mean with several others (Winer, 1962). As a result, they conclude wrongly that the difference was greater than the borderline significance difference between +1 scores for the +1 group and −1 scores for the −1 group. In fact, when we take into account the different relation of *t* values and significance levels for the Dunnett, the former difference turns out to be less than the latter, supporting Turiel.

8. The following discussion should be viewed in the light of the above remarks regarding Stage 2 and 'Stage 4½' since most of Haan's subjects scored 'Stage 2' were probably Stage 4½.

9. Such a viewpoint fails to acknowledge that it is impossible to define or describe a behaviour unambiguously without reference to underlying reasons or intentions (cf. Merleau-Ponty, 1963; Hamlyn, 1970; Taylor, 1964; Chomsky, 1959). In fact Haan *et al.* themselves are at pains to make clear the fundamental differences between the two types of activism, and to criticize a superficial equating of them (pp. 196—98).

10. For example, subjects who were conditioned 'up' showed much more pronounced modelling effects in the two-week post-test than did subjects who were conditioned 'down'. This result does not fit with the social learning notion that moral responses are simply habits, but it does fit well with the cognitive-developmental theory of uni-directional progress, and the related research findings in attempts to accelerate moral development (Turiel, 1966, 1969). Another finding with similar implications is that there was more change to the lower level by the higher level subjects than vice versa, a finding uninterpretable from a social learning point of view, but quite consonant with Kohlberg's theory, and with cognitive-developmental research on the relative difficulty of using reasoning at a level ahead of your present stage (Rest *et al.*, 1969). Additional evidence from Dworkin (1968) and LeFurgy and Woloshin (1969) suggests that social learning effects vary considerably with the subject's developmental level (Zinn, 1970).

11. Perhaps there is a confusion here with a different study of Holstein's (1973), in which she argues that because 23 per cent of an adolescent sample were two stages higher when retested after three years, they must have skipped a stage (cf. Smith and Firestone, 1973). A more obvious interpretation is that these individuals happened to pass through two consecutive stages in the period of three years. However, this seems dissonant with the longitudinal findings of Kohlberg and Elfinbein, and with the data presented in Table 1. It seems likely that scoring confusions of Stage 2 with 'Stage 4½' are implicated, since a majority of the subjects showing stage 'skipping' in Holstein's study were originally scored as Stage 2.

As far as sex differences are concerned, other studies by Turiel (1976) and Weisbrodt (1970), where educational level is controlled, show no significant sex differences in level of moral judgment attained.

12. In meta-theoretical terms, modern critical philosophy of science has come to view this issue as a conflict between the technical mode, which views all knowledge as *information*-based, and the hermeneutic mode, which emphasizes the pervasive priority of *interpretation* (Connerton, 1976; Radnitzky, 1970).

13. As Riegel (1975b) has indicated, Kohlberg has tended to succumb to a use of the 'stage' notion that has encouraged a taxonomic attitude towards development. A main source of misunderstanding is that it is no longer clear exactly what kinds of concrete reasoning the stages refer to, what moral concepts are, or what exactly 'structures' of reasoning imply about the relationships between these concepts. As a result, Kohlberg has unwittingly obscured what empirical claims are actually being made.

References

ALSTON, W.F. (1971). 'Comments on Kohlberg's "From is to Ought".' In: MISCHEL, T. (Ed) *Cognitive Development and Genetic Epistemology*. New York: Academic Press.

ARBUTHONOT, J. (1975). 'Modification of moral judgment through role-playing', *Develop. Psychol.*, 11, 3, 319—24.

BAKAN, D. (1966). 'The test of significance in psychological research', *Psychol. Bull.*, 66, 6, 423.

BANDURA, A. (1969). 'Social learning of moral judgments', *J. Pers. Soc. Psychol.*, 11, 3, 275—9.

BAUMRIND, D. (1975). 'It neither is nor ought to be'. In: KENNEDY, E. (Ed) *Psychology and Ethics*. Chicago: Loyola University.

BEILIN, H. (1971). 'Developmental stages and developmental processes'. In: GREEN, D.R., FORD, M.L.P. and FLAMER, G.B. (Eds) *Measurement and Piaget*. New York: McGraw-Hill.

BERKOWITZ, M. (1976). The role of dyadic interaction in moral judgment development: a test of the equilibration hypothesis. Unpublished MA Thesis, Wayne State University.

BERKOWITZ, M., BROUGHTON, J.M. and GIBBS, J.C. (1977). 'Equilibration in moral reasoning development: a new methodology'. Paper presented at the Seventh Annual Symposium of the Jean Piaget Society, Philadelphia.

BLATT, M. (1975). 'Studies on the effects of classroom discussion upon children's moral development', *J. Moral Educ.*, 4, 2, 129—61.

BOYD, D. (1972). From conventional to principled morality. Unpublished manuscript, Harvard University.

BOYD, D. (1976). Education toward principled moral judgment: an analysis of an experimental course in undergraduate moral education applying Lawrence Kohlberg's theory of moral development. Unpublished dissertation, Harvard University.

BROUGHTON, J.M. (1970). 'College regression' in moral development. Unpublished manuscript, Harvard University.

BROUGHTON, J.M. The development of natural epistemology in adolescence. Unpublished doctoral dissertation, Harvard University.

BROUGHTON, J.M. (in press). 'Dialectics and moral development ideology'. In: SCHARF, P. (Ed) *Reader in Moral Education*. New York: Winston.

BROUGHTON, J.M. and ZAHAYKEVICH, M.K. (1977). Review of Jane Loevinger's *Ego Development*, *Telos*, 32, Summer.

BUCK-MORSS, S. (1975). 'Socio-economic bias in Piaget's theory and its implications for cross-cultural studies', *Human Develop.*, 18, 35—49.

BUCK-MORSS, S. (in press). 'Piaget, Adorno and the possibilities of dialectical structures'. In: SILVERMAN, H.J. (Ed) *Piaget – Philosophy and the Human Sciences*, Stony Brook Studies in Philosophy, Vol. 4.

CASSIRER, E. (1923). *Substance and Function*. New York: Dover.

CHOMSKY, N. (1959). Review of B.F. Skinner's *Verbal Behaviour*. *Language*, 35, 26—58.

COHEN, J. (1962). 'The statistical power of abnormal/social psychological research', *J. Abnorm. Soc. Psychol.*, 65, 145.

COHEN, J. (1966). 'Some statistical issues in psychological research'. In: WOLMAN, B. (Ed) *Handbook of Clinical Psychology*. New York: McGraw-Hill.

CONNERTON, P. (Ed) (1976). *Critical Sociology*. New York: Penguin.

COWAN, P.A., LANGER, J., HEAVENRICH, J. and NATHANSON, M. (1969). 'Social learning and Piaget's cognitive theory of moral development', *J. Pers. Soc. Psychol.*, 11, 261—74.

DWORKIN, E.S. (1968). The effects of imitation, reinforcement, and cognitive information on the moral judgments of children. Unpublished doctoral dissertation, University of Rochester.

EDWARDS, C.P. (1975). 'Societal complexity and moral development: a Kenyan study', *Ethos*, 3, 505—27.

ELKIND, D. (1969). 'Conservation and concept formation'. In: ELKIND, D. and FLAVELL, J.E. (Eds) *Studies* in *Cognitive Development*. New York: Oxford University Press.

ERDYNAST, A. (1974). Improving the adequacy of moral reasoning. Unpublished dissertation, Harvard University.

FRAENKEL, J.P. (in press). 'The Kohlberg bandwagon: some reservations'. In: SCHARF, P. (Ed) *Reader in Moral Education*. New York: Winston.

GERGEN, K.J. (1976). 'Stability, change and chance in understanding human development'. Paper presented at the Life-Span Developmental Conference. Morgantown, West Virginia.

GIBBS, J.C. (1975). 'The Piagetian approach to moral development: an overview'. In: MEYER, J., BURNHAM, B. and CHOLVAT, J. (Eds) *Values Education: Theory/Practice/Problems/Prospects*. Waterloo, Ontario: Wilfrid Laurier University Press.

GIBBS, J.C. and FEDORUK, C.J. (1975). 'Experimentally induced change in moral judgment'. Paper presented at the symposium of the Jean Piaget Society, Philadelphia, June.

GIBBS, J.C., KOHLBERG, L., COLBY, A., and SPEICHER-DUBIN, B. (1976). 'The domain and development of moral judgment: a theory and a method of assessment'. In: MAYER, J. (Ed) *Essays on Moral Development*. Waterloo, Ontario: Wilfrid Laurier Press.

GILLIGAN, C. and KOHLBERG, L. (1974). 'From adolescence to adulthood: the rediscovery of reality in a post-conventional world'. Paper presented at the annual meeting of the Jean Piaget Society, June.

GUNZBERGER, D.W., WEGNER, D.M. and ANOOSHIAN, L. (1977). 'Moral judgment and distributive justice', *Human Devel.*, 20, 160—70.

HAAN, N., SMITH, M.B. and BLOCK, J. (1968). 'Moral reasoning of young adults: political social behaviour, family background, and personality correlates', *J. Pers. Soc. Psychol.*, 10, 185—201.

HABERMAS, J. (1975). *Knowledge and Human Interest*. Boston: Beacon Press.

HAMLYN, B.W. (1970). 'Conditioning and behaviour'. In: BORGER, R. and CIOFFI, F. (Eds) *Explanation in the Behavioural Sciences*. Cambridge, England: Cambridge University Press.

HICKEY, J. (1972). The effects of guided moral discussion upon youthful offenders' level of moral judgment. Unpublished doctoral dissertation, Boston University.

HOFFMAN, M. (1977). 'Personality and social development', *Annual Rev. of Psychol.*, 28, 295—323.

HOGAN, R. (1973). 'Moral conduct and moral character: a psychological perspective', *Psychol. Bull.*, 79, 4, 217—32.

HOGAN, R. (1974). 'On theoretical egocentrism and the problem of compliance', *Amer. Psychol.*, 30, 5, 533—40.

HOLSTEIN, C.B. (1973). 'A longitudinal study of family influences on adolescent moral judgment development'. Paper presented at the biennial meeting of SRCD, Philadelphia, March—April.

HUDSON, L. (1972). *The Cult of the Fact*. New York: Harper.

KEASEY, C.B. (1973). 'Experimentally induced changes in moral opinions and reasoning', *J. Personal. Soc. Psychol.*, 26, 1, 30—8.

KOHLBERG, L. (1958). The development of modes of moral thinking and choice in the years ten to sixteen. Unpublished doctoral dissertation, University of Chicago.

KOHLBERG, L. (1963a). 'The development of children's orientation toward a moral order: sequence in the development of moral thought', *Vita Humana*, 6, 11—33.

KOHLBERG, L. (1963b). 'Moral development and identification'. In: STEVENSON, H. (Ed) *Child Psychology*. Yearbook of National Society for the Study of Education. Chicago: University of Chicago Press.

KOHLBERG, L. (1968). 'Early education: a cognitive-developmental approach', *Child Devel.*, 39, 1013—62.

KOHLBERG, L. (1969a). 'Stage and sequence: the cognitive-developmental approach to socialization'. In: GOSLIN, D.A. (Ed) *Handbook of Socialization Theory and Research*. Chicago: Rand McNally.

KOHLBERG, L. (1969b). 'The relations between moral judgment and moral action'. Paper presented at the Institute of Human Development, University of California, Berkeley, March.

KOHLBERG, L. (1970). 'Education for justice: a modern statement of the Platonic view'. In SIZER, T. (Ed) *Moral Education*. Cambridge, Mass: Harvard University Press.

KOHLBERG, L. (1971). 'From is to ought: how to commit the naturalistic fallacy and get away with it in the study of moral development'. In: MISCHEL, T. (Ed) *Cognitive Development and Genetic Epistemology*. New York: Academic Press.

KOHLBERG, L. (1972). Mimeo Scoring Manual. Harvard Graduate School of Education.

KOHLBERG, L. (1973a). 'Continuities and discontinuities in childhood and adult moral development revisited'. In: BALTES, P.S. and SCHAIE, K.W. (Eds) *Lifespan Developmental Psychology—Personality and Socialization*. New York: Academic Press.

KOHLBERG, L. (1973b). 'The claim to moral adequacy of a highest stage of moral judgment', *J. of Phil.*, 70, 18, 630—46.

KOHLBERG, L. (1975a). 'Moralization: the cognitive-developmental approach'. In: LICKONA, T. (Ed)

Morality: Theory, Research and Social Issues. New York: Holt, Rinehart and Winston.

KOHLBERG, L. (1975b). 'Continuities and discontinuities revisited again'. Talk given at a colloquium on 'Dialectics and Development'. Wayne State University, Detroit, February.

KOHLBERG, L. (1975c). Moral Stage Scoring Manual. Mimeo, Center for Moral Education, Harvard, June.

KOHLBERG, L. (1975d). 'Response to critics'. Paper presented at the meeting of the Society for Research in Child Development, Denver, April.

KOHLBERG, L. and de VRIES, R. (1971). 'Relations between Piaget and psychometric assessments of intelligence'. In LAVATELLI, C. (Ed) *The Natural Curriculum*. Urbana, Illinois: ERIC.

KOHLBERG, L. and ELFINBEIN, D. (1975). 'The development of moral judgments concerning capital punishment', *Amer. J. Orthopsychiat.*, 16, 104—23.

KOHLBERG, L. and FREUNDLICH, D. (in press). 'Moral judgment in youthful offenders'. In KOHLBERG, L. and TURIEL, E. (Eds) *Moralization, the Cognitive-Developmental Approach*. New York: Holt, Rinehart & Winston.

KOHLBERG, L. and GILLIGAN, C. (1971). 'The adolescent as philosopher: the discovery of self in a post-conventional world', *Daedalus*, Spring, 1028—61.

KOHLBERG, L. and KRAMER, R. (1969). 'Continuities and discontinuities in childhood and adult moral development', *Human Devel.*, 12, 93—120.

KRAMER, R. (1968). Moral development in young adulthood. Unpublished doctoral dissertation, University of Chicago.

KREBS, R.L. (1967). Some relationships between moral judgment, attention and resistance to temptation. Unpublished doctoral dissertation, University of Chicago.

KREBS, D. and ROSENWALD, A. (in press). 'Moral reasoning and moral behaviour in conventional adults', *Merrill-Palmer Quarterly*.

KUHN, D. (1976). 'Short-term longitudinal evidence for the sequentiality of Kohlberg's early stages of moral judgment', *Develop. Psychol.*, 12, 2, 162—6.

KUHN, D. (in press). 'Mechanisms of cognitive and social development: one psychology or two?' In: BUSH, D. and FELDMAN, S. (Eds) *Cognitive Development and Social Development: Relationships and Implications*. Hillsdale, New Jersey: Lawrence Erlbaum.

KURTINES, W. and GREIF, E.B. (1974). 'The development of moral thought: review and evaluation of Kohlberg's approach', *Psychol. Bull.*, 81, 8, 453—70.

LeFURGY, W. and WOLOSHIN, G.W. (1969). 'Immediate and long-term effects of experimentally induced social influence in the modification of adolescents' moral judgements', *J. Pers. Soc. Psychol.*, 12, 104—10.

LEVINE, M. (1974). 'Scientific method and the adversary model', *Amer. Psychol.*, 29, 661—77.

LEWIN, K. (1931). 'The conflict between Aristotelian and Galileian modes of thought in contemporary psychology', *J. Gen. Psychol.*, 5, 141—77.

LIEBERMAN, M. (1973). 'Psychometric analysis of developmental stage data'. Paper presented at the Annual Meeting of the American Psychological Association, Montreal, August.

LOEVINGER, J. (1974). 'Issues in the measurement of moral development'. In: HOLTZMAN, W.H. (Ed) *Moral Development*. Publications of the International Conference on Testing Problems, Educational Testing Service, Princeton.

MERLEAU-PONTY, M. (1963). *The Structure of Behaviour*. Boston: Beacon Press.

MILGRAM, S. (1974). *Obedience to Authority*. New York: Harper and Row.

MORELLI, E. (1978). 'The sixth stage of moral development', *J. Moral Educ.*, 7, 2.

PETERS, R.S. (1971). 'Moral development: a plea for pluralism'. In: MISCHEL, T. (Ed) *Cognitive Development and Genetic Epistemology*. New York: Academic Press.

PIAGET, J. (1960). 'The general problems of the psychobiological development of the child'. In: TANNER, J.M. and INHELDER, B. (Eds) *Discussions on Child Development*, Vol. 4. London: Tavistock.

PINARD, A. and LAURENDEAU, M. '"Stage" in Piaget's cognitive-developmental theory: exegesis of a concept'. In: ELKIND, D. and FLAVELL, J.H. (Eds) *Studies in Cognitive Development*. New York: Oxford University Press.

PORTER, N. and TAYLOR, N. (1972). 'How to assess the moral reasoning of students: A teacher's guide to the use of Lawrence Kohlberg's stage-developmental method', *Profiles of Practical Education*, No. 8. Toronto: The Ontario Institute for Studies in Education.

RADNITZKY, G. (1970). *Contemporary Schools of Metascience*. Goteborg, Sweden: Scandinavian University Books.

REID, H.G. and YANARELLA, E.J. (1977). 'Critical political theory and moral development: on Kohlberg, Hampden-Turner and Habermas', *Theory and Society*, 4, 4, 505—42.

REST, J.R., TURIEL, E. and KOHLBERG, L. (1969). 'Level of moral development as a determinant of preference and comprehension of moral judgments made by others', *J. Personality*, 37, 225—52.

RIEGEL, K.F. (1975). Dialectical psychology and cognitive development. Talk given at a colloquium on 'Dialectics and Development', Wayne State University, Detroit, February.

RYAN, J. (1972). 'IQ — the illusion of objectivity'. In: RICHARDSON, K. and SPEARS, D. (Eds) *Race and Intelligence*. London: Penguin.

SALTZSTEIN, H.D., DIAMOND, R.M. and BELENKY, M. (1972). 'Moral judgment level and conformity behaviour', *Develop Psychol.*, **7**, 327—36.

SANDERS, S.L. and CONE, D.M. (1975). 'A critique of Kohlberg's theory of moral development from the viewpoint of interbehavioural psychology', *Interbehavioral Quarterly*, **6**, 2, 8—22.

SIEGEL, H. (1974). Kohlberg: evaluative status and moral adequacy. Unpublished manuscript, Department of Philosophy, Harvard University.

SIEGAL, M. (1975). Learning moral competence. Unpublished paper, Oxford University.

SMEDSLUND, J. (1961). 'The acquisition of the conservation of substance and weight in children, III: extinction of conservation of weight acquired "normally" and by means of empirical controls on a balance', *Scandinavian Journal of Psychology*, **2**, 85—7.

SMITH, J. and FIRESTONE, I. (1973). The development of moral judgment from childhood through maturity: a new social scale. Unpublished manuscript, Wayne State University.

SMYTHE, O. (1974). Kohlbergian moral development theory and the legacy of John Dewey. Unpublished manuscript, Department of Philosophy, Harvard University.

SULLIVAN, E.V. (in press). 'A study of Kohlberg's structural theory of moral development: a critique of liberal social science ideology'. In: SCHARF, P. (Ed) *Reader in Moral Education.* New York: Winston.

SUTTON, L.E. (1972). An investigation of invariant sequence in a cognitive-developmental theory of moral development. Unpublished master's thesis, Connecticut College.

TAYLOR, C. (1964). *The Explanation of Behaviour.* London: Routledge and Kegan Paul.

TAYLOR, C. (1971). 'Interpretation and the sciences of man', *Review of Metaphysics*, **25**, 3, 1.—51.

TOMLINSON, P. (1977). 'Some questions for Kohlberg'. Paper presented at the conference on Moral Development and Moral Education, University of Leicester, England, August 1977.

TRACY, J.J. and CROSS, H.J. (1973). 'Antecedents of shift in moral judgment', *J. Personal. Soc. Psychol.*, **26**, 2, 238—44.

TURIEL, E. (1966). 'An experimental test of the sequentiality of developmental stages in the child's moral judgments', *J. Pers. Soc. Psychol.*, **3**, 611—18.

TURIEL, E. (1969). 'Developmental processes in the child's moral thinking'. In: MUSSEN, P., LANGER, J. and COVINGTON, M. (Eds)*Trends and Issues in Development Psychology.* New York: Holt Rinehart and Winston.

TURIEL, E. (1972). 'Stage transition in moral development', In: TRAVERS, R.M. (Ed) *Second Handbook of Research on Teaching.* Chicago: Rand McNally.

TURIEL, E. (1974a). 'Conflict and transition in adolescent moral development', *Child Devel.*, **45**, 14—29.

TURIEL, E. (1976). 'A comparative analysis of moral knowledge and moral judgment in males and females', *J. Personal.*, **44**, 2, 195—208.

TURIEL, E. (1977). 'Conflict and transition in adolescent moral development, II: the resolution of disequilibrium through structural reorganization', *Child Devel.*, **48**, 634—7.

UNGER, R.M. (1975). *Knowledge and Politics.* New York: Free Press.

VAN DEN DAELE, L. (1968). 'A developmental study of the ego-ideal', *Genetic Psychol. Monographs*, **78**, 191—256.

WEBER, M. (1949). *The Methodology of the Social Sciences.* In: SHILS, E.A. and FINCH, H.A. (Eds) Glencoe, Illinois: The Free Press.

WEISBRODT, S. (1970). 'Moral judgment, sex and parental identification in adults', *Develop. Psychol.*, **2**, 396—402.

WHITE, C.B. (1975). 'Moral development in Bahamian school children: a cross-cultural examination of Kohlberg's stages of moral reasoning', *Develop. Psychol.*, **11**, 345—6.

WINER, B.J. (1962). *Statistical Principles in Experimental Design.* New York: McGraw Hill.

ZINN, V. (1970). 'Methodological issues in the study of the development of moral judgment'. Unpublished manuscript, Clark University.

11

Toward the Redevelopment of Kohlberg's Theory: Preserving Essential Structure, Removing Controversial Content

Bill Puka

ABSTRACT

Supposedly, Kohlberg's developmental theory has been lifted above alternative approaches by its reliance on sophisticated philosophical conceptions of moral reasoning and adequacy. Yet Kohlberg's use of these conceptions—his preference for individual rights and formal principles of justice—has been judged partisan and biasing by critics in psychology. This essay poses the prospect that Kohlberg's controversial philosophies are unnecessary to his empirical stage theory and can be eliminated without affecting it significantly. A decade or so of Kohlberg criticism has been unnecessary as well.

PHILOSOPHICAL PARTISANSHIP

When some observers contemplate Kohlberg's theory of moral development, they see a noble vision of goodwill in humankind. They see a picture of our inherent tendency to become respectful and fair-minded toward others. Other observers see a preposterous set of biases masquerading as scientific findings. These include biases toward rationalism and formalism, which search for absolute, universal laws amid the complex and subtle gradations of moral judgment. These also include biases toward the individualistic liberalism of Western democracies (''social contracts'') and toward the effete intellectual tradition of so-called Kantian deontology. Behind these cultural and intellectual biases, it is suggested, lurks the spectre of patriarchy. This bias pulls Kohlberg's vision of human civility away from its caring and relational side, its ''Female'' side.

247

Four assumptions form the moral foundation of Kohlberg's developmental theory, as he sees it. They also provide the ultimate targets for the major criticisms it has endured. These assumptions are: (1) that if morality is relative, we cannot speak of there being moral development, as opposed to mere change: (2) that an adequate morality must be universal; (3) that a developmental stage sequence is (or must be) defined from an end-point of ultimate adequacy or maturity; and (4) that this ultimate standard is a particular brand of justice. Critics hold that morality is culturally relative, or valid *for* certain individuals in certain contexts. They hold also that Kohlberg's entire stage sequence of development is tainted by having a very limited and faulty moral theme at the top. Under fire, Kohlberg has placed greater and greater effort into elaborating and justifying these assumptions. This has redoubled opposition to them.

There is an easier way out for Kohlberg's view, however, which sympathetic critics might have seen at the outset. (Years of wrangling might have been avoided if they had.) We might simply drop Kohlberg's main assumptions to test whether they are really necessary at all, to discover whether Kohlberg's view can stand without them. I would like to propose here that it can. Kohlberg's main assumptions were never needed in the first place, and can simply be dispensed with. This would leave his stage sequence (1–5) untouched, I suspect, while leaving the major Kohlberg criticisms nowhere to stand. It also would broaden the scope and variety of moral judgment research.

Observers may well wonder how such a radical proposal can be serious. If these main Kohlbergian assumptions were unnecessary, why would Kohlberg stand his entire theory directly upon them? Why would he claim, for example, that stage 6 principles of justice define the entire stage sequence and each stage within it, and that such principles also define the scope of morality itself and of moral judgment data? Why would Kohlberg cling to such a claim even in the face of such tenacious and damaging criticism over the decades, criticism that forecast the "toppling" of his entire view?

My answer to these questions is a somewhat psychological one, a speculation on Kohlberg's intellectual history. When Kohlberg entered the field of research on "morals," he encountered a relatively simple-minded relativism. A credible source of nonrelativistic thinking was needed simply to distinguish moral norms among the diversity of norm systems. Kohlberg turned to moral philosophy to find sophisticated distinctions between the moral and nonmoral, along with well-justified criteria of adequacy in moral reasoning.

If Kohlberg had continued to proceed as a psychologist at this point, he would have viewed such distinctions and criteria descriptively. This would mean two things. First moral philosophy would have been taken, in part, as a theoretical discipline peculiar to philosophers. Its positions would have been recognized as serving intellectual purposes which are peculiar to problems in theory building and the course of debate they spawned. On the other side, some aspects of the distinctions and criteria of philosophy would have been recognized as extending moral common sense and speaking to our spontaneous concerns in moral development. Only these would have occupied Kohlberg's attention.

From this selective, descriptive perspective, Kohlberg might have transported to psychology the various rival philosophical standards of moral relevance and adequacy. After all, it is such a diverse array that one finds in moral philosophy, as in common sense. Kohlberg might have formulated various cognitive-moral tracks relative to these different standards, by rational reconstruction, for purposes of comparison with each other and common sense. Alternatively Kohlberg might have transported only what is common to each rival philosophy and its standards. Then he might have gauged moral development from the bottom (or middle) up. As such, development would represent our increasing tendency not to ignore the variety of moral concerns posed by rival theories. And it would involve noticing these concerns from a variety of perspectives. This would contrast with our "progressive" tendency to cleave ever closer to one.

Instead, I believe, Kohlberg became a philosophical convert and partisan, to some extent. He became captivated by the philosophical vision of how morality should be reasoned ideally, reasoned in *theory*. And he decided that a particular philosophical tradition had defined the scope and adequacy of morality best. Then he set its view up as a somewhat a priori standard for moral psychology and development.

Again, there was some reason for doing this. Any philosophical conception in the area of morality seemed superior to those used in social research conceptions at that time. And the most prominent ethics were nonrelative or universalistic. Moreover, the Kantian tradition that Kohlberg favored seemed to have fewer fatal flaws than the main alternative, utilitarianism. Yet this partnership mired Kohlberg's view in more particularized and controversial assumptions than it needed. It left the view vulnerable to unnecessary criticism from philosophy itself, as well as psychology.

Practically speaking, Kohlberg's approach tended to narrow the seemingly legitimate scope of moral research. It excluded research into subjective or personal moralities, also into type moralities (of culture, class, gender), as opposed to general or social-institutional moralities. (Indeed, Kohlberg's philosophy hemmed in his own research). Any attempt by other researchers to broaden scope in the field seemingly had to be framed as a challenge to Kohlberg's "moral bias," rather than simply as "something else" of relevance to moral issues.

Critics have been quite justified then, I believe, in claiming the legitimacy of other moralities or "different voices" of morality. They have been justified in pointing out Kohlberg's philosophical partisanship. Yet they fall into the same sort of trap that snared Kohlberg when claiming that their moralities conflict with his, or constitute different versions of the phenomenon he researched. Gilligan's popular research on "justice focus" and "care focus" is a prime example. It seems to outline *type* moralities, which of their nature express certain social outlooks associated, perhaps, with gender. Kohlberg's research seeks a general morality, a morality that of its nature *must bridge* type moralities and the out-looks that fuel them. These two types of moralities can coexist and need not overlap. Certainly their functions diverge greatly, and so their adequacy should be judged by different standards. "Female" care focus seeks to endorse and nurture "natural" relationships whereas "male" justice focus seeks to protect individual autonomy. Kohlbergian morality seeks to ensure that the pursuit and expression of each morality, its values and interests, are respected equally.

It may be that Kohlberg's moral theme ultimately fails. It may reduce ulti-mately to a type morality. (That is, "justice reasoning" may reduce to "justice focus.") All allegedly general moralities may. But *this* bias claim must be supported relative to the other possibility that we have two different versions or levels or functions of morality involved, coexisting. A comparative critique of this sort has never even been attempted.

Likewise, while our personal or subjective values may be moral in some sense, they may not *develop* in the way of a general or even a type morality. They may not have a moral theme or cognitive organization which retains its identity as it goes through various transformations. They may not evolve through their own inherent powers or processes, as opposed to "being developed" or "shaped" from outside. We can call either process "development" if we wish, so long as we keep clear the crucial differences between inherent and noninherent development. Likewise, we may use the generic term "moral" when research-ing general, type, and personal morality, so long as the crucial differences in structure and purpose are made clear. Usually, using different terms promotes greater clarity e.g., "social learning" versus "development," "morality" ver-sus "ethics," or "morality" versus "moral ideology" or "personal values" and "conscience."

Dispensing with Kohlberg's philosophically partisan assumptions also pro-motes such clarity while broadening the moral scope of research and liberating Kohlberg's view from criticism. In sketching this prospect, we will touch lightly on the topic of relativism and then move on to stage 6.

Relativism and Universality

If there is any assumption that defines Kohlberg's approach, distinguishing it from socialization, it is "antirelativism." How can one speak of development in morality, of *progress* in the adequacy of moral reasoning, if moral views are merely a matter of individual preference or opinion, cultural tradition, or conven-tion? How can one hope for the sort of joint cooperation morality guides, asks Kohlberg, if each person has her or his own divergent standard for dealing with others? And if there is no valid moral view, valid for anyone, how can we engage in moral education without indoctrinating others in our favored ideology?

These three worries about relativism guided Kohlberg's effort to establish a standard of ultimate moral validity. Yet on analysis, each of these worries seems unfounded. Briefly, I will try to suggest why.

Kohlberg's discussion of relativism actually spans four versions of this view, without distinguishing them clearly. The first is "illogical relativism," which we will not consider. (It holds that because people in fact hold different moral opinions *therefore* all moral opinions are equally valid, or *therefore* there is no validity to the matter, or *therefore* everyone has a *right* to one's own opinions). The second is moral skepticism or reductionism, which holds that moral belief is merely a matter of taste, preference, or convention. It is relative to arbitrary factors rather than legitimating or validating ones such as "good reasons." The third and fourth hold that morality is relative to certain people or groups. It is valid for the individual or for a certain type of person, or for each society respectively. But it is not valid in general. (The fourth type assumes that morality is relative if it is not valid for everyone, valid "universally" rather than merely "in general." We will consider the third and fourth type together here for the sake of brevity.) Consider how Kohlberg's three worries may be dissipated with regard to moral reductionism first:

Moral Reductionism or Skepticism

1. Indoctrinative Education. If morality is simply a matter of preference, taste, or convention, then there can be no problem of indoctrination. There can be no (nonrelative) moral problem, at least. For there is no moral ground for objection, or no moral validity to that ground. So-called indoctrination is merely a play of conflicting tastes where one set of tastes wins out. Is the success of a new line of clothing in society indoctrination? Is it *morally* objectionable? Moral education would be a phenomenon of this sort within the first sort of relativism.

2. Progressive Development. If by morality we mean systems of taste, preference, or convention, then moral development research might investigate development in this realm. Muscles develop, and it is at least conceivable that skills do too, in their way. We speak of tastes and preferences as developing also, as becoming deeper and more subtle, increasingly discriminating and refined. Of course, such development may not be inherent or structural. It may have few aspects that are amenable to good reasoning. But certainly there are cognitive aspects to taste. We can give some reasons for liking one thing, disliking another. These would not be relevant reasons for moral nonrelativists, nor will changes in taste be *morally* progressive by their standards. But so what?

3. General Cooperation. Kohlberg's assumption that morality's *defining* function is to guide general cooperation seems faulty. At least it stands in need of justification. Kohlberg seems to derive this assumption from the social contract tradition in philosophy, which deals primarily with political and legal institutions, not moral ones. Such institutions are geared to overcoming divergencies in interest, of whatever sort. They treat moral beliefs and values as interests, without passing judgment on their validity for the most part. Democratic laws assure that this cooperation is voluntary, insofar as this is possible. Such laws may be based on various moralities, or simply on practicality. (If we coerce people they resist, and endlessly frustrating conflict results for all.) Democracy, whatever its moral character, may simply allow social relations to function more smoothly. Therefore if morality reduces to divergent tastes and preferences, such institutions can overcome their impediment to shared goals without tyranny. Morality need not be the chosen institution to "police" itself in this way.

At the same time, if one looks over the sorts of tastes, preferences, or conventions that are typically termed "moral," one does not find mere personal fiat or fashion. Rather one finds an emphasis on *preference* rather than taste, and a close association of preference to basic needs and interests. Relative moral preferences are tied very closely to motivational ultimates, in the way basic nonrelative moral principles are. (Indeed, this tie is a key criterion used by anthropologists to identify distinctively *moral* norms and conventions of other cultures.)

Kohlberg himself acknowledges that morality is relative—a matter of tastes, preference, and convention—everywhere but at its basic core. (This is recognized explicitly by stage 5 reasoning in Kohlberg's stage descriptions. See Appendix A.) Therefore, we must consult moral taste and preference *at its core* to see if it is really as varied, and as much an impediment to social cooperation, as Kohlberg believes. Indeed, I would hold, basic preferences lead us in the very opposite direction. For example, the (practical) need and preference to cooperate, at least minimally, is one of the most basic needs of all.

Moral Relativism or Nonuniversalism

1. Progressive Development. In the third and fourth type of relativism taken up by Kohlberg, it is assumed that moral views are more and less *valid*. They are valid for certain individuals or groups, rather than for everyone or for most people. On this basis there should be no problem to defining moral development. We simply use the standards of adequacy which a particular individual or type or group or culture sets. Then we chart development for each of them, relative to these respective standards. Alternatively, development might be charted in the way these standards are set in themselves, and deepened over time. This might be termed "metaethical" or "metacognitive" development. Of course we *may* evolve a very different type of theory here than the sort Kohlberg seeks. We *may* not find development at all. Still, we can conceive of it and research it to see if it occurs.

Note that Kohlberg's stages 1 through 5 do not universalize moral judgments. Indeed, stage 1 circumscribes them to one's own case and stage 2 to one's closest "associates." Later stages merely extend the process of generalizing moral judgments to larger and larger groups over time. Yet Kohlberg orders development among these nonuniversal ethics, focusing on their relative degree of strength.

   2. General Cooperation.   Assuming that cooperation is a subsidiary but significant function of morality, we must compare the relative assets and deficits of relative and nonrelative principles in fostering it. Nonrelative principles provide a more common basis for voluntary cooperation in an *ideal* sense, primarily. And this ideal sense is primarily theoretical or logical rather than social or psychological. Its cooperation "in principle" does not refer to ideal cooperation in actual life, to the sort of cooperation we can ideally expect given the actual facts of life. Kohlberg himself admits that very few adults actually reach his principled stages 5 and 6 in any society. Indeed, his theory holds that society is composed of individuals who define morality in holistically different ways, according to the structure of their stage. We can never hope that even most members of society can truly share nonrelative principles of morality as the self-legislatable basis for cooperation. Yet we find ourselves able to cooperate, using diverse moral perspectives and standards. Indeed Kohlberg's universal principles do not even seem able to foster *intellectual* agreement that they *are* universal principles, or that they have validity as the basis for universal cooperation.

   By contrast, relative principles seem to have actual validity *to us* or to our group, whether we be relativists or not. And if only to preserve their relative validity, we typically make compromises in our ethic in search of other normative bases for cooperation with those who hold different views. Oddly, Kohlberg never discusses the logic of moral compromise or accord using *different* (moral) standards and perspectives. Yet clearly much of the cooperation we engage in in life retains the different points of view of those involved and tries to coordinate them. It does not resort to an holistic "third system" of mutual regard.

   3. Indoctrinative Education.   If different moral views are valid for different people in different circumstances, then teaching a particular view (stage 6 justice) will be indoctrinative for some people. Yet Kohlberg's approach to moral education does not teach stage 6 morality. Indeed, it teaches no moral view, implicitly or explicitly. Rather it claims that moral development can not be taught. At best we can only stimulate people to construct morality for themselves. Kohlberg does this by posing or eliciting moral problems of various sorts and asking people to discuss them together.

   Of course holding moral discussions relies on democratic assumptions to some degree. Participants are allowed to speak their mind rather than towing "the official line" and no one is supposed to silence or threaten others during discussion. But in the typical classrooms Kohlbergians enter, there is no need to introduce such egalitarian norms of mutual consideration. They already exist for class discussion, at least on "opinionated" issues. This is due to democratic *laws.*

Of course Kohlbergians might enter less congenial settings (dictatorial or fundamentalist settings) where only "the true teaching" is allowed. And Kohlberg's nondogmatic approach may be seen as anathema. Here the problem of indoctrination is theirs, not Kohlberg's. And in objecting to such education, based on stage 6 principles, one is not engaging in indoctrinative education itself.

Suppose, however, that Kohlbergians did teach stage 6 morality directly. Indoctrination would be avoided here, so long as they also urged critical thinking on their view, and acknowledged the possible validity of alternative moralities. Indoctrinative education is not simply favoring one view in one's teaching. It is doing so without justifying that teaching well, or encouraging meaningful dissent.

END-POINTS/TOP-DOWN/STAGE 6 AND JUSTICE

As noted, Piaget, Kohlberg, and Gilligan claim that development is defined from its apex or end-point, the standard of cognitive adequacy or maturity. According to Kohlberg, the entire stage sequence is (and must be) defined relative to stage 6, as increasing approximations to it. Since stage 6 defines the fully adequate structure of moral reasoning, any form of normative thought which transcends it oversteps the moral realm as well. (It takes up more general issues of the worthy or meaningful life.)

Structurally, the conceptual differentiations and integrations of stage 6 are fully symmetrical and in full equilibration with the social environment. Morally, this means that all legitimate claims and responsibilities are fully recognized and correlated with each other. (Every right has a corresponding duty.) Moreover, the principle of just obligation which regulates them is fully reversible from all points of view—everyone ideally can see the reasonableness of this principle for all. Functionally this means also that stage 6 structure can yield concrete solutions to all moral problems. To philosophy, stage 6 represents the basic common-sense structure of the most adequate moral theory. Such theory is merely the elaboration and refinement of stage structure, according to Kohlberg.

In addition, Kohlberg claims that stage 6 structure, and the moral philosophy it grounds, is defined by the theme of egalitarian justice. This theme of rendering each "his" due, best captures the moral status of persons as of unconditional value by virtue of their capacity for purposive choice. The best account of such respect for persons and their rights, according to Kohlberg, is found in the formalist, deontological tradition, the Kantian tradition. Moreover, it is found in the liberal-egalitarian wing of that camp.

(These philosophers hold that the morality of actions comes from their inherent form or principle, from the *type* of action they are, e.g., lying. It does not come from the content or valence of their consequences, e.g., harm or disappointment, or the particular trait or virtue they express. They also hold that questions of basic respect for individual liberty cannot be overridden by majority will, or the desire to advance general welfare. Yet as members of society we individuals all must agree—contract—to provide fair opportunity to all, concerning the benefits of society available.)

The main theoretical criticisms of Kohlberg have focused on flaws and limitations of (a) justice theme (b) formal principles (c) Kantian deontology (d) liberalism (e) individual rights, or (f) some combination of these stances. Rights are said to reflect individualism. Principles show a kind of rigidity, abstraction, and impersonality. Justice shows a lack of compassion, concern, and helpfulness; it harbors a degree of callous disregard and the threat of violence. The liberal brand of justice reflects a Western cultural bias. It shows an intellectual bias as well, toward social contractarianism. And behind these flaws, biases, and limitations, according to critics, lurks the more fundamental bias of patriarchy.

Due to the holistic way Kohlberg conceives his theory, challenging any part rattles the entire edifice. However, the *logic* of Kohlberg's theory is independent of his particular conception of it, his theory of his theory. The particular thematic description Kohlberg offers of stage 6 is separable from the structural role stage 6 plays in the stage theory. And, of course, the end-point and standard of adequacy might come at a stage 7 or 8, rather than at the developmental stage after 5. Indeed, the standard of moral adequacy need not coincide with the standard of developmental maturity. There is no reason to suspect that natural commonsense development in moral reasoning reaches the full structural adequacy of intellectually reflective theories.

Even within Kohlberg's specific justice interpretation of stage 6, almost all controversial components are separable and dispensable. Let us see why. Kohlbergian "justice" is not justice in any distinctive thematic sense. Consider its "rights" component first. While Kohlberg's few reputedly stage 6 research subjects speak of "rights," it is unclear that they do so in a structural and spontaneously arising manner. (They may be speaking rhetorically or ideologically). Kohlberg has not offered a robust structural analysis of "rights reasoning" in particular, within stage 6 justice. Thus such "reasoning" might reflect socialization influences primarily, or intellectual reflection. (Indeed, Kohlberg's stage 6 "data" are normally cited from subjects called "Philosopher 1" or "Philosopher 3." Yet the form of development Kohlberg claims to measure is distinctively natural, the result of normal social interaction, not intellectual reflection). And as Rawls (1971) makes patently clear, a liberal-egalitarian theory may be constructed using duties and responsibilities alone. Therefore, when interpretively reconstructing the reasoning of respondents, Kohlberg might have left rights out entirely, and still captured structural justice. Sometimes he does just this in fact, speaking only of "legitimate claims" or "just claims." Such claims need not be rights, nor need they be individualized, as opposed to socially defined.

The same dispensability pertains to "justice" itself, as an overall moral theme. Kohlberg uses this term misleadingly, in a relatively archaic and amorphous sense, characteristic of Aristotle's *Ethics*. Justice in this sense does not focus on distinctive issues of merit, desert, or fair play, but on questions of what is right or respectful in general. And it bases its notion of respect on a prior sense of concern and affiliation. Kohlberg terms this sense "fellow-feeling." (Yet, as noted, Kohlberg's critics typically advocate concern and relationality as *rivals* to respect and justice.) In his most recent writings, Kohlberg refers primarily to respect rather than justice as the defining theme of morality and moral adequacy (Kohlberg, 1986).

Kohlberg's use of the term "principle" is similarly amorphous and all-embracing. Sometimes he seems to mean "rationale," or "line of reasoning." At other times he speaks of a principle being a "point of view." What stage 6 adds to stage 5, according to Kohlberg, is the background "moral point of view" from which stage 5 "rights" and social utility can be agreed to by all (Kohlberg, 1986). Surely Kohlberg's "rival themes" of relational caring or benevolence feature "rationales" or "lines of reasoning" at the center of their views. ("Try never to hurt others. Rather, do what is most nurturant or helpful for all concerned in a situation.") Certainly they offer a "point of view."

Critics often mistakenly charge Kohlberg with believing that adequate moral reasoning must actually apply principles or rules when deliberating. Actually Kohlberg holds that reasoning must *comply* with principles (rationales) to be adequate. This is a very different claim. Moreover, Kohlberg explicitly distinguishes rules and principles, rating the rule-based *style* or *type* of reasoning as inadequate, due to its "law and order" rigidity (Colby, Kohlberg, Gibbs, & Lieberman, 1983; Colby & Kohlberg, 1987).

Finally, nothing in the logic of respect requires that Kohlberg follow the social contract tradition or adhere to Western liberalism in particular. These are utterly separate "moral" orientations. (The latter two are primarily political, rather than moral orientations, as noted). Furthermore, the "liberal" notion that respecting each other's worth involves not only (a) noninterference in their liberty, but (b) actively *helping* them, is a matter of common sense, not intellectual theory. If I were to say that a person (or a Van Gogh, or a seashore) were of ultimate value and then I stood by while its source of value (or very existence) ebbed away, I would be "contradicting" my own belief. I would be acting irresponsibly as well. Likewise, if we as a society consider our members unconditionally valuable then let large segments of our community languish in poverty and illiteracy (with little opportunity to express their valuable capacities) we are "acting" inconsistently, irresponsibly. (Of course there may be some excuses for not taking *certain* paths to helping others, or for not bearing exorbitant costs when helping.)

Thus critics seem to go too far when criticizing Kohlberg's justice as individualistic and callous, rigid, and legalistic. It does not define moral adequacy in terms of mere "rights to noninterference." Critics seem to take Kohlberg's Kantianism too seriously as well. After all, Kant, like Kohlberg, was trying to account for the *commonsense* notion of the "golden rule." (The "golden rule" is the only "principle" in Kohlberg's theory, as we will see.)

Yet no doubt there is an ultimate partisanship in Kohlberg's metatheory that distinguishes it from themes of benevolence. For example, since Kohlberg identifies the source of human value in free will, and since "will" is primarily a psychological capacity, the individual will be accorded moral preference over social relationships in themselves. (As a follower of Mead, of course, Kohlberg sees psychological capacities such as autonomy in a social as well as individual sense. The individual is socially defined in this tradition.)

Moreover, since our just concern for people focuses on their will, rather than on the values or goals they choose or the virtues they express through choice, the nature and extent of our response to them will not be primarily compassionate. Nor will it extend to kindness on a regular basis. Kohlbergian respect is moved by threats to autonomy. It views need and deprivation in this way, rather than as heartfelt suffering prompting heartfelt aid. When those in need receive their equal share, their "just due," any remaining pain no longer has "legitimate" claims on justice.

These remaining Kohlbergian "biases" must be justified insofar as they play crucial roles in the actual stage theory. (Kohlberg adamantly asserts that they do. I will go on now to explain why they do not.) It is important to notice, however, that the justification called for here need only be *comparative*. Any complex moral view, such as "justice," will have flaws and limitations. So will any contrary view. Showing the flaws in justice is not enough to claim that utilitarianism or benevolence or relational caring has "equal validity" as an alternative, or even as a *component*. Such alternative views have age-old traditions in philosophy and have an equally long and well-documented reputation for inadequacy and incompleteness. Few attempts have ever been made to add them to the justice tradition for two very good reasons: (1) They seem incompatible with justice to the core, and; (2) They seem to detract more than they add, where complementarity seems possible. (Utilitarian views, especially, seem to endorse gross injustice.) The oft-heard suggestion that "care and justice" must be "balanced" in mature moral reasoning seems breathtakingly ignorant of the deep problems to be encountered.

The Ultimate Adequacy of Stage 6

Yet any moral theme, including justice or respect, is likely to fail the requirements of stage 6 structure. This is a good reason for dropping the ultimate adequacy claim here. As typically stated, in fact, Kohlberg's favored moral theme of stage 6 justice does not meet his own stage 6 requirements for moral adequacy. Consider a few reasons why.

1. Morally, justice and respect offer virtually no guidance regarding the pursuit of values and ideals. This includes personal and social values as well as ideals of one's own character development. Certainly going beyond the call of *duty,* as defined by justice, does not mean going beyond the scope of morality. There are morally exemplary people, and morally noble ideals. An adequate moral view must address them.

2. Values embody the moral dimension of goodness as contrasted to the dimension of right or justice. To Kohlberg's "respect logic," these values have moral standing only because they are chosen or held. Values are seen here as expressions of autonomy, for the most part. However, since justice respects *people* primarily, and respects them *equally* as *choosers,* it can not discriminate among better and worse value pursuits without discriminating against those who hold them. It lacks sufficient discrimination (differentiation) between the dimensions of equality and value *on principle.* Thus respect logic often puts morality on the wrong side of value disputes, or causes it to be indifferent (impartial) where it should not be. Examples abound everywhere, as when respect for equal rights to free speech actually *protects* Nazi hate mongering against the *appropriate* outrage of holocaust survivors.

To save face the logic of justice often calls this protection mere toleration. But justice *tolerates* Nazis in exactly the way it would *respect* them. And it prohibits the retaliation of Holocaust survivors just as it would the intentions of a thief or mugger.

3. Equal respect for persons *as equal persons* can not accord *degrees* or moral weight to personal responsibility or merit. Consider Kohlberg's famous Heinz dilemma. (Should a poverty-stricken husband steal a life-saving drug from its greedy inventor—a druggist—to save his wife?) According to Kohlberg, the stage 6 choice is simply to steal, out of respect for the wife's overriding claim to life. In Kohlberg's discussion of the solution one might expect to hear some provisions made for the druggist who, after all, has *some* claim to profiting from his "priceless" creation. One might expect some special provisions made to compensate Heinz, or even to excuse him from his ominous moral burden. In this case, after all, doing his duty means becoming a thief and going to jail. Yet no special provisions are mentioned by Kohlberg.

The same holds for the drowning person dilemma. Taking into consideration whether the drowning person jumped into the raging river on a lark, or to avoid capture for rape and murder, is considered discriminatory. The personhood of the drowning person counts most. But even if this were so, do these other factors count for nothing? If one is a cancer researcher passing by, with five familial dependents, need one bear the *same* serious risk of drowning to save a committed mass murderer as to save a highly successful peace activist? The disjunctive right/wrong logic of respect (of deontological ethics) seems bound to say "yes," or to commit injustice in its terms. The continuum logic of care and concern would better accommodate these degrees of responsibility.

4. Structurally, stage 6 justice may render all individual rights and duties symmetrical (correlative) from each person's point of view, as Kohlberg requires. Such neatness and completeness is desirable from the logical point of view and can avert confusion in decision making. But at stage 6 there is also a general principle of justice and several group, or social perspectives. There are special obligations acknowledged to friends and close relatives. Kohlberg offers no account of how these all correlate with each other. (Special obligations are typically asymmetrical, as in parents' obligations to children.) And if we add in the range of moral ideals, values and virtues that respect logic fails to address, the full logical symmetry of stage 6 seems highly questionable.

5. Stage 6 justice clearly can not solve all moral problems, even ideally. It fails systematically in cases where its interpersonal obligations are strongest and yet must be universalized on principle. For example, if we are to steal a needed drug for our dying wife, simply because she is a person, what are we to do for the starving multitudes? Are we to "storm the banks"? Are we strictly obliged to do so while others do almost nothing, thus making such drastic action necessary? Kohlberg has tried to address this sort of problem in various ways, never being satisfied with the logic of his approach.

In Kohlberg's higher-stage dilemmas we seem able to generate opposing solutions on stage 6 principles. In the lifeboat dilemma we may draw lots, as Kohlberg suggests, or go down together. The first solution seems impartial and self-chosen, but it equates justice in a positive sense with the luck of the draw. The second saves no lives but it also does not save some lives at the expense of others based on mere chance. In the case of aggression by one person on another it is unclear if equal respect prefers self-defense to pacifism. Does someone lose her or his personhood or unconditional value in the commission of a single right-violating act, attempted murder? If not, how can one prefer one's life to hers or his at stage 6 if the only defense means killing? Either way, through defense or nondefense, one life is lost. In one case one fails in one's duty to oneself. In the other, one violates another's right to life, killing him as a means to saving oneself.

(More elaborate and well-supported criticisms of stage 6 justice are provided elsewhere; Puka, 1986.)

A standard of moral adequacy (at stage 6) which outstrips perhaps the best moral theme (justice) we can offer it, is questionable. So is a theme which has moral flaws in its deepest logical core, as justice or respect seems to. Consider, therefore, a few suggestions for why we can abandon both.

Top-down Development

Despite what Kohlberg, Piaget, and Gilligan claim, development typically is not defined from an end-point of maturity. Certainly it *need* not be. Few (if any) sequences require an end-point to be ordered in progression. We all have been evaluating steps in processes or sequences all our lives, using piecemeal and comparative criteria. We compare one step with another, or two with a third. We compare steps in one sequence with those in an analogous one. We have judged Kohlberg's theory better than many of those before it without having some vision in mind of the ultimate or perfect developmental theory. The same has been true in rating critiques of his theory. We certainly have no standard of the ultimate critique, though we have seen many good ones and excellent ones. A piecemeal comparative process takes place when we note the deepening of our love relationships or assess progress in our careers. Indeed these processes characterize our assessments of intellectual and social history generally. The notion of an end-state or utopia in these contexts is extremely rare. Normally in fact, it is posed by extrapolating from nonultimate criteria, and from sequences of events we currently observe, rather than by dreaming up the ideal a priori.

In growth processes especially, where we can "get in on the ground floor" of observation, we typically chart growth from the bottom up, from nothing to anywhere else. We recognize a more developed muscle, or skill, or sense of taste, by looking at extremely undeveloped ones, and at movement away from that point. Likewise with cognition, almost any morally relevant change from the egocentric interest of Kohlberg's stage 1 will constitute moral development. This is so whether it moves toward utilitarianism, libertarianism, caring or kindness, or moral conventionalism. Of course, we *may* pose an ideal of the "perfect" marriage or job, the enlightened sage or moral exemplar. We *may* use it along with less ethereal methods to rate personal or social histories, their cycles of progress and regress. But this *need* not be so. (This is all my examples need illustrate.) And the pie in the sky quality of such standards hardly recommends them above more multifaceted and contextual approaches.

Yet Kohlberg claims actually to have used an end-point standard of Kantian justice to define the stage sequence and each stage in it. It was this standard of justice, supposedly, which defined which responses were morally relevant in the first place, and selected out those which remained relevant at more adequate stages. Thus whether an end-point was *needed* or not, or whether justice had to function as a standard of moral maturity, it actually did so in Kohlberg's case. As a result, the flaws we find in stage 6 and its justice theme should damn Kohlberg's whole scheme.

Whatever Kohlberg's *aims* or *efforts* for stage 6 justice in his theory, there are good reasons to believe they did not prove fruitful. (This is fortunate for his theory.) For one thing, it was not until 1983 that Levine and Hewer sat down with Kohlberg to chart the continuous progress of *justice* from stages 1–6 (see

Kohlberg, 1984, Chap. 3). This was the first time such a thematic analysis had taken place, despite the rhetorical emphasis on justice in Kohlberg articles. In some ways it did identify distinctively just forms of reasoning in the cognitive operations of equity, reciprocity, and equality. Yet in this new analysis it is never even *claimed* that justice is the only moral theme present at each stage. Nor is it demonstrated that justice is the *dominant* theme at *any* stage but stage 6. As a result it can not be shown that features of justice reasoning constitute the main "mechanism" of change from one stage to the other. This is remarkable for a theory of "justice development."

Rather what this analysis shows, I believe, is that moral reasoning involving at least some tacit notion of respect (equity and reciprocity) is present at stages 2 through 6. Even cursory analysis shows that the moral *focus* of the stages is elsewhere. It is on ethical egoism at stage 2, on conventional caring at stage 3, social stability and mutual preservationism at stage 4, and on the odd combination of social utilitarianism and libertarian rights at stage 5.

The motley structure of stage 5 raises the greatest question about the defining role of justice in the stage sequence. After all, stage 5 mixes the most individualistic (libertarian) of rights views with utilitarianism. Utilitarianism is the champion of *non*-Kantian, *non*deontological, *non*formalist morality. Liberal views of justice, such as those of Kohlberg and Rawls, were posed in direct opposition to the utilitarian alternative and to libertarian rights views as well. Moral philosophy has been *centered* on these precise debates for over a century.

Since 1978, Kohlberg has foresworn his traditional stage descriptions for new *operational* descriptions. These are derived from his newly validated scoring system and the thorough reanalysis of data on which it is based (see Kohlberg, 1984, Appendix A; Colby & Kohlberg, 1987). Only stages 1–5 are included here, as noted at the beginning of our discussion. This makes stage 5, with its mixture of rights and social utility or welfare, Kohlberg's highest (empirical) stage. An analysis of stage 5 provides a much more useful and accurate standard than stage 6 for a top-down reconstruction of the overall stage sequence. Primarily this is because each moral stage (2–5) features both a "group welfare" or "concern orientation" and an individual "respect orientation." Only stage 6 eliminates (or radically subverts) this duality. Kohlberg's recent claim that his notion of justice also encompasses care and concern might have been bolstered by focusing on the dual moral themes of each stage, and their fruition at stage 5.

Anne Colby is the main architect of the scoring system from which these new stage descriptions were drawn. She formulated the actual scoring categories and criterion judgments (in Vol. 1) on which stage scores are based. In describing their formulation, Colby is quite clear that stage 6 justice was *not* used in this process. (I base this claim on 10 years of personal communication.) Instead, scoring criteria were derived from a very close descriptive analysis of these data—from what respondents actually said. Very general, descriptive categories were used to determine the *moral relevance* of responses. These reflected concerns such as needs, liberty, respect, promise keeping, honesty, conscience, and so forth. The generality of these concerns and standards is shown by the sorts of quasimoral considerations which actually appear in the structure of early stages, considerations which have virtually nothing to do with the morality of justice.

Increasing moral adequacy was defined in the new stages primarily by *role* taking and *social perspective* taking, when accompanied by *any* moral "theme" within these broad categories of concern. Adequacy was defined also by the *logical* competence with which these roles were related to each other and to moral rationales.

Colby's account of stage-construction is verified by inspecting the scoring categories and standards in her manual. They encompass a variety of moral themes of which rights and justice are a minority (see, e.g., Kohlberg, 1984, p. 309; Colby & Kohlberg, 1987). And when social perspective-taking competence increases, relative to *any* major moral theme in this array, moral stage increases likewise. *This is the key.*

At stage 3 it is the competence to role take (for the first time), and to assume the peer perspective, that is primarily responsible for stage score. The *combination* of approval seeking, maintaining reputation, being caring and concerned, helpful and forgiving, honest and fair, provides the moral theme of this cognitive structure. Justice theme in particular does not determine stage score. If maintaining reputation, seeking approval, and being an honest and caring person were the only quasimoral norms present, stage 3 would still have to be seen as a moral advance over stage 2 egoism. Likewise, at stage 4 it is the capacity to take the perspective of society as a whole, and interrelate individual and group perspectives with it, that is primarily responsible for stage score.

The key to stage 5 is to distinguish the "law"-maintaining (stability-maintaining) norms of stage 4 from the "law"-creating or social contract functions of morality, then integrate them. In addition to a libertarian rights theme at this stage, themes of utilitarianism and perfectionism (ideal virtue) figure heavily. (Perfectionism holds us responsible for nurturing and expressing noble characters, ideal virtues, and worthy social ideals. Like utilitarianism, such a theme typically conflicts with deontological rights and justice.) Most important, *when research respondents adopt a utilitarian or ideal virtue theme by itself at stage 5 (without taking a rights orientation) they are still scored stage 5.* An ideal virtue theme typically focuses on benevolence, kindness, or love.

As a result, it becomes very difficult to see how "justice bias" at the top of Kohlberg's theory downscores respondents based on moral theme. (Indeed, there have never been hard data to support this exaggerated claim; see Gilligan, 1982, 1985; Walker, 1982.) It also becomes very difficult to see why eliminating the justice theme of stage 6, and stage 6 itself, would alter the stage sequence.

A crucial point of clarification is required here, before we conclude. Several prominent Kohlbergians who have read this manuscript fear that it undercuts the developmental character of Kohlberg's stage sequence. It seemingly leaves only five loosely related ethical systems which replace each other cognitively, the way particular beliefs or ideologies do. My account does not have such implications. It accepts the developmental continuity of logical, role-taking, and moral operations that become successively more differentiated, integrated, and equilibrated along Kohlberg's stage sequence. However, it questions the need and appropriateness of calling them justice operations. This is the main point. Suppose we assume, however, that Kohlberg, Levine, and Hewer have identified distinctive justice operations in Kohlberg's stages, the integrated operations of equity, reciprocity, universalizability, and equality. My account would then raise three questions: (1) Are these operations truly present all along these stage sequences? I see none at stage 1. Moreover tendencies toward inequality and toward restricting the scope of moral inclusion (versus generalizing or universalizing it) seem dominant at stages 2 and 3, perhaps even at stage 4; (2) Are these operations morally dominant along the stage sequence? I believe they are subsidiary or closely rivaled at stages 1–5; (3) Are these operations dominant among the types of operations that compose a moral stage—including logical, role-taking, and social perspective-taking operations—and in developmental transformations between stages? (So far, I believe, Kohlberg's stages are at least as much a matter of social reasoning on moral dilemmas as moral reasoning on social dilemmas.)

Kohlberg, Levine, and Hewer seem to assume that a developmental sequence requires the persistence of certain related operations throughout. These operations must define the moral reasoning, the "it," that is transformed, refined, amended, and reorganized along the developmental sequence. Like the end-point assumption for defining development, however, this persistence assumption seems unwarranted and unnecessary. To show inherent development only three observations are necessary: (1) continuity in structure (or function) and transformation of moral operations from each stage to its successor; (2) inclusion of the themes constituted by each stage within the domain of moral relevance; and (3) increasing moral-cognitive adequacy along the sequence of stage transformations. (Continuity and moral inclusion are the "it" of development.)

For centuries, metaphysicians sought some essential stuff, some "soul-substance," that persisted in people from conception to death (or beyond) to establish personal identity over time. How could a certain infant be the same person as the mature or aged person into which she or he grew, unless some personal essence remained the same or took on alterations with age? The *primary* answer, provided later, was that there was a relatively smooth and continuous transformation of each stage of this being into the next. And this continuous process of being was easily differentiated from closely allied or interacting processes. Thus even if the adult were radically different from the infant—if it had lost all memory of earlier life, with its early outlooks and beliefs, if it now possessed a body which had various organs and parts missing or added or at least grown into different sizes and shapes—it still constituted the same person. After all, it was a person, it fell in the domain of persons. And we were able to watch it being a person, after it first became one, all along the way. During that time, as it interacted with many other things and people and their processes of becoming and change, it never became enough like them to be more them than itself. Thus "it" seems to have retained "its" identity as the person "it" is. (Obviously this analogy is oversimplified and imperfect, i.e., merely an analogy; but hopefully it is instructive.)

CONCLUDING REMARKS

Viewing Kohlberg's stage sequence from its dominant "perspective-taking" dimension suggests that his theory charts the mere approach to moral thought, to minimal moral adequacy. It barely touches on the progression in adequacy, toward ultimate (philosophical) reasoning. Any form of moral cognition that cannot distinguish morality from immorality (at stage 2) or couch moral problems at the broader social levels at which they occur (at stage 3) is *grossly* deficient. Only at stages 4 and 5 does commonsense moral reasoning at least "cover all bases." Yet it does so very poorly, even at stage 4. Here it actually advocates majority tyranny, on occasion, alongside mutuality and tolerance. One does not need a particular or refined justice standard to chart such a humble cognitive entry into the moral realm.

REFERENCES

Colby, A., Kohlberg, L., Gibbs, J. & Lieberman, M. A. (1983). Longitudinal study of moral development, *SRCD* Monographs *48* (4).

Colby, A. & Kohlberg, L. (1987). *The measurement of moral judgment,* New York: Cambridge University Press.

Gilligan, C. (1982). *In a different voice,* Cambridge, MA: Harvard University Press.

Gilligan, C. (1985). A reply to critics. *Signs,* Winter.

Kohlberg, L. (1982/1984). *Essays in moral development* (Vols. 1, 2). New York: Harper & Row. (Kohlberg's articles "Stage and sequence" (1968), "From is to ought" (1971), and "Indoctrination versus relativity" can be found in these volumes.)

Kohlberg, L. (1986). The return of stage 6. In W. Edelstein & G. Nunner–Winkler (Eds.), *Zür Bestimmung der Moral* Berlin: Suhrkamp.

Puka, B. (1986). The majesty and mystery of Stage 6. In W. Edelstein & G. Nunner–Winkler (Eds.), *Zür Bestimmung der Moral.* Berlin: Suhrkamp.

Rawls, J. (1971). *A theory of justice,* Cambridge, MA: Harvard University Press.

Walker, L. (1982, June). *Sex differences in the development of moral reasoning: A critical review of the literature.* Paper presented at the Canadian Psychological Association, Montreal.

APPENDIX A

Level and Stage	What Is Right	Reasons for Doing Right	Social Perspective of Stage
LEVEL I—PRECONVENTIONAL			
Stage 1—Heteronomous Morality	To avoid breaking rules backed by punishment, obedience for its own sake, and avoiding physical damage to persons and property.	Avoidance of punishment, and the superior power of authorities.	Egocentric point of view. Doesn't consider the interests of others or recognize that they differ from the actor's; doesn't relate two points of view. Actions are considered physically rather than in terms of psychological interests of others. Confusion of authority's perspective with one's own.
Stage 2—Individualism, Instrumental Purpose, and Exchange	Following rules only when it is to someone's immediate interest; acting to meet one's own interests and needs and letting others do the same. Right is also what's fair, what's an equal exchange, a deal, an agreement.	To serve one's own needs or interests in a world where you have to recognize that other people have their interests, too.	Concrete individualistic perspective. Aware that everybody has his or her own interest to pursue and these conflict, so that right is relative (in the concrete individualistic sense).

(continued)

Level and Stage	What Is Right	Reasons for Doing Right	Social Perspective of Stage
LEVEL II—CONVENTIONAL			
Stage 3—Mutual Interpersonal Expectations, Relations, and Interpersonal Conformity	Living up to what is expected by people close to you or what people generally expect of people in your role as son, brother, friend, etc. "Being good" is important and means having good motives, showing concern about others. It also means keeping mutual relationships, such as trust, loyalty, respect and gratitude.	The need to be a good person in your own eyes and those of others. Caring for others. Belief in the Golden Rule. Desire to maintain rules and authority which support stereotypical good behavior.	Perspective of the individual in relationships with other individuals. Aware of shared feelings, agreements, and expectations which take primacy over individual interests. Relates points of view through the concrete Golden Rule, putting yourself in the other guy's shoes. Does not yet consider generalized system perspective.
Stage 4—Social System and Conscience	Fulfilling the actual duties to which you have agreed. Laws are to be upheld except in extreme cases where they conflict with other fixed social duties. Right is also contributing to society, the group or institution.	To keep the institution going as a whole, to avoid the breakdown in the system "if everyone did it," or the imperative of conscience to meet one's defined obligations.	Differentiates societal point of view from interpersonal agreement or motives. Takes the point of view of the system that defines roles and rules. Consider individual relations in terms of place in the system.

392

266

LEVEL III—POSTCONVENTIONAL, OR PRINCIPLED

Stage 5—Social Contract or Utility and Individual Rights	Being aware that people hold a variety of values and opinions, that most values and rules are relative to your group. These relative rules should usually be upheld, however, in the interest of impartiality and because they are the social contract. Some nonrelative values and rights, such as life and liberty, however, must be upheld in any society and regardless of majority opinion.	A sense of obligation to law because of one's social contract to make and abide by laws for the welfare of all and for the protection of all people's rights. A feeling of contractual commitment, freely entered upon, to family, friendship, trust, and work obligations. Concerns that laws and duties be based on rational calculation of overall utility, "the greatest good for the greatest number."	Prior-to-society perspective. Perspective of a rational individual aware of values and rights prior to social attachments and contracts. Integrates perspectives by formal mechanisms of agreement contract, objective impartiality, and due process. Considers moral and legal points of view: recognizes that they sometimes conflict and finds it difficult to integrate them.
Stage 6—Universal Ethical Principles	Following self-chosen ethical principles. Particular laws or social agreements are usually valid because they rest on such principles. When laws violate these principles one acts in accordance with the principle. Principles are universal principles of justice: the equality of human rights and respect for the dignity of individuals.	The belief as a rational person in the validity of universal moral principles, and a sense of personal commitment to them.	Perspective of a moral point of view from which social arrangements derive. Perspective is that of any rational individual recognizing the nature of morality or the fact that persons are ends in themselves and must be treated as such.

Kohlberg, 1976; see also Kohlberg 1969 and 1971 for other features of stages noted.

393

267

VOL. 81, No. 8   AUGUST 1974

Psychological Bulletin

THE DEVELOPMENT OF MORAL THOUGHT:
REVIEW AND EVALUATION OF KOHLBERG'S APPROACH [1]

WILLIAM KURTINES [2]   ESTHER BLANK GREIF

Florida International University   *Boston University*

This article examines and evaluates the evidence supporting Kohlberg's theory concerning the development of moral thought. A systematic review of the published research literature suggests that there are several conceptual and methodological problems with the approach. The problems include the derivation, administration, and scoring of the model's primary measurement device; the lack of evidence for both the reliability and validity of that device; and the absence of direct evidence for the basic assumptions of the theory. On the basis of the review, it seems that the empirical utility of the model has yet to be demonstrated.

Piaget's (1932) classic study, *The Moral Judgment of the Child,* provided the basis for much of the current psychological research in the area of moral judgment. His cognitive-developmental approach supplied a conceptual framework for the study of the growth of moral thought, and his "clinical method" furnished a widely used technique for assessing moral reasoning (e.g., Boehm, 1962; Haan, Smith, & Block, 1968; Kohlberg, 1969; MacRae, 1954; Rest, 1973; Turiel, 1966).

Perhaps the most influential and systematic extension of Piaget's theory and method can be found in the work of Kohlberg (1958, 1963a, 1963b, 1964, 1966a, 1966b, 1969). He has been instrumental in reviving and legitimizing the empirical study of moral development and has developed a major model of the growth of moral reasoning. Since its appearance in 1958, Kohlberg's paradigm has generated a great deal of research. Despite its demonstrated heuristic value, however, Kohlberg's model, like all theoretical systems,

must ultimately be evaluated empirically. It is therefore timely and appropriate that some attempt be made to determine how well this model has stood the test of time. Before discussing the model in detail, it is useful to review the basic assumptions of Kohlberg's system.

KOHLBERG'S APPROACH

Kohlberg's theory of moral development has its historical roots in the developmental theories of Baldwin (1906) and Mead (1934). As previously noted, however, its more immediate conceptual foundations lie in the cognitive-developmental theory of Piaget (1932). For Piaget, intellectual development consists of the successive transformation of cognitive structures in response to both internal and external pressures. The sequence of this development is set by the structure of the mind. Since the evolution of moral reasoning is assumed to reflect cognitive development, the order of moral development is also preset. This sequence involves a shift from heteronomous reasoning, in which adult rules are viewed as sacred and immutable, to autonomous reasoning, in which rules are viewed as human products.

For Kohlberg, as for Piaget, the development of moral reasoning proceeds through an

[1] The authors wish to thank Doris Entwisle, Robert Hogan, Constance Holstein, and Julian Stanley for their critical comments on an earlier version of this article.

[2] Requests for reprints should be sent to William Kurtines, Department of Psychology, Florida International University, Miami, Florida 33144.

invariant sequence of stages. Kohlberg, however, defined *six* different steps, each characterized by a separate type of moral reasoning. Moral reasoning becomes more sophisticated as development proceeds in a stepwise fashion through the stages. Ideally, the individual continues to develop until he is capable of reasoning and making judgments on the highest level (Stage 6). Kohlberg, like Piaget, viewed each stage as qualitatively different from the previous one. Each new stage is "a differentiation and integration of a set of functional contents present at the prior state [Kohlberg & Kramer, 1969, p. 99]."

Piaget's and Kohlberg's systems also differ on certain points. The primary differences lie in the number of stages of moral reasoning and the end point of development. Kohlberg's system is more highly differentiated; that is, it is based on six distinct stages rather than two general ones. The six developmental types are grouped into three moral levels and are shown in Table 1. Additionally, whereas for Piaget moral maturity is attained when an individual is capable of autonomous reasoning (for most people, around age 12), for Kohlberg moral maturity, defined as the capacity for principled (Stage 6) reasoning, is reached by very few people. Individuals who attain this level of moral reasoning do so in their late teens.

TABLE 1

LEVELS AND STAGES OF MORAL DEVELOPMENT

Level	Stage
I. Premoral level	1. Punishment and obedience orientation
	2. Naive instrumental hedonism
II. Morality of conventional role conformity	3. Good-boy morality of maintaining good relations, approval of others
	4. Authority-maintaining morality
III. Morality of self-accepted moral principles	5. Morality of contract and of democratically accepted law
	6. Morality of individual principles of conscience

Note. Data from Kohlberg (1963a, pp. 13–14).

The primary source for Kohlberg's derivation of his stages of moral reasoning was his doctoral dissertation (Kohlberg, 1958). To identify his stages of moral development, Kohlberg administered a variety of moral dilemmas to 72 middle-class and lower class boys (ages 10, 13, and 16) in suburban Chicago. The dilemmas were designed to present "a conflict between habitual conformity to a rule or authority as against a utilitarian or 'greatest good' response to situational values and social value objects [1958, p. 77]. From examination of the boys' responses to these situations, Kohlberg "isolated" six developmental types of value orientations: (1) obedience and punishment, (2) naively egoistic, (3) good boy, (4) authority and social-order maintaining, (5) contractual legalistic, (6) conscience or principles (cf. Kohlberg, 1969). These types provided the basis for the six stages of reasoning previously discussed. As Kohlberg (1958) himself noted, however, "The number of types we came out with was eventually rather arbitrary, and undoubtedly determined by the limits of variation of our particular population [p. 89]."

THE MORAL JUDGMENT SCALE

Only one method has been used to assess Kohlberg's stages—the Moral Judgment Scale. The purpose of the scale is to determine an individual's stage of moral development by examining his moral judgments and moral reasoning. Additionally, because of the hierarchical nature of the stages, the Moral Judgment Scale defines the individual's level of moral maturity.

The only relatively complete description of this scale and its contents is Kohlberg's dissertation (1958). The Moral Judgment Scale is a structured projective test consisting of nine hypothetical dilemmas either invented by Kohlberg or adapted from other sources. These same dilemmas apparently were used to derive the stages which the scale measures. Since research using the scale seems to be affected by some of its characteristics (e.g., lack of standardized administration procedures, a variable scoring system, and other features), we examine each in turn.

Administration of the Scale

To use the Moral Judgment Scale, an interviewer presents a subject with one dilemma at a time and the person must make a judgment about the situation and then justify his choice. The following is a frequently used example:

In Europe, a woman was near death from cancer. One drug might save her, a form of radium that a druggist in the same town had recently discovered. The druggist was charging $2,000, ten times what the drug cost him to make. The sick woman's husband, Heinz, went to everyone he knew to borrow the money, but he could only get together about half of what it cost. He told the druggist that his wife was dying and asked him to sell it cheaper or let him pay later. But the druggist said, "No." The husband got desperate and broke into the man's store to steal the drug for his wife. Should the husband have done that? Why? [Kohlberg, 1969, p. 379].

The interviewer encourages the subject to respond freely and asks probing questions to elicit additional responses, all of which are recorded. Since these probing questions vary in accordance with the subject's original judgment, each person receives a different set of questions. Further, because administration of all nine dilemmas is time consuming (taking approximately two hours), few researchers use them all. In fact, in eight of the published studies covered in this review, the mean number of dilemmas administered was 6.1 (see Table 2). Moreover, these researchers rarely reported which of the nine dilemmas they used, thereby raising the possibility that different studies used different situations. This lack of a standardized scale content contributes further to the difficulty of evaluating research results because not all of the situations are equally effective for assessing moral reasoning (cf. Kohlberg, 1958, p. 91).

The administration of the Moral Judgment Scale, then, is time consuming and variable. Not only do interview questions differ across subjects, but the number and content of dilemmas presented also vary across studies. As a consequence, generalizability of research results is problematical.

Several researchers (e.g., Haan et al., 1968) have used a five-item written version of the scale. This shorter form would, if properly standardized, eliminate some of the administration problems associated with the longer interview procedure (e.g., lack of generalizability). However, no published information concerning this scale is available.

Scoring of the Moral Judgment Scale

Scoring of the Moral Judgment Scale is based not on a subject's specific judgment to each moral dilemma, but rather on the reasoning which he gives in support of his judgment. The scale is complex and difficult to score. Precise scoring instructions are available only from Kohlberg personally, and extensive training is necessary in order to score protocols correctly. Although published descriptions of the scoring procedures are discrepant (see Table 2 for a list of the various scoring systems cited in the literature), examination of the literature reveals two main methods for scoring the protocols: a global system and a detailed system.

For global scoring, a subject receives a stage rating for each dilemma. "These ratings are based on intuitive weighting by the rater of the various elements included [in the response] and imply some feel for the types as a whole and some experience of the range of possible responses [Kohlberg, 1958, p. 91]." Scores based on these ratings can be reported in two ways: One can report a score for each stage (thereby giving a profile of percentage usage of stages), or one can report the dominant stage alone.

The detailed scoring system is more complex. Here scores are assigned to each "thought-content" unit, defined as "all of a subject's utterances which, taken together, seems to express a single moral idea [Fodor, 1972, p. 258]." These responses are assigned scores in accordance with an elaborate coding scheme devised by Kohlberg (1958). The system is based on 30 "general aspects of morality" (Kohlberg, 1963a), each defined by a six-level scale. After all thought-content units are assigned to stages, percentages of responses at each stage are computed. Results are then reported in at least one of three ways. In some studies, profiles of responses are used for analyses (e.g., 40% Stage 1, 30% Stage 2, 20% Stage 3, 10%

Stage 4, and 0% Stages 5 and 6; cf. Kohlberg, 1968). In other cases, a single total score is obtained by multiplying the percentage usage by weights assigned to each stage (e.g., $(0 \times 40) + (1 \times 30) + (2 \times 20) + (3 \times 10) + (4 \times 0) + (5 \times 0) + (6 \times 0) = 100$; cf. Fodor, 1972). This score is called a moral maturity score. Finally, in some studies analyses are based on only the dominant (modal) stage (e.g., Turiel, 1966) or on a mixed score (major and minor stages). From the detailed coding scheme, then, there appears to be three methods of reporting results. Combining these methods with the two possible ways for reporting results from the global scoring technique, one arrives at five possible combinations of scoring and reporting scores for the Moral Judgment Scale.

The variability and complexity of the scoring schemes for the Moral Judgment Scale have three major consequences for the evaluation of research conducted with the scale. First, the judgmental nature of the coding procedures introduces a potential for scorer bias. Standardized and objective scoring procedures would reduce the possibility of scores reflecting biases of individual judges. Second, the variability of scoring and reporting procedures confounds the interpretation of results. With both administration and scoring of the scale varying from study to study, it is difficult to estimate from the literature the extent to which results actually reflect differences among people. Finally, the intricate and often ambiguous nature of the scoring scheme almost surely discourages independent research, thereby preventing confirmation or disconfirmation of Kohlberg's model.

Other Features of the Scale

There are other features of the scale which may confound research results. First, the main characters in the dilemmas are male. Recognition of differential role expectations for males and females suggests that sex of the main character may influence an individual's judgments (cf. Magowan & Lee, 1970). It is not surprising then that, as defined by Kohlberg's scale, females appear to be less morally mature than males (Holstein, 1972; Kohlberg & Kramer, 1969).[3]

Second, not all of the dilemmas are independent in content; some are continuations of previous stories. For example, after the situation in which Heinz steals the drug for his wife, there occurs a sequence in which we learn that the drug did not cure her and, with only a few months to live, she is in agonizing pain. The subject must make a judgment about the justification for mercy killing. Because the purpose of the Moral Judgment Scale is to assess underlying reasoning rather than responses to specific situations, the lack of independence of the dilemmas necessarily reduces the range of responses it can elicit.

In addition to these content considerations, the Moral Judgment Scale is subject to problems common to all projective measures. For example, there is considerable evidence that scores on projective tests are influenced by IQ, social class, and verbal facility (cf. Entwisle, 1972; Jensen, 1959; Magowan & Lee, 1970). Also, both the age and the sex of the interviewer could influence a subject's responses (cf. Masling, 1960). Children may respond differently to younger and older, or male and female interviewers. Moreover, the examiner's freedom to ask probing questions adds an additional opportunity for the operation of experimenter bias. As Kohlberg (1958) explained,

[a child might] change and revise his decision . . . in response to what [he] . . . would see as "hints" in the probing as to what might be the answer preferred by the examiner. If one probes the reasons for a choice sufficiently, almost inevitably this probing is seen as implying that the choice is inadequate [pp. 118–119].

RELIABILITY

Reliability refers generally to accuracy of measurement. Ideally, a reliable instrument assesses a certain train or characteristic in a consistent and stable manner. Because of chance error in measurement, however, perfect reliability is virtually impossible to ob-

---

[3] C. B. Holstein. Moral Judgment Change in Early Adolescence and Middle Age: A Longitudinal Study. Paper presented at the biannual meeting of the Society for Research in Child Development, Philadelphia, March 1973.

tain. Consequently, reliability estimates are necessary in order to make reasonable interpretations of the scale scores (cf. Anastasi, 1968; Stanley, 1971).

Measurement theory bases reliability of scores on the distinction between true variation and error variation: The larger the ratio of true to error (or total) variance, the greater the reliability of a measure. Because many factors contribute to test variances, "their allocation to true and error variance could rightly be considered to be dependent upon the conditions and purposes of testing [Stanley, 1971, p. 363]." Thus determination of reliability involves not only use of statistical procedures but also a consideration of the functions of the test.

There are two major categories of scale reliability—estimates of temporal stability and estimates of internal consistency. Both deal with interindividual accuracy of measurement. The first is concerned with the stability of scores over time and the second, with homogeneity of measurement. In addition to scale reliability, it is also necessary to estimate the accuracy of individual scores and (in the case of subjective scoring) interscorer agreement. Intraindividual accuracy is usually assessed by estimating the standard error of measurement of a scale, and interrater reliability is commonly estimated by measuring agreement among independent scorers.

Temporal Stability

An estimate of the stability with which the Moral Judgment Scale measures a given individual's stage of moral reasoning would indicate the degree to which such scores reflect actual characteristics of the individual rather than random fluctuations resulting from the testing session. Because accurate assessment of stages is crucial for testing the assumptions of Kohlberg's model (e.g., invariance of sequence, reorganization of stages), an estimate of temporal stability is important.

Both test–retest and parallel form reliability measure stability of scores across time. Thus, an estimate of the temporal stability of the Moral Judgment Scale would indicate the degree to which an individual whose judgments fell at Stage 4 at Time 1 would also score at Stage 4 at Time 2. In all the published studies employing the Moral Judgment Scale, there are no reported estimates of temporal stability.

Consistency

Other forms of reliability concern homogeneity of test items. Applied to the Moral Judgment Scale, a consistency measure would estimate the degree to which dilemmas assess a similar dimension (viz., maturity of moral reasoning). While empirically keyed tests need not be homogeneous, a rationally devised test such as the Moral Judgment Scale should have considerable item homogeneity. If each dilemma taps a unique dimension, adding scores across dilemmas would be meaningless. For a total score to make sense, then, covariation among items must be positive and appreciable.

Several methods are available for assessing this type of reliability. The Kuder–Richardson coefficient, for example, estimates interitem consistency on the basis of intercorrelations among items. Split-half reliability involves a correlation between two comparable halves of a test. Although these procedures are applicable to the Moral Judgment Scale, there are no estimates of internal consistency to be found anywhere in the research literature.

Standard Error of Measurement

The most common way to assess the accuracy of an individual's test score is with the standard error of measurement, that is, the standard deviation of an individual's score. Suppose, for example, that a subject's score on the Moral Judgment Scale falls at Stage 3. Without an estimate of the standard error of measurement, one does not know whether this is $3 \pm .2$, 3 ± 1.2, or even 3 ± 3.0. Knowledge of the standard error of measurement not only clarifies the meaning of individual scores, it also facilitates the comparison of scores among individuals. Further, it is particularly important for the Moral Judgment Scale because a majority of an individual's responses are rarely at his modal stage. For example, a subject whose modal stage is 5 may have 45% of his responses at this stage, with 35% of his responses at Stage 4 and 20% at Stage 6. There are no reported estimates of this form of reliability in the published research literature.

Interrater Reliability

Interrater reliability indicates the degree to which independent raters agree concerning the nature of an individual's responses to a test item. Thus, it focuses on the scoring of a scale rather than the scale itself. This type of reliability, appropriate for subjectively scored instruments, has been reported for the Moral Judgment Scale.

The first estimates of interscorer reliability for the Moral Judgment Scale were reported by Kohlberg (1958). Product-moment correlations for global ratings for two of the nine dilemmas (2 and 7), using two raters (one of whom was Kohlberg), were .64 ($n = 44$) and .79 ($n = 36$). According to Kohlberg, differences in reliability between the situations are probably not random; rather, "This may be due to the differential values of the questions in representing the typology [p. 91]." If this is in fact the case, then reliability information for all dilemmas would help to determine which are the most scorable. Kohlberg did not compute reliability estimates for the detailed scoring system because "The coding operation, as opposed to the ratings, appeared to be concrete and objective enough to obviate assessing reliabilities [p. 92]."

Table 2 summarizes the studies reporting interscorer reliabilities for the Moral Judgment Scale.

Many other studies using the Moral Judgment Scale report no new interrater reliability, relying instead on previous estimates; these studies do not appear in Table 2. The correlations indicate an acceptable degree of reliability. A measure of actual agreement would be helpful for interpreting the scoring procedures, since the use of the product-moment correlation coefficient does not necessarily indicate absolute agreement between judges. For example, if Judge 1 rated Dilemmas 1 to 4 as representative of Stages 2, 3, 2, and 2, respectively; and Judge 2 rated the same dilemmas as representative of Stages 4, 5, 4, and 4, the product-moment correlation would be 1.0, but the judges

TABLE 2
SUMMARY OF PUBLISHED INTERSCORER RELIABILITY ESTIMATES FOR THE MORAL JUDGMENT SCALE

Study	Number of response protocols used	Number of dilemmas	Scoring procedure	Reliability estimate[a]
Product-moment correlations				
Fodor (1969)	10	9	detailed	.85
Fodor (1972)	10	9	detailed	.85[b]
Haan, Smith, & Block (1968)[c]	957	5	detailed	.82
Keasey (1971)	20	5	detailed	.87
Ruma & Mosher (1967)	10	6	not stated	.84
Turiel (1966)	48	9	detailed for one scorer; global for one scorer	.78
Interscorer agreement				
Haan, Smith, & Block (1968)	not given	5	detailed	85%
Rest, Turiel, & Kohlberg (1969)	not given	2	detailed	71%[d]
Saltzstein, Diamond, & Belenky (1972)	not given[e]	4	global	86%

[a] All estimates are based on correlations between two raters unless otherwise noted.
[b] Represents the mean correlation based on scoring by four raters.
[c] This study used the written version of the Moral Judgment Scale.
[d] Method of computation was not reported.
[e] The authors stated that agreement was based on 166 comparisons.

would not be in agreement on any of their ratings. There are some such estimates for certain subsets of items in the literature.

Haan et al. (1968), for example, provided such an estimate for five situations. By defining agreement as "either complete (both major and minor), major code only, or reversals of major and minor designations [p. 187]," they found that agreement between the two judges was 85%. Other studies report agreement of 71% and 86% (Rest, Turiel, & Kohlberg, 1969; Saltzstein, Diamond, and Belenky, 1972). Thus, these findings suggest that scoring for some dilemmas can be replicated. Evidence for the interscorer reliability of the entire coding and scoring procedure, however, would facilitate research in the area.

VALIDITY

Validity, in its most general sense, requires that a measure perform as would be expected on the basis of its underlying concepts. There are several methods for estimating validity (cf. Cronbach, 1971), two of which are particularly salient for this review. The first, predictive validity, concerns the effectiveness of a scale in predicting an external criterion. The second, construct validity, concerns the relationship between a scale and the theory from which it is derived. While the first form of validity can often be assessed more or less directly, construct validation is an inferential process which closely resembles the more general phenomenon of theory construction. Thus, a measure must be embedded in a "nomothetic" net, a matrix of empirical and logical relationships which provide its meaning (cf. Cronbach & Meehl, 1955).

Predictive Validity

Kohlberg's framework does not require a relationship between moral reasoning and moral action. Theoretically, individuals at different stages can exhibit the same behaviors using different types of reasoning, whereas individuals at the same stage can exhibit different behaviors using the same type of reasoning. However, Kohlberg (1969) himself suggested that there should be some relationship between moral reasoning and moral action, and several studies contain information bearing on this relationship. In order to justify six distinct stages, each stage should contribute to the prediction of nontest criteria, that is, all six stages should make better predictions than any subset of stages. The following review is neither detailed nor exhaustive; however, it does illustrate both the variety of procedures employed to validate the Moral Judgment Scale and the model of moral development, and the actual predictive utility of the six stages of moral reasoning.

The first study, by Haan et al. (1968), constitutes perhaps the major application of Kohlberg's technique to real world data. Among other things, the study attempted to identify differences in political and social activism associated with Kohlberg's stages. The study used two samples of college students and a group of peace corps volunteers. Level of moral reasoning was determined from a self-administered, five-dilemma ver-

sion of the Moral Judgment Scale. Using the detailed scoring technique, three judges trained by Kohlberg rated the protocols. Because only individuals "who could be assigned to one or another of five 'pure' moral types according to their responses to the Moral Judgment Scale [1968, p. 184]" were retained, 46% of the responding sample was excluded from the data analysis.

The most interesting behavioral findings concerned the activism–nonactivism criterion. Activism and nonactivism were defined as participation, or nonparticipation, in a free speech movement sit-in at Berkeley. For males, 75% of Stage 6 individuals were activists, 41% of Stage 5, 6% of Stage 4, and 18% of Stage 3 people were activists. However, the most striking finding of the study was the activism of Stage 2 males: 60% of them participated in the sit-in, the second highest percentage of the sample. The authors account for this unexpected finding with a distinction:

Principled arrestees [Stage 6] were more concerned with the basic issues of civil liberties and rights and the relationship of students as citizens within a university community. The IRs' [Stage 2] reasons were more often concerned with their individual rights in a conflict of power [p. 198].

The results, however, indicate that actual behavior of Stage 2 and Stage 6 males was similar, which raises questions about the discriminant and predictive validity of the stages.

Schwartz, Feldman, Brown, and Heingartner (1969), using a sample of college students, examined differences among Kohlberg's stages of moral development along two dimensions of moral conduct (cheating and helpfulness). Cheating was defined as using prohibited information on a vocabulary test, and helpfulness was defined as a willingness to aid a confederate in an experiment in which such help entailed a loss on the subject's part. Level of moral thought was determined from responses to four situations from Kohlberg's scale. The protocols were scored by Kohlberg using a detailed method. After the level of development was determined, those subjects who scored above the median for the group were classified as "high in level of moral thought" and the others were classified as "low." Of the two dependent variables, only cheating was related to the moral types: Highs cheated significantly less than lows. This result does support a distinction between the high and low end of Kohlberg's scale; however, it provides no evidence for the predictive validity of the individual stages.

Ruma and Mosher (1967) examined the relationship between several measures of guilt and Kohlberg's stages of development. Using a sample of 36 delinquent boys, they measured guilt with four separate indexes (e.g., the Mosher Guilt Scale) and assessed level of moral reasoning with six of Kohlberg's dilemmas. Ruma, who was trained by Kohlberg, scored the situations using the global method. Scores for level of moral reasoning were then intercorrelated with the measures of guilt. Three of the four measures were significantly related to level of moral reasoning, that is, higher moral reasoning was associated with higher measured guilt. Since, however, all but one of the subjects were at Stage 3 or below, the study provides no evidence for the validity of Stages 4, 5, and 6.

Fodor (1972) examined the relationship between delinquency and level of moral development. Using matched groups of delinquents and nondelinquents, he administered nine dilemmas from the Moral Judgment Scale. Protocols were analyzed using the detailed coding system and scores were computed by "weighing percentage usage by each stage by the score assigned that stage: i.e., from 0 to 5 [p. 258]." A comparison of mean scores for both groups revealed that delinquents received significantly lower scores than nondelinquents, thereby providing some validational support for the stages. However, Fodor also noted that mean scores for both groups fell at Stage 3, indicating that dominant stage does not distinguish between delinquents and nondelinquents. It is also worth noting that this study, like the one by Ruma and Mosher (1967), had few, if any, subjects above Stage 4.

Finally, an article by Saltzstein et al. (1972) dealt with the relationship between conformance in an Asch-type situation (cf. Asch, 1951) and levels of moral reasoning.

The sample consisted of 63 seventh-grade boys and girls. Conformity was assessed under two conditions: In the first, goal attainment was dependent upon group cooperation; in the second, it was dependent upon individual effort. Level of moral reasoning was determined with four situations using the interview technique. Protocols were scored by two of the authors and by Kohlberg using both the detailed and global methods. Saltzstein et al. found that Stage 3 subjects conformed most, Stages 2 and 1 next, and Stages 4, 5, and 6 least. These results provide only ambiguous evidence for a systematic relationship between measured level of moral reasoning and conformity. For example, while it is clear that Stage 3 types are conformers, there are no reported differences in the conformance of persons at Stages 4, 5, and 6.

Although this brief review is not exhaustive, it is representative and serves to illustrate several points. First, while Kohlberg's stages are moderately effective in discriminating between unsophisticated and sophisticated reasoning, there seems to be no evidence that each of the six stages by itself has discriminant validity or predictive utility. Second, it is hard to distinguish among the final three stages on the basis of existing evidence. Moreover, few published studies have included any sizable number of Stage 5 and Stage 6 types. In the study by Haan et al. (1968) in which these stages are represented, the results indicate that Stage 2 males are similar to Stage 6 males in their behavior. Finally, although the scale scores seem to have some behavioral correlates, it is not clear, for example, how Stage 3 delinquents (Fodor, 1972) differ from Stage 3 conformers (Saltzstein et al., 1972) or from Stage 2 political demonstrators (Haan et al., 1968); or why Haan et al. (1968) found such a high percentage of Stage 2 subjects among college students, while Schwartz et al. (1969), using a college sample, found none.

Construct Validity

Several lines of evidence are used to support two major assumptions of Kohlberg's model, namely, the invariant sequence and qualitative nature of the six stages of development. This is a problem in construct validation.

Rest, Turiel, and Kohlberg (1969) defined an invariant sequence as one

in which attainment of an advanced stage is dependent on the attainment of each of the preceding stages. It is further assumed that a more advanced stage is not simply an addition to a less advanced stage, but represents a reorganization of less advanced levels [p. 226].

In this article, Rest et al. stated that there are four major forms of evidence for the propositions of invariance and reorganizations:

age trends in various cultures and social classes supporting the ordering of the stages (Kohlberg, 1968); a Guttman "quasi-simplex" pattern in the correlations between the stages (Kohlberg, 1963[a]); and longitudinal studies of individual development (Kohlberg, 1970). Experimental evidence comes from a study by Turiel (1966), which is the point of departure for the present research [p. 226].

Two issues are at stake here (i.e., invariance and reorganization of stages) and each of the four forms of evidence is not necessarily relevant to both propositions. This evidence constitutes the primary construct validity for both Kohlberg's measure of moral judgment; and his theory of moral development; consequently, we examine each form of evidence in detail.

The first type of support for the notion of an invariant developmental sequence in the stages of moral judgment comes from cross-cultural trends. To demonstrate age trends in the development of moral reasoning, Kohlberg (1968) presented some data from an apparently unpublished study of moral reasoning in children in America, Taiwan, Mexico, Turkey, and Yucatan. Quantitative information concerning any of the samples is missing from the article (e.g., sample size is unspecified, characteristics of subjects are omitted, actual percentage scores are absent, range and standard deviation of scores are not reported). Further, there is no description of the method used to determine stage of moral reasoning in the various groups of cultures. The only usable information comes from five graphs (one for each country) which contain the mean percentage of children's responses at each of the six stages of moral reasoning

for three different age levels (10, 13, and 16 years).

The pattern of percentages of judgments on the graphs seem to lend moderate support for age trends across the first three stages. For example, the percentage of Stage 1 judgments does appear to decrease with increasing age (e.g., age 10 = 40%, age 13 = 10%, age 16 = 10%, for the American sample). However, because information concerning the actual number of children tested, the number of responses involved, the method of scoring, and the standard deviation of scores were all unreported, the actual size and significance of this decrease remains unclear. In view of the unknown reliability of the Moral Judgment Scale, this deficiency is an important one. Conclusions concerning the invariance of the first three stages, therefore, are at best tentative and ambiguous.

Evidence to support the invariance of the final three stages is less convincing. Further inspection of the graphs presented by Kohlberg (1968) reveals that, while approximately 7% of the 16-year-olds in America and Mexico used moral reasoning at Stage 6, 1% or less of the 16-year-olds in Taiwan reasoned at this stage. Moreover, *none* of the children in either Turkey or Yucatan were able to reach even Stage 5. Thus, Stage 5 reasoning is missing in two of the five samples, and Stage 6 reasoning is absent in three of the samples. Age trends in Stages 5 and 6 are clearly present only in the United States sample—the same group Kohlberg (1958) used to derive the stages.

In a 1967 study, Kohlberg reported this cross-cultural data in support of invariant age trends in the stages of development. This report presents only two of the original five samples. With regard to the absence of Stage 6 reasoning in the Taiwan sample, Kohlberg observed,

In general, the cross-cultural studies suggest a similar sequence of development in all cultures, although they suggest that the last two stages of thought do not develop clearly in preliterate village or tribal communities [p. 170].

In addition to being an inaccurate description of Taiwanese society, the absence of individuals in the final stages provides no

TABLE 3

QUASI-SIMPLEX CORRELATION MATRIX

Type of moral judgment	(Level I)		(Level II)		(Level III)	
	1	2	3	4	5	6
1	⁻⁻⁻					
2	.55	—				
3	−.41	−.19	—			
4	−.52	−.41	.18	—		
5	−.52	−.58	.09	.00	—	
6	−.37	−.43	−.29	−.07	.23	—

Note. Data from Kohlberg (1958).

evidence for age trends in these stages. Further, these data provide no support for the claim that the stages are universal.

The presence of response shifts in young children lends some support to the notion of age trends in moral reasoning in general. It does not, however, provide support for either the assumption of the sequential invariance of the stages or the qualitative nature of the stages. Kohlberg (1963a) has acknowledged that age trends themselves are not adequate evidence for his sequence of stages. As he observed,

While the age trends indicate that some modes of thought are generally more difficult or advanced than other modes of thought, they do not demonstrate that attainment of each mode of thought is prerequisite to the attainment of the next higher in a hypothetical sequence [pp. 15–16].

Thus, cross-cultural evidence for age trends, even if it were well documented, would provide no support for an invariant sequence of development.

"If our stages of moral thinking are to be taken as supporting the developmental view of moralization," said Kohlberg (1963a), "evidence . . . of sequentiality is required [p. 15]." The second major form of evidence for the invariant sequence comes from a Guttman "quasi-simplex" pattern of correlations among the stages (Kohlberg, 1958, 1963a). Kohlberg (1958) explained that Guttman's simplex is not an appropriate procedure because the stages in his model are not cumulative, but rather each new stage involves a restructuring of a previous stage. Therefore, he adopted the quasi-simplex procedure.

Using the original sample of 72 boys (ages 10 to 16), a single correlation matrix was derived from the intercorrelations of percentages of moral judgments made at each stage. If development proceeds sequentially, then adjacent stages should correlate more highly with each other than with more distant stages. Examination of the correlations in the matrix indicates that the general pattern is in the expected direction: In most cases, correlations decrease as one moves horizontally or vertically from the diagonal in the matrix (see Table 3).

Closer examination reveals, however, that the quasi-simplex provides no direct support for the invariance of the six stages. The correlations were computed for the stages in order, 1 through 6. Suppose, however, that one reversed the order of pairs of stages in each of the three levels (instead of 1, 2; 3, 4; 5, and 6 make the order 2, 1; 4, 3; 6, and 5), how would the pattern of correlations change? Table 4 contains an appropriately revised version of the matrix. As can be seen, the pattern of correlations is similar to that found in the first matrix; thus, each matrix seems to provide support for an invariant sequence of stages.

An even more serious criticism of this form of evidence centers on the sample used. Specifically, the correlations are based on moral reasoning responses of Kohlberg's (1958) original sample. Thus, the same responses used to derive the stage sequence are also used to provide evidence for the sequentiality of the stages. This is analogous to validating a test on the same sample from which it was derived. The lack of independence in the matrix greatly reduces the credibility of the quasi-simplex analysis.

The third form of evidence offered in support of the invariant sequence of Kohlberg's six stages of moral thought comes, according to Rest et al. (1969), from longitudinal studies of individual development. The only relevant published longitudinal data are contained in a study by Kohlberg and Kramer (1969). Based on Kramer's dissertation, the study is a follow-up of Kohlberg's original (1958) sample. Moral judgment scores were obtained for middle-class and lower class men. Within the middle-class sample, 29 subjects were 16 years old, 16 were 20 years old, and 13 were 24 years old. In the lower class sample, 35 subjects were 16 years old, 18 were 20 years old, and 8 were 24 years old. Moral reasoning was determined using the global method. No information is presented concerning the number of dilemmas used, the number of raters, or the interrater reliability.

To demonstrate the developmental invariance of the six stages, Kohlberg and Kramer presented two graphs (for middle-class and lower class boys) of moral judgment profiles at three ages. There were few significant changes in the moral judgment profiles of the samples over time, indicating that development (as Kohlberg defined it) is virtually complete by age 16. In both samples, at ages 16, 20, and 24, Stage 4 responses were more frequent than any other type, suggesting (as do several other studies) that the baseline response for most people is Stage 4. Not only do few people reach Stages 5 and 6, but there is no evidence in the study to show that (a) people who reach Stage 4 have gone through Stages 1, 2, and 3, and (b) people pass through these stages in a specified order. One can equally conclude that individuals skip from stage to stage in a random fashion. Finally, college students actually had lower stage sores than high school students. Although interpreted as a regression, the downward shift seems to indicate that the stage sequence is flexible. Thus, this longitudinal study provides no clear evidence for either the invariant developmental sequence or the reorganization of stages as postulated by Kohlberg.

The final important source of evidence for an invariant sequence comes from a series of experimental studies (Rest, 1973; Rest et al., 1969; Turiel, 1966). Overall, these studies provide some support for both sequential and hierarchical organization of the earlier stages of development. However, they fail to support the sequence for the last three stages. In the first study, Turiel (1966) attempted experimentally to induce changes in the stages of moral reasoning. The second two studies (Rest, 1973; Rest et al., 1969) were attempts to assess preference and comprehension

TABLE 4

REVISED QUASI-SIMPLEX CORRELATION MATRIX

Type of moral judgment	(Level I)		(Level II)		(Level III)	
	2	1	4	3	6	5
2	—					
1	.55	—				
4	−.41	−.52	—			
3	−.19	−.41	.18	—		
6	−.43	−.37	−.07	−.29	—	
5	−.58	−.52	.00	.09	.23	—

for the type of reasoning that characterizes each of Kohlberg's stages.

Turiel's study used 44 middle-class boys ranging in age from 12 years 0 months to 13 years 7 months. The experimental procedure was designed to test two main hypotheses: (a) The six stages of moral judgment form an invariant sequence, and (b) each stage represents a reorganization and displacement of the preceding stages. From these hypotheses, Turiel predicted that (a) because the sequence of development is fixed, subjects will be influenced more by reasoning one stage above their dominant stage than by reasoning further above, and (b) because the stages are progressively reorganized, subjects will reject reasoning at lower stages.

The design involved a pretest, to determine a subject's dominant moral stage; an experimental session, to expose subjects to moral reasoning different from their own; and a posttest interview, to assess the influence of the experimental procedure. The addition of a control group made the design a simple pretest-posttest control group design. While this procedure is unusually robust, allowing for the simultaneous control of a multitude of rival hypotheses (cf. Campbell & Stanley, 1966), a close examination of the study reveals that results were analyzed incorrectly and that the only meaningful comparisons produced negligible results. Because this study is frequently cited as major evidence for the invariant sequence of development, it must be examined in detail.

Initially, six dilemmas from the Moral Judgment Scale were administered to 69 males. Dominant stage of moral reasoning was determined by using both the global rating procedure and the detailed coding method. Because of difficulty in the classification of some people, 25 subjects were dropped from the sample leaving a total of 44 subjects. These subjects were assigned randomly to one of three treatment groups or to a control group ($n = 11$ per cell). After a two-week interval, subjects in the three experimental groups returned for the experimental procedures. During this phase, boys in each group were exposed to moral reasoning one stage below (-1 condition), one stage above ($+1$ condition), or two stages above ($+2$ condition) their own level of moral reasoning. The control group did nothing.

The final step of the experiment (the posttest) was conducted one week after the experimental manipulation when the experimental groups were retested using all nine situations (the same six used in the pretest plus the same three used in the experimental manipulation). The control group was retested with all nine situations three weeks after the pretest.

The obtained results were analyzed in two parts; both analyses are complex and difficult to understand. In the first and more confounded analysis, posttest responses to the same three situations used in the treatment conditions were examined. These scores were called the "direct scores" because "the experimental subjects were directly influenced on those three situations [Turiel, 1966, p. 614]." Direct scores were represented in terms of the average percentage of stage usage. For each of the three treatment groups and for the control group, responses were reported as -1, 0, $+1$, or $+2$ relative to the initial dominant stage of the subjects. Of all possible comparisons, two have direct relevance for the hypotheses of invariance and reorganization: (*a*) comparisons of the number of $+1$ scores in the $+1$ treatment group with the number of -1 scores of the -1 treatment group and the number of $+2$ scores of the $+2$ treatment group and (*b*) comparison of the number of $+1$ scores of the $+1$ treatment group with $+1$ scores of all other groups. That is, according to the hypotheses

of invariance and reorganization, people in the $+1$ treatment group should show a larger treatment effect than people in either the -1 treatment group or the $+2$ treatment group. For the first comparisons, control group scores were subtracted out, although the justification for this procedure is unexplained. A one-tailed t test between the corrected mean scores of the $+2$ treatment group and $+1$ treatment group did reach significance ($t = 3.55$, $p < .005$), suggesting that the $+1$ treatment was more effective than the $+2$ treatment. However, the one-tailed t test between the corrected mean scores of the -1 treatment group and the $+1$ treatment group was not significant ($t = 1.43$, $p < .10$). Thus, there appears to be no significant difference between the $+1$ and -1 treatments; both seem equally effective. (Turiel claimed that his hypothesis was supported because the results reached a "borderline level of significance"; this, however, is not true by usual standards.)

Additional support would be provided for the hypotheses of invariance and reorganization if it could be shown that the $+1$ treatment was generally more effective than the -1 treatment. Turiel (1966) claimed that the number of $+1$ scores of the $+1$ treatment group was higher than the number of $+1$ scores of any other treatment group. This claim is at best ambiguous, however, since the actual ts are unreported. Further, Turiel claimed that the number of -1 scores of the -1 treatment group was not significantly higher than the -1 scores of any other treatment group. For support, he noted that the difference between the -1 scores of both the -1 treatment group and the control group "did not reach significance" ($t = 1.66$, $p < .10$). This difference, however, is larger than the borderline level of significance ($t = 1.43$) offered in support of the major comparison ($+1$ and -1 scores). Thus, this secondary analysis provides only inconclusive support for the hypotheses of invariance and reorganization.

Even if the results were clear-cut, this entire analysis would still lack credibility because it is also confounded by a memory effect. During the experimental conditions, subjects were told possible responses to three moral dilemmas; in the posttest, they were asked to provide responses to the same dilemmas. Thus, rather than demonstrating the effects of the treatments, results obtained from subjects' responses may merely reflect the effects of memory, learning, and suggestion.

Turiel's second and only valid analysis compared pretest and posttest change scores. Each subject's scores on the six-item pretest were subtracted from his posttest scores for the same six items. This change score, called the "indirect score," reflected the effect of the experimental procedures. That is, pretest–posttest changes in an individual's moral reasoning were considered to reflect the exposure to reasoning different from his own.

Mean indirect scores were presented in a table according to treatment (-1, $+1$, $+2$, control) and stage level relative to pretest dominant stage (-1, 0, $+1$, $+2$). No variability measures were presented. There are three important points to note about the table. First, it is impressive in terms of the small effect due to the treatments. The mean change for all groups (disregarding signs) was 2.2%; the modal change was zero. It is little wonder, then, that Turiel reported "The evidence is only suggestive since significant findings were minimal [1966, p. 616]."

The second point to note in this table is that the mean change scores of the control group illustrate the probable unreliability of the Moral Judgment Scale. As noted above, none of the treatments produced any clearcut effects. Thus, it is interesting to examine the change scores of the control group. In the interval between the pretest and the posttest, the dominant stage scores of the control group decreased by 6.1%. This change was the largest obtained in the study. Furthermore, the largest change for any treatment group was a 5.7% move by the -1 group to the -1 stage, indicating that if there were any differences, the -1 treatment was more effective than $+1$ treatment. The second largest treatment change was a 4.5% increase in the $+1$ scores of the $+1$ treatment group. Over the same period of time, however, the -1 scores of the control group also increased

by 4.5%. This suggests that the control group spontaneously regressed in its moral judgments as far as the critical treatment group progressed. Thus, the low reliability of the dependent variable may have confounded the obtained results. Consequently, the instability of the moral judgment scores leaves open to question any interpretation of the observed changes in the treatment groups.

Third, the only comparisons that seem directly relevant to the hypothesis that the stages form an invariant sequence are those between the $+1$ change scores of the $+1$ treatment group and the -1 and $+2$ change scores of the comparable treatment groups. Once again, according to the hypotheses of invariance and reorganization, the $+1$ treatment should show a larger effect than either the -1 treatment group or the $+2$ treatment group.

The one-tailed t test indicated that the corrected mean [4] $+2$ change score of the $+2$ treatment group was statistically smaller than the $+1$ change score of the $+1$ treatment group ($t = 2.70$, $p < .025$). A second one-tailed t test between the corrected mean -1 change score of the -1 treatment group and the $+1$ change score of the $+1$ treatment group was not significant, although Turiel claimed that it reached a "borderline level of significance ($t = 1.46$, $p < .10$) [1966, p. 616]." Thus, the evidence for invariance of sequence or reorganization of stages is unconvincing.

Overall, Turiel's study provides only minimal support for the hypotheses of invariance and reorganization in the development of moral judgment. The results are qualified by several considerations. First, his article presented only two t tests directly relevant to the hypotheses of invariance and reorganization, and the actual differences obtained for these crucial comparisons were not significant. Second, treatment effects were quite small. While not necessarily problematic in itself, when interpreted in light of the possible unreliability of the dependent variable (the control group scores changed as much

---

[4] Corrected mean change scores were obtained by subtracting control group mean change scores from treatment group mean change scores.

as the treatment group scores), the obtained significance levels become suspect. Additionally, the −1 treatment was at least as effective in eliciting change as was the +1 treatment. Third, due to constraints of the experimental design, none of Turiel's subjects were at the Stage 5 or 6 levels (since the subjects were presented with reasoning two stages above their present stage, no subject could be higher than Stage 4). This leaves entirely untested the question of the invariance of the final three stages. Finally, other studies (using similar designs) indicate that it is possible to induce significant changes in moral judgment that run counter to developmental expectations (e.g., Bandura & McDonald, 1963). Thus, although Turiel's study is often cited as providing support for an invariant sequence in the development of moral judgment, in fact it does not.

The final two studies (Rest, 1973; Rest et al., 1969) attempt to show that the sequence of the stages of development form a hierarchical organization. The hierarchy is conceived of as one of complexity; each higher stage is viewed as logically more complex than the lower ones. The implication is that moral development concerns the capacity for making increasingly more sophisticated moral judgments. Both studies provide some evidence that the stages, as defined by Kohlberg, constitute a hierarchy of logical complexity. That is, the higher stages do seem to be more logically complex than the lower ones. However, the evidence does not demonstrate that actual development follows these six stages.

Both studies are similar in design and attempt to assess preference and comprehension for the types of reasoning characteristic of each of the stages in Kohlberg's model. The first study (Rest, 1973) contained 45 fifth- and eighth-grade children; the second (Rest et al., 1969) used 47 twelfth-grade students. The subjects were first administered a subset of dilemmas from the Moral Judgment Scale and their dominant stages were determined. They were then grouped by stage and administered a booklet containing two of the remaining dilemmas. After reading the situations, the subjects read the "advice" of

six friends. The advice of each friend was a pro and con argument for the solution to the dilemma. Each of the three sets of arguments was characteristic of the reasoning of stages below the subject's dominant stage (−1), directly above the subject's dominant stage (+1), and two above the subject's dominant stage (+2). Thus, the reasoning formed a continuum of simple-to-complex moral reasoning. After reading these arguments, subjects were asked to state which advice they thought best (preference) and to recapitulate the advice of each friend (comprehension).

Preference was consistently greater for moral reasoning higher than the subject's dominant stage. Comprehension was greater for the lower stages and decreased with higher stages. Thus, while the data do suggest that there is some shift in preference and comprehension (the subjects prefer stages above their own and comprehend those below), they do not show that the normal course of development (either within the individual or among groups) follows the six stages as defined by Kohlberg.

Counter Evidence

Few researchers employing Kohlberg's cognitive-developmental framework have reported findings which contradict the model. How can this relative absence of negative findings be explained? First, independent validation is made difficult by the nature of the scale itself. It has never been published and there is no readily available source of information describing its administration and scoring. Further, the methods and procedures concerning its use have changed continuously, although these modifications have not been publicly reported. The latest method of scoring is available only from Kohlberg himself. Second, the dearth of negative evidence may reflect the nature of the American research enterprise. As Entwisle (1972) remarked,

Even a complete survey of the literature can be misleading . . . because of the often remarked tendency of American authors to publish only positive findings, with lesser findings never reaching an editor's desk or even being rejected there [p. 385].

There are several considerations which suggest that the evolution of moral reasoning may not be as Kohlberg described it. First, one can question Kohlberg's (1963a) statement that the various stages of moral reasoning

represent structures emerging from the interaction of the child with his social environment, rather than directly reflecting external structures given by the child's culture [p. 30].

Several experimental studies (e.g., Bandura & McDonald, 1963; Cowan, Langer, Heavenrich, & Nathanson, 1969; Prentice, 1972) have argued that moral judgments are directly affected by social influence. These studies all demonstrate that it is possible to induce changes in moral judgments that run counter to cognitive-developmental predictions. Bandura and McDonald, for example, found that "children's judgmental responses are readily modifiable, particularly through the utilization of adult modeling cues [1963, p. 280]." While interpretations of the meaning of these results have been variable (cf. Cowan et al., 1969), the implications of the data are clear—modes of moral thought are subject to social influence; consequently, one would not necessarily expect them to follow a preset order.

A second line of evidence suggesting that Kohlberg's six stages do not form an invariant sequence comes from cross-sectional and longitudinal data (Holstein, 1972, see also Footnote 3). Over a three-year period, Holstein administered a written version of the Moral Judgment Scale (five dilemmas) to 53 families (children ages 13 to 16 and parents). Protocols were scored by an experienced coder (trained by Kohlberg).

Holstein's (1972, see Footnote 3) research is important for two reasons: It provides a detailed look at some cross-sectional and longitudinal data on moral reasoning, and it offers a systematic study of sex differences using the Moral Judgment Scale. In general, neither the cross-sectional, longitudinal nor sex-difference data support the notion of an invariant developmental sequence. For example, Holstein's data provide no direct evidence that development over the three-year period proceeded in a stepwise fashion; they suggest that there was considerable skipping of stages and much regression among the final

stages for both sexes. Furthermore, cross-sectional sex differences in modal response did not support the notion of an invariant sequence. For both the 16-year-old sample and the adult samples, the modal response for males was Stage 4, while at the same age the modal response for females was Stage 3. Kohlberg and Kramer (1969) noted this in their longitudinal study:

while girls are moving from high school or college to motherhood, sizeable proportions of them are remaining at Stage 3, while their male age mates are dropping Stage 3 in favor of the stages above it. Stage 3 personal concordance morality is a functional morality for housewives and mothers; it is not for businessmen and professionals [p. 108].

The obvious implication, according to the stage model, is that females are less developed in their moral reasoning than males.

The absence of support for a six-stage model does not imply that there are no trends in moral development. It simply indicates that Kohlberg's six specific stages may not be useful. There is some evidence to suggest that the reasoning which characterizes Kohlberg's final two stages can be viewed as alternative, but equally valid, forms of moral thought. For example, Hogan (1970) developed a 35-item scale designed to measure the disposition to adopt an instrumental or utilitarian attitude toward the law, as opposed to a disposition to invoke intuitive principles (Stages 5 and 6). The scale discriminates strongly between persons whose vocational choices reflect a belief in law and established procedures (e.g., policemen, ROTC seniors, etc.) and persons who believe in civil disobedience as a means for promoting social change. In addition, there are clear-cut personality differences between individuals characterized by both types of reasoning. Persons who invoke intuitive principles tend to be independent, innovative, and form creating; however, they also tend to be impulsive, opportunistic, and irresponsible. Persons who adopt utilitarian attitudes toward law are seen as reasonable, helpful, and dependable; on the other hand, they are also conventional and resistant to change. On the whole, the more mature individuals tend to cluster in the center of this dimension.

We have reviewed several sources of evidence which conflict with Kohlberg's model of moral development. These include results from experimental, cross-sectional, longitudinal, and personological research. Although most of this review concerned the absence of evidence for the invariance of Kohlberg's six stages of moral thought, there is also evidence indicating that the stages may not be invariant.

DISCUSSION

Research in the area of moral development has important implications for the understanding and explanation of human conduct. A great deal of work has been done using a cognitive model of moral development proposed by Kohlberg. As we have tried to show, however, the research done within this framework is beset with a multitude of problems which detract from the model's usefulness.

We divided these problems into four main areas. First, the intuitive derivation of the six stages of moral reasoning, which provide a foundation for this approach, resulted in an arbitrary set of stages whose general meaningfulness is not yet clear. Further, the scale developed to measure these stages of moral reasoning lacks standardization of both administration and scoring. Because the number of dilemmas used differs across studies, the actual content of the Moral Judgment Scale is constantly changing. This raises questions about the basis for comparison of results across studies; in effect, each study employs a unique scale. In the absence of evidence demonstrating that each dilemma taps the same cognitive dimension, there is no basis for making comparisons among studies using the Moral Judgment Scale. In addition to this limitation, meaningfulness is further attenuated by the absence of a standard scoring procedure. Until (a) a relationship between the global and detailed scoring schemes is established, (b) the reasons for using the five different schemes are elucidated, and (c) some general norms are published, interpretations of results obtained with the Moral Judgment Scale are tenuous. Finally and perhaps most importantly, the general unavailability of the scale discourages independent

research. Since the Moral Judgment Scale is the only means of assessing Kohlberg's stages, the absence of a complete and systematic published exposition of the scale's derivation, content, and psychometric properties is inexplicable.

Second, the reliability of the scale needs to be demonstrated. After 15 years of research with the Moral Judgment Scale, there are *no* reported reliability estimates for the scale itself. Further, evidence from experimental studies indicates that scores on the scale fluctuate greatly even over short periods of time. The only reported estimates are for the scoring scheme and most studies fail to report independent estimates. Uncertainty about the accuracy of measurement limits the utility of the measure.

A third problem concerns the predictive validity of the model. The validities of both the Moral Judgment Scale and Kohlberg's conceptual model rest on the assumption that moral development follows a six-stage invariant sequence and that the Moral Judgment Scale can assess these six stages. We have reviewed several studies representative of attempts to relate scores on the Moral Judgment Scale to nontest criteria. Despite some evidence suggesting that general trends in development are related to behavior, there is no clearly demonstrated connection between moral judgment, as measured by the Moral Judgment Scale, and moral action. Overall, predictive validity is minimal. There is no evidence to indicate that the six distinct stages, and particularly the final three stages, add predictive power to the scale or model beyond that which would be obtained with a simple dichotomous classification of high–low or mature–immature. This would not be particularly troublesome if there were no theoretical reason to expect a relationship between moral reasoning and moral behavior. However, the relationship, if any, between moral reasoning and moral behavior has not been clarified.

Finally, there seems to be little actual construct validation for the scale or model. A careful examination of the four types of evidence offered in support of the invariant sequence (viz., cross-cultural, statistical, longitudinal, and experimental) revealed that in actuality results do not support clearly the major assumptions of the developmental model. General cross-cultural age trends in early development provide no support for qualitative differences between stages or their sequential invariance. While the pattern of correlations in the quasi-simplex provided some support for the sequence, order of the stages within levels does not seem immutable. Longitudinal data demonstrated only that most males are at Stage 4 morality. Not only did the data fail to show that people go through the stages in a preset order, but it also failed to demonstrate that people go through each of the distinct stages at all. Furthermore, there is no support for the view that each new stage is a reintegration of the previous one and therefore qualitatively different.

Not only is there no clear-cut evidence supporting the assumptions of invariance of stages and their hierarchical nature, but there is also evidence suggesting that these assumptions may be incorrect. Several researchers have demonstrated that different types of moral reasoning may be learned. Further, the cross-sectional and longitudinal data from Holstein's study provide evidence suggesting that people do not develop through the stages of moral reasoning in the order set by Kohlberg. Finally, there is some evidence questioning the order of the final stages. Hogan (1970), for example, maintained that contractual legalistic (positive law) and principled conscience (higher law) moralities are both equally defensible moral postures. He also provided evidence that personality differences are important determinants of an individual's style of moral reasoning. Several lines of evidence, then, seem to suggest that moral development may not proceed in the fashion described by Kohlberg's model.

In view of these many problems, it is difficult to make a definitive statement about the utility of Kohlberg's cognitive-developmental model of moral development. After 15 years of research, the general lack of evidence for the model is suggestive. The possibility remains that the stages do reflect actual development and that the general lack

of evidence reflects the inadequacy of the measuring device used to assess the stages of moral reasoning. However, without additional information on the scale or an alternative way to assess stages of reasoning, we cannot know whether it is the scale, the model, or both that is problematic. Thus, we can only conclude that the value of the model remains to be demonstrated.

REFERENCES

Anastasi, A. *Psychological testing.* (3rd ed.) New York: Macmillan, 1968.

Asch, S. E. Effects of group pressure upon the modification and distortion of judgments. In H. Guetzkow (Ed.), *Groups, leadership and men.* Pittsburgh: Carnegie Press, 1951.

Baldwin, J. M. *Social and ethical interpretations in mental development.* New York: Macmillan, 1906.

Bandura, A., & McDonald, F. J. Influence of social reinforcement and the behavior of models in shaping children's moral judgments. *Journal of Abnormal and Social Psychology,* 1963, 67, 274–281.

Boehm, L. The development of conscience: A comparison of students in Catholic parochial schools and in public schools. *Child Development,* 1962, 33, 591–602.

Campbell, D. T., & Stanley, J. C. *Experimental and quasi-experimental designs for research.* Chicago: Rand McNally, 1966.

Cowan, P. A., Langer, J., Heavenrich, J., & Nathanson, M. Social learning and Piaget's cognitive theory of moral development. *Journal of Personality and Social Psychology,* 1969, 11, 261–274.

Cronbach, L. J. Test validation. In R. L. Thorndike (Ed.), *Educational measurement.* (2nd ed.) Washington, D.C.: American Council on Education, 1971.

Cronbach, L. J., & Meehl, P. E. Construct validity in psychological tests. *Psychological Bulletin,* 1955, 52, 281–302.

Entwisle, D. R. To dispel fantasies about fantasy-based measures of achievement motivation. *Psychological Bulletin,* 1972, 77, 377–391.

Fodor, E. M. Moral judgment in Negro and white adolescents. *Journal of Social Psychology,* 1969, 79, 289–291.

Fodor, E. M. Delinquency and susceptibility to social influence among adolescents as a function of moral development. *Journal of Social Psychology,* 1972, 86, 257–260.

Jensen, A. R. The reliability of projective techniques: Review of the literature. *Acta Psychologica,* 1959, 16, 108–136.

Haan, N., Smith, M. B., & Block, J. Moral reasoning of young adults: Political-social behavior, family background, and personality correlates. *Journal of Personality and Social Psychology,* 1968, 10, 183–201.

Hogan, R. A dimension of moral judgment. *Journal of Consulting and Clinical Psychology,* 1970, **35,** 205–212.

Holstein, C. B. The relation of children's moral judgment level to that of their parents and to communications patterns in the family. In R. C. Smart & M. S. Smart (Eds.), *Reading in child development and relationships.* New York: Macmillan, 1972.

Keasey, C. B. Social participation as a factor in the moral development of preadolescents. *Developmental Psychology,* 1971, **5,** 216–220.

Kohlberg, L. The development of modes of moral thinking and choice in the years ten to sixteen. Unpublished doctoral dissertation, University of Chicago, 1958.

Kohlberg, L. The development of children's orientations toward a moral order: I. Sequence in the development of moral thought. *Vita Humana,* 1963, **6,** 11–33. (a)

Kohlberg, L. Moral development and identification. In H. W. Stevenson (Ed.), *Child psychology, 62nd yearbook of the National Society for the Study of Education.* Chicago: University of Chicago Press, 1963. (b)

Kohlberg, L. Development of moral character and moral ideology. In M. L. Hoffman & L. W. Hoffman (Eds.), *Review of child development research.* Vol. 1. New York: Russell Sage Foundation, 1964.

Kohlberg, L. Cognitive stages and preschool education. *Human Development,* 1966, **9,** 5–17. (a)

Kohlberg, L. Moral education in the schools: A developmental view. *The School Review,* 1966, **74,** 1–30. (b)

Kohlberg, L. Moral and religious education and the public schools: A developmental view. In T. R. Sizer (Ed.), *The role of religion in public education.* Boston: Houghton Mifflin, 1967.

Kohlberg, L. The child as a moral philosopher. *Psychology Today,* 1968, **2,** 25–30.

Kohlberg, L. Stage and sequence: The cognitive-developmental approach to socialization. In D. A. Goslin (Ed.), *Handbook of socialization theory and research.* Chicago: Rand McNally, 1969.

Kohlberg, L., & Kramer, R. Continuities and discontinuities in childhood and adult moral development. *Human Development,* 1969, **12,** 93–120.

MacRae, D., Jr. A test of Piaget's theories of moral development. *Journal of Abnormal and Social Psychology,* 1954, **49,** 14–18.

Magowan, S. A., & Lee, T. Some sources of error in the use of the projective method for the measurement of moral judgment. *British Journal of Psychology,* 1970, **61,** 535–543.

Masling, J. The influence of situational and interpersonal variables in projective testing. *Psychological Bulletin,* 1960, **57,** 65–85.

Mead, G. H. *Mind, self, and society.* Chicago: University of Chicago Press, 1934.

Piaget, J. *The moral judgment of the child.* London: Routledge & Kegan Paul, 1932.

Prentice, N. M. The influence of live and symbolic modeling on promoting moral judgment of adolescent delinquents. *Journal of Abnormal Psychology,* 1972, **80,** 157–161.

Rest, J. R. The hierarchical nature of moral judgment: A study of patterns of comprehension and preference of moral stages. *Journal of Personality,* 1973, **41,** 86–109.

Rest, J., Turiel, E., & Kohlberg, L. Level of moral development as a determinant of preference and comprehension of moral judgments made by others. *Journal of Personality,* 1969, **37,** 225–252.

Ruma, E. H., & Mosher, D. L. Relationship between moral judgment and guilt in delinquent boys. *Journal of Abnormal Psychology,* 1967, **72,** 122–127.

Saltzstein, H. D., Diamond, R. M., & Belenky, M. Moral judgment level and conformity behavior. *Developmental Psychology,* 1972, **7,** 327–336.

Schwartz, S. H., Feldman, K. A., Brown, M. E., & Heingartner, A. Some personality correlates of conduct in two situations of moral conflict. *Journal of Personality,* 1969, **37,** 41–57.

Stanley, J. C. Reliability. In R. L. Thorndike (Ed.), *Educational measurement.* (2nd ed.) Washington, D.C.: American Council on Education, 1971.

Turiel, E. An experimental test of the sequentiality of developmental stages in the child's moral judgments. *Journal of Personality and Social Psychology,* 1966, **3,** 611–618.

(Received October 22, 1973)

Virtues and Habits in Moral Education*

R.S. Peters

Most moral philosophers since Aristotle have conceived of moral development in terms of the acquisition of virtues and have regarded habit-formation as an essential part of this process. Indeed Aristotle's celebrated 'paradox' of moral education dealt with the emergence of a rational form of virtuous conduct out of unreflective habits. Kohlberg, by contrast, regards what he calls 'a bag of virtues' as unimportant in morality. He also claims that processes of habit-formation, by means of which they are assumed to be established, are of secondary significance. The considerations which led him to this somewhat surprising view are as follows:

1. The Hartshorne-May investigation cast doubt upon the existence of stable character traits. In the case of honesty, low predictability was shown of cheating in one situation from cheating in another. The tendency of children to cheat depended on the risk of detection and the effort required to cheat. Noncheaters thus appeared to be more cautious rather than more honest. Peer-group approval and example also seemed to be an important determinant.[1]

2. Kohlberg claims that his own studies show that the decision not to cheat has something to do with the awareness of universal moral principles, not with principles concerned with the badness of cheating *per se*. Other good predictors of resistance to cheating are factors to do with ego strength. He concludes that the crucial determinants of moral development are cognitive. There are different conceptual levels in

---

*This article is an abridged version of "Moral Development: A Plea for Pluralism" published in *Cognitive Development and Epistemology* edited by Theodore Mischel (New York and London: Academic Press, 1971).

morality, and stability of character depends upon the level attained by the individual.

A. Traits and Principles

Before discussing the role of habit in morality, something must first be said about the dichotomy which Kohlberg makes between traits and principles. In his account of moral development a principled morality is contrasted with a morality of character traits. This is a strange contrast. Surely, being just or fair are paradigm cases of character traits. They are as much character traits as being honest, which is the virtue with which justice is often contrasted in Kohlberg's work. Yet fairness and justice are also paradigm cases of moral principles. To call something a "trait" of character is simply to suggest that someone has made a rule—for example, of honesty or of justice—his own. Whether a rule, which can also be regarded as a trait of character if it is internalized, is a principle depends on the function which the rule or consideration, which is personalized in the trait, performs. To call justice or concern for others principles is to suggest that backing or justification is provided by them for some more specific rule or course of action. We might, for instance, appeal to considerations of justice to back up a decision to give women the vote; gambling might be condemned because of the suffering which it brought on the relatives of gamblers. In these cases, justice and concern for others would be functioning as principles. Honesty, too, often functions as a principle in that it can be appealed to in condemning fraud and many other forms of deceit. The contrast, therefore, between traits of character and principles rests on no clear view of how the term "principle" functions.

There is, however, an important contrast which Kohlberg does not make between traits, such as honesty and justice, and motives such as concern for others. As we shall see, there are important differences between virtues which are motives and those which are character traits. But one obvious difference needs to be noted at this point: that concern for others develops much earlier in a child's life and does not require the same level of conceptual development to be operative as does justice or even honesty. *Prima facie*, too, there are grounds for thinking that it can be learnt or encouraged by the example of others. Of course, concern for others can be exhibited at different levels which vary according to a person's imagination and sophistication about what constitutes harm or welfare. But it certainly can get a foothold in a person's moral life earlier than justice, because it is not necessarily connected with rules and social arrangements, as is justice. This was one of the reasons which led Hume to distinguish the artificial from the natural virtues. It may, of course, take time for children to grasp that reasons for rules can fall under it *as a principle*. Kohlberg's stage theory may apply to it insofar as it comes to function as a principle—that is, as providing considerations that give backing to rules. But a different account must be given of how children become sensitized to such considerations than is given of how they come to be concerned about justice.

In talking about a principled morality we must not only distinguish motives from character traits such as justice and honesty. We must also note the peculiarities of a certain class of character traits that are both content-free and which do not, like motives, introduce teleological considerations. These are traits such as consistency, persistence, courage, determination, integrity, and the like. They are of a higher order and relate to the ways in which rules are followed or purposes pursued; they prescribe no particular rules or purposes, as do honesty and ambition. In ordinary language this group of character traits is intimately connected with what we call "the will." Kohlberg suggests the "ego-strength" variables correlate with the development of a principled morality. But this must necessarily be the case, for part of our understanding of a "principled morality" is that people should stick to their principles in the face of temptation, ridicule, and the like. But a different account must surely be given of their development than of that of a virtue like justice, for though it may be a necessary condition of a stable, principled morality that people should both be able to understand what justice is and assent to it, and that it should come to function as a principle for them in the sense of providing justifying reasons for a whole range of behavior, it is nevertheless not sufficient. There are many who can do all this but who still lack the courage, determination, integrity, and persistence to carry out what they see as just.

It looks, therefore, as if there is little validity in Kohlberg's distinction between principles and character traits. But a more positive finding of this brief examination is that there are distinct classes of virtues, the differences between which may prove to be important in considering the relationships between virtue and habit. To summarize, there are (a) highly specific virtues, such as punctuality, tidiness, and perhaps honesty, which are connected with specific types of acts, and which lack any built-in reason for acting in the manner prescribed—that is, are not motives, unlike (b) virtues, such as compassion, which are also motives for action. There are, then, (c) more artificial virtues, such as justice and tolerance, which involve more general condiderations to do with rights and institutions. Finally, there are (d) virtues of a higher order, such as courage, integrity, perseverance, and the like, which have to be exercised in the face of counter-inclinations.

When, therefore, Kohlberg criticizes a character trait type of morality on account of the specificity of character traits, it looks as if his criticism is based on the peculiar features of the character trait of honesty, on which most research has been done. Dishonesty has to be understood in terms of fairly specific situations such as cheating, lying and fraud. This is a feature of all type (a) virtues. Other virtues and vices, however, such a benevolence, cruelty, and integrity, are not tied down in this way to specific types of action, although about all such virtues the more sophisticated point could be made that what is to count as cases of them will vary from culture to culture. Kohlberg's criticism, therefore, depends on the pecularities of a particular class of character traits.

In general, however, this criticism follows analytically from the meaning attached to a principled morality; for principles pick out very general considerations, such an unfairness or harm to people, which can be appealed to in support of a number of rules. As many type (a) character traits, such as thrift, punctuality, chastity, and the like, represent internalized social rules whose justification depends upon appeal to more general considerations picked out by principles, their specificity, when compared with principles, is not surprising, for it is implicit in what we mean by a principle. But here again this depends very much on the examples taken. Punctuality and thrift manifestly require some further justification in terms of principles. Fairness and unselfishness, on the other hand, are also character traits, but there is nothing particularly specific about them. Indeed, they are internalizations of considerations which would normally be appealed to as principles. Consistency, integrity, determination, and the like are, as we have seen, character traits as well, but of a higher order and in no way tied down to specific acts.

It is important to realize too, that although principles pick out abstract considerations that can be appealed to in contexts of justification and moral uncertainty, for the most part they enter into our lives in a much more concrete, specific way. For most of us, for instance, the principle that we should consider people's interests is to be understood by reference to specific roles such as that of a father, teacher, citizen, etc., with the specific duties that are constitutive of them, and in following the more general rules that are internalized in the form of punctuality, tidiness, thriftiness, and the like. This was a point well made by Mill in his stress on the role of "secondary principles" in morality.

B. The Role of Habit

Kohlberg's contention that specific character traits, such as honesty, which function as habits, are of little significance in the moral life, is paralleled by his claim that learning theorists have produced no evidence of the influence of early forms of habit training on adult behavior.[2] Most of the evidence is negative—the effect of exposure to Boy Scouts, Sunday School, etc., and of the effect of earliness and amount of parental training on habits such as obedience, neatness, and so on.[3] This type of learning seems to be short-term, situation-specific, and reversible.

This lack of importance assigned to habit goes against a whole tradition of thought about moral development stemming from Aristotle. He too assigned a central place to cognitive factors in moral development insofar as he characterized this in terms of the gradual emergence of practical reason. But he conceded a major role to habits in morals and in moral education. He maintained[4] that the capacity given to us by nature to receive virtue is brought to maturity by habit. We acquire virtue by practice. Just as we become builders by building houses, so "we become just by doing just acts, temperate by doing temperate acts, brave by doing brave acts"[5]. It is therefore of great importance to see that children are trained in one set of habits rather than another. In their early years they cannot, of course, act bravely or justly in a full sense for they lack the appropriate knowledge and dispositions. But through instruction, praise and blame, reward and punishment by men who are already courageous and just, they can acquire action patterns which gradually become informed by a growing understanding of what they are doing and why.

How then is habit related to virtue in the life of a developed person, and how can a morality, which is firmly rooted in habit, provide the appropriate basis for a more rational reflective type of morality? An examination of the concept of "habit" may indicate answers to these questions which are also compatible with Kohlberg's contentions about habit formation; for it may well be the case that his contentions depend upon a limited conception of "habit" and on the peculiarities of the facets of morality on which he has concentrated his attention.

In order to raise questions about the role of habit in morality, it is necessary to distinguish three applications of the concept of "habit."[6]

We can speak, first, in a descriptive way about a person's habits or what he does habitually. Second, we can use explanatory phrases such as "out of habit," "from force of habit," and "a matter of sheer habit." Third, we can talk of certain things being learnt by a process of "habituation." Let us consider each of these applications of the concept of "habit" in relation to the types of virtue already distinguished in Section A.

Habits

When we use "habit" as a descriptive term, we are making certain suggestions about behavior. We are claiming, first, that it is something that the individual has done before and is likely to do again. It implies repetition arising from a settled disposition. Second, we suggest that it is the sort of thing that the individual *can* carry out more or less automatically. He does not have to reflect about it before he does it, to plan it in any way, or to decide to do it. But he may. If one of a man's habits is to get up early, it does not follow that he will not reflect about it on a particular occasion. It only suggests that he will not *have* to reflect on what he is doing on a particular occasion, that he *can* do this more or less automatically. Needless to say, also, there are many manifestations of automatic behavior that are not usually habits—for example, automatic writing.

What forms of behavior can be termed "habits"? Etymologically, the word suggests forms of behavior that one has in the way in which one has clothes. Habits, like clothes, express how a man holds himself. They thus can refer to his demeanor as well as to his clothes. Nowadays, we tend to confine the word to a person's settled dispostions which manifest themselves in behavior which, like clothes, he can put or take off at will. We do not, therefore, call dreaming a habit, nor do we speak in this way of stomach aches and facial tics. We thus can say that a man is in the habit of going for a walk before breakfast, that talking philosophy in the pub is one of his habits, or that he is habitually punctual and polite.

There are some forms of behavior which may be exercises of dispositions which we do not call "habits." For instance, we do not talk about sympathetic or angry behavior as "habits." This is because these forms of behavior are too deeply connected with our nature; they are not the sorts of behavior that we can put on and take off at will, like clothes. Also they are not the sorts of behavior which, even if repeated, we tend to perform automatically. If we did, they would cease to qualify as being sympathetic or angry in a full-blooded sense.

It might be thought that there is an incompatibility between habits and intelligence or reasoning. But if there is such a clash, it is not with this application of the concept of "habit." Ryle,[7] for instance, sees such an incompatibility. But that is because he does not distinguish between the three applications of the concept of "habit." He slides between talking descriptively of habits, which he regards as single-track disposition, and the use of explanatory phrases such as "out of habit." He also seems to think that all habits are developed by a particular form of habituation, namely drill, and incorporates this mistaken empirical assumption into his concepts of "habit." In actual fact, not all habits are single-track dispositions. Playing bridge or chess could be regarded as among a person's habits, and there is nothing single-track or unintelligent about activities of this sort. Indeed, there are writers who go up to the opposite extreme. Oakeshott, for instance, regards plasticity as one of the main features of habits. To use his own words: "Like prices in a free market, habits of moral behaviour show no revolutionary changes because they are never at rest."[8]

Habitual forms of behavior can involve reasoning as well as intelligence in the sense of adaptability. Indeed, we can talk about a habit of reflecting upon conduct.

Is there any reason, then, why virtues should not be described as habits, and are they of much importance in morality? Surely the importance of established habits in the moral life is manifest. Life would be very exhausting if, in moral situations, we always had to reflect, deliberate, and make decisions. It would also be very difficult to conduct our social lives if we could not count on a fair stock of habits such as punctuality, politeness, honesty, and the like, in other people. This applies particularly to those type *a* character traits, such as punctuality and tidiness, which are internalized social rules.

Habits, however, are not sufficient for the conduct of a person's moral life for at least three reasons. The first reason is that the different classes of virtues distinguished in Section A differ in their relation to habit, and it is important to understand what underlies Kohlberg's claim that only some situation-specific types of virtue, which form part of the "content" of morality, can be habits. Type(*a*)virtues, such as punctuality, tidiness, and perhaps honesty, seem to be the most obvious class of virtues which can be called habits, because they are connected with specific types of acts; so there seems to be no difficulty about the condition of automaticity being sometimes fulfilled. They also lack any built-in reason for acting in the manner prescribed. They are to be contrasted with type(*b*)virtues, such as compassion, which are also motives for action. It seems essential to the exercise of such virtues that feelings should be aroused, that one's mind should be actively employed on bringing about specific states of affairs. The concept of "habit" therefore cannot get a grip on virtues such as these. Nor can it get a grip on type(*c*), more artificial virtues, such as justice and tolerance, for a rather different reason. Being just, tolerant, or prudent involves much in the way of thought. Considerations have to be weighed and assessed.

The suggestion, therefore, that acting justly might be one of a man's habits sounds strange. Finally, type(*d*), higher-order virtues, such as courage, integrity, perseverance, and the like, would also be incongruously described as habits, because such virtues have to be exercised in the fact of counter-inclinations. It is, of course, part of our understanding of what can be considered a virtue that there should be counter-inclinations which might be operative. Otherwise there would be no point in the virtue in general. But it is only essential to some virtues, namely, those that involve some kind of self-control, that counter-inclinations must be present when they are exercised. Now insofar as this condition is realized, as it is in the case of virtues such as courage, it seems inappropriate to think of them as habits, for they require active attention. This would not be true, however, of all higher-order virtues—for example, consistency, which might be regarded as a habit.

The second reason for the insufficency of habit in the moral life is that those virtues which we can call habits have an incompleteness about them because the reason for behaving in the ways which they mark out is not internal to them, which is why we do not call virtues such as thrift, punctuality, and politeness motives. It is not suprising, therefore, that the Hartshorne-May enquiry found that children saw being honest as a way of escaping punishment or gaining approval. These may not be particularly good reasons for acting honestly, but some reason is required; people do not act *out* of honesty, as they act out of jealousy or compassion. Honesty, in other words, is a trait of character, not a motive. Ideally, acting honestly should be connected with considerations which provide a rationale for being honest, rather than considerations which are manifestly extrinsic to this form of behavior, such as the avoidance of punishment or the obtaining of approval. But such rationale is beyond the understanding of young children. So it is not surprising that, insofar as they are honest, they are honest for some extrinsic reason, as Aristotle saw in his account of how virtues are acquired under instruction.

This introduces a third point about the insufficiency of habits—when people are in non-routine situations, habits, by definition, can no longer carry them through. The question then arises, with virtues such as honesty and punctuality, as to what considerations become operative. If, as in the case of the children in the Hartshorne-May enquiry, or that of the Spartans when they went abroad, the sanctions of punishment and social approval are withdrawn, they may not continue to be honest. In their case the extrinsic considerations which supported their honesty were not such that honesty seemed sensible to them when being dishonest had no manifest disadvantages and some short-term advantage. Suppose, however, that, as Aristotle put it, "they understand the reason why of things," and connect being honest with some more general principle about human relationships—for example, respect for persons, concern for finding out what is true. They might then link particular manifestations of honesty, such as not cheating, or not lying, with further considerations falling under these principles. This would be what Kohlberg calls having a principled morality which, he claims, is the only stable sort. He usually links this with the acceptance of the principle of justice, but this is only a particular case of such a morality. What is important is that considerations deriving from such principles are reasons which always exist for various ways of being honest. Possible censure or punishment, on the other hand, do not always exist and they depend on the attitude of people generally to breaches of rules such as that of honesty. They provide reinforcements for rules rather than a rationale. If people have no rationale for rules, and only keep to them in conditions where there is positive or negative reinforcement for them, then they are ill-equipped to deal with situations of a non-routine sort where the usual reinforcements are absent. This points to the necessity for the development of reason in morals to provide a rationale for habit. Reason is a supplement to habit but not a substitute for it.

Out of Habit

It was noted that there seems to be no incompatibility between "habit," when used as a descriptive term, and intelligence and reasoning. But there is a clash when explanatory terms such as "out of habit" are used of behavior; for this phrase and others, such as "from force of habit," do suggest routine types of situations to which the concept of "intelligence" is not applicable. The condition of automaticity, of a stereo-typed form of behavior, seems more strongly implied. They also rule out the possibility that the individual who has done something has deliberated before he did it, has reflected or gone through any process of self-criticism or justification, or has seen what he does as a means to a further end. Of course he might, in the past, have formed this particular habit by some series of decisions involving deliberation, planning, justification, and other such exercises of reason. But if we say that a man does something, for instance, calls someone "sir" out of habit, we are denying that in this case any of the processes typically associated with reason have taken place. He might be able to give a reason for this if asked afterwards, but on this particular occasion he did not act with the end in view which he might specify if so pressed; it was not *his* reason.

"Out of habit" also rules out explanations of behavior which relate to features intrinsic to the behavior so explained. In other words, it rules out the suggestion that the individual did what he did for enjoyment, because of the satisfaction which it brought him, or for fun. It also rules out any suggestion of its being done out of a sense of duty. It claims nothing more than that this is the sort of thing that the individual tends to do because he has done it often before. To put it more technically, the explanation is in terms of the old psychological law of exercise.

In the life of any man, however rational, it is important that a great many things should be done out of habit. His mind is then set free to pay attention to things that are novel and interesting, and for which he has no established routine. Any complex skill, for instance, presupposes a number of component movements that are performed out of habit, and conversation would flag at meal times if most of our eating maneuvers were not performed out of habit. But what about the sphere of morality? Has this application of the concept of "habit" much relevance to this sphere?

Everything that was previously said about virtues which can be called habits would apply also *a fortiori* to the suggestion that they might be exercised out of habit. The only difference would be that more might be ruled out because the condition of automaticity seems to be more strongly suggested. To say that something is a habit is to say that it is the sort of behavior that an individual *could* perform without giving his mind to it, but to say that he performed it out of habit is to suggest that he did not give his mind to it. Obviously, therefore, type (b) virtues, which are motives, type (c) virtues, which involve much in the way of thought, and type (d) virtues, which involve self-control, should be ruled out. But even some type (a) virtues might seldom be exercised out of habit. Honesty, for instance, is exercised by means of a specific range of acts such as telling the truth, not cheating, and so on. But it would not often be exercised out of habit, because people are usually honest in the face of some sort of temptation, though they might be so disciplined that they become almost oblivious of this aspect of the situation. Honesty does not *have* to be exercised in the face of some counter-inclination as does a type (d) virtue such as courage. Thus, in a particular case, a man might be honest without being troubled much by counter-inclinations, and it might be said of him that he was honest out of habit. But this explanation of behavior is appropriate, in the main, to the more conventional virtues such as politeness, punctuality, and thrift.

Habituation

Thus far I have considered only one problem raised both by Aristotle and by Kohlberg, namely, that of the relationship between virtue and habit in the moral life. We must now address ourselves to another problem, that of the development of a rational morality out of a basis provided by early habit formation. In other words, we must study the relationship between the development of virtues and various forms of habituation.

Kohlberg, like Plato, emphasizes that the most important features of moral education are cognitive. The individual has to come to the grasp of principles and to connect particular rules like that of honesty with these instead of with extrinsic reinforcements such as praise and blame, reward and punishment. A grasp of principles, he maintains, cannot be directly taught: it can only develop with appropriate environmental stimulation, like the grasp of the causal principle or of the conservation of material things. This confirms Aristotle's point that children cannot, in the early stages of their lives behave like the just man. This means two things: first, that they cannot grasp the principle of justice, which is very abstract and difficult to grasp; and second, that they cannot raise questions about the validity of rules, that they cannot see that principles, such as that of justice, might provide a justification for other rules. As Piaget showed[9], it takes quite a time in the development of children before the notion of the validity of rules makes any sense to them, before they realize that they might be otherwise, and those rules they accept should depend upon the rationale which can be provided. Thus, in their early years, they cannot accept rules in a rational way or be taught rules by processes, such as explanation and persuasion, which depend upon the ability to grasp a rationale.

What, then, is to be said about early moral education? Must children first of all become habituated to following certain rules as Aristotle suggested, and can we conceive of a form of behavior which is learned in this way, developing into the rational form of behavior of Aristotle's just man or into Kohlberg's principled type of morality? We must first ask what is meant by "habituation." We use the term to describe a wide class of learning processes in which people learn by familiarizing themselves with, or getting used to, things, and by repetition. For instance, a boy might learn not to be afraid of dogs by a process of habituation, by being constantly in their presence and getting used to their ways. This type of learning might be contrasted with being instructed or with learning by insight. Drill is another obvious example of habituation.

Ryle, as has already been mentioned, not only thinks that habits are formed by the particular process of habituation known as drill but incorporates this belief into the meaning of "habit." This raises the question whether habits must be formed by *some* process of habituation, even if it is not the particular process of drill. It does not look as if this is a conceptual truth. Indeed, the *Oxford English Dictionary* explicitly states that there is no etymological ground for supposing that a habit must even be an acquired tendency. One might be led to think this because part of our understanding of "habit" is that a form of behavior should be repeated. We might therefore conclude that it was learned by repetition. But this is not necessarily the case. After puberty, for instance, one of a boy's habits might be to look long and lingerly at pretty girls. He did not have to learn to do this. He just found himself doing it. The explanation would be in terms of the maturation of the sex organs and consequent sensitization to girls, rather than in terms of any process of habituation, let alone drill.

Most habits, however, as a matter of empirical fact, are learned by some process of habituation. Not all of these are characterized by the sort of mindlessness that we associate with drill. If this were the case, the emergence of any rational type of morality out of processes of habituation would be a mystery. For instance, after reflection on the unsatisfactoriness of his daily pattern of life, a man can make a resolution to get up early; he can decide to make this one of his habits. In the early stages, when the alarm sounds, he may have to exhort himself, to rehearse his reasons for getting up early, and so on. When he has formed the habit, none of this deliberation and decision is necessary; but this is one way of forming a habit. Similarly, we can form habits intelligently in the context of an activity which has some overall end, such as a game of tennis. We may have to drill ourselves in particular movements, but we can learn also to make the movements in the context of a more widely conceived objective—for example, putting the ball where the opponent is not. Indeed, practice in situations where movements have to be varied in the light of changes in the situation is regarded by many as one of the best ways of forming habits, for this prevents too stereotyped a pattern of movements developing. Important, also, in the development of adaptable habits are the higher-order scruples connected with reason, such as having regard to whether what is done is correct, taking care, checking, and thinking of objections. These scruples are learned mainly by taking part in situations where actions and performances are criticized. Gradually, through a process of role playing, the learner becomes a constant critic of his own performances.

These ways of forming habits, in which reason and intelligence are involved, can be contrasted with other processes of habituation where a habit is "picked up" in ways which are explicable only in terms of laws of association, such as contiguity, recency, and frequency. In these cases, the learner may not be trying to master anything; there may even be a suggestion of automaticity. Something is done, for instance, which is associated with something pleasant, and it is repeated as in operant conditioning. Or some constant conjunction leads the individual to expect something without any connection being consciously noted—for example, the part played by serial probability in learning to spell. Alternatively, some mannerism, or form of behavior, is picked up by some process of imitation without any conscious modeling or copying. These principles may also be at work in cases where habits are deliberately formed, or where a person's mind is on what is being learnt. This is not being denied. For instance, in learning to spell, one can attempt to learn in a rational way by formulating rules. This can help learning; but at the same time one may also learn through "picking up" combinations of letters which frequently occur together. The point is that there are some processes of habituation where people fall into habits in ways which are explicable purely in terms of associative principles. But not all cases of habituation are like this.

Learning the Content of Morality (Type (a) virtues)

What then is to be said about the role of "habituation" in the moral sphere? Surely, it cannot refer to a process in which learning is explicable purely in terms of the principles of association. For, as in all cases of learning, one cannot apply some general theory of learning without paying careful attention to what it is that has to be learnt. And this is very complicated in the moral case, even if we take some type a virtue, such as honesty, which is to form part of the content of morality. Learning to be honest is not like learning to swim. It could not conceivably be picked up just by practice or by imitation; for a child has to understand what honesty is in order to behave in this way, and this presupposes all sorts of other concepts such as truth and falsehood, belief and disbelief, and so on. Such understanding cannot grow just by repetition and familiarity, though they may aid it. Similarly, extrinsic reinforcements, working by principles of association, may strengthen a tendency to behave in accordance with a rule, but the child has to understand what particular feature of his behavior is being singled out for attention. Parents often punish children for stealing, without appreciating that the child has not yet the grasp of concepts such as property, ownership, lending, giving, and the like which enable him to understand that it is stealing for which he is being punished. Such extrinsic reinforcers may help to mark out the relevant features of behavior by, as it were, underlining some aspect of it. But it is impossible to conceive how they could be suffcient to bring about understanding. Neither could understanding develop just through untutored "learning from experience": for "honesty" can only be exercised in relation to socially defined acts such as cheating and lying, and these could not be understood without initiation into a whole network of social practices. There must, therefore, be some kind of teaching of rules for moral education to get started at all. The content has to be exhibited, explained, or marked out in some way which is intrinsically rather than extrinsically related to it. This is a central feature of any process that can be called a process of teaching. Moral education is inconceivable without some process of teaching, whatever additional help is provided by various processes of habituation.

Although at an early stage there is no possibility of reason in the sense of justification being operative, there is ample scope for intelligence, for learning to apply a rule like that of honesty to a variety of situations which are relevantly similar. In other words, the rule can be taught in such a way that children gradually come to see the similarity between actions like that of lying and cheating. Parents can relate rules to their point even if children do not yet grasp the idea that their validity depends upon their point. And, surely, drawing attention to the consequences of their actions will help them to understand that actions have consequences. This at least will prepare the way for the stage when they grasp that the reasons for some rules of action depend upon consequences.

Sensitization to Principles (Type (b) and (c) virtues)

Kohlberg maintains that the assessment of actions in terms of their consequences is an important feature of a developmental stage in morality that cannot be taught by any kind of direct instruction. Children, like Socrates' slave, must come to see it, which is true enough; for this is not just a matter of information, like the height of St. Paul's cathedral, which simply has to be remembered rather than understood. But he also claims that "cognitive stimulation" can aid this process of coming to understand. And what else is that, apart from presenting some kind of content in different ways until eventually the appropriate connections are made? And, in the case of rules, this is surely done by teaching them intelligently, that is, by linking rules with other rules and with consequences which will eventually come to be seen as providing some point for them. Kohlberg also argues that some features of the situation in which rules are learned, for example, parental warmth, aid cognitive development because they provide a favorable climate for it. It may also be the case that some sorts of extrinsic aids, such as punishment, may encourage a rigidity or lack of intelligence in rule following that may become compulsive. These, however, are empirical questions which are largely still a matter for speculation. All I have been trying to do is to show how it is intelligible that acquiring habits in ways that are possible at an early stage should develop into a more rational way of following rules. I have been putting the same kind of case in the sphere of morals that I previously put when discussing the general relationship between forming habits and intelligence. It is not the case that habits have to be formed by a process like that of drill. They can be formed in the context of an activity which is more widely conceived. My argument is that learning habits in an intelligent way can be regarded as providing an appropriate basis, in the moral case, for the later stage when rules are followed or rejected because of the justification that they are seen to have or lack.

The encouragement of intelligent rule following, however, in relation to what Kohlberg calls the content of morality, is not the only thing that can be done in the early stages to prepare the way for principled morality. For, although a child may not be able, early in life, to connect rules with those considerations which are picked out by principles, he can become sensitive to considerations which will later serve him as principles. Psychologists such as Piaget and Kohlberg have failed to draw attention to this because of their preoccupation with type (c) virtues such as the principle of justice, which picks out very abstract considerations that are very difficult for a small child to grasp. If, however, instead of justice, we consider the status of type (b) virtues such as concern for others, I think that we may look at moral education in a very different light. The plight of others is much easier to grasp, and concern for it develops much earlier in children. If such concern is encouraged early in children, it can come to function later on as one of the fundamental principles of morality, when the child reaches the stage of being able to grasp the connection between many rules and their effect on other people.

Can anything be done early by training to sensitize children in this respect? Habituation seems the wrong sort of term to use in this context; for the last thing we want is to habituate children to the sight of suffering. Possibly, however, by exposing them a bit to the sight of suffering in others, or rather by not shielding them from situations where they will be confronted by it in a first-hand way, their sensitivity to it may be sharpened. It might also be argued that children can be encouraged to form the habit of paying attention to people's suffering rather than just concentrating on their own projects. This habit of mind would not itself be a virtue. But it might predispose children to be influenced by compassion on specific occasions. Again, this is a matter of speculation, but this sphere of the cultivation of appropriate forms of sensitivity is certainly one of the most crucial areas in the development of a principled form of morality. It is pointless to encourage children to reflect about rules, and to link them with general considerations of harm and benefit, if these considerations do not act as powerful motives for the person who can perform such calculations.

The Development of Self-Control (Type (d) Virtues)

When Aristotle spoke of the importance of habituation in moral education, perhaps he had in mind the particular type (d) virtues which are intimately connected with self-control. Indeed, Von Wright[10] has explicitly suggested that *all* virtues are forms of self-control. Habituation may be very important in the development of this particular class of virtues in that it may be necessary for people to be tempted, or made fearful, by situations which appear to them in a certain light. The more familiar they become with such situations, and with the internal commotions which they occasion, the more likely people are to be led by a variety of considerations to control their immediate responses. In the case of small children, the proper reasons for self-control are not readily apparent, and they are unable to link the manner of behavior with its proper justification. If, however, children are exposed to, for example, danger, and praised when they do not run away in terror, they may learn to control themselves for such extrinsic reasons. There is, of course, the danger that later on they will only display courage when the reinforcing conditions associated with the manner of behavior are present. But it could be argued that familiarity with both the external features of dangerous situations and with the internal commotions, which such danger occasions in them, carries over into situations in later life when they appreciate the proper reasons for being courageous. Like Aristotle's child, who learns to be temperate by behaving temperately under instruction, they are preparing themselves, by going through the motions of self-control, for the stage when they will have a more inward understanding of the reasons for the pattern of behavior that they are exhibiting. Habituation is important both in familiarizing children with the features of such situations and in developing the relevant action patterns that will enable them to deal practically with the emotions that may be aroused instead of being overcome by them.

Habituation may thus help to lay down a pattern of response that may be used in the service of more appropriate motives at a later stage.

Kohlberg nowhere deals with the development of this class of virtues which necessarily involve self-control. He might well claim, however, that even if people do learn to be courageous by some such process of habituation, there is no evidence of transfer. Like the Spartans they might display their courage only in very specific types of situations. Or people might become physically brave but moral cowards. To which it might be replied that, if moral courage is thought a desirable character trait to develop, it is difficult to conceive how it could develop without some kind of practice. Maybe there is not necessarily much transfer from situations requiring physical courage to those requiring moral courage, but some account must be given of how moral courage is developed. In this sphere the individual has to learn to accommodate himself not to dangers that threaten him in a palpable physical way, but to social threats and pressures such as ridicule, disapproval, ostracism, and so on. These sorts of reactions on the part of others can be evoked by a wide range of moral stances taken up by an individual. It is therefore possible for an individual to learn to cope with typical patterns of response on the part of others on the basis of a very limited number of issues on which he may make a stand. In other words, there is a built-in type of generality about this type of moral training. The English public school system of character training, derived from Thomas Arnold, is usually associated with team spirit and moral conformism. But equally strong in this tradition is the insistence that the individual should stick up for principles connected with "fair play" in the face of group pressure. Does Kohlberg think that an individual can in fact adhere to his favored principle of justice, when the screws are put on him, without some such training? And does he think that generations of British administrators, who, like the Romans, were able to maintain the rule of law with a fair degree of impartiality in situations where they were comparatively isolated and subject to social pressures, bribes, flattery, etc., were quite unaffected by the type of character training to which they were subjected at school? This seems, on the face of it, a most impausible assumption, but, of course, it would be an extremely difficult one to test.

Morality and the Development of Motivation

Sticking to a principle such as justice, however, should not be represented in too negative a light, as it might be by those who are overinfluenced by the Puritan tradition. There is also a strong positive aspect to it which is of great importance in considering the phenomenon of "will." This links with another central aspect of morality, to which Kohlberg pays too little attention, namely, the intimate connection between knowing the difference between right and wrong, and caring. It is not a logical contradiction to say that someone knows that it is wrong to cheat but has no disposition not to cheat, but it could not be the general case; for the general function of words like "right" and "wrong", "good" and "bad" is to move people to act. If there is no such disposition to act in a particular case, we would say that the person is using the term in an external sort of way, or that he is not sincere, or something similar to that. There is neither need nor time to defend such a generally accepted point about moral knowledge, though there has been no general acceptance, ever since the time that Socrates first put it forward, about the precise relationship between moral knowledge and action.[11]

Now, as Hume pointed out, justice is an artificial virtue which only gets off the ground when reason gets to work in social life. Hume equated "reason" with reasoning of the sort that goes on either in logic and mathematics or in science, and was led to think, therefore, that reason of itself provides no considerations that move people to act. On a broader view of "reason," however, it becomes readily apparent that there is a cluster of "passions" closely connected with it without which its operation would be unintelligible. I am referring not just to the passion for truth, but also to other passions which are intimately connected with it such as the abhorrence of the arbitrary, the hatred of inconsistency and irrelevance, the love of clarity and order, and, in the case of nonformal reasoning, the determination to look at the facts. These passions both provide point to theoretical enquiries and transform the pursuit of practical purposes.

When Kohlberg talks of the principle of justice, it is not clear whether he means the formal principle that no distinctions should be made without relevant differences or more particularized versions of this in distributive or commutative justice. But any application of this principle must involve some kind of abhorrence of arbitrariness and of inconsistency if it is to be operative in any individual's life. Also, as Kohlberg maintains that it presupposes becoming aware of some "universal structural dimensions in the social world," some focused attention to the facts of the social world is also involved. How do such rational passions develop? What helps to foster them? Kohlberg, like Piaget, postulates some kind of intrinsic motivation which leads children to assimilate and accommodate to what is novel and to develop their latent capacities. But there is a great difference between sporadic curiosity and the passions which cluster round the concern for truth. Does not the encouragement and example of adults and older children play any part in their development? Without them a child's understanding of justice would be very external. He might know what justice is, but might not care about it overmuch. To apply the principle seriously, the child has to develop not only an abhorrence of the arbitrary, but also a more positive concern for the considerations that determine relevance. How do children come to care? This seems to me to be the most important question in moral education; but no clear answer to it can be found in Kohlberg's writings.

Is Kohlberg Prescribing a Morality?

In discussing the adequacy of Kolberg's account of the role of habit in moral development distinctions were made between different classes of virtues. These seemed to be of some significance in assessing his account of processes of development. But they are of even more fundamental significance if we survey Kohlberg's conception of moral development from an overall ethical standpoint; taking these distinctions seriously might lead us to reflect that Kohlberg is really prescribing one type of morality among several possibilities. "Morality" can be used as a classificatory term by means of which a form of interpersonal behavior can be distinguished from custom, law, religious codes, and so on. But in ethics and in the practical task of bringing up children, this does not take us very far; for it would involve us in the most feeble form of the naturalistic fallacy to argue that, because we term a form of behavior "moral," this behavior is one which should be pursued or encouraged. Nothing about what ought to be or to be done follows from the empirical fact that we use a word in a certain way. It might well be, for instance, that a form of behavior, in which justice plays such a prominent part, might accord very well with our usage of "moral." But that is neither here nor there if anyone is troubled by the general question "What are there reasons for doing?" or by more particular questions about how he is to bring up his children.

Even within this principled form of morality considered thus far, there are, in fact, different emphases open. For instance, one might think that the most important things to encourage in children were sympathy, compassion, concern for others, and the like. One might not be particularly concerned about consistency or about the virtue of justice, which one might think of as being a rather niggardly one. Similarly, one might think that courage, integrity, autonomy, or other such excellences ought to be encouraged without being overly concerned about the substantial rules or purposes in relation to which these

higher-order traits were exercised. Finally, one might not be too impressed with the interpersonal realm. One might go along with Gauguin
and say that painting pictures was the thing, or advocate some other
type of worthwhile activity. This form of activity, it might be said, is so
valuable that considerations of an inter-personal sort would have to be
set aside. All of these are possible moral positions in the general sense
that reasons could be given for behaving in the ways suggested and for
bringing up one's children accordingly. Of course, an attempt might be
made to introduce some kind of unity into the moral life either by
attempting to show that all such considerations were derived from one
type of consideration, as did the Utilitarians, or by arbitrarily demarcat-
ing the sphere of the moral, as did Kant. But *prima facie* it appears to
be a difficult enterprise, and it is certainly not one upon which
Kohlberg has embarked. His account of moral development might
therefore be considered to be one-sided in that it has been erected on the
features of a limited interpretation of morality.

A further point must be made, too, about any moral system in
which justice is regarded as the fundamental principle: it cannot be
applied without a view, deriving from considerations other than those
of justice, about what is important. This point can be demonstrated only
very briefly, but it is one of cardinal importance. When we talk about
what is just or unjust, we are applying the formal principle of reason—
that no distinctions should be made without relevant differences, either
to questions of distribution, when we are concerned about the treatment
which different people are to receive, or to commutative situations,
when we are concerned not with comparisons but with questions of
desert, as in punishment. In all such cases some criterion has to be
produced by reference to which the treatment is to be based on *relevant*
considerations. There must therefore be some further evaluative
premise in order to determine relevance. Without such a premise, no
decisions can be made about what is just on any substantial issue. In
determining, for instance, what a just wage is, relevant differences must
be determined by reference to what people need, to what they contribute to the community, to the risk involved, and so on. To propose any
such criteria involves evaluation. This opens up obvious possibilities for
alternative emphases in morality in addition to those already mentioned. But are these emphases to be put on the "formal" or on the
"content" side of Kohlberg's account of moral development? When we
begin to look at his system in this more detailed way, it must become
apparent that it is either implicitly prescriptive or so formal that it is of
only limited significance for those who are interested in moral education, or moral development, in a concrete way. His findings are of

unquestionable importance, but there is a grave danger that they may become exalted into a general theory of moral development. Any such general theory presupposes a general ethical theory, and Kohlberg himself surely would be the first to admit that he has done little to develop the details of such a general ethical theory. Yet without such a theory the notion of "moral development" is pretty insubstantial.

Notes

1. L. Kohlberg, "Development of Moral Character and Ideology" in *Review of Child Development Research*, Volume I, edited by M. L. Hoffman (New York: Russell Sage Foundation, 1964).

2. L. Kohlberg, "Moral Education in the Schools," *School Review*, 74, 1966, pp. 1-30.

3. L. Kohlberg, "Development of Moral Character and Ideology," p. 388.

4. Aristotle, *Nicomachean Ethics*, Book II, Chapter 1, edited by J. A. K. Thompson (Hammondsworth: Penguin, 1955).

5. *Ibid.*

6. See also R. S. Peters, "Reason and Habit: The Paradox of Moral Education" in *Moral Education in a Changing Society* edited by W. R. Niblett (London: Faber, 1963) and A. C. Kazepides, "What Is the Paradox of Moral Education?", *Proceedings of the Twenty-fifth Annual Meeting of the Philosophy of Education Society*, Denver, 1969.

7. G. Ryle, *The Concept of Mind* (London: Hutchinson, 1948), p. 42-43.

8. M. Oakeshott, "The Tower of Babel," *Rationalism in Politics* (London: Methuen, 1962), p. 65.

9. J. Piaget, *The Moral Judgment of the Child* (London: Routledge, 1932).

10. G.H. Von Wright, *The Varieties of Goodness* (London: Routledge, 1963), Chapter VII.

11. G. Ryle, "On Forgetting the Difference Between Right and Wrong," *Essays in Moral Philosophy* edited by A.I. Meldon (Seattle: University of Washington Press, 1958).

The Justification of
Conceptual Development Claims

WOUTER van HAAFTEN

1. Introduction

In this paper [1] I would like to discuss whether it is possible to justify conceptual development claims. By conceptual development I mean, roughly, any form of development in which our conceptualisation of (some part of) reality changes in a fundamental way. And by a conceptual development claim I mean, roughly, any contention that a later stage in conceptual development is somehow better or more adequate than preceding ones. My question is: how can such claims be argued for? Part of what makes this an interesting problem is, that the possibility of defence is dependent on the development to be defended.

The justification of conceptual development claims is relevant to the philosophy of education, firstly, because such claims are presupposed in many of our everyday deliberations about human development and education. In thinking about what we try to achieve in education, we are in fact often comparing developmental stages (in a sense to be specified hereafter). In defining and defending aims of education we put forward conceptual development claims. Secondly, several influential developmental theories, in particular within the cognitive-structuralistic paradigm, either make or imply such claims. For instance, Piaget's theory (or theories) about several forms of (intellectual) cognitive development, Kohlberg's moral development theory, Selman's theory about the development of social perspective taking (Selman, 1980), Oser's theory of religious development (Oser & Gmünder, 1984) and Parsons' aesthetic development theory (Parsons, 1987) all more or less clearly suggest not only that there are qualitatively different stages in the child's cognitive development, but also that the later stages are more adequate than prior ones. It is not always sufficiently clear, however, what precisely is involved in such a conceptual development claim, and much less how it could be justified. I consider it to be one of the tasks of a philosophy of education to unearth and analyse such basic tenets of relevant psychological theories (cf. van Haaften *et al.*, 1986).

The central term 'development' is used rather loosely in these theories. In general, they certainly do not want to restrict themselves to a purely biologistic perspective; more often the basic position is interactionistic. In order to deal with such theories in an adequate way, we should not exclude in advance any possible *cause* of conceptual change, be it maturation or learning and education. The relation between the explanation of conceptual development and the justification of conceptual development claims is then complicated. On the one hand, they are closely connected, in at least three ways. First, an educator will have his reasons to further certain forms of development and to discourage other forms. Secondly, persons who go through any form of conceptual development themselves may have their reasons, however vague and intuitive, to prefer certain basic new insights once attained, and therefore to stick to them instead of backsliding to earlier ideas. In both cases the motives and convictions, the deliberations and justifications of the educator and the developing person respectively may constitute part of the explanation of the developmental process. Thirdly, the theorist will have some reasons to build his model of conceptual development the way he does. (He has reached a certain level of development himself, after all.) But then this model is guiding his research to a considerable degree. Kohlberg, for instance, after having admitted that he had not been successful in bridging the gap "from is to ought" (Kohlberg *et al.*, 1983; cf. Kohlberg, 1971, 1981; van Haaften, 1984) in his later writings more clearly acknowledged the normative presuppositions of his theory of moral development. Not only did he show how specific types of reasons for moral judgements can be distinguished for each stage, he also wanted to indicate why a later developmental stage is to be considered "more moral" than previous ones, which may serve as part of the explanation why people develop through the stages in that way. Developmental theory in that case seeks to establish not merely why people think they ought to prefer the later stage, but also why they ought to prefer it. The theory tries to formulate a *rationale* of development.

On the other hand, the psychological explanation of conceptual development and the justification of development claims do not, of course, coincide. First of all that would suggest a far too rational and reflective character for conceptual developmental processes [2]. There are many causes of development, only one of which might sometimes be a more or less considered preference for the later stage[3]. Secondly, the more advanced stages are more reflective in general. But there are considerable differences in this regard amongst cognitive-structural domains. Morality, for instance, is more intrinsically connected with the notion of justification than other domains are. That means that, whereas all theories are interested in the typical intra-stage kinds of reasoning, moral development and moral development theory may be more sensitive to reasoned inter-stage comparisons and preferences than other forms of conceptual development. Thirdly, all connections notwithstanding, there remains the principal difference between the (psychological) question what people *do* hold to be valid reasons and the (philosophical) question as to what *could* possibly be valid reasons for a conceptual development claim.

I must leave aside many interesting questions concerning the relation between causes in the explanation of conceptual developmental processes and reasons in the validation of conceptual development claims, including whether or not every conceptual developmental theory by its very nature presupposes some conceptual development claim. My concern will not be with explanatory problems here. I would like to concentrate on the justificatory issue. I am looking for some of the *conditions of the possibility* of a *justification* of such claims. Surprisingly, apart from Kohlberg's famous but unsuccessful argument "from is to ought" and the many analyses and criticisms it has received, not very much systematic attention has been paid to this vital question, so far as I can see, perhaps owing to its constantly being mingled with explanatory problems in general or, as in the work of Piaget (cf. Chapman, 1988b, pp. 331 ff.), with epistemological questions concerning the possibility of novelty and progress in developmental processes.

In the following I propose to distinguish two main lines that might be taken in a defence of conceptual development claims. They have to do with our basic ideas as to why this peculiar form of development should come about at all. They imply two fundamentally different notions of conceptual development and two divergent potential foundations of conceptual development theories. I have in mind (a) the reduction of inconsistencies and (b) the improvement of criteria of judgement, as two different kinds of reason why later developmental stages might be considered better than prior ones. The principle of inconsistency reduction means that later stages are in some way more consistent than earlier ones. The principle of criteria improvement means that judgements (e.g. moral judgements) that are made in the later stage are more adequate because the criteria used in making these judgements in the later stage are qualitatively better than those used before.

But, one may ask, are these two principles really different? Is not the reduction of inconsistencies brought about precisely by the later stage's using better judgemental criteria? And are not those criteria considered better precisely because they reduce inconsistencies? I will argue that this is not so, or at least that this cannot always be the case. In other words, I want to show that the principle of inconsistency reduction does not always work; and that at least in those cases another type of reason is needed to endorse the claim that later stages are more adequate than earlier stages in conceptual development.

I shall first in § 2 clarify some meta-theoretical points concerning conceptual development claims. Then, in § 3, I shall discuss the principle of inconsistency reduction as a possible basis for the defence of conceptual development claims. Strong arguments can be given in favour of this principle. There are, however, some conditions of its use and some severe limitations in its applicability, which I indicate in § 4. I argue that the principle of inconsistency reduction cannot be effective for the moral, the aesthetic or the religious domain. Next, I introduce the principle of criteria improvement as an alternative, and in § 5 I try to formulate some of the conditions which will have to be met in order for the justification of conceptual development claims to be possible along this line. Finally, I tentatively suggest in § 6 that a specific, and in my opinion acceptable, naturalistic or developmental bridge from 'is' to 'ought' will be involved in this connection.

2. Conceptual Development Claims

Whenever we call a certain process a *development* we have criteria in mind. Firstly, there are criteria determining our use of the word 'development'. For instance, it is often maintained that by speaking of development it is implied that some qualitative change must be involved, not merely quantitative as in growth. Secondly, we may be thinking of criteria concerning the specific domain of development referred to. Different criteria are used, for instance, for moral, or aesthetic or religious development. Thirdly, we must have at least some criteria in mind which are relevant to the differences between developmental stages within the domain, according to which we distinguish the stages.

First a word about the criteria for the term. Many analytical philosophers take the view that the use of this word is misleading in educational contexts from the very start, because of its connections with the biological sphere. Hamlyn in an influential article argues that "to see a state of a thing as a stage in its development we must be able to see it as connected essentially in some way with an end-state which is in some way the rationale of the thing itself. We must be able to see the acorn not just as a lump of vegetable matter but as, given the fulfilment of certain conditions, a future oak tree" (Hamlyn, 1975, pp. 32,33). The explanation of events which constitute stages of a developmental process can therefore according to him be brought under the general heading of functional or teleological explanation (p. 34). In this perspective it must be misleading to speak of intellectual or moral *development*. For in such domains learning is necessarily involved. There must be an acceptance of standards of rationality and rightness, and these have to come from outside the individual (p. 36). Hamlyn concludes that education can have little to do with development; it may at best provide the right conditions for the developmental process to come off (p. 38).

This argument will be inescapable, if one fully accepts Hamlyn's analysis of development. However, Elliott (1975) in a reply has argued that the word 'development' is used in various ways, constituting a family of cases (p. 43). Some of the uses in education are related to the biological concept, not all of which fulfil the rather strict conditions laid down by Hamlyn. It would therefore be legitimate as well as natural for us to use the word in an educational context. Elliott in fact suggests that, in some cases at least, not using the word might be more misleading than using it. Furthermore, Wright (1986) has convincingly shown that the concept of development does not necessarily imply a natural end-state, nor necessarily exclude public (e.g. moral) standards in learning. Education and conceptual development can therefore be much more closely connected than was admitted by Hamlyn. I find some comfort in these observations to leave it open for the word 'development' to be used in the broader sense as is done in cognitive-developmental theories like those mentioned above. For the moment, I will take for granted as necessary conditions for its use only (1) that developmental stages are qualitatively different, and (2) that each stage in a series (of two or more) is necessary for its successor. In particular, my use of the term here will not prejudge anything concerning the nature of the transitions and not exclude learning as a possible cause of development.

When we think of development as a form of qualitative change, we need to be able in principle to give an indication as to what that change consists in. Now as soon as we formulate to that end certain essential differences emerging in the course of some particular sort of development, we have thereby in a sense discerned *stages*. This is the case both in our ordinary talk about development and in developmental theories. In the latter we might, following a lead of Habermas (1981, II, p. 218), distinguish between a *logica* and a *dynamica*, as two mutually indispensable parts of any developmental theory. In the *logica* the stages are defined and their logical relations determined. The *dynamica* is concerned with the developmental processes and the principles of their explanation. What we are here concerned with is then only the stages as they are defined or reconstructed in the *logica*. The justifcatory question regards the stages in the *logica* in particular in so far as their qualitative differences are relevant in their comparison. That admits of a use of the term 'stage' in a rather minimal sense, in which there need be no indication about how the actual developmental processes take place. The sharp distinction between the stages in the *logica* does not, for instance, imply any suggestion of abrupt stage transitions; the real processes may be entirely gradual and smooth. Nor need there be any allegation of ages in relation to the stages so discerned. Nor is it implied that individuals should at all times function or react in accordance to one single stage in cognitive development. It is important to see that in this minimal sense, stages do *not describe* actual states. As yet they are simply an indication of *some characteristics* that are essential in the type of development in question at a certain moment as opposed to what is considered essential to it at other moments. These characteristics then are the distinctive criteria for the stages.

The same is true for our everyday talk about development, e.g. in education. Again we refer to certain criteria which define the stage under discussion over against one or more other stages. Reference to these criteria may be explicit, but will be made mostly in an entirely implicit way. The criteria may be vague and imprecise; or like some psychological theories they may distinguish up to six or more developmental stages, together constituting a developmental pattern. But in either case we use certain distinctive criteria. These are necessary if we are even to conclude that a certain development does not actually happen. No developmental theory and no thinking about development in general, as long as the notion of development is taken to imply some form of qualitative change, can do without this minimal notion of stages.

Stages should also not always be thought of in so vast and comprehensive a sense as to cover a whole "domain of reality" or "mode of knowledge and experience" (Hirst & Peters, 1980) like those of morality or aesthetic experience or formal logic and mathematics [4]. It is more likely that within such domains there are (smaller) developmental dimensions, besides aspects that do not show any development (van Haaften *et al.*, 1986), perhaps rather more like Piaget had in mind when he introduced the expression "structures d'ensemble" which, however, misled so many authors (cf. Chapman, 1988b, pp. 343 ff.).

In the following I shall depart from the notion of a stage in this minimal sense. But now it is important to realise that in conceptual development (as opposed to, e.g. development of oak trees or butterflies) criteria are involved at two levels (van Haaften, 1988). On the one hand we use or presuppose the above-mentioned criteria in our comparing developmental stages. On the other hand—and this is typical of conceptual development—there are the criteria which, with*in* each stage, are used or presupposed in moral or aesthetic (etc.) judgement. In discussing what ought to be done in the situation of Kohlberg's Heinz dilemma, for instance, moral judgement criteria are applied. People formulate their own moral judgements, and they discuss the moral judgements of other persons. In this, as Kohlberg has shown, different persons use different sets of judgement criteria which are characteristic of different stages in moral development. This illustrates how, in this type of development, the *stage criteria* defining the distinct stages refer to the different sorts of *judgement criteria* people use. But the two types of criteria should not be confused. Judgement criteria relate to judgements; stage criteria relate not to judgements, but to the various sets of judgement criteria.

It is also important to see that in conceptual developmental stages two issues always come into play simultaneously, like two sides of the same coin. On the one side, each conceptual development stage is characterised by its specific criteria for what would be adequate judgements in its domain. What develops in, for example, moral development is not so much the answer to questions about what ought to be done in certain situations, but rather the crucial concepts and criteria which in trying to answer such questions are being used. On the other side, and at the same time, this implies a *stage specific conception of the domain of reality in question*, e.g. a particular conception of morality: a certain fundamental idea, typical of that stage, as to what moral judgements and what morality itself are all about, a notion of what is essential to morality as such. In other words, to use a different set of moral judgement criteria amounts to having a new idea, however implicit, of what morality *is* [5]. Or perhaps we should rather say, conversely, that the various sets of judgement criteria form an expression of the respective basic conceptions of the domain. But in any case, the judgement criteria simultaneously lay down for a certain stage (a) what are considered adequate ways of reasoning in the domain concerned, and (b) what is considered adequate in the conception of that domain[6].

In sum, with the term 'stages' in the context of conceptual development I shall refer to various characteristic (sets of) criteria of judgement within a certain domain of reality. In terms of the minimum notion of a stage, the *logica* of a conceptual development theory thus formulates (proposes) a *pattern* of qualitatively different sets of judgement criteria which developing persons in principle are supposed to be able to apply [7] successively in course of time. And as we noted that the conception of the relevant domain of reality itself accordingly develops simultaneously, we might also say that the *logica* tries to define or reconstruct a developmental pattern of different types of *foundations* of our successive ways of conceptualising reality in that domain [8]. A conceptual development claim can be said to bear upon such successive foundations.

We should make one more distinction before we can go ahead and address the problem of the justification of conceptual development claims. A conceptual development claim contains a descriptive part and an evaluative part. The descriptive part, i.e. the description or reconstruction of the developmental pattern, refers to the criteria according to which the developmental stages in the relevant domain are to be distinguished, thus to the respective sets of judgement criteria. The evaluative part appeals to or presupposes additional criteria according to which it can be decided that certain stages are better (or worse) [9] than others. As to the relation between both partial claims, we may notice that an evaluative claim always relates to certain distinct stages (to at least two of them, whether more or less precisely defined) and therefore necessarily presupposes and, at least implicitly, always refers to some descriptive claim.

The foregoing considerations were meant to clarify the notion of conceptual development claims. A conceptual development claim is involved both in our everyday talk and in scientific theory as soon as it is contended or implied that a later stage in some type of conceptual development is in a certain respect better than prior stages. Clearly that is an evaluative claim, which presupposes a descriptive claim in which the relevant stages are distinguished. As we shall see, the justification requirement of the evaluative claim may impose restrictions on what can be admitted as stages in the descriptive sense. Now let us turn to some problems that are central to the justification of conceptual development claims.

3. First Principle: inconsistency reduction

What in general can be said in support of a conceptual development claim? To begin with, let us mention very briefly some approaches that are not satisfactory. The most naive line would be straightforwardly to identify the better with the later. The later stage is considered better because it is later in development. This would involve an obvious genetic (naturalistic) fallacy. Nor can it be adequate just to point to the fact that new things are learned in the course of development (in addition to which it may be stressed that they cannot subsequently be un-learned), without making it sufficiently clear why this learning process or the new things learned constitute an improvement. In that case, learning something is simply taken to be good by definition. It is not fallacious but insufficient to argue that certain intermediate stages are necessary conditions of, or necessary transits to, a final (or at least to some later) stage. Everything then comes to depend on the justification of the conceptual development claim with regard to that later or final stage; and a further explanation would be required, of course, as to why an individual, who as yet can have no access to that final stage, should go through the intermediate stages [10].

Now let us look at the principles which I mentioned at the outset: (a) inconsistency reduction and (b) criteria improvement. First, (§§ 3 and 4) about inconsistency reduction. Albeit rather implicit, this appears to be an often invoked principle in theories within the cognitive-structural paradigm (cf. Mischel, 1971; Kohlberg, 1976, 1984; Habermas, 1983; Kitchener, 1986; Chapman 1988a). A later stage is considered better if it is more consistent somehow (or less inconsistent) than its forerunners. I believe that a strong case can be made for this principle. I see two main lines of argument which endorse it.

A first line of argument in favour of the more coherent stage n is: that stage n will provide (and in the course of evolution appears to have provided) a better survival probability than the foregoing stage $n-1$. Now this argument can take different shapes. Perhaps during the evolutionary process mankind has developed a direct inclination towards conceptual consistency, and so also a preference for the more coherent conceptual development stages. That may be part of an *explanation* of conceptual development in 'naturalistic' or evolutionary terms. Evolution then has 'wired' us this way: less coherent thinkers, or persons who did not develop sufficiently coherent conceptualisations in time, simply could not produce the requisite offspring before being taken out of circulation. (Perhaps this would also be an explanation why there are so few new developmental stages during the long period of maturity!) But my point here would be that the better conceptualiser's better chance of success in the struggle for life can also be a strong argument in *justification* of the evaluative claim that the more coherent stage n is to be preferred to the less coherent stage $n-1$.

A second way of endorsing the principle of inconsistency reduction is by appealing to a so-called transcendental–pragmatic argument (cf. Peters, 1966, 1973; Apel, 1973, 1986). Such an argument is of an entirely different kind. It does not refer to extrinsic considerations like survival chance, but claims that the principle of inconsistency reduction is valid because it is also a principle which sustains and is presupposed in any sort of serious reasoning, including deliberations concerning the validity of the principle itself.

The gist of the argument, adapted to the defence of conceptual development claims is this: We could not profitably argue about anything if we were to allow ourselves all kinds of contradictions and inconsistencies. If we seriously want to reason at all, we need to be consistent or at least to try and reduce inconsistency wherever we can. In other words, *in* reasoning we implicitly but necessarily already adhere to the principle of inconsistency reduction. Its acceptance is part of what it is to reason. Thus, as soon as one raises the question which of two stages in development should be preferred, the more or the less consistent one, the answer to that question has in fact been given. For to raise this question seriously means that one is willing to weigh arguments as best as one can. And that means that inconsistencies should be reduced wherever and whenever possible, and thus that the more consistent stage should be preferred. Or, to put it the other way round, any attempt to defend rationally the thesis that the less coherent conceptualisational stage should be preferred would result in a form of self-contradiction, as what one intends to argue for (inconsistency) conflicts with what one in arguing intends to achieve (consistency). This is why the argument is sometimes called a transcendental–pragmatic argument: it points to the *pragmatic* self-contradiction that is involved in arguing against the content of a principle that in the act of seriously trying to argue has been adopted already.

I do not, of course, want to suggest that this kind of reasoning is actually and in so many words employed by the developing person, but only that in principle a justification of conceptual development claims seems to me to be viable along these lines. Perhaps we may regard it as a philosophical formulation of what normally guides our reasonings in an entirely implicit way.

4. Limitations of the Inconsistency Reduction Principle

Both the survival argument and the transcendental argument can provide strong support for the principle of inconsistency reduction, but there are some limitations to this principle. Clearly, it can only be effective *where inconsistencies can in principle arise*. The question is, however, whether that is really always possible. In order to explain this point I have to first make a distinction between internal and external forms of inconsistency. Let us speak of internal inconsistency if, in an analysis (in a reflection by the developing person, or in an analytical reconstruction by the theoretician) of what are leading concepts or judgement criteria typical of a certain stage, those concepts or criteria are found to be mutually conflicting, so as to produce inconsistent conceptualisations in the relevant domain. On the other hand, we may speak of external inconsistency if some of our concepts or criteria are not in accordance with reality, so that our conceptualisations turn out to be inconsistent with certain (new) experiences.

Now, whenever different stages should appear to be so internally inconsistent to various degrees, a preference for the more consistent stage can be successfully defended by an appeal to the principle of inconsistency reduction and the arguments sustaining it. Clearly the transcendental argument applies; and the survival argument may also, where internal inconsistencies produce external inconsistency as well. The situation is different, however, where there are no internal inconsistencies, so that the only possible inconsistencies under discussion are *external*. It is here that we may best see what are some conditions for the use and some limits in the radius of the principle of inconsistency reduction.

First a brief word about some *conditions for the applicability* of the principle. Conflicts or confrontations between our conceptions and reality can only arise if we can have access to reality (or if reality can have access to us) at least partly independently of our own conceptual framework. This is possible if two requirements are met, one metaphysical and one epistemological. The metaphysical requirement is that we acknowledge a form of (indirect) realism. In this respect we should be clear about the notion 'constructivism', which is handled in a rather sloppy way in theories that present themselves as constructivist (Kitchener, 1986). Sometimes the term is used in a sense suggesting that in conceptual development we completely construct or reconstruct reality. In that case, reality can only be the reality of our construction. The result is some form of idealism, which precludes any role for conflict between our conceptions and reality 'itself' as a factor in conceptual development. Therefore in the context of the present discussion 'constructivism' can only mean that in conceptual development we construct and reconstruct our ways of conceptualising reality in confrontation with an (at least partly) independently existing world—which implies some form of ontological realism.

The epistemological requirement is that, contrary to suggestions in conceptual development theories (e.g. Kohlberg, 1969, p. 388; but also 1981, 1984), the conceptual framework which is characteristic of a developmental stage should not be holistic, that is to say, at least not in such a way that every relevant experience one might have is entirely shaped or modelled by it. For, evidently, in that case again a conflict with reality could not originate. In this sense, too, there must be some possibility of confrontation with an independent world. I should add that if this seems to suggest that we are to accept that there can be *un*conceptualised experience this is emphatically not so intended. We need only accept the less problematic thesis that the specific concepts and criteria which define a stage are limited in number and in scope so that not all experience is in their grip. We might rather see them as core concepts, fermenting but not determining overall our conceptualisations at a certain time. Confrontation with an independent world thus means: confrontation between experiences that are structured by the stage-specific concepts or criteria and experiences that are not so structured.

These are two (necessary, not sufficient) conditions for the possibility of a confrontation with an independent reality which is presupposed in the notion of external inconsistency. This requirement is also crucial for the *limitations in the radius* of the principle of inconsistency reduction. These limitiations have to do with the essential differences between the various domains of cognitive development. We may take moral development as the example again. Most philosophers agree that in moral reasoning two different kinds of judgement are necessarily involved: *empirical* or descriptive (aspects of) judgements about certain qualities of the persons or objects or situations in question; and *normative*, viz., evaluative or prescriptive (aspects of) judgements about how in general such properties of persons or objects or situations are to be evaluated, or about what in general in such situations ought to be done. Usually these two sorts of judgement are completely and inextricably interwoven in everyday practice. But analytically, and in our *arguing about* practical situations we should distinguish carefully between the factual (in principle observational) aspects, on the one hand, and our evaluations and perhaps our prescriptions based on them, on the other. They are of a radically different type. I accept this traditional distinction between the 'is' and the 'ought' [11]. Let me give an example. We may (empirically) observe that certain persons have been tortured [12] in jail. We immediately find this highly condemnable. Reasoning strictly, however, we may conclude that things as we observe them are objectionable only if the normative (non-empirical) premise is added that (say) any form of torture is immoral and condemnable in deference to human life. Just noticing or reporting the traces of violence is not enough to constitute a moral judgement about what is so observed. A moral judgement can only be made from some moral perspective on what one sees happening. In the moral domain, therefore, the empirical data require an essential non-empirical complement.

As regards the justification of moral conceptual development claims this means the following: In any discussion about moral problems some cognisance of the relevant facts about the (in principle observable) objects or situations in question is presupposed. Therefore the persons discussing the issue must be in some developmental stage in the domain of physical cognition. That is, they (mostly unconsciously) apply certain non-moral judgement criteria in their weighing the empirical claims that are being made. Furthermore, the discussion might switch over to the question as to what are the most adequate judgement criteria in this respect, and thus involve conceptual development claims over different stages with their different sets of judgement criteria in the physical domain. For instance, a preference for the judgement criteria that are characteristic of Piaget's conservation stage (as compared to non-conservation) may well be defended with an appeal to the principle of inconsistency reduction. In the moral domain, however, there are not only the indispensable empirical observations, with the empirical judgement criteria involved in our reasoning about them, but also, and necessarily, our moral evaluations of the situation in question. Persons discussing moral issues, therefore, must be in some moral development stage as well. That is, they apply certain normative judgement criteria in weighing the normative contentions that are being put forward. Furthermore, the discussion might be extended to the question as to what are the *most adequate moral judgement criteria*, and thus involve conceptual development claims in the moral domain.

Now my point is that because moral, i.e. normative, criteria form a decisive part of our moral reasoning and of our concept of morality, empirical reality cannot possibly provide a *sufficient* endorsement of conceptual development claims in this domain. Normative judgement criteria are necessarily involved as well in the evaluation of moral judgements. Which means that the notion of *external* inconsistency is principally inadequate as a criterion for the comparison of moral stages, because they are defined by their different (sets of) moral judgement criteria. It would be a category mistake to invoke the criterion of external inconsistency here [13].

To this it might be objected that in moral deliberations what we actually do is try to minimise potential conflicts in our relations with other persons by seeking an optimal balance between the various interests of people in society. Is that not an empirical stage criterion, at least in principle? Kohlberg once took this line (1973)— which sharply contrasted with his otherwise typically Kantian inspirations. But the objection misses the point altogether. Our question was: if stages are characterised by their respective sets of judgement criteria, how can we decide which one of certain sets of *moral* judgement criteria is to be preferred to which other ones? Can external inconsistency reduction in principle be a criterion to choose between them? And my suggestion was that it can not. The reason for this is not so much that it would be impossible to choose between utilitarian and Kantian moral perspectives on such grounds, but rather that no stage whatsoever can be preferred on empirical grounds in this domain because its primary judgement criteria are non-empirical. Perhaps we may in certain situations be able to decide empirically which actions will result in the greatest good for the greatest number of persons concerned (or whatever variant of utilitarian criterion is opted for). In that sense we do have an empirical measure, once this normative judgement criterion has been fixed. We cannot, however, establish in this way the correctness of the normative judgement criterion itself.

The choice [14] of an *empirical judgement criterion*, like "quantity is determined by the height of liquid level in the glass" therefore "the higher the level, the more you have" (as in Piaget's non-conservation stage), *can* in principle be corrected by experience. The point is not that we are able to observe empirically whether the level of glass *x* or of glass *y* is higher, but that we can discover by experience that such a judgement criterion, which makes this measure of quantity, is inadequate because it produces inconsistencies. Thus, inconsistency reduction can in principle provide a reason why conservation criteria should be preferred. The choice of a *normative judgement criterion*, however, like "to be (morally) good is: not being punished" or "you are a good boy if you are never punished" (as in Kohlberg's stage *1*) or "to be (morally) good is to further whatever is conducive to the greatest good for the greatest number of persons concerned" (as in his stage *5*), *can not*, on the basis of experience, turn out to be right or wrong. Of course one can find out empirically whether act *x* or act *y* results in more punishment. So, if one opts for this criterion, one will be able to decide between *x* and *y*, or between judgements purporting that *x* or that *y* should be done [15]. Similarly, one may be able to determine empirically whether act *x* or act *y* is more in accordance with the utilitarian criterion. So, if one wants to apply this criterion, one may be able to decide what (morally) is the best thing to do. But one cannot *by experience* discover whether this judgement criterion itself is (morally) adequate. There can be no discrepancy between a normative judgement criterion and reality, because the moral criterion only *selects from* reality (as it is observed or known) those elements that are taken to be morally relevant. *A fortiori*, it will be impossible to decide on the basis of experience that the judgement criterion of stage *5* is a better moral judgement criterion than that of stage *1*. External inconsistency reduction principally cannot be a (stage) criterion when we have to decide between different (sets of) normative judgement criteria.

At this point the objection may be raised that I have neglected the important role of social conflict. Have I not been using too narrow a notion of potential conflict with empirical reality? Should that not include the opinions and sayings of other people, which may be contrary to our own conceptions and expectations? The first answer to this must be, I think, that we should clearly distinguish between questions about transition factors or *causes* in developmental processes (belonging to the *dynamica*) on the one hand, and questions about *reasons* in support of conceptual development claims (over stages, as defined in the *logica*) on the other. Certainly, conflicting opinions further developmental processes in many ways. They may, for instance, make people rethink the issue. But the fact that there is a conflict does not show who is in the right. Conflicts about what may count as good reasons cannot themselves be the grounds for the decision [16]. Our primary question is: What sorts of argument can or cannot (and for what reasons) be *valid* in this particular context?

But what if there are stages which induce more conflict than others? The following argument is sometimes put forward in defence of post-conventional moral judgement. At the conventional level the word of parents or teachers or religious leaders is typically accepted as a judgement criterion. Such authorities, however, are then found to be regularly contradicting themselves, or one another. The resulting inconsistencies allegedly can be resolved by passing to post-conventional principled reasoning, and the inconsistency reduction would be a good reason for preferring the post-conventional stage. This argument calls for the following comments: (1) Principled judgement may well ask for more rather than less conflict, in comparison just with following the nearest authorities. The answer to this, in turn, will be perhaps that it is not simply conflicts with the environment which have to be overcome, but rather the conflict-inducing criteria, and that this is what can be achieved by turning to principles. But then, as not just any principle will be acceptable, a *qualitative* stage criterion (and not just inconsistency reduction) will be required to choose the *right* principles. (I will come to this type of stage criteria in the next section.) Furthermore, (2) although, admittedly, the heteronomy of the conventional level is often inconsistent, it need not be. In principle, conventional authority-following judgement can be entirely consistent, if the criteria in question are defined precisely enough (for instance by stipulating some hierarchy among the various authorities, etc.). Thus, although in practice there may be a lot of uncertainty at this level, perhaps *causing* people to search for better judgement criteria, this does not imply that the improvement is necessarily to be found in a transition to post-conventional forms of reasoning. If both stages can be consistent, a preference for the latter cannot be justified by appealing to the principle of inconsistency reduction.

If the argument thus far is correct, then it will be clear that the same holds for *all* cognitive domains where empirical considerations are only part, and in a sense not the most essential part of the story. This is just as much so in, for example, aesthetic and religious judgement, and therefore in aesthetic and religious conceptual development, as it is in moral judgement and development. Conflicts with the empirical elements in the aesthetic or religious domain may affect the inherent conceptualisations of empirical reality, but they do not touch the core which typically creates the *aesthetic* or *religious* judgement. In all such domains of development empirical reference is just as indispensable as it is, at the same time, crucially insufficient. Such judgements presuppose the possibility of empirical reference, but they use it in a way which is determined by their primary normative judgement criteria. To give one more example, from aesthetic development theory: by the criterion of realistic representativeness (as in Parsons' stage 2) painting x may be found to be more successful than painting y, whereas by the criterion of expressiveness (as in Parsons' stage 3) painting y may be judged to be the most beautiful. In either case one of the paintings may satisfy the criterion one uses better than the other. But it makes no sense to say that the stage 3 criterion itself results in less conflict with reality than the stage 2 criterion. Empirical considerations cannot in principle help us out in this way if we want to justify conceptual development claims over stages in these domains.

So far, I have been trying to show that there are some very serious limitations in the scope of the inconsistency reduction principle. It will work only where developmental stages are internally inconsistent, or where they can be externally inconsistent. In this connection we should now observe that in actual theories of moral and aesthetic and religious development (like those of Kohlberg, Parsons, and Oser) in general stages as described are *not internally inconsistent*. Individuals may be internally inconsistent, perhaps they always are, and that may make them continually search for improvement. But the developmental stages, as reconstructed in the (*logica* part of the) respective theories, do not (and on the minimum stage concept, not) contain internally inconsistent sets of judgement criteria. If the argument given above is correct, however, there can be *no external inconsistency either* in these domains. This means that the principle of inconsistency reduction is ineffective here for the justification of conceptual development claims. At least for these types of cognitive development we shall have to find other ways of supporting claims that later stages are better than prior ones.

5. Second Principle: better judgement criteria

This rejection of the inconsistency reduction principle drives us towards the second fundamental principle of conceptual development that I mentioned at the outset, which I referred to as improvement of judgement criteria. It is clear by now that we may have to appeal to it at least in all those cases in which the principle of inconsistency reduction fails. It has, however, severe difficulties of its own.

On this principle, successive stages are more adequate, not (quantitatively, so to speak) because of their decreasing inconsistencies, but (qualitatively) because their respective sets of judgement criteria are increasingly better. That is, if the set of judgement criteria which is considered typical of stage n is compared to the set of judgement criteria which is held characteristic of stage $n-1$ or perhaps more generally stage $n-m$, the set of judgement criteria of stage n must be argued to be a better set of judgement criteria. The judgement *criteria themselves* (taken together) must be better, where the inconsistency effects of the compared stages cannot provide the argument. The following is a tentative suggestion as to how conceptual development claims might be sustained along the lines of this principle. It will not be possible to give the argument as it is actually required in the concrete situation, because this will be different now for every domain and every stage. On the second justificatory principle there is no single one criterion, like that of the reduction of inconsistencies, which can be applied anywhere. We can, however, try to formulate some *requirements for stages* that seem to be necessary conditions for such claims to be so justifiable (§5); and then sketch some elements of the structure of a justification of this kind (§6).

Four such requirements seem to be fairly obvious. Firstly, it follows from the above discussion that stages, as reconstruction, should be internally consistent. And there is another reason for this requirement. As we are dependent in our comparisons on the characteristics of the various stages, it would be rather difficult if we had to compare bunches of inconsistencies: how could we decide between them? In defining stages in conceptual development, which are typically characterised by their different sets of judgement criteria, this first requirement of internal consistency means that the judgement criteria within each relevant stage must be mutually compatible.

Secondly, in the foregoing we have taken for granted, in fact as part of the definition of the notion of development itself, that stages are qualitatively different. But there is an additional reason in this connection, also, for holding to that requirement. An evaluative conceptual development claim would make less sense if the development were only a matter of increase according to some fixed criterion (as in growth). Rather, the point of a conceptual development claim precisely seems to be that there is some qualitative improvement. It is in that sense that qualitatively different stages are discerned. In the same way, if our discussion on aims of education concerns conceptual development, we typically talk about what the crucial differences are and thereby again we compare qualitatively different stages. This second requirement would then imply that each new stage must have different judgement criteria. Or at least that each new stage should have a qualitatively different *set* of them. Not all criteria themselves need to be different, but the totality of criteria per stage need to be.

Thirdly, stages must be retrospectively comparable. Without comparison there could be no justification of any preference. Our notion of conceptual development implies that the developing person will not be able to compare stages prospectively. That stages are qualitatively different means that in general the developing person cannot yet quite understand the point of stage $n+1$ while being in stage n. For if he could, he might just as well jump to the highest stage at once. But however this may be and in whatever way the insight into the higher stage is reached at a certain moment, the justification of a conceptual development claim presupposes at least *retrospective* comparability. And this in turn requires that stages as specified in the *logica* should not be substitutive in such a rigorous manner that the core concepts of former stages would get lost or become unrecognisable in the later stages. I am not quite sure what this third requirement involves with regard to the judgement criteria. Does it mean that the total set of criteria of any stage n must somehow *comprise* the total set of criteria of stage $n-1$? Would that be possible only if each new stage adds new criteria to the total set of the former stage? (Notice, however, that even such cumulativity of *criteria* would not by itself rule out new stage structures resulting each time, thus leading to entirely new perspectives or conceptualisations.)

Fourthly, each stage is a necessary condition for its successor stage. Again, this requirement may appear quite natural, but it is important, as I shall try to explain in the next section. It also imposes considerable restraints upon what can be admitted as stages in conceptual development. The character of this conditionality is peculiar. It is not a matter of logical necessity in the strict sense (i.e. on penalty of logical contradiction). But neither is it just a simple and straight-forward physical necessity. For it concerns the conditions of the possibility and development of validity itself, only in the light of which the whole question of legitimation could arise. Yet the conditionality is not of a purely transcendental character, because it is only this specific form of validity, which would not have existed without its particular developmental genesis, that invited the justificatory question in this particular stage. The logical character of the justification of a conceptual developmental claim depends essentially on the specific stage reached by the person who provides the justification, in ways to be elaborated in §6; but theoretically the question of justification as such could come up in any stage. Perhaps we may name it a *transcendental-genetic* conditionality. In each stage, the previous stages are a necessary condition for the possibility of the forms of conceptualisation and justification that can be considered adequate.

Incidentally, a *transcendental-pragmatic* argument (not unlike the one given in §3) would be appropriate in the defence of an—admittedly purely theoretical, yet theoretically indispensable—*very first step* [17] in the sort of cognitive development that we are considering here, say from stage *0* to stage *1*: namely from the stage in which there is not yet any arguing to the stage in which the minimally required (rational) deliberations have become possible for the first time. In this case it may be argued that stage *1*—once reached!—*must* (rationally) be preferred to stage *0*. But I shall not go further into this here (cf. van Haaften, 1984) [18].

6. A Natural Bridge from 'is' to 'ought'

Internal consistency, qualitative difference, retrospective comparability, and prior stage conditionality as described above are, I suggest, some necessary conditions if the relevant evaluative conceptual development claim is to be justifiable along the lines of the second principle and without resourse to inconsistency reduction. Such conditions help guarantee the consecutive order of the stages in the *logica* [19]. They are clearly not sufficient, however, for the justification of the conceptual development claim. Even if the judgement criteria of stage *n* encompass those of stage *n-1*, and even if that would allow us to conclude that stage *n* cannot be *worse* as regards judging than its preceding stage *n−1*, that still certainly would not be sufficient reason to conclude that stage *n* is now also better than stage *n−1*. In the following, I should like to make some tentative remarks concerning what seem to me intriguing elements in the structure of any justification on the basis of the principle of better judgement criteria.

Let us first look at the relation between stages once again. Prior stages are the *condition* for the possibility of the justification of the conceptual development claim to be given (§5). Prior stages however are not the *ground* in this justification. In our justification we refer to earlier stages because we compare them, but we do not appeal to them. This is because justifications typically take place within a certain conceptual framework; and, in the context of conceptual development theory, to say that somebody is in a certain stage is to make a reference to the conceptual framework in terms of which at that moment he would justify his judgements (van Haaften, 1987). The interrelated core concepts and criteria, which are typical of a certain stage, form the foundations of judgement and justification in that stage (cf. §2). The foundations of the last stage reached determine in an essential way the potential forms of justifications that can be given at that time, for stages in conceptual development are characterised precisely by the kinds of reasons which can be adduced for judgements in the relevant domain.

We may now observe three significant points with regard to the person (me) who undertakes to justify a conceptual development claim (whether I am the theoretician or the developing person who is the object of the theoretician's claims). The first is, that I must myself have passed through (or at least have reached) the stages the claim is about. I must know the stages in question from the inside. Otherwise I would not be able adequately to compare them [20]. Therefore the comparison can at most be about the last stage reached, stage n, and its forerunner, stage $n-1$.

More important is the connected second point: it is also only in stage n that I am able to 'see' and recognise what is involved in what must be one indispensable *ground* (reason) for the conceptual development claim that stage n is better than stage $n-1$. In this respect it is not merely a material condition for me to have reached stage n. An argument in defence of the conceptual development claim requires certain factual premises; and in this case the crucial *factual* premises of the argument must necessarily point to the specific qualities of the stages compared. It is precisely the particular character of stage n which is my reason to prefer it to its precursor. Again, it is not our question here what made me reach stage n. Perhaps in stage $n-1$ I more or less unconsciously felt discontent with one of the judgement criteria, and in trying to refine it I came to project and reorganise my form of judgement so as to bring about a new and qualitatively different perspective on the relevant issues (cf. Piaget's notion of reflective abstraction, e.g. Piaget, 1977). However, this is not our problem now. The question here is what reason I may adduce if I want to justify my preference for the new stage. That reason is: the specific character of stage n as compared to stage $n-1$.

However, legitimately to argue an evaluative claim we need not only factual premises, but also a relevant *normative* premise. Accordingly, to endorse the conceptual development claim, there must be not only factual premises concerning the stages involved in the comparison, but also a normative premise in the form of a criterion by which those stages with their specific qualities can be evaluated. What can this criterion be? I think the answer is—and that is my third point—that the only relevant criterion we dispose of to judge conceptual development stages in a certain domain of reality is *our conception of the essence of the domain of reality in question*. Thus, for instance, the only relevant criterion by which to judge moral stages is what we acknowledge to be the essence of morality. That is the decisive criterion if we have to decide what is the most adequate stage in moral development, for we have no other compass to go by.

Remember now the distinctions made in the second section, between judgement criteria and stage criteria; and between the 'two sides of the coin' of conceptual development stages. Take moral judgement as the example again. In general, each stage in moral development is characterised by its specific moral judgement criterion (or set of criteria), according to which we evaluate singular moral judgements. Thus, the moral judgement criterion of stage n is the criterion according to which in stage n we evaluate singular moral judgements (and acts, etc.). And, at the same time (the other side of the coin), this epitomises our conscious or unconscious ideas about what the essence of morality is. The descriptive moral stage criteria, which determine how moral judgement stages are to be discerned, are precisely given by the various ways in which within each singular stage moral judgements are evaluated (particularly, the types of reasons that are given for the evaluations). That means that in this case of stage n, the descriptive moral stage criterion is precisely given by the moral judgement criterion/criteria of stage n. The evaluative moral stage criterion determines how the various moral stages, which are thus distinguished, are to be (relatively) evaluated. As we saw, that criterion is determined by our conception as to what morality essentially consists in. But then each stage is characterised simultaneously by its specific way of judging moral judgements and (on the other side of the same coin) by its own specific conception as to what is the essence of morality. Thus the question what is the best moral stage (the normative stage question), which is dependent on the criterion by which moral stages are to be evaluated, is of necessity decided for me by what to the best of my knowledge is the essence of morality. And that, in turn, is given by the moral development stage I am in now, stage n. Such is the situational structure of the justification that can be given by me, being in stage n.

What I have said above may sound circular. Notice first that no 'is' – 'ought' fallacy is involved in the account, however. There was no leap from the factual premise that there are such and such stages, amongst which is n which I am in now, to the normative conclusion that one particular stage, n, is the best one. To reach this conclusion I have used certain factual premises about the stages in question together with an additional normative premise, viz., that the stage which best satisfies the criteria implied by what to the best of my knowledge is the essence of morality must be considered the best moral stage. That seems an acceptable argument.

Notice further that in actual developmental processes we may very often move beyond a certain stage without accepting such a step as an improvement. Not every change in perspective means progress. What I have proposed is an analysis of the structure of a possible justification of a conceptual development claim *if* such a claim is put forward. There is no automatism. And good reasons are required all the same.

The peculiarity we are faced with seems to result from the fact that the criteria of stage n are *fact and norm* at the same time. To be in stage n is to be convinced that such and such criteria of judgement and the related conception of morality are the most adequate criteria and conception. That is factually what I am convinced of. That is the character of stage n as compared with other stages. And at the same time it is the only possibly relevant norm for me to use in evaluating stages of moral development. This is the fundamental form of validity that I, being in stage n, am able to bring to the argument. In this sense my development *produces* the possibility of the required justification.

We may look upon this situation as just a typical predicament of conceptual development and of conceptual development claims, in so far as they are made and perhaps justified. How could it be otherwise in human thinking, which admits of qualitative change? For the justification of a conceptual development claim that stage n is better than stage $n-1$, it is necessary for us to have reached stage n. Further, only stage n can provide us with the relevant facts on which the claim can be based. And finally it is also stage n which produces the relevant norm according to which we can judge the relevant facts. There is no fallacious 'is' – 'ought' deduction involved. On the contrary, we might rather contend that what we find here in conceptual development is a *natural* naturalistic bridge from 'is' to 'ought' [21]. The argument from within stage n is non-fallaciously deductive; and the developmental structure of the argumentation situation produces non-deductively the naturalistic bridge. It is my conviction, although I cannot substantiate it, that here lay Kohlberg's intuition when he formulated his 'is'—'ought' argument (Kohlberg, 1971, 1981; cf. Boyd, 1986).

There is no *logical* circularity in this, because we can very well distinguish between a justification within a certain conceptual framework (that is the justification of e.g. moral judgements, on the basis of the stage specific evaluative judgement criteria) on the one hand and a justification *of* a certain conceptual framework (the justification of the conceptual development claim about this stage, characterised by its stage-specific judgement criteria, as compared to former stages) on the other hand. There is, however, what might be called an *anthropological* circularity involved: the circle which is closed in the developing person for whom (or in whom) the *foundations* of the first type of justification and the foundations of the second type coincide in his convictions concerning what makes up the essence of the domain in question. In the end, it is the developing person who forms the transcendental-genetic condition of the possibility of all justification, including justifications of conceptual development claims.

But, finally, aren't we then entirely in the hands of relativism? Now that I am in stage n, I seem to be caught in the fact-norm coincidence of stage n. I was not beforehand, because at that time I could not yet see the point of stage n's norms, and not afterwards, because if I ever reach a later stage I will reject this norm in favour of the norm of stage $n+1$ (cf. Rest, 1983, p. 592). This sounds disquieting because of its relativistic overtones. There may be some relief, however, if we realise two points. Firstly, the fact–norm coincidence of this stage n will dissolve in the next stage. And, what is more, as soon as we then accept the conceptual development claim which is typical of stage $n+1$ because of its new norm (involving its particular fact–norm coincidence), we may consider stage n as justified in its proper place in the developmental pattern, because of its being a necessary condition for the now accepted stage $n+1$.

Secondly, depending on how in our meta-theory requirements we can improve the stage such as those mentioned in §5 (in particular the prior stage conditionality requirement together with the retrospective comparability requirement) the proposed norms used in the defence of conceptual development claims are certainly not completely arbitrary or relativistic in the usual sense. Of course such norms are relative to stages! But the developmental stages themselves are related in very specific ways. So that when people severely disagree, there is a limited number of conceivable situations. Either they are in the same developmental stage, in which case they can in principle appeal to shared criteria in order to settle their differences of opinion concerning this or an earlier stage about which the conceptual development claim was put forward; or they are in different stages, in which case two possibilities are open. On the one hand, they may differ in stages reached within the same developmental pattern. This is the usual case in education—perhaps definitive of it. It implies severe limitations in possibilities of justification in this context (cf. van Haaften, 1988), and the resulting discussions (think of the piano lessons!) are familiar enough. Where stages are indeed such that their qualitative dissimilarity leads to prospective inaccessibility, it is an inherent curtailment that justifications can only be given and argued about with regard to stages which both parties have reached or passed through [22]. One can only hope for some growing confidence along the way; and further find comfort in the idea that later in the course of development there may be an opportunity for a justification *ex post facto*. On the other hand, however, people may be in different stages because of a fork in the developmental pattern. In that case they can only try to go back to a knot of common insights and from there see how far they can come to build new agreements. Although forks in developmental patterns have not often been proposed in developmental theories—each theory concentrating on just one particular developmental line—they do not seem to be impossible.

Let me just very briefly summarise. During processes of conceptual development there may be fundamental changes in our perspectives on certain parts of reality, and in our ways of making and evaluating judgements concerning those parts of reality. Sometimes we may formulate and compare some of the crucial concepts or criteria involved. Often then, either implicitly or explicitly, a conceptual development claim is put forward, purporting that a later developmental stage (with its characteristic concepts and criteria) is better or more adequate than prior ones. Claims of the same sort are made by theories of conceptual development (Piaget, Kohlberg, etc.). My question was: how can such conceptual development claims be justified? Or, can we say something about the conditions of the possibility of such justifications? One important basic principle sustaining such a project may be the inconsistency reduction principle, i.e. the principle that a later stage be less inconsistent than its forerunner(s). Strong reasons can be adduced in favour of this principle. But, as I have tried to show, it is severely limited in scope. Moral, aesthetic and religious development claims cannot be justified along these lines. That invited the question whether there can be other strategies in the defence of conceptual development claims. As an alternative, I proposed that there might be a preference for certain stages, not because they are more consistent than their precursors, but because their characteristic core concepts and criteria may themselves be regarded as more adequate than those of prior stages. In this connection I made some tentative suggestions, firstly about some of the conditions which stages must satisfy for such a kind of justification of conceptual development claims to be possible, and secondly about the typical structure and predicament of the then requisite forms of argumentation.

Correspondence: Wouter van Haaften, Institute of Philosophy and History of Education, University of Nijmegen, Erasmusplein 1, 6525 GE Nijmegen, the Netherlands.

NOTES

[1] Originally presented at the Annual Conference of the Philosophy of Education Society, April 1989. I wish to thank R.K. Elliott for his very helpful suggestions for improvement.

[2] Suggestions in this direction can be found in the work of Kohlberg, but they are strongly emphasised in Habermas' 'constructivistic' concept of learning inspired by him (e.g. Habermas, 1983).

[3] Rational preference for stage $n+1$ even may only be fully possible once that stage has been reached. In that case the preference could only prevent backsliding to stage n from stage $n+1$ and not really be a transition factor. Much depends here on how, theoretically, stages and their relations are conceived of.

[4] I shall however, for the sake of convenience, often unqualifiedly take moral development as an example.

[5] Judgements which cannot be measured against the judgement criteria are not so much wrong but rather inapt or inadequate. Compare it to the rules of chess: if you were to move the bishop like a rook, you would not so much make a wrong move; you rather would do something which is not a chess move at all, according to the current definition of the game. Only *within* the range of the judgement criteria can there be such things like better or worse judgements. On the other hand, judgement criteria do not completely determine what the right answers to concrete questions in the relevant domain must be. But, as in chess, they do have a clear normative impact.

[6] I do not want to say that (a) and (b) are necessarily co-extensive.

[7] It should be emphasised that the application of the judgement criteria and the conception of the domain in question are not necessarily conscious. Mostly they are not. However, in the justification of a conceptual development claim they will have to be made explicit.

[8] These foundations of conceptual *stages* should not, of course, be confused with foundations of conceptual *stage theories* like the two principles mentioned at the outset.

[9] When I speak of conceptual development claims unqualifiedly, I mean positively evaluative claims.

[10] In the following I will neglect such potential intermediate stages.

[11] Not to be confused with the problem of the theory-ladenness of observation. That no observation is 'pure' leaves unimpeded the distinction between the observational or empirical and the (non-observational) evaluative aspects of our judgements. Thus, although it is true that (judgements about) physical properties are often just as much dependent on certain implicit measurement norms as evaluative judgements are dependent on implicitly accepted moral or aesthetic norms, this does not put those two sorts of norms on a par.

[12] It may be objected that with the use of certain terms, like 'torture', we have already introduced a strongly evaluative element. However, we can quite well distinguish the descriptive and the evaluative aspects within the meaning of a word.

[13] It should be once more emphasised that in actual practice there is of course nothing like a neat separation between our getting informed about the facts and our coming to an evaluation. We can, however, in an analysis distinguish between those two aspects of reasoning. And in moral justifications, I think, we should always try to do so as much as we can.

[14] I do not want to suggest by this formulation that anybody in the non-conservation stage would deliberately make such choices. We are not concerned here with what makes people go through developmental stages at all. In this context, not of explanation but of justification, the question is only what *could* be *valid* reasons *if* one (doubtlessly in a later stage in this case) has to defend certain preferences.

[15] We know by experience that we do not like to be punished. But to want to avoid punishment does not

imply that one should want to avoid the *criterion* of punishment avoidance. Even less does it follow that one should for that reason prefer a different moral judgement criterion.

[16] Even if arguments are convincing to the persons involved and so constitute causal transition factors, they may not be sound. This is stage-dependent, however; cf. §6.

[17] It seems to me an important feature of the argumentation given, that it is *not* dependent on the indication or characterisation of a starting-point; nor for that matter of an end point or *telos* of conceptual development (cf. Chapman, 1988a). No more is needed than that the (minimally defined) stages are considered in relation to each other.

[18] A transcendental-pragmatic argument, unlike Kant's transcendental argument, is not a form of deductive reasoning and therefore not vulnerable to the problem of regression (Kuhlmann, 1987).

[19] This does of course not preclude the possibility that *persons* backslide to earlier stages; that would be a process to be accounted for in the *dynamica* (*vide supra*).

[20] Perhaps this is too strong. It may not be necessary for me to have gone through certain (logically prior) stages myself in order to be able to compare their essentials in an adequate way. This point is particularly relevant if historical and collective forms of development are taken into consideration (e.g. the development of the sciences).

[21] Not to be confused with the type of argument briefly referred to at the end of §5, which might be seen as providing a transcendental–pragmatic bridge from *is* to *ought*.

[22] Thus only persons both in stage *n* and/or higher stages *n+x* can only argue about conceptual development claims concerning only stage *n* and stages *n-y*.

REFERENCES

APEL, K.O. (1973) *Transformation der Philosophie. Band II: Das Apriori der Kommunikationsgemeinschaft* (Frankfurt/Main, Suhrkamp).

APEL, K.O. (1986) Die transzendentalpragmatische Begründung der Kommunikationsethik und das Problem der höchsten Stufe einer Entwicklungslogik des moralischen Bewußtseins, *Archivio di Filosofia, LIV*, pp. 107–157.

BOYD, D.R. (1986) The Oughts of Is: Kohlberg at the Interface between Moral Philosophy and Developmental Psychology, in: S. MODGIL & C. MODGIL (Eds) *Lawrence Kohlberg: consensus and controversy* (Philadelphia, Falmer Press) pp. 43–63.

CHAPMAN, M. (1988a) Contextuality and directionality of cognitive development, *Human Development, 31*, pp. 92–106.

CHAPMAN, M. (1988b) *Constructive Evolution. Origins and Development of Piaget's Thought* (Cambridge, Cambridge University Press).

ELLIOTT, R.K. (1975) The concept of development: a reply to Professor Hamlyn, *Proceedings of the Philosophy of Education Society*, 9, pp. 40–48.

HAAFTEN, A.W. VAN (1984) Een ontwikkelingstheoretische benadering van de "is-ought question" [A developmental approach to the is-ought question], *Pedagogische Studiën, 61*, pp. 272–281.

HAAFTEN, A.W. VAN, KORTHALS, M., WIDDERSHOVEN, G.A.M., DE MUL, J. & SNIK, G.L.M. (1986) *Ontwikkelingsfilosofie. [Philosophy of Development]* (Muiderberg, Coutinho).

HAAFTEN, A.W. VAN (1987) Rechtvaardiging en fundering [Justification and foundation]. *Pedagogische Verhandelingen, 10*, pp. 56–65.

HAAFTEN, A.W. VAN (1988) Can moral education be justified in moral education?, in: B. SPIECKER & R. STRAUGHAN, (Eds) *Philosophical Issues in Moral Education and Development* (Milton Keynes, Open University Press), pp. 17–42.

HABERMAS, J. (1981) *Theorie des kommunikativen Handelns* (2 Vol.) (Frankfurt/Main, Suhrkamp).

HABERMAS, J. (1983) *Moralbewußtsein und kommunikatives Handeln* (Frankfurt/Main, Suhrkamp).

HAMLYN, D.W. (1975) The concept of development, *Proceedings of the Philosophy of Education Society*, 9, pp. 26–39.

HIRST, P.H. & PETERS, R.S. (1980) *The Logic of Education* (London, Routledge & Kegan Paul).

KITCHENER, R.F. (1986) *Piaget's Theory of Knowledge, Genetic Epistemology and Scientific Reason* (New Haven, Yale University Press).

KOHLBERG, L. (1969) Stage and sequence. The cognitive-developmental approach to socialization, in: D.A. GOSLIN, (Ed.) *Handbook of Socialization Theory and Research* (Chicago, Rand McNally), pp. 347–480.

KOHLBERG, L. (1971) From is to ought: how to commit the naturalistic fallacy and get away with it in the study of moral development, in: T. MISCHEL, (Ed.) *Cognitive Development and Epistemology* (New York, Academic Press), pp. 151–235.

KOHLBERG, L. (1973) The claim to moral adequacy of a highest stage of moral judgement, *Journal of Philosophy*, 70, pp. 630–646.

KOHLBERG, L. (1976) Moral stages and moralization: the cognitive-developmental approach. in: T. LICKONA (Ed.), *Moral Development and Behavior: Theory, Research and Social Issues* (New York, Holt, Rinehart & Winston), pp. 151–202.

KOHLBERG, L. (1981) *Essays on Moral Development, Vol. I: the philosophy of moral development* (San Francisco, Harper & Row).
KOHLBERG, L. (1984) *Essays on Moral Development, Vol. II: the psychology of moral development* (San Francisco, Harper & Row).
KOHLBERG, L., LEVINE, C. & HEWER, A. (1983) *Moral Stages, A Current Formulation and a Response to Critics* (Basel, Karger).
KUHLMANN, W. (1987) Was spricht heute für eine Philosophie des kantischen Typs?, in: W. R. KÖHLER, W. KUHLMANN, & P. ROHS (Eds) *Philosophie und Begründung* (Frankfurt/Main, Suhrkamp), pp. 84–115.
MISCHEL, T. (1971) Piaget: cognitive conflict and the motivation of thought, in: T. MISCHEL (Ed.) *Cognitive Development and Epistemology* (New York, Academic Press), pp. 311–355.
OSER, F. & GMÜNDER, P. (1984) *Der Mensch, Stufen seiner religiösen Entwicklung, Ein strukturgenetischer Ansatz* (Zürich/Köln, Benziger).
PARSONS, M.J. (1987) *How We Understand Art, A Cognitive Developmental Account of Aesthetic Experience* (Cambridge, Cambridge University Press).
PETERS, R.S. (1966) *Ethics and Education* (London, George Allen & Unwin).
PETERS, R.S. (1973) The justification of education, in: R. S. PETERS (Ed.) *The Philosophy of Education* (Oxford, Oxford University Press), pp. 239–267.
PIAGET, J. (1971) *The Construction of Reality in the Child* (New York, Basic Books).
PIAGET, J. (1977) *Recherches sur l'abstraction réfléchissante* (Paris, Presses Universitaires de France).
REST, J.R. (1983) Morality, in: J.H. FLAVELL & E. MARKMAN (Eds) *Manual of Child Psychology, Vol. III: Cognitive Development* (New York, Wiley) pp. 556–629.
SELMAN, R.L. (1980) *The Growth of Interpersonal Understanding* (New York, Academic Press).
WRIGHT, L. (1986) The concept of development and its legitimacy in the philosophy of education, *Journal of Philosophy of Education*, 20, pp. 39–50.

ACKNOWLEDGMENTS

Kohlberg, Lawrence. "The Claim to Moral Adequacy of a Highest Stage of Moral Judgment." *Journal of Philosophy* 70 (1973): 630–46. Reprinted with the permission of the Journal of Philosophy, Inc., Columbia University, and the author. Courtesy of the *Journal of Philosophy*.

Simpson, Elizabeth Léonie. "Moral Development Research: A Case Study of Scientific Cultural Bias." *Human Development* 17 (1974): 81–106. Reprinted with the permission of S. Karger, AG. Courtesy of Yale University Sterling Memorial Library.

Sullivan, Edmund V. "A Study of Kohlberg's Structural Theory of Moral Development: A Critique of Liberal Social Science Ideology." *Human Development* 20 (1977): 352–76. Reprinted with the permission of S. Karger, AG. Courtesy of Yale University Sterling Memorial Library.

Shweder, Richard A. "Liberalism as Destiny." *Contemporary Psychology* 27 (1982): 421–24. Copyright 1982 by the American Psychological Association. Reprinted by permission. Courtesy of Yale University Sterling Memorial Library.

Murphy, John Michael and Carol Gilligan. "Moral Development in Late Adolescence and Adulthood: A Critique and Reconstruction of Kohlberg's Theory." *Human Development* 23 (1980): 77–104. Reprinted with the permission of S. Karger, AG. Courtesy of Yale University Sterling Memorial Library.

Locke, Don. "Cognitive Stages or Developmental Phases? A Critique of Kohlberg's Stage-Structural Theory of Moral Reasoning." *Journal of Moral Education* 8 (1979): 168–81. Reprinted with the permission of Carfax Publishing Co. Courtesy of Yale University Sterling Memorial Library.

Puka, Bill. "The Majesty and Mystery of Kohlberg's Stage 6." In Thomas E. Wren, ed., *The Moral Domain: Essays in the Ongoing Discussion between Philosophy and the Social Sciences* (Cambridge, MA: MIT Press, 1990): 182–223. Reprinted with the permission of MIT Press. Courtesy of Yale University Divinity Library.

Locke, Don. "The Illusion of Stage Six." *Journal of Moral Education* 9 (1980): 103–09. Reprinted with the permission of Carfax Publishing Co. Courtesy of Yale University Sterling Memorial Library.

Straughan, Roger. "Why Act on Kohlberg's Moral Judgments? (Or How to Reach Stage 6 and Remain a Bastard)." In Sohan Modgil and Celia Modgil, eds., *Lawrence Kohlberg: Consensus and Controversy* (Philadelphia, PA: Falmer Press, 1985): 149–57. Reprinted with the permission of The Falmer Press. Courtesy of Yale University Sterling Memorial Library.

Haan, Norma. "Hypothetical and Actual Moral Reasoning in a Situation of Civil Disobedience." *Journal of Personality and Social Psychology* 32 (1975): 255–70. Copyright 1975 by the American Psychological Association, Inc. Reprinted by permission. Courtesy of Yale University Sterling Memorial Library.

Gibbs, John C. "Kohlberg's Moral Stage Theory: A Piagetian Revision." *Human Development* 22 (1979): 89–112. Reprinted with the permission of S. Karger, AG. Courtesy of Yale University Sterling Memorial Library.

Holstein, Constance Boucher. "Irreversible, Stepwise Sequence in the Development of Moral Judgment: A Longitudinal Study of Males and Females." *Child Development* 47 (1976): 51–61. Reprinted with the permission of the Society for Research in Child Development. Courtesy of Yale University Sterling Memorial Library.

Broughton, John. "The Cognitive-Developmental Approach to Morality: A Reply to Kurtines and Greif." *Journal of Moral Education* 7 (1978): 81–96. Reprinted with the permission of the *Journal of Moral Education*. Courtesy of Yale University Sterling Memorial Library.

Puka, Bill. "Toward the Redevelopment of Kohlberg's Theory: Preserving Essential Structure, Removing Controversial Content." In William M. Kurtines and Jacob L. Gewirtz, eds., *Handbook of Moral Behavior and Development: Volume 1: Theory* (Hillsdale, NJ: Lawrence Erlbaum Associates, Publishers, 1991): 373–93. Reprinted with the permission of Lawrence Erlbaum Associates, Inc. Courtesy of Yale University Sterling Memorial Library.

Kurtines, William and Esther Blank Greif. "The Development of Moral Thought: Review and Evaluation of Kohlberg's Approach." *Psychological Bulletin* 81 (1974): 453–70. Copyright 1974 by the American Psychological Association. Reprinted by permission. Courtesy of Yale University Medical Library.

Peters, R.S. "Virtues and Habits in Moral Education." In Donald B. Cochrane, Cornel M. Hamm, and Anastasios C. Kazepides, eds., *The Domain of Moral Education* (New York, NY: Paulist Press, 1979): 267–87. Article originally published in *Cognitive Development and Epistemology*. Reprinted with the permission of Academic Press, Inc. Courtesy of Yale University Divinity Library.

van Haaften, Wouter. "The Justification of Conceptual Development Claims." *Journal of Philosophy of Education* 24 (1990): 51–69. Reprinted with the permission of Carfax Publishing Co. Courtesy of Yale University Sterling Memorial Library.